TO LEAD THE WORLD

EDITED BY MELVYN P. LEFFLER AND JEFFREY W. LEGRO

TO LEAD THE WORLD

*American Strategy after the
Bush Doctrine*

OXFORD
UNIVERSITY PRESS

2008

OXFORD

UNIVERSITY PRESS

Oxford University Press, Inc., publishes works that further
Oxford University's objective of excellence
in research, scholarship, and education.

Oxford   New York
Auckland   Cape Town   Dar es Salaam   Hong Kong   Karachi
Kuala Lumpur   Madrid   Melbourne   Mexico City   Nairobi
New Delhi   Shanghai   Taipei   Toronto

With offices in
Argentina   Austria   Brazil   Chile   Czech Republic   France   Greece
Guatemala   Hungary   Italy   Japan   Poland   Portugal   Singapore
South Korea   Switzerland   Thailand   Turkey   Ukraine   Vietnam

Published by Oxford University Press, Inc.
198 Madison Avenue, New York, New York 10016

www.oup.com

Oxford is a registered trademark of Oxford University Press

Library of Congress Cataloging-in-Publication Data
To lead the world : American strategy after the Bush
doctrine / edited by Melvyn P. Leffler and Jeffrey W. Legro.
      p.   cm.
Includes bibliographical references and index.
ISBN 978-0-19-533098-4; 978-0-19-536941-0 (pbk.)
   1. United States—Foreign relations—2001– —Philosophy.
   2. National security—United States.   3. Security, International.
4. World politics—21st century.   5. Bush, George W. (George Walker),
            1946– —Political and social views.
   6. Bush, George W. (George Walker), 1946– —Influence.
   I. Leffler, Melvyn P., 1945–   II. Legro, Jeffrey.
         JZ1480.A5T65 2008
      327.73—dc22   2007045232

3 5 7 9 8 6 4 2

Printed in the United States of America
on acid-free paper

Acknowledgments

THE MILLER CENTER of Public Affairs at the University of Virginia provided generous support and funding for this project. In particular, we would like to thank Gerald L. Baliles, the director of the Miller Center, and J. Michael Mullen, assistant director. Our cochairs in the Governing America in a Global Era program, Sid Milkis and Brian Balogh, offered superb advice whenever we encountered difficult issues.

To facilitate an exchange of ideas on the future of U.S. national security strategy, the Miller Center hosted a two-day workshop titled "After the Bush Doctrine: National Security Strategy for a New Administration" on June 7–8, 2007. The event required tremendous effort on the part of our extraordinarily talented Miller Center colleagues and support staff, especially Chi Lam. Our thanks to them and to John Owen for their contributions to the workshop. Additionally, we are extremely grateful to David S. Broder, Fareed Zakaria, and David Brooks, who moderated our discussions, and to William Kristol and Leslie H. Gelb, who provided incisive commentary.

Many other people helped to bring this project to fruition. Our graduate research assistants—Seth Center, Louis-Blaise Dumais-Lévesque, and Daniel McDowell—did an outstanding job. Susan Ferber, our editor at Oxford, took the time to attend the workshop and offered thoughtful advice throughout the preparation of the manuscript. Anne Carter Mulligan, program coordinator at the Miller Center, supervised this project from its inception with a rare blend of competence, diligence, tact, and good humor. Her assistance has been indispensable to the timely completion of this book.

Most of all, we thank our authors for their illuminating contributions and enthusiastic collaboration.

Contents

Contributors

Barry Eichengreen is the George C. Pardee and Helen N. Pardee Professor of Economics and Professor of Political Science at the University of California, Berkeley. Eichengreen's latest book is *The European Economy since 1945: Coordinated Capitalism and Beyond*.

Niall Ferguson is the Laurence A. Tisch Professor of History at Harvard University and a *Los Angeles Times* columnist. He recently authored *The War of the World: Twentieth-Century Conflict and the Descent of the West*.

Francis Fukuyama is the Bernard L. Schwartz Professor of International Political Economy at the Johns Hopkins School of Advanced International Studies and author of *America at the Crossroads: Democracy, Power, and the Neoconservative Legacy*.

G. John Ikenberry is the Albert G. Milbank Professor of Public and International Affairs in the Department of Politics and the Woodrow Wilson School of Public and International Affairs at Princeton University. He is the author of *After Victory: Institutions, Strategic Restraint, and the Rebuilding of Order after Major Wars*, which won the 2002 Schroeder-Jervis Award.

Douglas A. Irwin is the Robert E. Maxwell '23 Professor of Arts and Sciences in the Department of Economics at Dartmouth College and author of *Free Trade under Fire*, now in its second edition.

Robert Kagan is Senior Associate at the Carnegie Endowment for International Peace and monthly columnist for the *Washington Post*. He most recently wrote *Dangerous Nation: America in the World, 1607–1898*.

David M. Kennedy is the Donald J. McLachlan Professor of History at Stanford University. He won the Pulitzer Prize for History for *Freedom from Fear: The American People in Depression and War, 1929–1945.*

James Kurth is the Claude Smith Professor of Political Science at Swarthmore College. He is the author of numerous articles on foreign policy and international relations and is Senior Fellow at the Foreign Policy Research Institute, where he serves as editor of its journal, *Orbis.*

Melvyn P. Leffler is the Edward R. Stettinius Professor of American History in the Corcoran Department of History and cochair of the Governing America in a Global Era program at the University of Virginia's Miller Center of Public Affairs. A Bancroft Prize winner, he most recently published *For the Soul of Mankind: The United States, the Soviet Union, and the Cold War.*

Jeffrey W. Legro is the Compton Professor of World Politics, Chair of the Woodrow Wilson Department of Politics, and cochair of the Governing America in a Global Era program at the University of Virginia's Miller Center of Public Affairs. He is the author of *Rethinking the World: Great Power Strategies and International Order.*

Charles S. Maier is the Leverett Saltonstall Professor of History at Harvard University. He is the author of *Among Empires: American Ascendancy and Its Predecessors,* among other works on global history.

Samantha Power is Professor of Practice in Public Policy at the John F. Kennedy School of Government at Harvard University. Her book *"A Problem from Hell": America and the Age of Genocide* was awarded the 2003 Pulitzer Prize for General Nonfiction.

Stephen Van Evera is Professor of Political Science at the Massachusetts Institute of Technology. He is the author of *Causes of War: Power and the Roots of Conflict* and of many articles on U.S. foreign and national security policy.

TO LEAD THE WORLD

Introduction
Melvyn P. Leffler
and Jeffrey W. Legro

FOR MANY AMERICANS, the past decade has been a bewildering era. They have seen their country attacked and their husbands, sons, wives, and daughters sent to war in faraway places. They have read about orange alerts and red alerts. They have waited on long lines at airport security checks. They know that defense expenditures have soared and that Homeland Security has mushroomed. They have seen gruesome daily headlines about the carnage in Iraq, the strife in Afghanistan, and the turmoil in Pakistan. They read about the suicide attacks that were prevented or aborted in Europe, and they know, darkly, that terrorists are at work from North Africa to Southeast Asia, from the United Kingdom to Russia to China. With perils abounding, Americans want a national strategy that makes sense.

U.S. leaders grasp the anxieties on Main Street as well as on Wall Street. They recognize, moreover, that terrorism is just one aspect of a complicated international landscape. Other threats—a nuclear Iran, an irrational North Korea, a revisionist China or Russia, a vulnerable international economy—could be even more dangerous. They do not want to be caught unawares and unprepared—for the sake of their country, for the sake of their careers, for the sake of their sanity—should the unthinkable happen.

Yet they know the world is changing rapidly and that their ability to foresee future dangers is limited. They have read the *9/11 Commission Report*: the "system," it emphasized, "was blinking red." Yet neither Democratic nor Republican administrations took notice. Trapped in a cold war view of threats, those earlier decision makers suffered from a "failure of imagination" and were blind to the gathering storm of terrorism.[1] History can repeat itself. Terrorism has replaced the cold war in the national psyche, but that new specter may similarly hinder imagination about impending dangers. Late at night, when their staffs have left, when the overwhelming demands of daily tasks are barely met, the president and his or her top advisers must wonder anxiously whether new warning lights are blinking, unseen. They need to know, as we all do, what the path ahead might look like, what threats and opportunities are most significant, and how the United States can best prepare.

This volume is conceived with the hope that it will stimulate creative thought about the planning and implementation of national security policy. It is about how the United States can recover from an especially tumultuous period in its foreign relations. It is about U.S. strategy after the Bush doctrine.

A Starting Point

The administration of George W. Bush published two national strategy statements. The first statement, issued in September 2002, aroused enormous controversy, and the second did not flinch from its predecessor's most controversial propositions. The strategy appeared to be a radical departure from the policies that had defined America's approach to world affairs throughout the cold war and beyond. Seemingly abandoning containment, deterrence, and a reliance on collective action, the Bush strategy called for a policy of unilateral action and preventive war: "Given the goals of rogue states and terrorists, the United States can no longer rely on a reactive posture as we have in the past. The inability to deter a potential attacker, the immediacy of today's threats, and the magnitude of potential harm that could be caused by our adversaries' choice of weapons, do not permit that option. We cannot let our enemies strike first."[2]

The emphasis on a unilateral, preemptive initiative shaped the administration's reactions to the terrorist attacks of 9/11. President Bush and his advisers decided to destroy the Taliban government in Afghanistan, which had provided shelter to the al Qaeda movement, and to overthrow the government of Saddam Hussein in Iraq for supposedly developing weapons of mass destruction and conspiring with terrorists to attack the United States and its allies. The wars in Afghanistan and Iraq form the core of the war on terror. They have consumed thousands of American lives, probably hundreds of thousands of Iraqi and Afghan lives, and vast sums of money, likely to exceed two trillion dollars by the end of the decade. They are worth the cost, says President

George W. Bush, if they will contribute to a safer, more peaceful world, conducive to the spread of freedom and democracy.

More than any president in recent history, President Bush has defined the nation's security in terms of the promotion of freedom around the world. All people, he stresses, want freedom. And freedom everywhere, he claims, is essential for the safety of the United States. "The survival of liberty in our land," he stated in his second inaugural address, "increasingly depends on the success of liberty in other lands. The best hope for peace in our world is the expansion of freedom in all the world."[3] America's principles, according to Bush, should shape U.S. decisions on international cooperation, foreign assistance, and the allocation of resources.[4]

Bush's strategy statements contain much more than platitudes about the value of human freedom and dignity. They outline policies that go far beyond the emphasis on unilateral, preemptive military action. Focusing considerable attention on the advantages of an open international economy, they espouse the importance of global economic growth through free markets and free trade. They stress the importance of disseminating the rule of law, promoting sound fiscal, tax, and financial policies, and nurturing investments in health and education. They state that fighting poverty is a "moral imperative," and they envision doubling the size of the world's poorest economies within a decade. Fighting disease, they acknowledge, is as important as fighting poverty; indeed, it is a key to fighting poverty. And notwithstanding the emphasis placed on anticipatory unilateral action, the administration's strategy statements acknowledge the importance of strengthening ties with partners, energizing alliances in Asia, and building and expanding the North Atlantic Treaty Organization (NATO).[5]

However comprehensive the strategy statements have been, the war on terror and the struggles in Iraq and Afghanistan have consumed the attention of the administration and its critics. In the past few years, book after book has appeared discussing the shortsightedness and ineptitude of the administration's actions in Iraq.[6] So vast is this literature and so focused has been the administration's defense of its actions in Iraq that most of us have lost sight of the larger issues of national security. Yet the larger context is essential for evaluating the merits of the case in Iraq. Probing questions have arisen about the centrality of that conflict for the war on terror in general. And even more fundamental inquiries have arisen about the logic of a war on terror when some commentators maintain that the threat has been hugely exaggerated, that the concept itself—a war on terror—unwisely conflates terrorist groups, and that it makes little sense because terror is a tactic, not an adversary.[7] And in its second term, the Bush administration itself appears to have backed away in practice from the defining traits of its doctrine, such as preventive action, unilateralism, and aggressive democratization.[8] The puzzle that faces America is: what should come next?

The Aim

Many have debated Bush's foreign policy.[9] Critiquing the president's actions in Iraq is easy; examining Bush strategy overall is more challenging but still unsatisfying unless one can outline better alternatives. The purpose of this volume is to call on some of the nation's foremost thinkers on foreign policy to lay out their thoughts about the road ahead. The contributors were chosen carefully, representing a mix of political predilections and personal experience. They come from the right, the center, and the left of the political spectrum; some have served in government positions and some have not. They represent diverse scholarly specialties, including historians, political scientists, economists, and international relations experts. They are renowned for their writings on diplomacy, public policy, human rights, international institutions, military strategy, and trade and financial practices.

They all faced the same assignment—to write a concise national security strategy statement. They were not to dwell on defending or attacking current policy but to focus on framing advice for future officials. We challenged them to:

Identify and assign priority to the greatest threats facing the nation.
Define the overall goals of national strategy.
Reconcile values and interests.
Integrate economic and military initiatives.
Incorporate trade, budgetary, and payments issues.
Delineate acceptable trade-offs between domestic objectives and foreign policy goals.
Illuminate the role of human rights and democratic impulses.
Ponder whether institutions of national governance need to be rearranged.
Outline a desirable architecture of international institutions, agreements, and alliances.
Inform us how to regain respect in the world and ensure our security at the same time.

In short, they faced a formidable task. We knew the contributors would focus on different aspects of the agenda reflecting their priorities and biases. Still, they would have to defend them against a larger matrix of issues and concerns. The aim was to nurture the best thinking about overall national strategy that might inform public debate and guide officials in the future. Governing America in a global era is a formidable task; our mission is to engender the wisest thinking about the overall enterprise.

Crucible of Strategy

Although each of the contributors has taken his or her own unique approach to this assignment, the chapters should be examined against a set of strategic criteria that forces critical analysis about national purpose and national interest. Of course, these are contentious concepts, and reasonable people should argue fiercely about their meaning. Still, U.S. policy makers must come to grips with a number of tasks and must make choices. They will have to decide whether the nature of world politics is changing and how that affects strategy making. They must identify the most significant threats and opportunities, and they must determine how resources should be allocated to meet those dangers. They must be attuned to new opportunities for maximizing the security and welfare of their own citizens, as well as those abroad—whose well-being will benefit the United States. They must ponder whether they should take a leadership role in the international arena, simply react to events, or distance themselves as much as possible from the turbulence in the world; whether to try to maintain the country's dominant global position or redirect its energies inward; whether to retain massive military capabilities or concentrate on counterinsurgency. They must determine how hard they should try to spread U.S. values concerning democracy, human rights, and capitalism to other countries. They must garner the support of U.S. citizens and those of other countries—or offer a plan as to why such mobilization is not needed.

These are not theoretical criteria. The lessons of the past suggest that when issues of this sort have been ignored or handled badly, the consequences have been hurtful to the nation's interests; when they have been attended to with success, the results have been beneficial not only for Americans, but for others as well.

The United States has typically prospered when its leaders have understood the nature of the changing world. George Washington recognized the nation's vulnerable geopolitical position when he set forth one of the nation's most enduring strategic concepts: no entangling alliances. This was not a design for disengaging from the world; at the time it was an intelligent formula for safeguarding the nation's security by avoiding embroilment in Europe's recurrent wars, many of which emanated from rivalries in the New World. When U.S. officials have not been equally attuned to the evolving international landscape, the results have been doleful—as was the case in the

1930s, when the United States failed to readjust its economic and military policies and forfeited an opportunity to play a constructive role in the quest for global stability and prosperity.

Foreseeing the main threats that challenge the nation's security is a formidable task, and getting it right is vitally important. During World War I, American officials were able to imagine that a German victory on the continent would constitute a threat to U.S. commercial and political interests. Accordingly, President Woodrow Wilson mobilized the country for intervention. Yet he failed to foresee the magnitude of the strategic and economic problems that would emanate after the war from his failure to deal adequately with reparation and war debt issues.

Even when threats are accurately identified, leaders must match means and ends. In 1823, President James Monroe declared that the Western Hemisphere was closed to further colonization; any attempt by European monarchical (and mercantilist) powers to extend their systems to any portion of the Western Hemisphere would be regarded as dangerous to the peace and safety of the United States. But Monroe had no ability to enforce his doctrine. Of course, he realized that he could rely on British military capabilities to deter France and Spain from intervening and reestablishing their presence in the New World, but Monroe and his successors had no ability to offset British power, the principal threat to U.S. well-being and security. At the end of the nineteenth century, when Secretary of State John Hay issued the famous Open-Door notes calling on the great powers to allow equal commercial opportunity within their spheres of influence inside China and to respect China's territorial integrity, he, too, had no ability to support his policy. The open-door policy beautifully encapsulated the mixture of commercial ambition and ideological zealotry that characterized U.S. strategic thinking, but it invited contempt abroad for the absence of military force to buttress American diplomatic principles.

Nonetheless, the record of U.S. diplomacy is not one of unremitting error, as many Americans think. At various times, U.S. officials have moved proactively to create opportunity for the country and to promote stability for the world. During World War II, they conceived institutions, such as the United Nations, the International Monetary Fund, and the World Bank, that were designed to overcome the problems that had beset the international economy after World War I. They also recognized the need to establish a favorable balance of power in Europe and Asia. In the 1960s, President John F. Kennedy initiated the Peace Corps to address third-world development and burnish the U.S. image in the competition with the Soviet Union. In the 1970s, President Richard M. Nixon reversed more than two decades of U.S. policy, opened relations with the People's Republic of China, and tried to use Beijing to counter the burgeoning military power of the Soviet Union. And in the wake of Gorbachev's reforms and the toppling of the Berlin Wall, George Herbert Walker Bush worked assiduously to bring a unified Germany into the NATO alliance.

Throughout their history, Americans have debated the position and role of the United States in world politics. Until 1945, they mostly preferred to disengage from conflicts in Europe, focus on territorial expansion in North America, thwart perceived dangers in the Western Hemisphere, and promote their trade. After World War II, U.S. officials made a different set of choices and decided that the country should play the role of hegemon and stabilizer in international politics—that was a choice. Twenty-five years before—after World War I—that choice had been rejected. Whatever role it assumes in the future, the United States must develop military and economic capabilities and deploy them in a way that matches its aspirations, thus raising difficult choices about levels of military spending, the desirability of volunteer versus professional armies, the balance among conventional, nuclear, and counterinsurgency forces, and the trade-offs between domestic priorities, such as universal health care, and strategic goals.

The United States has often attempted to spread its political, economic, and social values to other countries. Yet in doing so it has had to face difficult trade-offs with security and economic interests. Woodrow Wilson wanted to universalize American principles. Peace, he insisted, required that the European powers embrace U.S. principles: freedom of the seas, equal commercial opportunity, self-determination of peoples, and arms limitation. He did not, however, sufficiently acknowledge the practical requirements and burdens that inhered in such a vision. Nor could he persuade Europeans or Americans to support him. Years later, Nixon and Henry Kissinger attempted to strip U.S. policy of its ideological fervor but, in so doing, produced a policy that many Americans found to be deeply troubling. Today, the tension between values and interests often involves choices between supporting democracy and human rights and retaining the loyalty or stability of authoritarian governments, such as in Pakistan, Saudi Arabia, or China, that benefit the United States.

Finally, U.S. leaders must create support for their strategy without generating myths that later constrain effective adaptation. Truman's mobilization of the country to battle Communism, for example, produced an ideological fervor that blinded the country to subsequent disagreements between Soviet and Chinese Communists. Ronald Reagan seemed to master the balance more ably—he rallied the country to build strength to cope with the Soviet threat and then adjusted his vision and mobilized domestic support to exploit new opportunities to cooperate with Soviet leader Mikhail Gorbachev, a cooperation that helped to bring the cold war to an end.

The lessons of the past can certainly be debated. But, ultimately, policy makers do need to formulate policy based on an appreciation of the international landscape, an assessment of threats, a calculation of objectives, and an integration of values and interests. Policy makers must assign priorities and make critical trade-offs on such key issues as international leadership, military dominance, the use of force, the promotion of democracy, the United States' global image, and participation in international institutions. Once priorities are sorted through, means and ends must be reconciled, resources need to be assigned, and instruments of governance designed. Disparate bureaucracies must be mobilized in pursuit of shared goals, and public opinion must be garnered to support the overall mission. These undertakings are the necessary requisites of any strategy.

What's Ahead

The contributors set forth provocative ideas. As readers will see, they agree that threats abound, but they believe that threats have been misconstrued by President Bush and his advisers. Some focus, as does James Kurth, on the mishandling of the Sunni insurgents in Iraq, whereas others, such as Niall Ferguson, are skeptical about the priority accorded to preempting terrorism and downright scornful of the war in Iraq. Preemptive unilateralism, in Ferguson's view, diverts attention from endemic religious strife throughout the Middle East, as well as from the vulnerabilities in the world economy. Other commentators, such as Robert Kagan, worry that while the United States is immersed in a quagmire in Iraq, China is rising as a formidable adversary and Russia is recouping its strength. Still other contributors, such as Stephen Van Evera, G. John Ikenberry, Douglas A. Irwin, and Barry Eichengreen, maintain that officials are so enveloped by traditional thinking and spending habits that they are failing to address the challenges of global warming, pandemics, proliferation of weapons of mass destruction (WMDs), energy shortfalls, and trade and budgetary deficits. Vacuous rhetoric about freedom and democracy, writes Samantha Power, conceals a flawed strategy that obfuscates real interests and tangible objectives. Deeds, she insists, are far more important than words; and the deeds, argue Charles S. Maier, Francis Fukuyama, and David M. Kennedy, must attenuate religious fervor and social and economic inequality, promote justice, and show a respect for the principles of sovereignty abroad and popular will at home. And almost all the contributors agree that unilateralist instincts must be disciplined or resisted and that collaboration and multilateralism must be restored.

We do not attempt to foreshadow their views at length: the chapters speak powerfully for themselves. The contributors do often clash sharply in what they see ahead and how the United States should respond. We make no attempt to smooth over disagreements or to generate a false consensus. Our aim is not to produce a single strategic vision or recommendation for a future administration. Instead, in the concluding chapter, we explicate the debates that run through the chapters. The goal is to clarify in vibrant colors the nature of the trade-offs involved in choosing between different scenarios and options. Americans do need to think clearly about a complex world, but that does not mean oversimplifying inherent dilemmas. We also save one additional critical task for the conclusion—articulating the key assumptions and principles that almost all the authors, sometimes implicitly, do accept. Differences aside, these principles will likely be central to any American foreign policy, and it is essential to identify them and consider whether they offer a viable basis for effective planning.

Making strategy is tough, and more than one intelligent observer has argued that composing strategy statements is a waste of time, or perhaps even worse. Yet no one involved in the national security community would argue against thinking through goals, interests, and threats. No one would dispute that means and ends must be reconciled and that to do so one must have a sense of priorities. And no one would dismiss the importance of values in thinking through the utility and appeal of any particular policy. Such matters are indispensable for the security and prosperity of the American people and, indeed, for the security and prosperity of peoples around the globe.

Yet formulaic and comprehensive documents such as those designed for submission to Congress, and even those more secret national strategy statements that were so important to waging the cold war, have had serious deficiencies. They conflate and they generalize; they often sound like menus; rarely do they contain the interpretive insights that transform strategic vision into strategic policy. The following chapters are intended to address the essential ingredients that must be incorporated into the making of national security policy. In their eclectic ways, we hope that they will stimulate debate and dialogue about goals, interests, threats, values, and institutions. Our aim is to encourage critical thinking about priorities and trade-offs. If the United States is to lead the world, as all our contributors think it should, we need creative thought and, yes, imagination, about some of the most daunting and most important issues of our times.

Notes

1. Thomas Kean and Lee Hamilton, *9/11 Commission Report* (Washington, DC, 2004), 254, http://govinfo.library.unt.edu/911/report/index.htm.

2. *The National Security Strategy of the United States of America* (Washington, DC: The White House, 2002), 15; also see *The National Security Strategy of the United States of America* (Washington, DC: The White House, 2006).

3. Inaugural address (January 20, 2005), http://www.whitehouse.gov/news/releases/2005/01/20050120-1.html.

4. *National Security Strategy* (2002), 4.

5. For fighting poverty as a "moral imperative," see ibid., 14; for expanding the "circle of development" and "building the infrastructure of democracy," see *National Security Strategy* (2006), 31–34.

6. See, for example, Bob Woodward, *State of Denial: Bush at War, Part III* (New York: Simon & Schuster, 2006); George Packer, *The Assassins' Gate: America in Iraq* (New York: Farrar, Straus, & Giroux, 2005); Thomas E. Ricks, *Fiasco: The America Military Adventure in Iraq* (New York: Penguin, 2006); Ron Suskind, *The One Percent Doctrine: Deep Inside America's Pursuit of Its Enemies since 9/11* (New York: Simon & Schuster, 2006).

7. Zbigniew Brzezinski, *The Choice: Global Domination or Global Leadership* (New York: Basic Books, 2004); Robert Jervis, *American Foreign Policy in a New Era* (New York: Routledge, 2005); John E. Mueller, *Overblown: How Politicians and the Terrorism Industry Inflate National Security Threats, and Why We Believe Them* (New York: Free Press, 2006).

8. Philip H. Gordon, "The End of the Bush Revolution," *Foreign Affairs* 85 (July/August 2006).

9. Including us. See, for example, Melvyn P. Leffler, "9/11 and American Foreign Policy," *Diplomatic History* 29 (June 2005): 395–413; Jeffrey W. Legro, *Rethinking the World: Great Power Strategies and International Order* (Ithaca, NY: Cornell University Press, 2005), 166–172.

ONE

A Farewell to Geopolitics
Stephen Van Evera

WHAT GRAND STRATEGY should the United States adopt in the post-9/11 era?

The balance-of-power concerns that shaped U.S. grand strategy from 1917 to 1991 have faded sharply. The nuclear revolution has made conquest among great powers impossible. As a result, other great powers now pose far less threat to U.S. national security than they did in the past.

At the same time a grave new threat to the security of all major powers has arisen: terrorism with weapons of mass destruction (WMDs). This threat stems from two phenomena: the spread of WMD materials and technology and the rise of terrorist groups that aspire to mass killing.

Threats to the global commons, especially global warming and threats to global public health, also seem increasingly serious.

These new dangers pose a common threat to all major powers. And they cannot be defeated without common action by those powers.

Three policies are called for:

- The world's major powers should organize themselves into a grand alliance, or concert—along the lines of the 1815 Concert of Europe—to take united action against WMD proliferation, WMD terrorism, and threats to the global commons. The United States should lead in creating and sustaining this new concert.
- The United States should reorient its national security policies and programs toward counterterror and countering WMD proliferation while downgrading efforts to prepare for war against other major powers.

- Programs to protect the environment and global public health should be given far higher priority in U.S. foreign policy.

American Strategy, 1917–1991: Keep Industrial Eurasia Divided

From 1917 to 1991 American national security policy focused on maintaining the political division of industrial Eurasia. American policy makers noted that industrial Eurasia (Europe plus Japan) in toto had somewhat more industrial power than the United States. They observed that modern military power was distilled from industrial power. They therefore feared that any state that controlled all of industrial Eurasia could exploit its superior economic resources to build a war machine superior to America's. Such a state, they feared, might project its power across the Atlantic and threaten or even conquer the United States. Hence officials in Washington persistently opposed the expansion of states that reached for Eurasian hegemony, fighting bitter wars to contain Germany from 1917 to 1918 and 1941 to 1945 and a long cold war to contain the Soviet Union from 1947 to 1989.

American leaders sold these struggles to the U.S. public with crusading rhetoric of a battle between dictatorship and democracy—as wars of a "free" world against tyranny, waged to save others from evil. The U.S. public largely bought these idealistic arguments. Today many Americans still believe that the United States fought the wars of 1917 through 1989 for idealist reasons. In fact, however, U.S. policy makers acted largely for power-political reasons. They worried that a Eurasian hegemon would possess the power to injure the United States, and worked to prevent any Eurasian hegemony for that reason.[1] The U.S. policy makers' logic paralleled the balance-of-power logic that guided traditional British policy toward the European continent, leading Britain to contain the expansion of France under Louis XIV, Napoleonic France, Czarist Russia, Wilhelmine Germany, and Nazi Germany.[2]

Terrorism was not considered a significant threat to the United States between 1917 and 1991. Very little terror was directed against the United States during these years. Nor was nuclear proliferation considered a prime threat. During the first five-plus decades of the nuclear era (1945–2001), nuclear proliferation was seen as a worry but one that was subordinate to geopolitical concerns.

Threats to the global commons seemed remote. The global climate seemed unthreatened. Threats to U.S. public health were recognized, but solutions to these threats were not believed to lie in protecting global public health.

The Fading of Geopolitical Threats after 1991

The danger that a Eurasian hegemon might appear and threaten the United States largely disappeared after the Soviet Union collapsed in 1991.

There is now no plausible candidate for Eurasian hegemony on the horizon. China comes closest, but not very close.[3] Someday China may rival the United States in military power, but that day is decades away.[4] And even then China will pose little geopolitical threat to the United States for four reasons.

First, geography makes China a markedly less plausible candidate for Eurasian hegemony than was Germany in 1917 and 1941 or the Soviet Union in 1947. Germany and the Soviet Union were adjacent to large industrial regions of Europe that they could invade over land. In contrast, China is not adjacent to large, vulnerable industrial regions. Europe's industrial areas are very far from China. Japan is a major industrial region near China, but it lies across a vast water barrier from the Asian mainland. A conventional Chinese invasion of Japan across this imposing water barrier would be nearly impossible. China therefore does not have important industrial targets that it might conquer within easy reach. Geography naturally precludes China from gaining a wider industrial empire.

Second, if China nevertheless does somehow conquer other industrial regions, it will gain little strength by doing so. The reason is that today's postindustrial knowledge-based economies are far harder for a conqueror to harness to aggressive purposes than were the smokestack economies of the 1940s and 1950s. Postindustrial economies depend on free access to technical and social information. This access requires some domestic press freedom and access to the Internet, foreign publications, and foreign travel. But the police measures needed to subdue a conquered society require that these channels be controlled because they also serve as carriers of subversive ideas. Thus key elements of the economic fabric now must be ripped out to maintain control over conquered polities. Conquerors must stifle the productivity of those they conquer in order to control them, leaving conquerors with little or no net economic gain. This is a marked change from the smokestack era, when societies could be conquered and policed with far less collateral harm to their economies.

Third, the rising power of nationalism guarantees that China will pay large costs to police any empire that it conquers. The age of empire on the cheap has passed with the spread of nationalist ideas, small arms, and guerrilla tactics. A Chinese reach for empire will likely collide with effective resistance of the kind that defeated the Soviet Union in Afghanistan (1979–1989) and the United States in Vietnam (1961–1975).

Fourth, and most important, the nuclear revolution makes great powers virtually unconquerable. Any state with a secure nuclear deterrent is secure from conquest, as it could annihilate any attacker. And a secure deterrent is far easier to maintain than to threaten, so nuclear powers can defend themselves even against states with many times their economic power. As a result, the United States could defend itself against China even if China grew to become the world's largest economy, conquered its neighbors, and then found a way to harness their industrial power for war. Under such exceedingly far-fetched circumstances, China still could not conquer the United States without first developing a nuclear first-strike capability against the United States. But a Chinese nuclear first-strike capability is a pipe dream and will remain so. It would require an implausibly overwhelming Chinese economic superiority over the United States. An economically fast-growing and politically unchecked China could never gain such vast economic superiority even in a best-case scenario for China. A Chinese nuclear first-strike capability against the United States is not in the cards. Therefore, a plausible Chinese threat to U.S. sovereignty can be ruled out for the foreseeable future.

For these reasons, addressing geopolitical threats should have far less priority in U.S. national security policy than in the past. Other major powers are not the danger to U.S. security that they once were. Even a vast increase in the assets possessed by China—or Russia or the major European powers—would leave them unable to threaten the sovereignty of the United States. The United States can therefore afford to put much less priority on limiting their power.

Three New Dangers: WMD Spread, WMD Terrorists, Threats to the Global Commons

As geopolitical threats have faded, three dangerous new threats have emerged.

WMD Proliferation

The global security of nuclear weapons and materials has deteriorated in recent years. The Soviet collapse made Soviet nuclear weapons, materials, and scientists more available to terrorists. Enough nuclear material to make tens of thousands of atomic bombs remains in poorly secured Russian facilities, ripe for theft or sale to terrorists.[5]

The advance and spread of technology is lowering the cost of developing WMDs. Even such poor states as North Korea can now afford it. This trend will continue in coming decades as new means of mass destruction emerge from the advances of bioscience and perhaps nanoscience. A megatrend toward the proliferation of WMD capabilities is appearing.[6]

New nuclear proliferators have appeared on the scene. The 1980s and early 1990s saw large counterproliferation successes: South Africa abandoned the bomb, Argentina and Brazil shelved their nuclear programs, and Ukraine, Kazakhstan, and Belarus dismantled their Soviet-legacy nuclear arsenals. Momentum seemed to be with the nonproliferation regime. More recently, things have ominously reversed. India and Pakistan tested nuclear weapons in 1998, North Korea has developed and built nuclear weapons, and Iran has moved further toward developing them. Pakistan's nuclear technology has been spread to others by the renegade leader of Pakistan's nuclear program, A. Q. Khan.

WMD Terrorists

A new breed of terrorists who aspire to mass killing has appeared. The years 1988 to 1995 saw the emergence of terrorist groups—the Islamist al Qaeda (1988) and the Japanese group Aum Shinrikyo (1994/1995)—that pursue mass murder and would use nuclear weapons or other WMDs if they had them.

Before the 1990s students of terror assumed that no terrorists aspired to commit mass murder. The watchword was that "terrorists want lots of people watching, not lots of people dead."[7] Terrorists were assumed to operate in the realm of pragmatic politics in pursuit of defined political aims.

The appearance of al Qaeda and Aum Shinrikyo proved this assumption wrong. Some terror groups do aspire to vast destruction. In 1998 Osama bin Laden proclaimed that "to kill Americans...civilian and military—is an individual duty for every Muslim who can do it in any country in which it is possible."[8] A former al Qaeda press spokesman, Suleiman Abu Ghaith, claimed that al Qaeda had a right to kill four million Americans, including two million children.[9] Clearly, al Qaeda will use WMDs to commit immense murder if it finds the opportunity.

More terrorist groups that aspire to mass killing will likely appear in future years. Millenarian ideas are on the rise in all five major world religions.[10] Such thinking, which views catastrophic events as a good thing, offers a rationale for nihilistic WMD attacks. Hateful forms of nonmillenarian fundamentalist religious beliefs are also on the rise across the globe. The problem of mass murder fueled by violent religious ideas will get worse before it gets better.

Together, the spread of WMDs and the appearance of groups that aspire to mass killing face the United States with a serious threat of WMD terrorism, now and for many years to come.

Emerging Dangers to the Global Commons

If unchecked, climate change could wreak large injury to civilization. Vast damage to global agriculture and to coastal regions could ensue. Scores or hundreds of millions of people could be made homeless by rising ocean waters and desertification of farmlands. This danger is shared by all humanity, as every society will suffer, albeit to different degrees, from the calamity.

Other common threats include the H5N1 avian flu virus, other emerging infectious diseases, and the appearance of antibiotic resistance among known infectious diseases. These dangers seem minor—until they arrive. (The 1918 flu epidemic killed 675,000 Americans, more than both world wars combined. Wilhelm II's Imperial German Army and Hitler's Wehrmacht were bad, but flu bugs were worse.) These diseases pose a common threat because they will ignore borders and threaten everyone. The danger they pose is growing with greater interaction between the human and animal worlds and with irresponsible use of medicine, which is creating antibiotic-resistant strains. At the same time, the potential to address these dangers by common action is growing as our understanding of infectious disease expands. Diseases that once were invincible can now be mitigated or defeated by effective common action. Both the threat and the opportunity to defeat the threat are growing.

Climate change and emerging infectious diseases pose common problems that must be addressed by common action taken jointly with other states. Unilateral action by individual states will not be enough.

An American Strategy to Address the New Threats

A U.S. strategy to counter these new threats—WMD terror and threats to the global commons—should have three elements.

Create and Sustain a Concert of Cooperation among the World's Major Powers

In 1815 the victorious powers that had defeated Napoleon feared more mass revolutions like the French Revolution. They also feared conflict among themselves, partly because they worried that interstate warfare would weaken their regimes, bringing on the revolutions they hoped to avoid.[11] To address these problems, they created a Concert of Europe. Under the Concert they agreed to cooperate to repress revolution across Europe while also agreeing on rules to resolve or contain their mutual conflicts.

Today the world again faces a threat from below, this time from WMD terrorists. The world also faces other common threats, especially to the climate and to global public health. A concert of cooperation among the major powers is again needed to address these shared dangers.[12]

A concert is both possible and necessary. It is possible because the world's major states now pose little threat to each other—far less than they did before the nuclear revolution. As noted earlier, nuclear weapons have made conquest among major powers almost impossible. As a result, competition for security, which fueled much conflict among great powers in the past, has greatly abated.[13] In this way, nuclear weapons have freed the major powers to cooperate against other dangers. Because the powers are less dangerous to each other, they can more easily make common cause to solve other problems.

A concert is also possible because all major powers are threatened by WMD terror and by dangers to climate and health.[14] Being jointly menaced by these threats, they have a common interest in defeating them and so share a common interest in cooperating to defeat them. None will be tempted to say, "those problems threaten you, not us, so we won't help," because they imperil everyone.[15] All will be inclined to cooperate as long as they understand this.

A concert is necessary because WMD proliferation cannot be contained and WMD terror cannot be defeated without common action by the world's great powers. Nor can the climate be protected or global health be preserved by unilateral action by one country.

Counterterror policies often are only as strong as their weakest link. For example, if terrorist groups find haven anywhere, as they did in Afghanistan in the 1990s, they can flourish. One refuge is all they need. Hence every state must deny WMD terrorists access to their own and their neighbors' territory. Exceptions cannot be allowed.

Efforts to police WMD spread and WMD terrorists often are best enforced by threat of economic sanctions against miscreant states.[16] But sanctions are effective only if all major industrial states participate. They are far weaker if a single major state defects. Thus the coalition against WMD spread and WMD terrorists must include every major industrial state.

Broad common action is also required to protect climate and health. No state can protect itself by its unilateral action from the harmful effects of fossil-fuel burning by other countries. No state can fully protect itself from pandemic diseases that emerge from other societies. Instead, a key defense lies in proactive collective public health measures abroad to prevent the emergence of pandemic diseases wherever they might occur.

Can the United States catalyze such a broad cooperation? The United States forged and sustained vast coalitions of states, commanding most of the world's economic power, during World War II and the cold war. If the United States could fashion broad cooperation then, it can surely do it today.

The new concert would require much global consensus building but only modest and feasible institution building. Some new institutions will be needed, but most concert functions could be implemented through existing institutions, such as the North Atlantic Treaty Organization (NATO) and other alliances, the United Nations (UN), the International Atomic Energy Agency (IAEA), Interpol, and the Proliferation Security Initiative (PSI). A concert strategy is not impossibly ambitious.[17]

Other U.S. policies should be subordinated to the need to create and maintain the new concert.

First, and most important, the United States–China rivalry must be kept within bounds so that U.S.-Chinese cooperation against WMD proliferation and WMD terror is maintained. As noted earlier, China will likely rise in relative power for some years, perhaps becoming a peer competitor to the United States someday. A global power shift is under way. History warns that power transitions are dangerous and hard to manage. History further warns that the two strongest powers often clash, as each is the main threat to the other.

If China's ascent is mismanaged, the danger of a United States–China cold war, or even a hot war, will arise. Such conflicts would spell disruption of U.S.-Chinese cooperation against WMD terror and other common threats. This disruption of U.S.-Chinese cooperation would gravely threaten U.S. and global security. Instead, the United States must manage China's rise in a way that maintains U.S.-Chinese cooperation against the new threats.

Second, the United States should eschew strategies and tactics that harm its ability to lead a global coalition as it pursues its war on al Qaeda and its other foreign policy objectives. Instead, it should harmonize its other policies with the requisites of building and sustaining American global leadership. Specifically, the United States should conserve its global legitimacy and avoid policies that undermine it.

This means that the United States should pursue preventive war only in extremis, because preventive war casts the United States in the role of aggressor and so can undercut its legitimacy in the eyes of others. Preventive war should remain as an option but should be waged only with substantial international approval. Accordingly, the 2002 "Bush doctrine," which embedded unilateral preventive war in U.S. strategy as a regular instrument of policy, should be dropped.[18]

The United States should also avoid policies that require counterinsurgency, as counterinsurgent action inexorably draws the United States into brutal police work that presents an ugly face to the world. Scandals such as that of Abu Ghraib are likely whenever U.S. forces are asked to conduct counterinsurgency. The best answer is to avoid counterinsurgencies except in extremis. This means avoiding aggressive wars and the occupations they often entail. Instead, U.S. strategy should prefer more indirect and less violent instruments of influence abroad. As a first resort, it should rely on economic sanctions, military action by allies and armed proxies, forceful argument and persuasion through public diplomacy, and occasional covert action—not aggressive war. It should attract others to help with these tasks by persuading them that they will benefit from America's success. This requires adopting policies and rhetoric that persuade others that America acts to further their interests as well as its own and that American success will improve their lot.

Accordingly, the United States should speak in respectful tones to other governments. Before taking action, it should consult these governments on policies that affect their interests and make a plausible show of reflecting those interests in its policies. It should avoid cutting an imperious profile.

Since 2001 the United States' standing around the world has plummeted as publics and elites elsewhere have reacted in allergic fashion to the policies and rhetoric of the George W. Bush administration.[19] What went wrong? The Bush administration regularly broke the rules I outline here. It waged preventive war against Iraq without much international blessing, and in 2002 it adopted a doctrine of waging unilateral preventive wars, prompting arguments overseas that the United States is an aggressor that acts without regard for the broader interest. It entangled itself in a counterinsurgent campaign in Iraq that presents a grim spectacle to the world, arousing others against the United States. It treated other governments brusquely, often leaving them feeling unconsulted or disrespected.[20] It sometimes spoke in bullying tones toward others. It presented the arrogant and imperious John Bolton as its face to the world as UN ambassador.

The Bush administration refused, reduced, or ended U.S. participation in a number of international institutions and treaties that are popular abroad. Specifically, it moved to weaken a draft UN accord to limit small arms traffic, it blocked a proposal to strengthen the 1972 treaty banning the production of biological weapons, and it refused to join or remain in a range of treaties, including the Kyoto Protocol on global warming, the International Criminal Court, and the 1972 Anti-Ballistic Missile (ABM) Treaty.[21] Some of these treaties were flawed, but the administration rarely offered to fix them. Instead, it framed its rejection of these treaties in sharp language that seemed to deny that the United States has an obligation to help solve the problems these treaties address. This sharp language fostered an impression abroad that the United States cannot be trusted to act in the common interest of civilized societies. Some in the conservative movement have further raised eyebrows by talking of the need for an American empire.[22] The United States cannot lead a global concert until these policies are changed. Instead, the United States must adopt policies and rhetoric that demonstrate that the United States will act to protect the common global welfare.

Third, the United States must build its diplomatic capacity. American statecraft skills have atrophied in recent years, as the State Department has been poorly funded. American capacity for public diplomacy (shaping ideas abroad) has also atrophied. These skills must be redeveloped if the United States is to lead a global coalition.

Redirect U.S. National Security Resources toward the New Security Threat: WMD Terror

How shall the United States apply the power of a U.S.-led concert to defeat the WMD terror threat?

U.S. declaratory policy should identify the threat of WMD terror as the prime threat to U.S. national security. And the United States should, together with its concert allies, wage the war on WMD terror on every relevant front. Six specific missions should be pursued. Together these six missions form an effective counterterror strategy.[23]

Mission no. 1: The military-intelligence offensive. The U.S.-led concert must be prepared to deter regimes from giving haven to al Qaeda by credibly threatening military action against them if they aid al Qaeda. It must be prepared to oust such regimes by force if deterrence fails, as it ousted the Taliban from power in Afghanistan in 2001–2002. It must be ready to build the strength and legitimacy of states such as Pakistan that are willing to root WMD terrorists from their own territory but are too weak to do so.

The United States must also sustain a global intelligence offensive aimed at rolling up al Qaeda networks through police work. This should be done largely in cooperation with allied intelligence agencies.

This offensive should be highly selective. It should focus only on terror networks that threaten WMD attack against the United States or its concert allies. It should be conducted with heavy reliance on proxies and in cooperation with allies. Sideshows against secondary nuisances, such as Saddam's Iraq or Assad's Syria or local terror groups that do not threaten WMD attacks, should be avoided.

Mission no. 2: Securing weapons of mass destruction and limiting WMD proliferation. All necessary steps should be taken to ensure that terrorists cannot gain access to nuclear weapons or other WMDs.[24] Loose nuclear weapons and materials in Russia and elsewhere must be secured. Nuclear proliferation, especially to potential rogue states such as Iran and North Korea, must be stemmed. This is best done by forging a broad coalition of states to energetically apply both sticks and carrots, including economic sanctions and security guarantees, to persuade potential proliferators to agree in negotiations to forswear nuclear weapons. Discussion of ousting the regimes of potential proliferators should stop, as such talk only feeds the nuclear appetites of these regimes. Force should be used only as a last resort.

The nuclear nonproliferation regime should be bolstered and tightened. The 1970 Nuclear Nonproliferation Treaty (NPT) erred in allowing nonnuclear states to build uranium enrichment and plutonium production facilities; states can build such facilities as a move toward nuclear weapons and then withdraw from the treaty and build weapons when they are ready. This loophole should be closed. This will require a new system to provide nuclear reactor fuel to states that agree to forgo uranium enrichment or plutonium production.

The international community should establish a new principle that states have civil legal liability for any damage ensuing from terrorist use of their WMDs. This would give potential proliferators reason to fear that their national WMD programs will bring them major economic harm. The worried finance ministries and business communities of potential proliferators, fearing endless lawsuits if their armed forces lost control of a nuclear weapon or other WMD, would become powerful lobbies against proliferation. All governments would have greater reason to secure existing WMD arsenals. As a result, WMD proliferation would be prevented, and WMD security would improve.

Mission no. 3: Homeland security. The U.S. homeland should be hardened against attack. The current U.S. homeland security program is more a palliative to calm a worried public than a real security program. Instead, the United States should seriously pursue homeland security. The action agenda this requires is well known: reform of the FBI; integration of local police, fire departments, and public health laboratories into homeland security; better control of U.S. borders; greater security for U.S. nuclear reactors, chemical plants, railroads, and ports from terrorist attack; and a rewriting of U.S. insurance laws governing terrorist incidents to give businesses an incentive to harden their infrastructure against an attack.[25]

Mission no. 4: Waging a war of ideas. The al Qaeda terror threat will persist until the terms of debate in the radical wing of the Muslim world are changed. A program to bring this change in the Islamist terms of debate must be developed. Otherwise al Qaeda will always find new recruits and places to hide.

Mission no. 5: Ending inflammatory conflicts. Al Qaeda feeds on warfare. It exploits the Israel-Palestinian conflict, the India-Pakistan conflict in Kashmir, the wars in Chechnya and Iraq, and past conflicts in Bosnia, Kosovo,

East Timor, and Somalia in its propaganda, painting Muslims as victims in these conflicts whether or not they are. It also uses these conflicts as a training ground for its terrorists. Accordingly, the United States should work to dampen conflicts throughout the Mideast region. Mitigating these conflicts would take important cards out of al Qaeda's hands.[26] Toward this goal the United States must develop and use its peacemaking capacity.

Mission no. 6: Saving, resuscitating, or intervening in failed states. Failed states are incubators for terror. They provide potential havens in which terrorists can establish bases for training and organizing. The United States should therefore develop state capacity for preventing or ameliorating state failure; or it should develop a strategy for directly applying American power to destroy WMD terrorist elements in failed states using U.S. Special Forces, local proxies, or other elements of U.S. power.[27]

All six missions—even homeland security—can be better performed with cooperation from other states. However, broad cooperation by other states is essential only for the first two missions, the military-intelligence offensive and the securing of WMDs and limiting of WMD spread. A concert strategy is serving its main purpose if broad cooperation on these two missions is achieved. Specifically, a concert strategy asks that all states firmly police WMD terrorists on their own territory, assist efforts to police WMD terrorists in neighboring states and client states, share global intelligence on terrorists, and cooperate fully with global efforts to secure and contain the spread of WMDs. Help on other issues will be needed from some states, but not from most. Thus a concert strategy does not make impossibly large demands of others. It asks only for feasible and reasonable cooperation.

Performing the six counterterror missions will require large innovations in U.S. national security policy. The United States should put relatively fewer resources into traditional military functions—army, navy, air force—and relatively more resources into counterterror functions. The first two missions, the military-intelligence offensive and securing and limiting proliferation of WMDs, require capable conventional forces. But both missions also require intelligence and postconflict management capabilities, including capacities for state building and conflict resolution in conquered societies; and the second mission requires robust diplomatic skills to persuade others to lock up loose nukes and bolster the NPT. The other four missions—homeland security, the war of ideas, ending inflammatory conflict, and saving, resuscitating, or policing failed states—require largely nonmilitary capabilities. To defeat the WMD terror threat, therefore, the United States must not only maintain strong conventional military forces but also build up nonmilitary instruments: intelligence, homeland security, diplomacy for locking down loose WMDs around the world, and the capacities to wage a war of ideas, to end conflicts that breed terror, and to rescue failed states. The organizations that will do these things—U.S. intelligence agencies, local law enforcement, the Coast Guard, the Center for Disease Control, local public health agencies, the Cooperative Threat Reduction Initiative (CTR), the State Department Office of Public Diplomacy, the Agency for International Development, and others—must be strengthened.[28]

Elevate the Protection of the Global Environment and Global Public Health to Higher Priority in U.S. Foreign Policy

These goals are viewed as minor concerns in U.S. foreign policy making. They deserve far higher priority, commensurate with their importance to the national welfare. A solution to climate change will require especially large political effort by U.S. political leaders.

To stem climate change we must replace the global coal and oil industries with new clean-energy industries. The chief barriers to this transformation are more political than technical or economic. The transformation can be achieved at feasible cost by phasing in a steep global carbon tax or a tight cap on carbon emissions in a carbon cap-and-trade system. A carbon tax or carbon cap will spark an explosion of new clean-energy technologies and businesses by giving clean-energy producers the upper hand against carbon energies in the marketplace. But a carbon tax or carbon cap will also be fiercely resisted by the coal and oil industries.[29] Defeating them will require an immense political effort. The clean technologies and industries we need can be created; what is needed is the political will to enact the global carbon tax that will create them.

Selective Engagement: A Supporting Element for a Concert Strategy

Before the WMD terror threat became manifest, I favored a U.S grand strategy that Robert Art calls *selective engagement*.[30] Selective engagement still makes sense and should be pursued along with a concert strategy. This works because the two strategies are complementary: a selective-engagement strategy helps establish the preconditions for the broad cooperation that a concert strategy requires. Concert should now be the prime strategy, with selective engagement playing a supporting role.

A selective-engagement strategy defines America's prime interest to lie in the preservation of peace and order among the world's major states and economic regions. It assumes that war among major powers or in economically important areas can harm American economic and cultural interests and can therefore spread to engulf the United States, and so it should be prevented. The main threat to the United States is no longer conquest but war itself. The United States prevents such war by deterring aggression among the world's major powers and among states in important regions.

Such a policy prevents conflict by raising the cost of aggression for aggressor states and making preemptive or preventive aggression less necessary for status quo powers. It mimics the policy of Bismarck's Germany toward central Europe from 1871 to 1890. In those years Bismarck bolstered peace in Germany's neighborhood by weaving a network of defensive alliances among Germany's neighbors, with Germany at the center of the network. Bismarck believed that Germany might be drawn into any new war on its periphery; that Germany therefore had an interest in peace among these states; that war is more likely when governments believe conquest is easy, as aggressors then believe they can aggress successfully, and status quo powers, being more worried, seek to secure themselves by aggression; and that peace could therefore best be preserved by giving German security guarantees to Germany's neighbors in order to raise the cost of aggression and increase the level of security among these neighbors. Bismarck's policy was a striking success: Europe was unusually peaceful during the years 1871–1890.[31] Under selective engagement the United States would pursue a parallel policy in three major regions:

- In Europe the United States would preserve peace by maintaining the NATO alliance, thereby offering a security guarantee to all NATO states, and by offering security guarantees to non-NATO states, conditioned on their willingness to respect the rights of others.
- In East Asia the United States would continue to guarantee the security of Japan, South Korea, Australia, New Zealand, and Taiwan, conditioned on their willingness to behave peacefully toward others. The United States would also reach security understandings with other Asian states, including China.
- In the Middle East the United States would guarantee the security of Israel, conditional on its willingness to agree to peace on reasonable terms with the Arabs. ("Reasonable terms" are essentially those of the four major peace plans that have been widely discussed in recent years: the Clinton parameters of December 2000, the 2003 Geneva Accord, the 2003 Ayalon-Nusseibeh or "People's Voice" initiative, and the Saudi plan of March 2007. These plans call for near-full Israeli withdrawal from the Palestinian territories occupied by Israel in 1967, including Arab East Jerusalem and the Muslim holy places on the Jerusalem Temple Mount, in exchange for full and final peace, with

no return of Palestinian refugees to Israel, who instead would receive financial compensation for lost land and homes.)

The Middle East cannot be stable if Israel is not secure, and the United States should look toward eventual (post–Arab-Israeli peace) Israeli membership in NATO to ensure that security. The United States should also pursue as a goal a wider security order in the Mideast region that would dissuade aggression by all against all. The Mideast will be more peaceful if all states in the region are secure, and the United States should seek to create this security.

The details of U.S. policy will differ across these three regions. But in all three places U.S. policy would include a common core principle: the United States will punish aggression by any state and aid any victim of aggression, unless that aggression is justified by accepted international norms.

A selective-engagement strategy complements a concert strategy because it works to reduce conflict among the world's major powers. Reducing such conflict is also a prime goal and a prime precondition of a concert strategy.

Impediments to Adopting a Concert Strategy

Powerful foreign and domestic forces will likely oppose the adoption of a concert strategy unless there is strong leadership for such a strategy.

Special Interests: Foreign Lobbies, the U.S. Defense Establishment

Unlike other great powers, the United States has a peculiar custom of allowing foreign lobbies free run of its national capital. As a result, foreign lobbies often play a large role in shaping U.S. foreign policies.[32] Several of these lobbies will take a dim view of a U.S. concert strategy. Taiwan's influential lobby works to prevent détente between the United States and China. It will therefore oppose a concert strategy that would entail building U.S.-Chinese cooperation. Accordingly, its agents and allies in the United States will argue in the U.S. media that China poses a security threat to the United States and that the United States can best address this threat by adopting confrontational policies toward China. (The Taiwan lobby already makes this argument and has won important people in Washington to its view, wrong though it is.) Elements of the Israel lobby that align with Israel's rightist Likud party are leery of tight U.S.-European relations, as Europe is critical of Likud's expansionist policies, so these elements will not be enthused about tighter ties between the United States and Europe.[33]

Some Eastern European states, including Poland and the Baltic states, have lobbies that will oppose tighter U.S.-Russian cooperation. Proponents of a concert strategy will have to overcome the disruptive action of these lobbies.

Important elements of the U.S. national security establishment will oppose a concert strategy. The raison d'être of most of the U.S. military establishment is defense against the military threat posed by other great powers. It has ably fulfilled this mission for the past century. It will not easily accept a new concert strategy that makes it less important, thus undercutting its claim for big budgets, while putting other nonmilitary government agencies in more important national security roles. The defense establishment is comfortable having the United States in an adversarial stance toward Russia and China, as this justifies big military budgets, so it will reflexively oppose policies of closer cooperation with those states. It will also favor policies that impede such cooperation. For example, we can expect the U.S. defense industry and its friends in Congress to continue pushing for national missile defense, which creates friction with Russia, and for unduly large U.S. weapons sales to Taiwan and for unconditional U.S. support for Taiwan, which create friction with China.[34]

A concert strategy serves the U.S. national interest. That interest is diffuse and has no powerful lobby to represent it. Foreign lobbies and the defense establishment represent far narrower interests, but these interests are concentrated and organized.[35] A strong law of politics holds that concentrated and organized interests trump the general unorganized interest, even when the unorganized general interest is far larger (as in this case). An American concert strategy would need to overcome this dynamic.

American Cultural Insularity and Lack of Global Governing Expertise

America's capacity to execute a concert strategy is limited by the insularity of American culture and the atrophied diplomatic capacities of the U.S. government. Americans know little about the world. They speak few languages. They rarely go abroad. They would rather watch football and *Survivor* than learn of faraway lands and peoples. As a result, few are prepared to become effective global political managers.

The American federal government is unready for the task of global political manager. As noted earlier, the U.S. State Department is poorly funded and has few reserves of expertise on which to draw.

Directing a global concert is a very demanding task. It requires intense focus and deep knowledge of global affairs on the part of the government and the public. These are not America's strong suits.

Americans are poorly informed about current world politics and international history. As a result, the American public has little grasp of the facts that support the case for a concert strategy. This makes public support for a concert strategy unreliable.

For example, most Americans are unaware that the United States rode to victory in both world wars and in the cold war on the backs of its allies. In fact, the United States achieved success largely through others' sacrifices. Yet the American popular myth holds that those wars were won by American heroes and heroics. This urban legend leaves the U.S. public susceptible to the common argument that cooperation with other states provides few benefits and that allies are pests or freeloaders that the United States can do without.

What is the true picture? In World War I the United States suffered 126,000 military deaths, compared with 7,295,000 total military deaths among its thirteen allies. Thus U.S. military deaths constituted only 1.7 percent of the total among the Allied powers.[36] In World War II the United States suffered 408,000 military deaths, compared with 10,780,000 military deaths among its eighteen allies.[37] Thus U.S. military deaths made up only 3.6 percent of the Allied total in World War II. U.S. allies also made large sacrifices to win the cold war. In all three struggles the United States' allies were essential to its success.

A concert strategy will lack broad public support unless such facts are widely understood. The public must appreciate that the United States did well abroad in the twentieth century only because it forged and led broad alliances. Its great triumphs rested on successful diplomacy that persuaded others to stand with America and share the cost of war. Without allies the United States would have paid a terrible price for victory, if it had won at all. And it will pay a terrible price in the twenty-first century if it goes forward alone, without locking arms with others.

Another example: Americans are broadly unaware of the geopolitical national security concerns (outlined earlier) that led the United States to check German and Soviet expansion in the past century. Hence they are unaware that these geopolitical concerns are obsolete and do not apply to China today. Hence they accept erroneous arguments that China's rise requires the same confrontational response as the past rise of Germany and the Soviet Union.

The U.S. public's ignorance of world affairs makes it susceptible to false claims from special interests who oppose a concert policy for self-serving reasons. A concert policy requires a foundation of strong public support. That support requires a broad public grasp of world politics. Absent that public understanding, special interests may destroy a concert policy by deceiving a gullible public into opposing it.

Neoconservatives have largely shaped U.S. foreign policy in recent years. Their key policy ideas and prescriptions are contrary to the requisites of a concert strategy.[38] American policy must turn away from neoconservative ideas to conduct a successful concert strategy. These specific neoconservative ideas and policies should be downgraded or dropped:

- *Unilateral action.* Neoconservatives have a penchant for acting alone. They often see allies as a hindrance, and they disdain international institutions. But unilateralism is a recipe for defeat in the war on terror. The United States cannot quell the terrorists without broad international cooperation. Victory against terror requires many helping hands, just as it did in both world wars and in the cold war.

- *Preventive war.* Neoconservatives argue that preventive war should be a regular tool of statecraft, but, as noted earlier, the United States should wage preventive war only in extremis. A preventive war is an aggressive war, and as such it tends to provoke a wary or even encircling reaction from others unless it is pursued with some international blessing.

- *Bullying and big-stick diplomacy.* Neoconservatives broadly believe that compliance by others is better won by threats than by conciliation. In their view, sticks work better than carrots. Waving the mailed fist makes friends. They believe in the bandwagon theory of alliances, which holds that states align more often with the most threatening state in the neighborhood. They disbelieve its antithesis, balance-of-threat theory, which holds that states align against the most threatening state and that waving the mailed fist brings self-encirclement. Of course sometimes threats succeed, but history shows that balancing behavior prevails over bandwagoning and that bullying conduct usually wins more enemies than friends, especially when directed at major powers.[39] Accordingly, a concert policy requires that the United States abandon the tone of bullying and intimidation favored by neoconservatives and instead approach others in a more respectful fashion. Bullying should usually be saved for instances when it can be defended as legitimate—for example, with states that have violated important international norms.

- *Empire.* Neoconservatives believe that empire is both feasible and at times necessary. They favor the creation of a broad American sphere of influence, or empire, in the Middle East. Such a policy will arouse wide opposition around the world, as empire is broadly considered illegitimate in the postcolonial era.

- *The silent treatment.* Neoconservatives believe that talks with other states are often a form of appeasement—a demonstration of weakness that invites predation. Hence they often favor a policy of limiting or refusing talks with states with whom the United States has had friction (such as North Korea, Iran, and Syria at various times in recent years). In fact, talks are not a favor to others. Talks can be a forum for offering assurances but also for twisting arms and sowing fear. They are a setting for conveying and explaining threats and for receiving concessions or even surrender from others.

Successful coercive diplomacy requires talks. Coercive power cannot be converted into compliance by others without discussions in which the coercing state explains to the target state what compliance is desired, how it will be measured, and what punishment will ensue if the compliance is not forthcoming. And, of course, cooperation by others cannot be arranged without talks. The global political leadership that a concert strategy requires cannot be exerted without talking with all relevant players.

Neoconservatives also hold views that impede the development of an effective specific counterterror policy. They generally reject the view that WMD terror is the prime threat to U.S. security. Specifically, they underestimated the threat posed by nonstate actors both before and after 9/11, believing instead that state-sponsored terror or aggression poses the greater danger.[40] This leads them to favor allocating too few resources to the WMD terror threat. They also believe that deterring or smashing states is an adequate answer to the terror danger. Against Saddam Hussein, many neoconservatives believed that all else would fall into place once the United States defeated the Iraqi army. Hence they failed to see the need to prepare for postwar problems. Against al Qaeda, they have focused on the need to prepare to smash the armies of hostile states while neglecting the need to develop other tools of statecraft, including the capacity to wage a war of ideas, to dampen conflicts among others, to prevent or address state failure, or to lock down loose WMD materials abroad. Their counterterror strategy rests on the false premise that only terror groups with state sponsors can really harm the United States, so defeating terror requires only defeating or deterring these state sponsors. Their belief in this false premise ensures that they will not develop an effective strategy for countering terror.

Neoconservative ideas are almost exactly wrong for the new age. Neoconservatives would reduce American cooperation with other major powers, instead featuring U.S. unilateralism, exactly when U.S. national security requires more cooperation. Neoconservatives would fail to focus on the greatest threat to the United States, the WMD terror problem. Neoconservatives would pursue an American empire in the Middle East in an age when a reach for empire is no longer feasible and is also likely to worsen the terror threat to the United States by provoking more Muslims to join the jihadis. It is ironic that neoconservatives have risen to power at the moment at which their ideas least fit the times.

Conclusion

Never in modern times have the world's major powers had less reason to compete with each other or more reason to cooperate to solve problems that jointly threaten them all. Current conditions resemble the conditions of 1815, when all the major powers felt endangered by a common threat from below—mass revolution—and cooperated against it. Today the world's major powers are jointly menaced by another threat from below—WMD terror—and by threats to their shared climate and global public health that they must address together. These challenges threaten the whole world and cannot be solved by the unilateral action of a single power. It is therefore both possible and necessary for the world's major states to cooperate to address these problems.

Accordingly, the United States should forge and sustain a broad cooperation against these common problems. It should also refocus its foreign and security policy to address them. This is the best grand strategy for achieving national security in the new era.

Notes

1. Valuable surveys of past American grand strategy are Robert J. Art, *A Grand Strategy for America* (Ithaca, NY: Cornell University Press, 2003), 178–197; Art, "A Defensible Defense: America's Grand Strategy after the Cold War," *International Security* 15, no. 4 (Spring 1991): 5–53 (see 10–23); and Christopher Layne, *The Peace of Illusions: American Grand Strategy from 1940 to the Present* (Ithaca, NY: Cornell University Press, 2006), 15–117.

On the role that balance-of-power logic played in American entry into World War II see also G. R. Sloan, *Geopolitics in United States Strategic Policy, 1890–1987* (New York: St. Martin's, 1988), 113–116 (on Franklin Roosevelt's prewar thought). For examples of prewar balance-of-power thinking in the United States see Livingston Hartley, *Is America Afraid?* (New York: Prentice-Hall, 1937), 47–50, 69–75, 138–143, 175; Walter Lippmann, "The Atlantic and America: The When and Why of Intervention," *Life* 10, no. 14 (April 7, 1941): 84–92; and, discussing these, John A. Thompson, "The Exaggeration of

American Vulnerability: The Anatomy of a Tradition," *Diplomatic History* 16, no. 1 (Winter 1992): 23–43 (see 36–37).

Such arguments later formed the core of the case for a policy of anti-Soviet containment advanced by its principal intellectual architects, including George Kennan and Walter Lippmann. On Kennan, see John Lewis Gaddis, *Strategies of Containment: A Critical Appraisal of Postwar American National Security Policy* (New York: Oxford University Press, 1982), 25–88. On Lippmann, see Walter Lippmann, *U.S. Foreign Policy: Shield of the Republic* (Boston: Little, Brown, 1943), 162–164. Lippmann's book predates the cold war, but his later writings assume the same balance-of-power logic it expresses. For other civilian and military planners who held similar views, see Melvyn P. Leffler, "The American Conception of National Security and the Beginnings of the Cold War," *American Historical Review* 89, no. 2 (April 1984): 346–381 (see 356–358, 370, 374, 377); and Leffler, *A Preponderance of Power: National Security, the Truman Administration, and the Cold War* (Stanford, CA: Stanford University Press, 1992), 10–13 passim.

2. Winston Churchill summarized this traditional British logic: "For four hundred years the foreign policy of England has been to oppose the strongest, most aggressive, most dominating Power on the Continent, and particularly to prevent the Low Countries from falling into the hands of such a Power.... Faced by Philip II of Spain, against Louis XIV under William III and Marlborough, against Napoleon, against William II of Germany, it would have been easy and must have been very tempting to join with the stronger and share the fruits of his conquest. However, we always took the harder course, joined with the less strong Powers, made a combination among them, and thus defeated and frustrated the Continental military tyrant, whoever he was, whatever nation he led. Thus we preserved the liberties of Europe." Winston S. Churchill, *The Gathering Storm* (New York: Bantam, 1961), 186–187.

Kennan echoed these arguments in 1951: "It [is] essential to us, as it was to Britain, that no single Continental land power should come to dominate the entire Eurasian land mass. Our interest has lain rather in the maintenance of some sort of stable balance among the powers of the interior, in order that none of them should effect the subjugation of the others, conquer the seafaring fringes of the land mass, become a great sea power as well as land power, shatter the position of England, and enter—as in these circumstances it certainly would—on an overseas expansion hostile to ourselves and supported by the immense resources of the interior of Europe and Asia"; George F. Kennan, *American Diplomacy, 1900–1950* (New York: New American Library, 1951), 10. For similar statements, see Gaddis, *Strategies of Containment*, 29, 57, and 201, quoting Kennan, National Security Council Report 7 (NSC 7), and John F. Kennedy.

3. Discussing the likely scope and implications of China's rise are Robert J. Art, "The United States and the Rise of China: Implications for the Long Haul," in *China's Ascent: Power, Security, and the Future of International Politics*, ed. Robert S. Ross and Zhu Feng (Ithaca, NY: Cornell University Press, 2008); Joseph S. Nye, "The Challenge of China," in *How to Make America Safe: New Policies for National Security*, ed. Stephen

Van Evera (Cambridge, MA: Tobin Project, 2006), 73–77; and Edward Steinfeld, "Getting China Right," in Van Evera, *How to Make America Safe*, 79–85.

4. Developing this point are Nye, "Challenge of China," and Steinfeld, "Getting China Right."

5. On the danger of insecure nuclear materials, see Graham Allison, *Nuclear Terrorism: The Ultimate Preventable Catastrophe* (New York: Times Books, 2004), 143–150, 177; Matthew Bunn and Anthony Wier, *Securing the Bomb 2006* (Cambridge, MA, and Washington, DC: Project on Managing the Atom, Harvard University and Nuclear Threat Initiative, 2006), and resources at the Nuclear Threat Initiative Web site (http://www.nti.org) and the Managing the Atom Web site (http://www.managingtheatom.org).

6. A worrying forecast that WMD technology will continue to develop and spread dangerously is found in Martin Rees, *Our Final Hour: A Scientist's Warning: How Terror, Error, and Environmental Disaster Threaten Humankind's Future in This Century—On Earth and Beyond* (New York: Basic Books, 2003), 1–71.

7. Terrorist analyst Brian Jenkins in 1974, quoted in Louise Richardson, *What Terrorists Want: Understanding the Enemy, Containing the Threat* (New York: Random House, 2006), 141.

8. In 1998, quoted in Anonymous [Michael Scheuer], *Through Our Enemies' Eyes: Osama bin Laden, Radical Islam, and the Future of America* (Washington, DC: Brassey's, 2002), 59.

9. In 2002 Abu Ghaith announced on an al Qaeda–affiliated Web site, http://www.alneda.com: "We have a right to kill 4 million Americans—2 million of them children—and to...wound and cripple hundreds of thousands." Quoted in Allison, *Nuclear Terrorism*, 12. A portrait of the jihadis' worldview and violent intentions is provided by Mary Habeck, *Knowing the Enemy: Jihadist Ideology and the War on Terror* (New Haven, CT: Yale University Press, 2006).

10. Daniel Benjamin and Steven Simon, *The Age of Sacred Terror* (New York: Simon & Schuster, 2002), 91–94, 419–446.

11. On the Concert, see Robert Jervis, "From Balance to Concert: A Study of International Security Cooperation," *World Politics* 38, no. 1 (October 1985): 58–79; and Paul W. Schroeder, *The Transformation of European Politics, 1763–1848* (Oxford, UK: Oxford University Press, 1994).

12. Also arguing for a U.S. grand strategy focused on building international cooperation to take joint action is Richard N. Haass, "Is There a Doctrine in the House?" *New York Times*, November 8, 2005; and Nina Hachigian and Mona Sutphen, *The Next American Century: How the U.S. Can Thrive as Other Powers Rise* (New York: Simon & Schuster, 2008).

13. I argue that security concerns were a common motive for past wars in Stephen Van Evera, *Causes of War: Power and the Roots of Conflict* (Ithaca, NY: Cornell University Press, 1999), 125–128, 185–190, 203–206.

14. Thus, ironically, nuclear weapons both pose a prime security problem and allow the solution to that problem. The possibility of nuclear weapons in the hands of nondeterrable terrorists compels the major powers to cooperate against

it. Nuclear weapons in the hands of major powers allows this cooperation by dampening security competition among them.

15. Even nontargeted states will be gravely damaged if a nuclear terrorist attack occurs, as a nuclear attack anywhere in the industrial world will likely implode the global trading system, causing a deep worldwide economic depression. There will be no haven from the economic havoc that ensues from a nuclear terror attack.

16. On the effectiveness of sanctions, see Daniel W. Drezner, "The Hidden Hand of Economic Coercion," *International Organization* 57 (Summer 2003): 643–650; and Kimberly Ann Elliott, "The Sanctions Glass: Half Full or Completely Empty?" *International Security* 23, no. 1 (Summer 1998): 50–65.

17. A thoughtful discussion of the requisites for global governance in the new era is Francis Fukuyama, *America at the Crossroads: Democracy, Power, and the Neoconservative Legacy* (New Haven, CT: Yale University Press, 2006), 155–180.

18. The Bush doctrine was framed in the *National Security Strategy of the United States of America* (Washington, DC: The White House, 2002). A friendly description is Keir A. Lieber and Robert J. Lieber, "The Bush National Security Strategy," *U.S. Foreign Policy Agenda, An Electronic Journal of the U.S. Department of State* 7, no. 4 (December 2002), http://usinfo.state.gov/journals/itps/1202/ijpe/pj7-4lieber.htm (accessed January 21, 2008). For more critical discussions, see Fukuyama, *America at the Crossroads*, 81–94; and the "Defense Strategy Review" page of the Project on Defense Alternatives at http://www.comw.org/qdr/.

19. On global views of the United States, see "America's Image Slips, but Allies Share U.S. Concerns over Iran, Hamas," *Pew Global Attitudes Project*, http://pewglobal.org/reports/display.php?ReportID=252 (accessed June 13, 2006). This survey reports that favorable opinions of the United States have fallen sharply since 1999–2000 and are at new lows in some important countries.

20. In 2003 *Newsweek*'s Fareed Zakaria wrote: "Having traveled the world and met with senior government officials in dozens of countries over the past year, I can report that with the exception of Britain and Israel, every country the administration has dealt with feels humiliated by it"; Fareed Zakaria, "The Arrogant Empire," *Newsweek*, March 24, 2003, 18–33 (see 29). Jorge Castañeda, Mexico's reformist foreign minister until January 2003, said of Latin American officials: "We like and understand America. But we find it extremely irritating to be treated with utter contempt"; ibid., 29. A retired senior Turkish diplomat, Ozdem Sanberk, remarked that U.S. abrasiveness helped prevent Turkish support for the 2003 U.S. attack on Iraq: "The way the U.S. has been conducting the negotiations has been, in general, humiliating"; ibid., 33.

21. A summary of these unilateral policies is found in Stephen Schlesinger, "War against Havens for Terrorism: Examining a New Presidential Doctrine," in *The Maze of Fear: Security and Migration after 9/11*, ed. John Tirman (New York: New Press, 2004), 155–168 (see 155–157).

22. See, for example, Frank J. Gaffney, "Worldwide Value," *National Review Online* 5 (2004): 1–3. Gaffney proposed seven ambitious goals for the second Bush administration, including regime change in Iran and North Korea "one way

or another." A critical discussion is found in Jim Lobe, "Neocon Wish List," *Foreign Policy in Focus* (November 11, 2004): 1–2. For more discussion of imperial ideas in the conservative movement, see G. John Ikenberry, "America's Imperial Ambition," *Foreign Affairs* 81, no. 5 (September/October 2002): 44–60; Thomas E. Ricks, "Empire or Not? A Quiet Debate over U.S. Role," *Washington Post*, August 21, 2001; and Kevin Baker, "American Imperialism, Embraced," *New York Times Magazine* (December 9, 2001): 53–54.

23. I develop this argument in Stephen Van Evera, "Bush Administration, Weak on Terror," *Middle East Policy* 13, no. 4 (Winter 2006): 28–38; and in Stephen Van Evera, "Assessing U.S. Strategy in the War on Terror," *Annals of the American Academy of Political and Social Science* 607, no. 1 (September 2006): 10–26.

24. An excellent agenda for action to secure nuclear weapons and materials is found in Allison, *Nuclear Terrorism*, 140–209.

25. A valuable survey of homeland security issues is provided by Stephen E. Flynn, *America the Vulnerable: How Our Government Is Failing to Protect Us from Terrorism* (New York: Harper Perennial, 2005).

26. My argument is from Stephanie Kaplan, who argues in a forthcoming political science Ph.D. dissertation (Massachusetts Institute of Technology) that war is a tonic for terrorist propaganda making, recruiting, network building, and training and thus serves as a general breeding ground for terrorists. She concludes that war prevention and war termination should be a centerpiece of U.S. counterterror policy.

27. A thoughtful discussion of intervention against terrorists in failed states is provided by David Ignatius, "Sept. 10 in Waziristan: What Will Be Done about al Qaeda's Camps?" *Washington Post*, July 31, 2007.

28. Today the agencies that would lead in a serious war on al Qaeda take a far backseat to the military services in budget allocation. Specifically, in 2006 the United States spent $454 billion for the military services and their support. In the same year, the United States spent only $40 billion on homeland security; only $1.31 billion on locking down loose nuclear weapons and materials through the CTR; and only $1.36 billion on public diplomacy. Thus U.S. spending on the military was 11 times its spending on homeland security, 347 times its spending on locking down nuclear weapons and materials, and 334 times its spending on the war of ideas. The United States is like a midget with a strong right arm: powerful in one regard, but only one. For sources, see Van Evera, "Bush Administration, Weak on Terror," 35 and notes 17, 31, and 32 on pp. 37, 39.

29. Efforts by coal and oil producers to purvey self-serving myths about global warming are described by Ross Gelbspan, *Boiling Point: How Politicians, Big Oil and Coal, Journalists and Activists Are Fueling the Climate Crisis* (New York: Basic Books, 2004).

30. On selective engagement, see Art, *Grand Strategy for America*, 121–171.

31. I develop and offer evidence for Bismarck's argument that war is more likely when conquest is easy in Van Evera, *Causes of War*, 117–239.

32. A revealing window on how foreign lobbies operate in Washington is provided by Ken Silverstein, "Their Men in Washington: Undercover with

D.C.'s Lobbyists for Hire," *Harper's Magazine* (July 2007): 53–61. Silverstein demonstrates that even the most odious foreign interests can hire very capable former U.S. government officials with strong connections to the government and the press.

33. On the Israel lobby, see John J. Mearsheimer and Stephen M. Walt, *The Israel Lobby and U.S. Foreign Policy* (New York: Farrar, Straus, & Giroux, 2007). A criticism is found in Abraham H. Foxman, *The Deadliest Lies: The Israel Lobby and the Myth of Jewish Control* (New York: Palgrave, 2007).

34. The U.S. defense establishment will also resist redirecting U.S. defense efforts toward the WMD terror threat, as I recommend here. No organization likes to have its budget cut or its mission changed.

35. More broad-based domestic groups may also oppose elements of a concert strategy. For example, some human rights groups will object to cooperation under a concert with states that violate human rights, such as China and Russia.

36. Allied military deaths in World War I were as follows: Russia, 2,950,000; France, 1,630,000; Britain, 1,000,000; Italy, 950,000; Romania, 375,000; Serbia/Yugoslavia, 128,000; United States, 126,000; Belgium, 88,000; Australia, 60,000; Canada, 55,000; India, 25,000; New Zealand, 16,000; Portugal, 13,000; and Greece, 5,000. Data from Ruth Leger Sivard, *World Military and Social Expenditures 1985* (Washington, DC: World Priorities, 1985), 11.

37. Allied military deaths in World War II were as follows: Soviet Union, 7,500,000; China, 1,350,000; France, 475,000; Poland, 445,000; United States, 408,000; Yugoslavia, 400,000; Britain, 350,000; Belgium, 110,000; Canada, 39,000; Australia, 34,000; India, 24,000; New Zealand, 17,000; Greece, 10,000; South Africa, 9,000; Netherlands, 6,000; Ethiopia, 5,000; Mongolia, 3,000; Norway, 2,000; and Brazil, 1,000. Data from Sivard, *World Military and Social Expenditures 1985*, 11.

38. An example of neoconservative thinking on foreign policy is found in David Frum and Richard Perle, *An End to Evil: How to Win the War on Terror* (New York: Random House, 2004). Other neoconservative foreign policy analysts include Kenneth Adelman, John Bolton, Max Boot, Thomas Donnelly, Frank Gaffney, Frederick Kagan, Robert Kagan, Charles Krauthammer, William Kristol, Michael Ledeen, Danielle Pletka, Norman Podhoretz, Michael Rubin, and David Wurmser. For informative coverage of the neoconservative policy community, see http://www.lobelog.com.

39. On bandwagoning and balancing and the prevalence of the latter over the former, see Stephen M. Walt, *The Origins of Alliances* (Ithaca, NY: Cornell University Press, 1987), 17–33, 147–180, 263–266, 274–280.

40. Before 9/11, the Bush administration took the terror threat lightly, despite warnings from terror experts. See Van Evera, "Bush Administration, Weak on Terror," 35–36.

TWO

End of Dreams, Return of History
Robert Kagan

THE WORLD HAS become normal again. The years immediately following the end of the cold war offered a tantalizing glimpse at the possibility of a new kind of international order, with nations growing together or disappearing altogether, ideological conflicts melting away, cultures intermingling, and increasingly free commerce and communications. But that was a mirage, the hopeful anticipation of a liberal, democratic world that wanted to believe the end of the cold war did not just end one strategic and ideological conflict but all strategic and ideological conflict. People and their leaders longed for "a world transformed."[1] Today the nations of the West still cling to that vision. Evidence to the contrary—the turn toward autocracy in Russia or the growing military ambitions of China—is either dismissed as temporary aberrations or denied entirely.

The world has not been transformed, however. Nations remain as strong as ever, and so too do the nationalist ambitions, the passions, and the competition among nations that have shaped history. The world is still "unipolar," with the United States remaining the only superpower. But international competition among great powers has returned, with the United States, Russia, China, Europe, Japan, India, Iran, and others vying for regional predominance. Struggles for honor and status and influence in the world have once again become key features of the international scene. Ideologically, it is not a time of convergence but of divergence. The competition between liberalism and absolutism has reemerged, with the nations of the world increasingly lining up, as in the past, along ideological lines. Finally, there is the fault line between modernity and tradition, the violent struggle of Islamic fundamentalists against the powers and the modern secular cultures that, in their view, have penetrated and polluted their Islamic world.

How will the United States deal with such a world? Today there is much discussion of the so-called Bush doctrine and what may follow it. Many believe the world is in turmoil not because it is in turmoil but because George W. Bush made it so by destroying the new hopeful era. And when Bush leaves, it can return once again to the way it was. Having glimpsed the mirage once, people naturally want to see it and believe in it again.

The first illusion, however, is that Bush really changed anything. Since the end of World War II, at least, American leaders of both parties have pursued a fairly consistent approach to the world. They have regarded the United States as the "indispensable nation"[2] and the "locomotive at the head of mankind."[3] They have amassed power and influence and deployed them in ever widening arcs around the globe on behalf of interests, ideals, and ambitions, both tangible and intangible. Since 1945 Americans have insisted on acquiring and maintaining military supremacy, a "preponderance of power" in the world rather than a balance of power with other nations.[4] They have operated on the ideological conviction that liberal democracy is the only legitimate form of government and that other forms of government are not only illegitimate but transitory. They have declared their readiness to "support free peoples who are resisting attempted subjugation" by forces of oppression, to "pay any price, bear any burden" to defend freedom, to seek "democratic enlargement" in the world, and to work for the "end of tyranny."[5] They have been impatient with the status quo. They have seen America as a catalyst for change in human affairs and employed the strategies and tactics of "maximalism," seeking revolutionary rather than gradualist solutions to problems. Therefore they have often been at odds with the more cautious approaches of their allies.[6]

When people talk about a Bush doctrine, they generally refer to three sets of principles: the idea of preemptive or preventive military action; the promotion of democracy and "regime change"; and a diplomacy tending toward "unilateralism," a willingness to act without the sanction of international bodies such as the United Nations Security Council or the unanimous approval of its allies.[7] It is worth asking not only whether past administrations acted differently but also which of these principles any future administration, regardless of party, would promise to abjure in its foreign policy. As scholars from Melvyn P. Leffler to John Lewis Gaddis have shown, the idea of preemptive or preventive action is hardly a novel concept in American foreign policy.[8] And as policy makers and philosophers from Henry Kissinger to Michael Walzer have agreed, it is impossible in the present era to renounce such actions a priori.[9] As for "regime change," there is not a single administration in the last half-century that has not attempted to engineer changes of regime in various parts of the world, from Eisenhower's CIA-inspired coups in Iran and Guatemala and his planned overthrow of Fidel Castro, which John F. Kennedy attempted to carry out, to George Herbert Walker Bush's invasion of Panama to Bill Clinton's actions in Haiti and Bosnia. And if by *unilateralism* we mean an unwillingness to be constrained by the disapproval of the UN Security Council, by some North Atlantic Treaty Organization (NATO) allies, by the Organization of American States (OAS), or by any other international body, which presidents of the past allowed themselves to be so constrained?[10]

These American traditions, together with historical events beyond Americans' control, have catapulted the United States to a position of pre-eminence in the world. Since the end of the cold war and the emergence of this "unipolar" world, there has been much anticipation of the end of unipolarity and the rise of a multipolar world in which the United States is no longer the predominant power. Yet American predominance in the main categories of power persists as a key feature of the international system. The enormous and productive American economy remains at the center of the international economic system. American democratic principles are shared by over a hundred nations. The American military is not only the largest but the only one capable of projecting force into distant theaters. Chinese strategists see the world not as multipolar but as characterized by "one superpower, many great powers," and this configuration seems likely to persist into the future absent either a catastrophic blow to American power or a decision by the United States to diminish its power and international influence voluntarily.[11]

The anticipated global balancing has for the most part not occurred. Russia and China certainly share a common and openly expressed goal of checking American hegemony. They have created at least one institution, the Shanghai Cooperation Organization, aimed at resisting American influence in Central Asia, and China is the only power in the world, other than the United States, engaged in a long-term military buildup. But Sino-Russian hostility to American predominance has not yet produced a concerted and cooperative effort at balancing. China's buildup is driven at least as much by its own long-term ambitions as by a desire to balance the United States. Russia has been using its vast reserves of oil and natural gas as a lever to compensate for its lack of military power, but it either cannot or does not want to increase its military capability sufficiently to begin counterbalancing the United States. Overall, Russian military power remains in decline. In addition, the two powers do not trust one another. They are traditional rivals, and the rise of China inspires at least as much nervousness in Russia as it does in the United States. At the moment, moreover, China is less abrasively confrontational with the United States. Its dependence on the American market and foreign investment and its perception that the United States remains a potentially formidable adversary mitigate against an openly confrontational approach.

In any case, China and Russia cannot balance the United States without at least some help from Europe, Japan, India, and at least some of the other advanced democratic nations. But those powerful players are not joining the effort. Europe has rejected the option of making itself a counterweight to American power. This is true even among the older members of the European Union (EU), among whom neither France, Germany, Italy, nor Spain proposes such counterbalancing, despite a public opinion hostile to the Bush administration. Now that the EU has expanded to include the nations of Central and Eastern Europe and the Baltic states, who fear threats from the East, not from the West, the prospect of a unified Europe counterbalancing the United States is practically nil. As for Japan and India, the clear trend in recent years has been toward closer strategic cooperation with the United States.

If anything, the most notable balancing over the past decade has been aimed not at the American superpower but at the two large powers China and Russia. Japan, Australia, and even South Korea and the nations of Southeast Asia have all engaged in "hedging" against a rising China. This has led them to seek closer relations with Washington, especially in the cases of Japan and Australia. India has also drawn closer to the United States and is clearly engaged in balancing against China. Russia's efforts to increase its influence over what it regards as its "near abroad," meanwhile, have produced tensions and negative reactions in the Baltics and Eastern Europe. Because these nations are now members of the EU, this has also complicated EU-Russian relations. On balance, traditional allies of the United States in East Asia and in Europe, although their publics may be more anti-American than they were in the past, nevertheless pursue policies that reflect more concern about the powerful states in their midst than about the United States.[12] This has provided a cushion against hostile public opinion and offers a foundation on which to rebuild American relations with these countries after the departure of Bush.

The Iraq war has not had the effect expected by many. Although there are reasonable-sounding theories as to why America's position should be eroding as a result of global opposition to the war and the unpopularity of the current administration, there has been little measurable change in the actual policies of nations other than their reluctance to assist the United States in Iraq. In 2003 those who claimed that the U.S. global position was eroding pointed to electoral results in some friendly countries: the election of Schröeder in Germany, the defeat of Aznar in Spain, and the election of Lula in Brazil.[13] But if elections are the test, other, more recent votes around the world have put relatively pro-American leaders in power in Berlin, Paris, Tokyo, Canberra, and Ottawa. As for Russia and China, their hostility to the United States predates the Iraq war and, indeed, the Bush administration. Chinese rhetoric has, if anything, been more tempered during the Bush years, in part because the Chinese have seen September 11 and American preoccupation with terrorism as a welcome distraction from America's other preoccupation, the "China threat."

The world's failure to balance against the superpower is the more striking because the United States, notwithstanding its difficult interventions in Iraq and Afghanistan, continues to expand its power and military reach and shows no sign of slowing this expansion, even after the 2008 elections. The American defense budget has surpassed $500 billion per year, not including supplemental spending totaling over $100 billion on Iraq and Afghanistan. This level of spending is sustainable, moreover, both economically and politically.[14] As the American military budget rises, so does the number of overseas American military bases. Since September 11, 2001, the United States has built or expanded bases in Afghanistan, Kyrgyzstan, Pakistan, Tajikistan, and Uzbekistan in Central Asia; in Bulgaria, Georgia, Hungary, Poland, and Romania in Europe; and in the Philippines, Djibouti, Oman, and Qatar. Two decades ago hostility to the American military presence began forcing the United States out of the Philippines and seemed to be undermining support for American bases in Japan. Today, the Philippines is rethinking that decision, and the furor in Japan has subsided. Overall, there is no shortage of other countries willing to host U.S. forces, a good indication that much of the world continues to tolerate and even lend support to American geopolitical primacy, if only as a protection against more worrying foes.[15]

Predominance is not the same thing as omnipotence. The fact that the United States has more power than everyone else does not mean it can impose its will on everyone else. American predominance in the early years after World War II did not prevent the North Korean invasion of the South, a Communist victory in China, the Soviet acquisition of the hydrogen bomb, or the consolidation of the Soviet empire in Eastern Europe—all far greater strategic setbacks than anything the United States has yet suffered or is likely to suffer in Iraq and Afghanistan. Nor does predominance mean the United States will succeed in all its endeavors, any more than it did six decades ago.

By the same token, foreign policy failures do not necessarily undermine predominance. Some have suggested that failure in Iraq would mean the end of predominance and unipolarity. But a superpower can lose a war—in

Vietnam or in Iraq—without ceasing to be a superpower if the fundamental international conditions continue to support its predominance. So long as the United States remains at the center of the international economy and the predominant military power, so long as the American public continues to support American predominance, as it has consistently for six decades, and so long as potential challengers inspire more fear than sympathy among their neighbors, the structure of the international system should remain as the Chinese describe it: one superpower and many great powers.

This is a good thing, and it should continue to be a primary goal of American foreign policy to perpetuate this relatively benign international configuration of power. The unipolar order with the United States as the predominant power is unavoidably riddled with flaws and contradictions. It inspires fears and jealousies. The United States is not immune to error, like all other nations, and because of its size and importance in the international system those errors are magnified and take on greater significance than the errors of less powerful nations. Compared with the ideal Kantian international order, in which all the world's powers would be peace-loving equals, conducting themselves wisely, prudently, and in strict obeisance to international law, the unipolar system is both dangerous and unjust. Compared with any plausible alternative in the real world, however, it is relatively stable and less likely to produce a major war between great powers. It is also comparatively benevolent, from a liberal perspective, for it is more conducive to the principles of economic and political liberalism that Americans and many others value.

American predominance does not stand in the way of progress toward a better world, therefore. It stands in the way of regression toward a more dangerous world. For the choice is not between an American-dominated order and a world that looks like the EU. The future international order will be shaped by those who have the power to shape it. The leaders of a post-American world will not meet in Brussels but in Beijing, Moscow, and Washington.

If the world is marked by the persistence of unipolarity, it is nevertheless also being shaped by the reemergence of competitive national ambitions of the kind that have shaped human affairs from time immemorial. During the cold war, this historical tendency of great powers to jostle with one another for status and influence, as well as for wealth and power, was largely suppressed by the two superpowers and their rigid bipolar order. Since the end of the cold war, the United States has not been powerful enough, and probably could never be powerful enough, to suppress by itself this normal tendency of nations. This does not mean that the world has returned to multipolarity, as none of the large powers is yet attempting to compete with the superpower for global predominance. Nevertheless, several large powers are now competing for regional predominance, both with the United States and with each other.

National ambition drives China's foreign policy today, and although it is tempered by prudence and the desire to appear as unthreatening as possible to the rest of the world, the Chinese are powerfully motivated to return their nation to what they regard as its traditional position as the preeminent power in East Asia. They do not share a European, postmodern view that power is passé; hence their now two-decades-long military buildup and modernization. Like the Americans, they believe that power, including military power, is a good thing to have and that it is better to have more of it than less. Perhaps more significant is the Chinese perception, also shared by Americans, that status and honor, and not just wealth and security, are important for a nation.

Japan, meanwhile, which in the past could have been counted as an aspiring postmodern power—with its pacifist constitution and low defense spending—now appears embarked on a more traditional national course. Partly this is in reaction to the rising power of China and concerns about North Korea's nuclear weapons. But it is also driven by Japan's own national ambition to be a leader in East Asia or at least not to play second fiddle or "little brother" to China. China and Japan are now in a competitive quest to augment their own status and power and to prevent the other's rise to predominance, and this competition has a military and strategic, as well as an economic and political, component. Their competition is such that a nation such as South Korea, with a long, unhappy history as a pawn between the two powers, is once again worrying about both a "greater China" and the return of Japanese nationalism. As Aaron Friedberg commented, the East Asian future looks more like Europe's past than its present.[16] But it also looks like Asia's past.

Russian foreign policy, too, looks more like something from the nineteenth century. It is being driven by a typical, and typically Russian, blend of national resentment and ambition. A postmodern Russia simply seeking integration into the new European order, the Russia of Andrei Kozyrev, would not be troubled by the eastward enlargement of the EU and NATO, would not insist on predominant influence over its "near abroad," and would not use its natural resources as means of gaining geopolitical leverage and enhancing Russia's international status in an attempt to regain the lost glories of the Soviet empire and of Peter the Great. But Russia, like China and Japan, is moved by more traditional great-power considerations, including the pursuit of those valuable if intangible national interests: honor and respect. Although Russian leaders complain about threats to their security from NATO and the United States, the Russian sense of insecurity has more to do with resentment and national identity than with plausible external military threats.[17] But that does not make insecurity less a factor in Russia's relations with the world. Indeed, it makes finding compromise with the Russians all the more difficult.

One could add others to this list of great powers with traditional rather than postmodern aspirations. India's regional ambitions are more muted, or are focused most intently on Pakistan, but it is clearly engaged in competition with China for dominance in the Indian Ocean and sees itself, correctly, as an emerging great power on the world scene. In the Middle East there is Iran, which mingles religious fervor with a historical sense of superiority and leadership in its region.[18] Its nuclear program is as much about the desire for regional hegemony as about defending Iranian territory from attack by the United States.

Even the EU itself, in its way, expresses a pan-European national ambition to play a significant role in the world, and it has become the vehicle for channeling German and French, if not British, ambitions in what Europeans regard as a safe supranational direction. Europeans seek honor and respect, too, but of a postmodern variety. The honor they seek is to occupy the moral high ground in the world, to exercise moral authority, to wield political and economic influence as an antidote to militarism, to be the keeper of the global conscience, and to be recognized and admired by others for playing this role.

Islam is not a nation, but many Muslims express a kind of religious nationalism, and the leaders of radical Islam, including al Qaeda, do seek to establish a theocratic nation or confederation of nations that would encompass a wide swath of the Middle East and beyond. Like national movements elsewhere, Islamists have a yearning for respect, including self-respect, and a desire for honor. Their national identity has been molded in defiance against stronger and often oppressive outside powers and also by memories of ancient superiority over those same powers. China had its "century of humiliation." Islamists have more than a century of humiliation to look back on, a humiliation of which Israel has become the living symbol, which is partly why even Muslims who are neither radical nor fundamentalist proffer their sympathy and even their support to violent extremists who can turn the tables on the dominant liberal West, and particularly on a dominant America which implanted and still feeds the Israeli cancer in their midst.

Finally, there is the United States itself. As a matter of national policy stretching back across numerous administrations, Democratic and Republican, liberal and conservative, Americans have insisted on preserving regional predominance in East Asia, the Middle East, the Western Hemisphere, until recently Europe, and now, increasingly, in Central Asia. Since the end of the cold war, beginning with the first Bush administration and continuing through the Clinton years, the United States did not retract but expanded its influence eastward across Europe and into the Middle East, Central Asia, and the Caucasus. The United States, too, is more of a traditional than a postmodern power, and though Americans are loath to acknowledge it, they generally prefer their global place as "No. 1" and are equally loath to relinquish it. Once having entered a region, whether for practical or idealistic reasons, they are remarkably slow to withdraw from it until they believe they have substantially transformed it in their own image.

The jostling for status and influence among these ambitious nations and would-be nations is a second defining feature of the new post–cold war international system. Nationalism in all its forms is back, if it ever went away, and so is international competition for power, influence, honor, and status. If the United States chose to accept a diminished global role, to become one among equals, the world would surely devolve into a more equal multipolar competition. These more equal powers would not be any more committed to international laws and institutions than nations have been throughout history. They would settle disputes as great and lesser powers have done in the past, sometimes through diplomacy and accommodation but often through confrontation and wars of varying scope, intensity, and destructiveness. One novel aspect of such a multipolar world is that most of these powers would possess nuclear weapons. That could make wars between them less likely, or it could simply make them more catastrophic.

People who believe that a multipolar order would be preferable to the present American predominance often succumb to a basic logical fallacy. They believe that the international order the world enjoys today exists independently of American power. They imagine that in a world in which American power was diminished, the aspects of international order that they like would remain in place. But that is not the way it works. International order does not rest on ideas and institutions. It is shaped by configurations of power. The international order we know today reflects the distribution of power in the world since World War II, and especially since the end of the cold war. A different configuration of power, a multipolar world, in which the poles were Russia, China, the United States, India, and Europe, would produce its own kind of order, with different rules and norms reflecting the interests of the powerful states that would have a hand in shaping it. Would that international order be an improvement? Perhaps for Beijing and Moscow it would. But it is doubtful that it would suit the tastes of enlightenment liberals in the United States and Europe.

The current order, of course, not only is far from perfect but also offers no guarantee against major conflict among the world's great powers. Even under the umbrella of unipolarity, regional conflicts involving the large powers may erupt. War could erupt between China and Taiwan and draw in both the United States and Japan. War could erupt between Russia and Georgia, forcing the United States and its European allies to decide whether to intervene or suffer the consequences of a Russian victory. Conflict between India and Pakistan remains possible, as does conflict between Iran and Israel or other Middle Eastern states. These, too, could draw in other great powers, including the United States.

Such conflicts may be unavoidable no matter what policies the United States pursues. But they are more likely to erupt if the United States weakens or withdraws from its positions of regional dominance. This is especially true in East Asia, where most nations agree that a reliable American power has a stabilizing and pacific effect on the region. In Europe, too, the departure of the United States from the scene—even if it remained the world's most powerful nation—could be destabilizing. It could tempt Russia to an even more over-bearing and potentially forceful approach to unruly nations on its periphery.

In the Middle East, competition for influence among powers both inside and outside the region has raged for at least two centuries. The rise of Islamic fundamentalism does not change this. It only adds a new and more threatening dimension to the competition, which neither a sudden end to the conflict between Israel and the Palestinians nor an immediate American withdrawal from Iraq would change. The region and the states within it remain relatively weak. A diminution of American influence would not be followed by a diminution of other external influences. An American withdrawal from Iraq will not return things to "normal" or to a new kind of stability in the region. It will produce a new instability, one likely to draw the United States back in again. The alternative to American predominance in the region is not balance and peace. It is further competition.

The alternative to American regional predominance, in short, is not a new regional stability. In an era of burgeoning nationalism, the future is likely to be one of intensified competition among nations and nationalist movements. Difficult as it may be to extend American predominance into the future, no one should imagine that a reduction of American power or a retraction of American influence and global involvement will provide an easier path.

Complicating the equation, and adding to the stakes, is that the return to the international competition of ambitious nations has been accompanied by a return to global ideological competition. More precisely, the two-centuries-old struggle between political liberalism and autocracy has reemerged as a defining characteristic of the present era.

The assumption that the death of Communism would bring an end to disagreements about the proper form of government and society seemed more plausible in the 1990s, when both Russia and China were thought to be moving toward political, as well as economic, liberalism. Such a development would have produced a remarkable ideological convergence among all the great powers of the world and heralded a genuinely new era in human development.

But those expectations have proved misplaced. China has not liberalized but shored up its autocratic government. Russia has turned away from imperfect liberalism decisively toward autocracy. Of the world's great powers today, therefore, two of the largest, with over 1½ billion people, have governments committed to autocratic rule and seem to have the ability to sustain themselves in power for the foreseeable future, with evident popular approval.

Many assume that Russian and Chinese leaders do not believe in anything, and therefore they cannot be said to represent an ideology, but that is mistaken. Communism and liberal capitalism are not the only ideologies the world has ever known. The rulers of China and Russia do have a set of beliefs that guide them in both domestic and foreign policy. They believe that autocracy is better for their nations than democracy. They believe it offers order and stability and the possibility of prosperity. They believe that for their large, fractious nations, a strong government is essential to prevent chaos and collapse. They believe that democracy is not the answer and that they are serving the best interests of their peoples by holding and wielding power the way they do. This is not a novel or, from a historical perspective, even a disreputable idea. The European monarchies of the seventeenth, eighteenth, and nineteenth centuries were thoroughly convinced of the superiority of their form of government. Only in the past half-century has liberalism gained widespread popularity around the world, and even today some American thinkers exalt "liberal autocracy" over what they, too, disdain as "illiberal democracy." If two of the world's largest powers share a common commitment to autocratic government, autocracy is not dead as an ideology.

The foreign policies of such states necessarily reflect the nature and interests of their governments. The world looks very different from Moscow and Beijing than it does from Washington, London, Berlin, and Paris. In Europe and the United States, the liberal world cheered on the "color revolutions" in Ukraine, Georgia, and Kyrgyzstan and saw in them the natural unfolding of humanity's proper political evolution. In Russia and China, these events were viewed as Western-funded, CIA-inspired coups that furthered the geopolitical hegemony of America and its (subservient) European allies. The two autocratic powers responded similarly to NATO's intervention in Kosovo in 1999, and not only because China's embassy was bombed by an American warplane and Russia's Slavic orthodox allies in Serbia were on the receiving end of the NATO onslaught. What the liberal "West" considered a moral act, a "humanitarian" intervention, leaders and analysts in Moscow and Beijing saw as unlawful and self-interested aggression. Americans and Europeans went to war not on the basis of international legality but in service of what they regarded as a "higher law" of liberal morality.

For those who do not share this liberal morality, such acts are merely law-less, destructive of the traditional safeguards of national sovereignty. But it is precisely toward a less rigid conception of national sovereignty that the liberal world of Europe and the United States would like to go. Ideas that are becoming common currency in Europe and the United States—limited sovereignty, "the responsibility to protect," a "voluntary sovereignty waiver"—all aim to provide liberal nations with the right to intervene in the affairs of nonliberal nations. The Chinese and Russians, and the leaders of other autocracies, cannot welcome this kind of progress.

This is more than a dispute over the niceties of international law. It concerns the fundamental legitimacy of governments, which, at the end of the day, is a matter of life and death. Autocrats can hardly be expected to aid in legitimizing an evolution in the international system toward "limited sovereignty" and "the responsibility to protect." For even if the people and governments pushing this evolution do not believe they are establishing the precedent for international interventions against Russia and China, the leaders of those nations have no choice but to contemplate the possibility and to try to shield themselves. China, after all, has been a victim of international sanctions imposed by the U.S.-led liberal world, and for killing far fewer people than did the governments of Sudan or Zimbabwe. Nor do China's rulers forget that if the liberal world had had its way in 1989, they would now be out of office, probably imprisoned, possibly dead.

Because autocratic governments have a vital interest in disputing liberal principles of interventionism, they will often resist efforts by the liberal international community to put pressure on other autocracies around the world. Many in the United States and Europe have begun complaining about Chinese policies that provide unfettered aid to dictatorships in Africa and Asia, thereby undermining American and European efforts to press for reforms in countries such as Zimbabwe and Burma. To ask one dictatorship to aid in the undermining of another dictatorship, however, is asking a great deal. Chinese leaders will always be extremely reluctant to impose sanctions on autocrats while they themselves remain subject to sanctions for their own autocratic behavior. They may bend occasionally so as to avoid too-close association with what the West calls "rogue regimes." But the thrust of their foreign policy will be to support an international order that places a high value on national sovereignty.

Neither Russia nor China has any interest in assisting liberal nations in their crusade against autocracies around the world. Moreover, they can see their comparative advantage over the West when it comes to gaining influence with autocratic governments in Africa, Asia, or Latin America, governments that can provide access to oil and other vital natural resources or that, in the case of Burma, are strategically located. Moscow knows that it can have more influence with governments in Kazakhstan and Turkmenistan because, unlike the liberal West, it can unreservedly support their regimes. And it is a simple matter of addition that the more autocracies there are in the world, the less isolated Beijing and Moscow will be in international forums such as the United Nations. The more dictatorships there are, the more global resistance they will offer against the liberal West's efforts to place limits on sovereignty in the interest of advancing liberalism.

The general effect of the rise of these two large autocratic powers, therefore, will be to increase the likelihood that autocracy will spread in some parts of the world. This is not because Russia and China are evangelists for autocracy or want to set off a worldwide autocratic revolution. This is not the cold war redux. It is more like the nineteenth century redux. In the nineteenth century the absolutist rulers of Russia and Austria shored up fellow autocracies, in France, for instance, and used force to suppress liberal rebellions in Germany, Italy, and Spain. China and Russia may not go that far, at least not yet. But Ukraine has already been a battleground between forces supported by the liberal West and forces supported by Russia. The great power autocracies will inevitably offer support and friendship to those who feel besieged by the United States and other liberal nations. Autocrats and would-be autocrats will know that they can again find powerful allies and patrons, something that was not as true in the 1990s.

Moreover, China and, to a much lesser extent, Russia provide a model for successful autocracy, a way to create wealth and stability without political liberalization. This is hardly novel, of course. Hugo Chávez did not need China to show him the possibilities of successful autocracy, least of all in Latin America. In the 1970s autocratic regimes such as Pinochet's Chile, the Shah's Iran, and Suharto's Indonesia also demonstrated that economic success could come without political liberalization. But through the 1980s and 1990s the autocratic model seemed less attractive, as dictatorships of both right and left fell before the liberal tide. That tide has not yet turned in the other direction, but the future may bring a return to a global competition between different forms of government, with the world's great powers on opposite sides.

This has implications for international institutions and for American foreign policy. It is difficult to speak of an "international community" with any confidence. The term suggests agreement on international norms of behavior, an international morality, even an international conscience. The idea of such a community took hold in the 1990s, at a time when the general assumption was that the movement of Russia and China toward Western liberalism was producing a global commonality of thinking about human affairs. But by the late 1990s it was already clear that the international community lacked a foundation of common understanding. This was exposed most blatantly in the war over Kosovo, which divided the liberal West from both Russia and China and from many other non-European nations. Today, it is apparent on the issue of Sudan and Darfur. In the future, incidents that expose the hollowness of the term *international community* will likely proliferate.

As for the UN Security Council, after a brief awakening from the cold war coma, it is falling back to its former condition of near-paralysis. The agile diplomacy of France and the tactical caution of China have at times obscured the fact that the Security Council on most major issues is clearly divided between the autocracies and the democracies, with the latter systematically pressing for sanctions and other punitive actions against Iran, North Korea, Sudan, and other autocracies and the former just as systematically resisting and attempting to weaken the effect of such actions. This is a rut that is likely to deepen in the coming years.

The problem goes beyond the Security Council. Efforts to achieve any international consensus in any forum are going to be more and more difficult because of the widening gap between the liberal and autocratic governments. The current divisions between the United States and its European allies that have garnered so much attention in recent years are going to be overtaken by the more fundamental ideological divisions, and especially by growing tensions between the democratic transatlantic alliance and Russia.

The divisions will be sharper where ideological fault lines coincide with those caused by competitive national ambitions. It may be largely accidental that two of the world's more nationalistic powers are also the two leading autocracies, but this fact will have immense geopolitical significance.

Under these circumstances, calls for a new "concert" of nations in which Russia, China, the United States, Europe, and other great powers operate under some kind of international condominium are unlikely to succeed. The early-nineteenth-century Concert of Europe operated under the umbrella of a common morality and shared principles of government. It aimed not only at the preservation of a European peace but also, and more important, at the maintenance of a monarchical and aristocratic order against the liberal and radical challenges presented by the French and American revolutions and their echoes in Germany, Italy, and Poland. The Concert gradually broke down under the strains of popular nationalism, fueled in part by the rise of liberalism.

Today there is little sense of shared morality and common political principle among the great powers. Quite the contrary. There is suspicion and growing hostility and the well-grounded view on the part of the autocracies that the democracies, whatever they say, would welcome their overthrow. Any concert among them would be built on a shaky foundation likely to collapse at the first serious test.

These features of the international scene do not require the United States to engage in a blind crusade on behalf of democracy everywhere at all times, nor to seek a violent confrontation with the autocratic powers. American foreign policy should, however, be attuned to these ideological distinctions and recognize their relevance to the most important strategic questions.

The United States should pursue policies designed both to promote democracy and to strengthen solidarity among the democracies. It should join with other democracies to erect new international institutions that both reflect and enhance the shared principles and goals of democracies. One possibility might be to establish a global concert or league of democracies, perhaps informally at first, but with the aim of holding regular meetings and consultations among democratic nations on the issues of the day. Such an institution could bring together Asian and Pacific nations with the European nations—two sets of democracies that have comparatively little to do with each other outside the realms of trade and finance. The institution would complement, not replace, the UN, the Group of Eight (G8), and other global forums. But it would at the very least signal a commitment to the democratic idea, and in time it could become a means of pooling the resources of democratic nations to address a number of issues that cannot be addressed at the UN. If successful, it could come to be an organization capable of bestowing legitimacy on actions that liberal nations deem necessary but that autocratic nations refuse to countenance—as NATO conferred legitimacy on the conflict in Kosovo, even though Russia was opposed.

Some will claim that such an organization will only create divisions in the world. But those divisions are already there. The question now is whether there is any way to pursue American interests and liberal democratic ends despite them.

Others will worry that European democracies are either unwilling or unable to share the burden in pursuing common goals with the United States. That may be true. But there is still reason to hope that an effort to reinvigorate democratic solidarity may increase European willingness to take on such burdens, especially when it coincides with the increasingly autocratic and belligerent behavior of Russia and the continuing rise of autocratic China.

In such an international environment the United States should prefer democracy over autocracy and use its influence to promote the former when opportunities arise. This is more than just a matter of moral preference, although Americans often cannot avoid expressing and acting on that preference. But in a world in which autocracies increasingly look for allies in fellow autocracies, the democracies will want to do the same. The United States should discourage moves toward autocracy in democratic nations, both by punishing steps that undo democratic institutions and by providing support to those institutions and individuals who favor democratic principles. It should isolate autocratic governments when possible while rewarding democracies for their continuing efforts to maintain liberal democratic systems. History suggests that external influences, especially by the global superpower, have a positive if not determinative influence on the political course nations take. The United States should express support for democracy in word and deed without expecting immediate success. It should support the development of liberal institutions and practices, understanding that elections alone do not guarantee a steady liberal democratic course. But neither should Americans lose sight of the centrality of free and fair elections for both democracy and true liberalism.

This does not mean that promoting democracy can or should be the only goal of American foreign policy, no more than should producing wealth, fighting terrorism, preventing the spread of nuclear weapons, or any other national goal or ambition. There will be times when promoting democracy, like any other primary goal, will have to take a backseat to other objectives. But as the hardheaded Dean Acheson put it, Americans "are children of freedom" and "cannot be safe except in an environment of freedom."[19]

The emphasis on democracy, liberalism, and human rights has strategic relevance in part because it plays to American strengths and exposes the weaknesses of the autocratic powers. It is easy to look at China and Russia today and believe that they are simply getting stronger and stronger. But one should not overlook their fragility. These autocratic regimes may be stronger than they were in the past in terms of wealth and global influence. But they do still live in a predominantly liberal era. That means that they face an avoidable problem of legitimacy. They are not like the autocracies of nineteenth-century Europe, which still enjoyed a historical legitimacy derived partly from the fact that the world had known nothing but autocracy for centuries. To be an autocrat today is to be constantly concerned that the powerful forces of liberalism, backed by a collection of rich, advanced nations, including the world's only superpower, will erode or undermine the controls necessary to stay in power. Today's autocracies struggle to create a new kind of legitimacy, and it is no easy task. The Chinese leaders race forward with their economy in fear that any slowing will be their undoing. They fitfully stamp out signs of political opposition partly because they live in fear of repeating the Soviet experience. Having watched the Soviet Union succumb to the liberal West, thanks to what they regard as Mikhail Gorbachev's weakness and mistakes, they are determined to neither show weakness nor make the same mistakes.

Vladimir Putin shares both their contempt for Gorbachev and their commitment to the lessons learned from his downfall. In a nice historical irony, the Russian leader, in order to avoid a Russian denouement, is trying to adopt a Chinese model of modern autocracy, using oil and gas wealth instead of entrepreneurship to buy off the Russian elite as he consolidates power in the name of stability and nationalism. In both countries, the renewed international competition among ambitious nations is helpful in this respect. It allows the governments to charge dissidents and would-be democrats as fifth-columnists for American hegemony. In Russia's case, it has been easy for Putin to tarnish liberal democrats by associating them in the popular mind with past policies of accommodation and even subservience to the United States and the West.

Nevertheless, the Chinese are not just pretending when they claim that their deep internal problems make them hesitant to pursue a more adventurous foreign policy. Leaders in Beijing rightly fear that they are riding a tiger at home, and they fear external support for a political opposition more than they fear foreign invasion. Even promoting nationalism as a means of enhancing legitimacy is a dangerous business, because in Chinese history nationalist movements have evolved into revolutionary movements.

The Russian regime is also vulnerable to pressures from within and without, for, unlike China, Russia still maintains the trappings of democracy. It would not be easy for a Russian leader simply to abandon all pretense and assume the role of tsar. Elections must still be held, even if they are unfair or are mere referenda on the selection of the leadership. This situation provides an opportunity for dissidents within and liberals on the outside to preserve the possibility of a return to democratic governance in Russia. It certainly would be a strategic error to allow Putin and any possible successor to strengthen their grip on power without outside pressures for reform, for the consolidation of autocracy at home will free the Russian leadership to pursue greater nationalist ambitions abroad. In these and other autocracies, including in Iran, promoting democracy and human rights exacerbates internal political contradictions and can have the effect of blunting external ambitions, as leaders tend to more dangerous threats from within.

In most of the world today—in Asia, Europe, Latin America, and even Africa—the idea of supporting democracy against autocracy is not very controversial, though there are heated debates over precisely how to do it. The issue becomes more complicated when one turns to the Middle East, where some observers believe the Arab people are simply not ready for democracy and where the prospect of electoral victories by Islamist movements seems to some the worst possible outcome. Should the United States and others promote democracy in the Middle East, too?

Part of the answer comes if one turns the question around and asks: Should the United States support autocracy in the Middle East? That is the only other choice, after all. There is no neutral stance on such matters. The United States is either supporting an autocracy through aid, recognition, amicable diplomatic relations, and regular economic intercourse, or it is using its manifold influence in varying degrees to push for democratic reform. The number of American thinkers who believe that the United States should simply support Middle Eastern autocrats and not push for change at all is small, and the number of policy makers and politicians who support that view is even smaller.[20]

The main questions, then, are really a matter of tactics and timing. But no matter whether one prefers faster or slower, harder or softer, there will always be the risk that pressure of any kind will produce a victory for radical Islamists. Is that a risk worth taking? A similar question arose constantly during the cold war, when American liberals called on the United States to stop supporting third-world dictators and American conservatives and neoconservatives warned that the dictators would be replaced by pro-Soviet Communists. Sometimes this proved true. But at other times such efforts produced moderate democratic governments that were pro-American. The lesson of the Reagan years, when pro-American and reasonably democratic governments replaced right-wing dictatorships in El Salvador, Guatemala, the Philippines, and South Korea, to name just a few, was that the risk was, on balance, worth taking.

It may be worth taking the risk again in the Middle East, and not only as a strategy of democracy promotion but as part of a larger effort to address the issue of Islamic radicalism by accelerating and intensifying its confrontation with the modern, globalized world.

The Islamists' struggle against the powerful and often impersonal forces of modernization, capitalism, and globalization is a fact of life in the world today. Much of this fight has been peaceful, but some of it has been violent and now, oddly, poses by far the greatest threat of a catastrophic attack on the mainland of the United States.

It is odd because the struggle between modernization and globalization on the one hand and traditionalism on the other is largely a sideshow on the international stage. The future is more likely to be dominated by the struggle among the great powers and between the great ideologies of liberalism and autocracy than by the effort of some radical Islamists to restore an imagined past of piety. But of course that struggle has taken on a new and frightening dimension. Normally, when old and less technologically advanced civilizations have confronted more advanced civilizations, their inadequate weapons reflected their backwardness. Today, the radical proponents of Islamic traditionalism, though they abhor the modern world, nevertheless not only are using the ancient methods of assassination and suicidal attacks but also are deploying the weapons of the modern world against it. Modernization and globalization inflamed their rebellion and also armed them for the fight.

It is a lonely and ultimately desperate fight, for in the struggle between tradition and modernization, tradition cannot win—though traditional forces armed with modern technology can put up a good fight. All the world's rich and powerful nations have more or less embraced the economic, technological, and even social aspects of modernization and globalization. All have embraced, albeit with varying degrees of complaint and resistance, the free flow of goods, finances, and services and the intermingling of cultures and lifestyles that characterize the modern world. Increasingly, their people watch the same television shows, listen to the same music, and go to the same movies. And, along with this dominant modern culture, they have accepted, even as they may also deplore, the essential characteristics of a modern morality and aesthetics: the sexual, as well as political and economic, liberation of women; the weakening of church authority and the strengthening of secularism; the existence of what used to be called the counterculture; free expression in the arts (if not in politics), which includes the freedom to commit blasphemy and to lampoon symbols of faith, authority, and morality—these and all the countless effects of liberalism and capitalism unleashed and unchecked by the constraining hand of tradition, a powerful church, or a moralistic and domineering government. The Chinese have learned that although it is possible to have capitalism without political liberalization, it is much harder to have capitalism without cultural liberalization.

Today radical Islamists are the last holdout against these powerful forces of globalization and modernization. They seek to carve out a part of the world in which they can be left alone, shielded from what they regard as the soul-destroying licentiousness of unchecked liberalism and capitalism. The tragedy is that their goal is impossible to achieve. Neither the United States nor the other great powers will turn over control of the Middle East to these fundamentalist forces, if only because the region is of such vital strategic importance to the rest of the world. The outside powers have strong internal allies, as well, including the majority of the populations of the Middle East who have been willing and even eager to make peace with modernity. Nor is it conceivable in this modern world that a people can wall themselves off from modernity, even if the majority wanted to. Could the great Islamic theocracy that al Qaeda and others hope to erect ever completely block out the sights and sounds of the rest of the world, and thereby shield its people from the temptations of modernity? The mullahs have not even succeeded at doing that in Iran. The project is fantastic.

The world is thus faced with the prospect of a protracted struggle in which the goals of the extreme Islamists can never be satisfied because neither the United States nor anyone else has the ability to give them what they want. The West is quite simply not capable of retreating as far as the Islamic extremists require.

If retreat is impossible, perhaps the best course is to advance. Of the many bad options in confronting this immensely dangerous problem, the best may be to hasten the process of modernization in the Islamic world. More modernization, more globalization, faster. This would require greater efforts to support and expand capitalism and the free market in Arab countries, as many have already recommended, as well as efforts to increase the public access to the world through television and the Internet. Nor should it be considered a setback if these modern communication tools are also used to organize radical extremism. That is unavoidable so long as the radical Islamist backlash persists, which it will for some time to come.

Finally, the liberal world should continue to promote political modernization and liberalization, support human rights, including the rights of women, and use its influence to support repeated elections that may, if nothing else, continually shift power from the few to the many. This agenda, too, will produce setbacks. It will provide a channel for popular resentments to express themselves and for radical Islamism itself to take power. But perhaps this phase is as unavoidable as the present conflict. Perhaps the sooner it is begun, the sooner a new phase can take its place.[21]

Throughout all these efforts, whose success is by no means guaranteed and certainly will not occur any time soon, the United States and others will have to persist in fighting what is, in fact, quite accurately called the "war on terrorism." Now and probably for the coming decades, organized terrorist groups will seek to strike at the United States, and at modernity itself, when and where they can. This war will not and cannot be the totality of America's worldwide strategy. It can only be a piece of it. But given the high stakes, it must be prosecuted ruthlessly, effectively, and for as long as the threat persists. This will sometimes require military interventions when, as in Afghanistan, states either cannot or will not deny the terrorists a base. That aspect of the "war on terror" is certainly not going away. One need only contemplate the American popular response should a terrorist group explode a nuclear weapon on American soil. No president of any party or ideological coloration will be able to resist the demands of the American people for retaliation and revenge, and not only against the terrorists but against any nation that aided or harbored them. Nor, one suspects, will the American people disapprove when a president takes preemptive action to forestall such a possibility—assuming the action is not bungled.

The United States will not have many eager partners in this fight. For, although in the struggle between modernization and tradition the United States, Russia, China, Europe, and the other great powers are roughly on the same side, the things that divide them from each other—the competing national ambitions and ideological differences—will inevitably blunt their ability or their willingness to cooperate in the military aspects of a fight against radical Islamic terrorism. Europeans have been and will continue to be less than enthusiastic about what they emphatically do not call the "war on terror." And it will be tempting for Russian and Chinese leaders to enjoy the spectacle of the United States bogged down in a fight with al Qaeda and other violent Islamist groups in the Middle East, just as it is tempting to let American power in that region be checked by a nuclear-armed Iran. Unfortunately, the willingness of the autocrats in Moscow and Beijing to run interference for their fellow autocrats in Pyongyang, Tehran, and Khartoum increases the chances that the connection between terrorists and nuclear weapons will eventually be made.

When the cold war ended, it was possible to imagine that the world had been utterly changed: the end of international competition, the end of geopolitics, the end of history. When in the first decade after the cold war people began describing the new era of "globalization," the common expectation was that the phenomenon of instantaneous global communications, the free flow of goods and services, the rapid transmission of ideas and information, and the intermingling and blending of cultures would further knit together a world that had already just patched up the great ideological and geopolitical tears of the previous century. "Globalization" was to the late twentieth century what "sweet commerce" was to the late eighteenth—an anticipated balm for a war-weary world.

In the 1990s serious thinkers predicted the end of wars and military confrontations among great powers. John Ikenberry recently described the post–cold war era, the decade of the 1990s, as a liberal paradise:

> The Cold War ended, democracy and markets flourished around the world, globalization was enshrined as a progressive historical force, and ideology, nationalism and war were at a low ebb. NAFTA, APEC, and the WTO signaled a strengthening of the rules and institutions of the world economy. NATO was expanded and the U.S.-Japan alliance was renewed. Russia became a quasi-member of the West and China was a "strategic partner" with Washington. Clinton's grand strategy of building post–Cold War order around expanding markets, democracy, and institutions was the triumphant embodiment of the liberal vision of international order.[22]

And perhaps it was these grand expectations of a new era for humankind that helped spur the anger and outrage at American policies of the past decade. It is not that those policies are in themselves so different or in any way out of character for the United States. It is that to many people in Europe and even in the United States, they have seemed jarringly out of place in a world that was supposed to have moved on.

As we know, however, both nationalism and ideology were already making their comeback in the 1990s. Russia had ceased to be and no longer desired to be a "quasi-member" of the West, partly because of NATO enlargement. China was already on its present trajectory and had already determined that American hegemony was a threat to its ambitions. The forces of radical Islam had already begun their jihad, globalization had already caused a backlash around the world, and the juggernaut of democracy had already stalled and begun to tip precariously.

After World War II, another moment in history at which hopes for a new kind of international order were rampant, Hans Morgenthau warned idealists against imagining that at some point "the final curtain would fall and the game of power politics would no longer be played."[23] But the world struggle continued then, and it continues today. Six decades ago American leaders believed that the United States had the unique ability and the unique responsibility to use its power to prevent a slide back to the circumstances that produced two world wars and innumerable national calamities. Although much has changed since then, America's responsibility has not.

Notes

1. This was the title chosen by former president George H. W. Bush and his national security adviser, Brent Scowcroft, for their account of American foreign policy at the end of the cold war.

2. Second inaugural address of William J. Clinton, January 20, 1997.

3. Dean Acheson, quoted in Robert L. Beisner, *Dean Acheson: A Life in the Cold War* (New York: Oxford University Press, 2006), 372.

4. See Melvyn P. Leffler, *A Preponderance of Power: National Security, the Truman Administration, and the Cold War* (Stanford, CA: Stanford University Press, 1992).

5. The quotations are, of course, from Harry Truman, John F. Kennedy, Bill Clinton, and George W. Bush.

6. See Stephen Sestanovich, "American Maximalism," *National Interest* (Spring 2005).

7. Critics obviously do not mean that the Bush administration literally acts alone, as even in Iraq the United States had a number of allies. It had more partners in that war than George H. W. Bush had in its invasion of Panama and than Bill Clinton had in his intervention in Haiti. *Unilateralism* apparently is a relative term and depends for its interpretation on circumstances.

8. Melvyn P. Leffler, "9/11 and American Foreign Policy," *Diplomatic History* 29, no. 3 (June 2005); John Lewis Gaddis, *Surprise, Security, and the American Experience* (Cambridge, MA: Harvard University Press, 2005).

9. In Walzer's view, traditional legal arguments against preventive war look "different when the danger is posed by weapons of mass destruction, which are developed in secret, and which might be used suddenly, without warning, with catastrophic results." Not only might preventive action be "legitimate" under such circumstances, but so would "unilateral action" without a Security

Council authorization. The "refusal of a U.N. majority to act forcefully" was not "a good reason for ruling out the use of force by any member state that can use it effectively." Michael Walzer, "The Hard Questions: Lone Ranger," *New Republic* (April 27, 1998): 10–11. Kissinger's argument is similar. See Henry Kissinger, "Iraq Poses Most Consequential Foreign-Policy Decision for Bush," *Los Angeles Times*, August 8, 2002.

10. To review the behavior of the most recent administrations: The Reagan administration sought no international authorization for its covert war against the Sandinistas or its arming of guerrillas in Angola and Afghanistan, and it sought neither UN nor OAS support for the invasion of Grenada. The first Bush administration invaded Panama without UN authorization and would have gone to war with Iraq without authorization if Russia had vetoed action at the Security Council. The Clinton administration bombed Iraq over the objection of UN Security Council permanent members, and went to war in Kosovo without UN authorization.

11. Rosalie Chen, "China Perceives America: Perspectives of International Relations Experts," *Journal of Contemporary China* 12, no. 35 (2003).

12. This is what William Wohlforth predicted almost a decade ago. See William C. Wohlforth, "The Stability of a Unipolar World," *International Security* 24, no. 1 (Summer 1999).

13. See, for instance, G. John Ikenberry, "Strategic Reactions to American Preeminence: Great Power Politics in the Age of Unipolarity" (working group paper prepared for the National Intelligence Council, July 2003).

14. American defense spending remains historically low as a percentage of gross domestic product (GDP), about 4 percent. (In the Reagan years, it reached nearly 8 percent. During the early years of the cold war, it was well over 15 percent.) Nor is the size of the defense budget a political issue, even among Democrats. Both Barack Obama and Hillary Clinton currently call for increases in the size of U.S. ground forces, for instance, which is a huge additional expense.

15. For the most thorough discussion of worldwide trends that run counter to the prediction of balancing, see Keir A. Lieber and Gerard Alexander, "Waiting for Balancing: Why the World Is Not Pushing Back," *International Security* 30, no. 1 (Summer 2005): 109–139.

16. Aaron L. Friedberg, "Europe's Past, Asia's Future?" *SAIS Policy Forum Series*, no. 3 (October 1998).

17. A recent editorial in the *Economist* ("Pining for the Cold War," May 14, 2007) artfully provides the view of the world as seen from Moscow, that "Russia is a strong, sovereign and prosperous country, surrounded by enemies and traitors who are bent on undermining its geopolitical power. Upstarts such as Estonia and Poland are trying to spoil Russia's far more important relationships with proper European countries, such as Germany or France. The freshly baked European Union (EU) members act on the instructions of America, a hypocritical and arrogant dictator of the world order, which pretends to be a democracy but in fact is closer to the Third Reich."

18. "Whether the U.S. likes it or not, Iran is a major regional power with great political and spiritual influence. It is in the United States' interests to accept Iran's influence as a reality, though it may be a bitter pill to swallow, and to stop leveling accusations against the Islamic Republic based on prejudices"; *Tehran Times*, May 15, 2007.

19. Quoted in Beisner, *Acheson*, 152.

20. After September 11, 2001, most observers agreed that American support for autocratic regimes in Egypt and Saudi Arabia was the "principal source of resentment" of the terrorists who launched the attack on the United States and that therefore a policy of simply supporting autocrats in those and other Middle Eastern countries would be a mistake. See Samantha Power, "U.S. Democracy Promotion: Failure or Folly?" (remarks delivered at the Pell Center for International Relations and Public Policy, Newport, RI, April 10, 2006).

21. See, for instance, Reuel Marc Gerecht, *The Islamic Paradox* (Washington, DC: AEI Press, 2004).

22. G. John Ikenberry, "Liberal International Theory in the Wake of 9/11 and American Unipolarity" (paper prepared for the seminar on IR Theory, Unipolarity and September 11th—Five Years On, NUPI [Norwegian Institute of International Affairs], Oslo, Norway, February 3–4, 2006).

23. Hans J. Morgenthau, "The Mainsprings of American Foreign Policy: The National Interest vs. Moral Abstractions," *The American Political Science Review* 44, no. 4 (December 1950): 838.

THREE

Beyond Statecraft
Charles S. Maier

THERE ARE MOMENTS in history when foreign policy—the strategies by which any nation seeks to regulate its relations with other countries—surges beyond its usual routines, recognizes historical actors outside the nation-state framework, and seeks to address new agents of world politics. The founders of the American Republic addressed an implicit Enlightenment global public and invoked "a decent respect for the opinions of mankind" when they declared independence. Although they negotiated very traditionally with the established states of Europe, their claim to nationhood envisaged a broader concept of foreign relations. The French revolutionaries of 1792 addressed a community of would-be revolutionary supporters abroad (as would the Bolsheviks of 1917). Looking at the terrible stalemate of World War I from the standpoint of a neutral United States, Woodrow Wilson hypothesized a democratic public opinion that would cast aside an old diplomacy and create a global community guaranteeing peace and self-determination.

Certainly these expansive concepts of international relations can produce tragic miscalculation, disorder, and disillusion. The former colonists of 1776 succeeded but by skillful diplomacy and exploitation of monarchical rivalries. The French triggered a quarter century of spiraling warfare. President Wilson's results are still debated. Responding to genuine popular aspirations abroad is one thing; simple evangelism is another; and the calamitous war in Iraq reveals the difference. Nonetheless, there are moments when global conditions seem to dictate that foreign policy address a far more inclusive public than the usual framework of nation-states and that it encompass a new range of concerns. This is the situation today. Foreign policy must still retain the traditional instruments of diplomacy and security for a world of states, but it also needs to develop a new repertory for national societies in their own right as they are caught up in wrenching transformations that their political systems only partially control.

So, too, global society no longer comprises just the sum of the world's nation-states. It has become a far more fluid aggregate of communities, sometimes local, sometimes contained within particular countries, but increasingly transnational and unbordered, caught up in crises of faith and values, grasping possibilities for unprecedented material development but angered, too, by how inequitable these opportunities are. Traditional foreign policy works with the organizational scaffolding of states and nations but hardly with the turbulent flux of societal change.

The United States did not create the world of social turmoil and the vast inequalities that afflict many societies. But we cannot ignore that American policies, with their resolute faith in the power of market-driven change, have helped to advance the global processes that themselves require an enhanced foreign policy. Chalmers Johnson resurrected the term *blowback* after 9/11 from a 1954 CIA report on the U.S. role in unseating the Iranian premier, Mohammed Mossadegh, the year before.[1] In effect, the United States and the other wealthy industrial states are experiencing and will continue to face a broad current of socioeconomic and cultural blowback; indeed, claims more profound than the merely reactive term *blowback* suggests. A generation ago policy makers liked to talk about the revolution of rising expectations. Today we confront expectations that are less rising than frustrated; we confront the belief that the U.S. "regime" often blocks the global diffusion of wealth and civic change. Of course, for vast numbers of non-Americans, the United States still represents a positive force. Nonetheless, in a world of six billion people, the fevered hopes or frustrations of even a small minority can make for incalculable politics.

So the argument that follows is simple, but the dilemma is profound. American international policy faces broad popular mentalities—claims, on the one hand, for global equity or, on the other, for a sort of transcendental vindication: the fervent, not the meek, shall inherit the earth. These claims can be represented by governments and leaders who appear—indeed, often are—demagogic and dangerous to our notions of global order. Even more destabilizing is the fact that these currents spill over boundaries and are unrestrained by the framework of nation-states. But states—with some assistance from the United Nations (UN) and the still gossamer fabric of nongovernmental organizations (NGOs)—remain the instruments with which we must channel these passions. Statecraft may not be enough, but we certainly have to start there—with the understanding, however, that statecraft will have to encompass broader concerns and methods than it has during the past eight years.

Unfortunately, the United States confronts this challenge at a singularly vulnerable moment. The country is burdened by its leadership's reckless policies in Iraq and heedless privileging of wealth and inequality at home. Still, to participate in a policy debate implies accepting the American assumption that the future is never foreclosed and that once again the country can attempt another quadrennial fresh start. Underlying this confidence, at least for some, perhaps, lies the touching American belief in immunity from history. When, as in the past few years, history actually disappoints or punishes, we ask, like Job, "Why do bad things happen to nice people?" The answer in this case has involved complacency, overconfidence, and the radical refusal to take into account the complexities of other societies. The American narrative, however, always allows scope for repentance, individual or collective, and beginning anew. And so, even while still mired in Iraq; while still preoccupied by the fragility of our porous frontiers, whether as a barrier to terrorists or as a checkpoint for the masses of immigrants we rely on for uncomplaining labor; and, furthermore, deep in individual and collective debt, we trust in historical redemption—receiving it and bestowing it.

Indeed, post-Bush foreign policy has already begun. The interval of American swagger is winding down. From the viewpoint of this writer, no administration since the 1920s has done more to squander the earlier foreign policy achievements of the United States, which were considerable. No congressional opposition has so supinely acquiesced in the fantasies of the executive. In few other eras did the media so give up the task of skeptically interrogating national leaders, objectives, and methods. Still, the intoxicating confidence in unipolar power and "indispensable" nationhood, the reckless oversimplification of world politics, and the post–cold war binge of self-congratulation have hopefully ended.

The timing of the inflection point is typical enough. Postwar American foreign policy has traditionally altered course not with changes of administration but during the last year or two of an outgoing presidency. Eisenhower's cold war stance abated after 1958 once John Foster Dulles had to retire and the president sought to ease confrontation with Moscow; Carter's effort to prolong détente was jettisoned by the late 1970s, first with the concern about Soviet midrange missiles and then the Afghanistan and Iranian crises; Reagan caught observers and Mikhail Gorbachev off guard by offering the zero option at Reykjavik. The George W. Bush regime began to modify its defiance after the 2006 congressional elections. Donald Rumsfeld's resignation, the withdrawal of the Bolton nomination to the UN, Paul Wolfowitz's collapse at the World Bank, and a different discourse from Secretary of State Condoleezza Rice all suggested a more measured policy.

Readers need not share my critical assessment of the past six or seven years to follow the argument developed in this chapter, which in fact is not about the policies of the Bush presidency. Fortunately, the administration's dismaying adventures may not make a fatal difference. Policy makers in most countries abroad, as well as in our own forgiving, if divided, nation, seem not to want to dwell on America's mistakes and choices of 2001–2006. It is easier for most of us to move on. Grieving families in Iraq and the United States can cope with the wreckage. As a country, we do have the opportunity, undeserved or not, for a fresh start. But as we think about the reconstruction of American foreign policy, it is important to understand that it involves far more than military interventions, the war on terrorism, or even traditional diplomacy.

States, Societies, and the Social Passions

International politics has long involved not just the relations between states but the balance of social and political forces within them, and it does so now more than ever. *Explicit* foreign policy presupposed a world of states and nations, firm territorial boundaries, coalitions and rivalries. Traditional diplomatic history was the way we told its story. We can term the effort to have an impact on the forces within polities "below" the level of states' *implicit* foreign policy. Implicit foreign policy addresses a world of social movements, popular aspirations, and resentments often unstructured by parties and regimes and often spilling across national borders. Periodically, political leaders have made clumsy efforts to bypass official representatives: Citizen Genêt sought to lobby American opinion on behalf of the French Republic; Woodrow Wilson implied to the Germans in October 1918 that getting rid of Kaiser William II would make it easier to achieve an armistice agreement. Half a year later he tried unsuccessfully to appeal to the loftier instincts of the Italian people over the heads of their leaders on the Fiume issue at the Paris peace conference. Regime change and ideological reeducation clearly became an objective in World War II. But by implicit foreign policy I mean an effort to influence the social bases of politics. Statesmen did not always acknowledge, indeed sometimes did not recognize, that they were trying to influence social structures, although in the aftermath of war it was easier than at other times. In fact, most major efforts at international settlement have involved interrelated efforts to make social hierarchies conform to the conditions needed for international stability. Stabilization has rested on the functional alignment of social structure and state policies.

Consider some of the major junctures in international politics. The Congress of Vienna evokes for most of us a club of aristocratic statesmen rearranging European borders and installing hereditary rulers for the sake of legitimacy and stability. Measured by the rarity of major European war in the nineteenth century, its achievement was relatively robust; but underlying it was an unavowed effort to guarantee rule by landed elites that slowly (but only slowly) had to share their domestic influence with financial, industrial, and scientific or bureaucratic elites. A predominantly agrarian-based social hierarchy, enforced early on by counterrevolutionary interventions across borders, was as important to the settlement as the equilibrium between states and the consultation among rulers.

The post–World War I settlement was notoriously less successful. Its architects did not mollify the forces of aggrieved German nationalism, and it is not clear that they could have durably done so. But the Wilsonian societal base they wagered on—essentially stable middle-class democracy—proved too feeble as well, excluding as it did the aspirations of a revolutionary proletariat with a foothold in Russia and depriving many members of its hoped-for constituency outside Russia of economic stability. For a few years in the mid-1920s, financial and business leaders worked across national lines to restore the socioeconomic conditions that might sustain the peace treaties, including the return of prosperity, the temporary supremacy of German (and Japanese) moderates, and a reestablished colonial domain for the British and French. A new ideology of business-government "associationism" (to use Herbert Hoover's term) based on industrious middle-class producers replaced the more atomistic Wilsonian vision of autonomous citizen voters. But the world economic crisis undermined the societal underlay required for the explicit settlement to hold.

The post–World War II settlement associated with Yalta "worked" in that the leaders superintending it abandoned any hope for a single socioeconomic infrastructure and accepted the partition of Europe and of postcolonial nations in Asia. The peace of the Communist world was ensured by party dictatorship and the elimination of capitalist property. The tensions that might have returned to the West were eliminated by a Keynesian settlement that gave the temporarily strong working classes welfare states and reasonably full employment and the assurance of American participation and economic aid so that the economic deprivations of the interwar era would not occur.[2] President Kennedy envisaged a similar social goal in the Alliance for Progress, although the means provided were insufficient for the vast task of stabilizing Latin America.

In each of these cases the relations between states were reinforced (or undermined) by the social and economic structures within them. Indeed, I believe it a rule that any successful foreign policy be "in sync" with domestic social organization. This is not to claim that one of these domains is causally prior to the other. Political analysts deploy such spatial metaphors as "underlying" or refer to the "social base" of politics, but the world of states and traditional international affairs shapes the currents of society as much as the other way around. Both domestic and international stability (which does not preclude evolutionary change) depend on some sort of congruence.

Any successful foreign policy in the years to come will likewise have to operate in two arenas at once: the relatively traditional milieu of rivalry and cooperation among nation-states and a new (or revived), more populist domain of aspirations, resentments, and unrest organized through the media and in the streets. And although the first arena may be easier to deal with than it was during much of the twentieth century, the second has become more inflamed and challenging. I hesitate to use the term *ideologies* to describe the mass sentiments now in play, for they are less coherent and less structured, whether as social analyses or as narratives of transformation, than were the classical ideologies, whether liberalism, Marxist socialism, or nationalism. (Nationalism, in any case, divided populations across frontiers and thus helped to reinforce the political units that are the subjects of traditional statecraft.) The movements and currents in play today are the new (or revived) volatile passions generated in the vortex of cultural and economic change. They divide societies within even as they sometimes generate international conflict. Any successful foreign policy will have to address their concerns and assuage their grievances in order to stabilize the world of nation-states.

Indeed, the realm of political sentiments has become so inflamed that a very wise and rational French political scientist has asked whether the "passions" were not returning after two centuries in which one had thought that they might be restrained by interests or by commerce. "What is at stake," Pierre Hassner has written, "is the confrontation between an ethos of rational calculation, founded on readily understandable interests...and an ethos of pride, honor, and glory founded on military and warrior virtues, even on the search for death, inflicted or suffered, and sometimes on the intoxication of self-mutilation and self-destruction."[3] Hassner cites a long list of American statements that incorporated this murky warrior ethos by reputable commentators from Robert Kagan to Max Boot, one of today's leading cheerleaders for repeated combat. As Hassner recognizes, there is a "left" as well as a "right" enthusiasm: the search for radical equality or, more precisely, the hatred of inequality, of distinctions of fortune and wealth, the passion to burn the chateau. These impulses, right and left, have been described since Homer and the Old Testament, recognized by Hobbes and Machiavelli, Nietzsche and Freud, Oswald Spengler, and Samuel Huntington. They were approved by Carl Schmitt and Ernst Jünger or by such American heroes as General Patton and Ernest Hemingway. Since the Enlightenment, however, leading thinkers such as Adam Smith, Immanuel Kant, J. S. Mill, and Auguste Comte and almost all practitioners of the social sciences have believed that such impulses must wither away under the impact of a modern industrial economy or could be confined to the sphere of games and sports. Their premise was not so much that men were rational in a pure sense but that the material goods they might enjoy for themselves and their families had become more important than the deprivations they could inflict on others. Rationality meant recognition of this allegedly self-evident calculation. Commerce must trump war.[4] And the supposed fact that history was a one-way street at the end of which this impulse would prevail, whether through rational bureaucratic action or profound psychological transformation, was what constituted modernity. But perhaps the fires of apocalyptic desire merely smoldered underground and were doomed to break out again from time to time.

The Impact of Religion

What are the passions that so agitate our societies today? What communities both generate these emotion-laden beliefs and are simultaneously shaped by them? As newscasts and pundits continually reiterate, the newer sources of these public emotions are religious revival and economic globalization, which I consider in turn. Although these forces exert a fundamental impact on international relations, they are hardly controlled by the traditional instruments of international or military policy. Indeed, they are developments that American policy helped often to sponsor but that yielded unforeseen dilemmas.

The nation-state has acted contradictorily toward these alternative sources of social mobilization. It has sought to curb religious power, at least over public life, but simultaneously to liberate economic energies. The modern Western state claimed many of its powers precisely to master the sometimes murderous clash of religions. For three centuries, the trajectory of state power ascended, and the claims of religion were on the defensive. But the zenith of this particular cycle of secularism at least was reached in the 1970s, and since then, with an exception made for Western Europe, the pendulum has swung back. Americans today are divided on this countertendency, which is reflected in the blue-state, red-state face-off. In any case, religious loyalties have become powerful enough to shape those encompassing orientations of personal life that modern commentators call "identities." They have become fervent enough among some groups to justify the violence that ethnic purification had most recently claimed and, indeed, to add suicidal martyrdom to the behavior that has been sanctioned and sanctified. Europe and America looked with alarm toward the rise of Islamist parties, who hoped to make the states that they organized vehicles for installing Islamic law. Iran's revolution of 1978–1979 brought the most spectacular Islamist victory. Since then, the introduction of *shariya* has advanced in many Muslim societies. Afghanistan was still embroiled in strife over these issues while a Muslim program was advancing in hitherto secular Turkey. Egypt and Algeria only precariously resisted Islamists, who did not seem far from wholesale militant rebellion. Postinvasion Iraq was wracked by inner Muslim violence that the occupying Americans seemed unable to control.[5]

But Islam did not emerge as the only militant faith. The Indian Janata Party (JNP) and its successor, the Bharatija Janata Party (BJP), incorporated militant Hindu currents, and Hindu-Muslim communal violence periodically flared in India and made Indian-Pakistani relations far more problematic. Thailand was yielding to Buddhist claims. The zealotry of some Zionist settlers had exerted a major influence in the Israeli state, making renunciation of the 1967 territorial gains virtually impossible for almost forty years and helping to inflame wider regional Middle Eastern disputes. Despite its own constitutional guarantees of religious impartiality and freedom, the United States had become a society in which continuing appeals to divine guidance—some constantly invoking it, others confidently claiming it had already been granted—made large claims on public affairs and helped define the deep political divisions at home. Most secularists maintained that the issue in all these situations was not really the quality of personal belief but the claim that religion should play an important role in establishing public policies. But how could those who fervently believed in the truth of their respective dispensations simply renounce reforming legislative frameworks they found immoral? The result was, as it had been for five centuries, some bitter contests over books and borders—but also over bodies, in particular women's bodies.

This is one reason that religious revival at the beginning of the twenty-first century has so troubled secularists. It has often been associated with views of gender and female roles that seem retrograde in light of the advances made by women in the preceding generation. Religious revival might in fact empower women within certain spheres, namely the domestic, and observance of strict practices might bring its own sense of fulfillment. Still, in many ways orthodoxy has seemed to limit their overall freedom and their roles, whether sexual, familial, or institutional. At the level of urbanized elites, such restrictions might be easier to leave behind, but in traditionalist communities they have remained powerful. Thus the preeminent challenge of a godly world has not been that of terrorism, although that might remain a danger. It is the conviction that ultimately public norms cannot acquiesce in what liberals like to claim are purely private matters.

There had been several answers in the historical past to the problem of religious conflict and violence. Old empires, such as the Ottoman, had sought to allow religious communities a sort of ritual autonomy under their own spiritual leaders. The millet system allowed for state toleration of non-Islamic faiths so long as they accepted the secular authority of the sultan and understood that Islam enjoyed a position of supremacy within the polity. In Western Europe, the answer to Protestant-Catholic conflict was either suppression of one faith by another or, once that proved too costly in terms of bloodshed and violence, a geographical division of souls. Communities of faith, and the princes who protected them, reached compromises on the basis of territorial confederalism. Protestants and Catholics did so in Central Europe in 1555 with the Peace of Augsburg and again in 1648 with the treaties of Westphalia. In the Low Countries, Protestants and Catholics migrated or fled to the respective territorial enclaves: the United Provinces of the North, the Spanish Netherlands to the South. Eventually Hindus and Muslims, Shiite and Sunni Muslims might achieve a similar equilibrium. Nonetheless, it is clear that arriving at such a balance through decades of bloodshed is a long and discouraging process. The third solution, trying to establish the state on a plane above religious communities and declaring that it would permit and protect individual commitments but would not privilege communal identities, took the longest to develop. It required the prior development in the seventeenth and eighteenth centuries of sophisticated notions of toleration. It worked best and most extensively in the United States. It was a great achievement, although it seemed periodically to come under pressure. Americans, mostly in the red states but also confused secularists, sometimes decided that it would be intolerant to oppose the popular search to enrich political life with creedal impulses.

In any case, the new claims of faith have roiled not only our own domestic life but also foreign policy. Issues of funding reproductive medicine abroad or the appropriate response to terrorism have obviously erased many of the distinctions between international affairs and domestic affairs. Insofar as foreign policy issues come into play, it seems to me that the guidelines for American policy should not in theory betray the principles we accept at home. Still, the line between compromise and betrayal is a fine one. On the level of states, foreign policy involves continuous compromise, as we have sought to practice for thirty years on human rights issues, maintaining principles but not usually cutting off relations with states that do not observe them. There will be conflicts from time to time, and they will have to be resolved on a case-by-case basis.

American policy must at least recognize that not every political movement or party that seeks to organize around the basis of a religious commitment necessarily poses a threat of repression. Despite fears, the Indian JNP has become integrated into everyday democratic politics in that huge country. The Christian Democratic parties in Europe—originally envisaged at the turn of the twentieth century—became a major force for liberal-democratic reconstruction after Fascism and World War II. Their adherents claimed inspiration from the moral legacy of Christianity, an all-purpose ideological basis, which often meant little more than anti-Communism and sometimes seemed hypocritical in light of their members' acquiescence in Fascism. Still, Christian Democracy became the basis for the centrist and conservative reconstruction in Europe over the past sixty years. Some moderate Islamic parties, most prominently newly elected Turkish president Abdullah Gül's Justice and Development Party (AKP), may evolve as similar forces. Ankara is hardly Qum. If Washington can discriminate among the spectrum of forces, it will encourage the moderate option.

The Repoliticization of Inequality

American foreign policy is likely to become increasingly burdened by the impact of globalization—whether defined as cross-border openness to investment, to trade, or to migration—and of global poverty. The number of people living on less than a dollar a day—the World Bank's criterion for extreme poverty—declined in the 1980s and 1990s but remains over a billion, while the number of those earning between a dollar and two dollars has gone up, although the combined percentage of these very poor has probably declined.

The issue of poverty is not identical with that of globalization but is likewise immensely politicized. Latin America remains the region with the highest degrees of inequality due to factors such as land ownership, polarized regimes, and the like.[6] It is also the region in which populist regimes or policies most explicitly challenge the presence of American capital. Such a tradition has been recurrent in so-called Latin American populism: the leaders of Venezuela and Bolivia have embraced this rhetoric; Argentina's leaders are recurringly tempted by it. Whether Hugo Chávez's regime comes to grief or not is still to be decided. But it is a good bet that his sort of appeal and politics will prove attractive in many other locations. If "Evita-land" seems far away, let us recall that a governor of Louisiana built a large political movement on these sentiments in the 1930s before he was assassinated.

The economic literature on the impact of globalization and the tendencies toward inequality remain dismayingly contradictory. UN agencies and those studies produced under their input follow the traditionally pro-redistribution concerns that have marked UN reports at least since the Brandt report and the heyday of the United Nations Conference on Trade and Development (UNCTAD). National Bureau of Economic Research (NBER)-oriented material comes to the opposite conclusions; the World Bank reports highlight strategies that can target growth to poverty reduction. Classical trade theory has demonstrated ever since the days of Smith and Ricardo that unconstrained exchange should increase everyone's welfare in absolute terms. Market exchange over time, at least when accompanied by technological advance, has apparently made wider and wider groups of people better and better off. Nonetheless, the poor in countries with a lot of unskilled labor do not always improve their lot by freer trade. Free-trade advocates such as Jagdish Bhagwati insist that free trade is pro-poor; the critics say that trade theory is "worse than wrong, it is dangerous" or that, despite the World Bank, "growth is failing the poor."[7]

Recent studies, in fact, suggest ambiguous results: income inequality can increase or decrease even as growth goes forward. Inequality *between* societies may be decreasing, whereas inequality *within* societies is increasing. Others argue that overall inequality within societies, as measured by Gini indices, may be decreasing but that the lowest deciles, 1–4, and the highest decile, 10, are pulling away from the central 50 percent of the populations in deciles 5–9. It may also be that inequality may be decreasing but that risk-averse households may feel uncomfortable about the uncertainty of their future position within a society.[8] So, too, growth may be increasing, inequality may be decreasing, but the fact that households in traditional occupations may lose their livelihood may arouse great passion.

Economists may lament the inflammatory language and the muddy concepts. They also often narrow the politically relevant issues. As some point out, if the assembler of athletic shoes in Malaysia gets a formerly unavailable income of two dollars per day but corporate headquarters nets a substantial profit based on that wage rate, there will be debate over the equity involved. Moreover, the new wage opportunity does not mean that most of those participating in this collective process of material improvement would voluntarily have chosen the conditions under which they were taking part. Certainly for centuries those working as agricultural producers for landlords understood that they were often in a highly dependent power relationship. If not formally bound to their fields, they usually fell into a continuous indebtedness that effectively constrained their market participation. They confronted arrangements—employers, investors, purchasers—that they had no voice in choosing. This does not mean that most working men and women do not find satisfaction from their labor—the money that they earn, the fellowship of the workplace, the pride of workmanship. But relatively few among the world's working population have been able to choose where they work, how they work, what rewards they might reap, and whether they can even continue working.

The impact on labor in the advanced industrial societies adds to the stakes of the issues concerning the developing or stagnant countries.[9] Critics of globalization in the United States or Europe are concerned, obviously, with the impact on local workers and not just those in the outer world. In these countries, including our own, the issues of job security (or job loss) and immigration are salient. In recent months, more and more articles in the informed press have also pointed to the vast enrichment at the very top of income earners and wealth holders within the United States. This points to a critical political fact: the foreign-policy debates over global inequality cannot be kept separate from discussions of domestic policies. Although the United States is the wealthiest society in the world (and ranks just after such very small banking centers as Luxembourg in per capita gross national product [GNP]), the stagnation of real family income and the growing enrichment of America's moneyed classes will increase the salience of inequality issues. A wise policy agenda must address both the domestic and the international tendencies at the same time, because both will be subject to similar critiques and angry reactions.

For the sake of simplification, call those who believed in the benevolence of markets, who prized the growth and wealth they brought, and who were willing to accept their ever more transnational impact *Smithians*. They tended to deny that power was a relevant variable in well-functioning market activity. Call those who felt that the human cost or the inequality produced was too high for the possible rewards offered *the Left*. When Marxist systems collapsed at the end of the 1980s, the Left was discredited throughout the world, outside of such die-hard enclaves as China, North Korea, Vietnam, and Cuba. From 1980 until century's end, the Left was in disarray, the Smithians triumphant. Francis Fukuyama, in effect, heralded their victory, along with that of democratic liberalism.

The Smithians, moreover, have largely set the terms of debate. The accepted rhetoric of the respectable press continually referred to labor market reform, which from a union viewpoint meant the capacity of entrepreneurs to lay off labor. This did not mean that capitalists had to positively want to lay off workers or dismantle health and pension systems. They just could envisage no alternatives in light of globalization. Only in the Nordic countries did job retraining and refitting seem to allow quick restructuring; but the largest of these countries, Sweden, had a population of only nine million. Elsewhere the process was far less easy. Eventually after, say, a decade of stagnant employment figures (as in Germany, but only the former West Germany), the restructured economy could start to reabsorb labor. The political leaders in charge of Western states sometimes protested but did not really disagree. They saw themselves as administrators of territorial units confronting trans-territorial forces; and, in contrast to the sphere of religion, they felt that there could be no effective opposition to the domain of markets. Although the U.S. economy created employment and jobs, there was malaise about the attrition of manufacturing employment; the new positions were often in retail-connected services, such as large stores or call centers, and the working conditions were subject to harsh criticism. Consequently, the Smithian scenario seems less benevolent and certainly likely to be more contested during the coming decades. It is a reasonable prediction in 2007 to suggest that the criticisms and the countervailing pressures, including populism, as well as protectionism, will probably grow more serious in the years to come. We can hear the tectonic plates of the great age of international capitalism grinding against each other.

The issue of whether or not the liberalization of trade, investment, and financial markets produces more winners than losers is not what counts here. Even those growing better off can feel resentment at others who are rewarded far more handsomely. What is at stake is the reaction of so many people who feel themselves displaced, marginalized, and victims of processes they cannot control. Postadolescents, stalled in the bleak holding pattern of urban joblessness or short-term make-work positions, understand that burning automobiles focuses the attention of the media. Riots have a performative function even if they seem economically irrational. Street theater—consider Paris in 1789, 1848, or 2007, Watts in 1967, Columbia University in 1968, or Seattle and Geneva in 2006—makes the great and the good take notice. Sometimes the dramas get good reviews, as in East Berlin and Prague in 1989, and sometimes horrified reactions. Sometimes they produce beneficial changes—those that expand opportunity and redress inequality—and sometimes they evoke mere repression. But like battlefield confrontations they introduce moments of unpredictability. Even if they may be sympathetic to the protestors' cause, those who have positions of some predictable comfort do not really want history up for grabs, at least not their own. But once again, history seems more ransom to the unpredictable.

If the politics of populism becomes more appealing abroad, it will also become more tempting at home. Many liberals have sought to minimize the growing danger and unfairness of vast inequality by claiming that Americans value equality of opportunity but not result. Such a distinction has proved to be in many respects a comforting evasion. But equality of opportunity has often remained a myth. And ultimately the ever-greater skewing of income and wealth such as that which characterized the opening of the new century suggests that the game is not merely played for high stakes but is fundamentally unfair. Cupidity is not one of the self-evident rights cited by the Declaration of Independence. Ultimately these discrepancies will seem just unacceptable and will provoke forceful reactions. Such reactions will not be justified as a simple counterclaim. They will be explained in terms of God's wrath or historical dialectic or an alternative vision of human rights. The poor will not win in such a conflict, they never do; but the security of life will disappear for everyone. If market outcomes come to seem unjust at home, this will have an impact on how sacred they appear abroad.

Most commentators have debated whether such events can reverse the great trend toward free trade, untrammeled capital movements, and mass migrations that have characterized the past forty years. They have raised the specter of 1914 and 1929–1931. But a setback to world trade and prosperity is not the only danger involved. Globalization, poverty, and inequality create an international structure in which organized states have less capacity to cope with polarizing social conflicts. It will bring great disruptive potential, to a degree between favored and less favored nations, and increasingly within all these countries. It is obvious that some political leaders will think it advantageous and idealistic to challenge, if not a growing inequality, certainly a growing perception of truly elite enrichment. The post-Castroite transition in Cuba, as *norteamericano* developers attempt to build their casinos on the Havana waterfront, will probably sharpen at least the rhetorical confrontations.

So what does this have to do with foreign policy? The United States is rightly understood to be the leading site of the Smithians and the privileged. On a global scale, the power that has helped to structure global markets has so far helped to channel flows of wealth to inventive entrepreneurs in the United States, to the advanced industrial and postindustrial societies, and, increasingly, to the countries of East and South Asia. Its critics abroad see its firms as the vanguard of exploitative capital. It is doubtful that enough of them will read *The Economist* to offset this powerful view. The divisions of world politics will not mobilize states, as such, but leaders who will speak for the disinherited and with rude and troubling voices. Their power will not be keyed to states alone but to transnational class formations.

Within the United States, at least through 2006, these moods were more than offset by the cultural and religious mobilization that the Republican Party has managed so well. But on a world scale, the political outcome of religious mobilization is less certain. Will oxygenated religious faith cancel out economic grievances and preach social conservatism, as it did in the nineteenth century, or will it work at cross-purposes? In Latin America, Rome has partially reined in the social radicalism of liberation theology, and the spread of evangelical religion can likewise temper economic radicalism. The political valence of reenergized faith commitments cannot be taken for granted. Obviously in the Middle East, the contest (often within Islamic states) is still open. Traditional foreign policy will not have much leverage when—as Yeats once put it, listening to the rising winds—it confronts those "imagining in excited reverie/That the future years had come/Dancing to a frenzied drum."[10] The alliances of those who feel dispossessed and those privileged groups with an interest in a far more genteel politics will not be easy. Some answers are suggested later, but first I critique the responses that will be insufficient.

Farewell to Westphalia

Throughout the twentieth century scholars and political leaders made the now familiar observation that democracy transforms the conditions under which statesmen must work, rendering their high-level world more volatile and dangerous. Practitioners and historians have repeatedly cited the democratization of foreign policy since the era of Woodrow Wilson and David Lloyd George as a force that was transforming international relations. Walter Lippmann throughout his career was an ambivalent observer of the force of public opinion. George Kennan and Henry Kissinger alike as prudential practitioners have lamented the intrusion of mass passions into foreign policy. Kissinger, in particular, has suggested that mobilization of public opinion undermined the capacity to conduct a policy of détente. Others have contended that democratic advances were a beneficial force. Proponents of the democratic peace theory (which I think badly flawed, but that is not the issue here) remain convinced that democracy will inhibit the recourse to interstate violence. So what is new in the observations made here?

What is happening now is somewhat different: states themselves are becoming less and less the site for the exercise of public power. Foreign relations, traditionally conceived, have consisted of the way states manage their relative independence within a world of multiple actors. What political scientists have long modeled as the Westphalian system—so called from the European treaties of the mid-seventeenth century that recognized a large number of sovereign states all acutely aware that they were fated to compete against each other—is inexorably being transformed. In the decades to come, any national leadership will be confronted by problems in which national states and traditional national security doctrines will prove less and less sufficient for navigating the deeper currents of global history. Indeed, according to the head of the State Department's Policy Planning Staff, the Bush administration has itself sought to overcome the tradition of Westphalia.[11]

This may not be wise policy, although attempting to reverse a settlement that helped fragment an empire follows logically from recent de facto U.S. imperial ambitions. States serve as paradoxical instruments of history. For many centuries they have both condemned human societies to recurring violence and simultaneously served as their major line of defense against it. As Hannah Arendt reminded us, they have provided what security is available for life and property, and often for liberty, too, but they have also generated recurrent insecurity.[12] Nevertheless, like it or not, their central role in the production of security and insecurity is ending. Their dual role is devolving in two different directions. Increasingly, as we have suggested, transnational constellations of class and faith generate disorder while supranational associations endeavor to provide order. If the preeminent task of foreign policy is to provide a community's security, its practitioners will have to tame the first and strengthen the second.

Why this devolution of the nation-state? Let's remember that it has been under way since at least the 1970s, and not just for the reasons usually cited. Not just because states are increasingly delegating powers and functions to supranational associations, whether regional such as the European Union (EU), or functional, such as the World Trade Organization (WTO), or global, such as the UN. And not just because of the processes we term *globalization*, although the consequences of globalization are profound. Neither, despite a whole new set of bureaucracies and interests that thrive on depicting lurid dangers, are states simply failing to meet the challenges presented by terrorist networks acting together across boundaries. Nor, finally, are states becoming merely more constrained by the inevitable frictions that arise among them, by prisoners' dilemma games and "security traps" that have been analyzed so abstractly. Over the past sixty years, states have learned how to deal with these more cautiously. Nuclear deterrence helped concentrate the mind.

And yet this condition has been changing ever since the last third of the twentieth century, beginning even before American commentators signed on to celebrate our benevolent global supremacy. Although states control military resources, the resources for mastering so many of the collective emotions that move crowds and that ultimately make or break regimes have been less and less under their control. Paris and Prague gave premonitory signs of that fact in 1968; Tehran and the guerrilla war in Afghanistan pointed to the new infusion of mass politics at the end of the 1970s. Between 1989 and 1991, the force of popular mobilization was revealed within the states of the Communist world. The adversaries of Communism rejoiced in that fact, and political observers ascribed this mass capacity to the institutions of civil society, which made them sound like a force for liberation. Civil society comprised churches, unions, a free press, and prodemocracy advocates in general—whatever networks were not controlled by the state. Political commentators forgot that in the 1970s many of those in responsible political, academic, and corporate positions were often lamenting that an excess of democracy was making Western societies ungovernable. Inflation, bloated welfare systems, powerful unions, and unruly students seemed a disaster in the making. In the 1980s such mass mobilization, now safely confined to the decrepit Communist world, became a cause for celebration. What seemed to triumph were precisely the principles long championed by American and other advocates of democracy. Our side and our principles won the great ideological struggle. What seemed to follow was that U.S. policy should work for the continued success of democracy, construed as the reliance on elections and popular rule, and not merely the attainment of human rights, that is, the rule of law and the security of persons and property.

In the post-1989 celebrations, we took little cognizance of the fact that the passions that sent protesters to the streets to topple Communist regimes might also come to shake the governing capacity of non-Communist states. Sauce for the goose, sauce for the gander: the trilateralist critiques of "overloaded democracy" had largely been forgotten with the collapse of Communism. Had they had a point? As much as friction between states, the challenge to every state's mastery of its foreign policy environment is the collective passions that arise from "outside" or "below" the system of high politics. We witness the dismantling of governability, which states since 1650 or so worked so arduously to centralize within their respective institutions, but which has now threatened to erode under the pressure of popular resentments and hopes. Fareed Zakaria pointed out that democratic political systems might not ensure liberal outcomes or results that ensure the rule of law and the protection of property.[13] Any observers of the electoral outcomes at the end of that model democracy, the Weimar Republic, might have drawn the same conclusion.

States no longer have a monopoly on power in the realms of economics or of faith, both of which have become and are likely to remain sites of intense conflict, if not violence. Any American "foreign" policy must address these domains, but it cannot do so with the traditional resources of the territorial state, not even of a quasi-imperial state. Foreign policy is, in fact, an insufficient concept for dealing with these loci of conflict, for it suggests that the structures of ambassadors and diplomacy and interstate relations constructed in the state systems of the seventeenth century and after encompass the total realm of politics outside the domestic. It presupposes a firm territorial mapping, albeit a pluralist one. But even had the events and policy responses of the period since 9/11 not debilitated the American position, the new challenges could not be met on a territorial basis alone.

Certainly, international issues as traditionally conceived will persist. International society always finds it difficult to accommodate the rise of new ambitious powers and the weakening of old ones. Managed badly, as between, say, 1900 and 1950, such transitions produce what Robert Gilpin termed hegemonic wars.[14] The rise of China as a geostrategic giant—no matter how cautious its leadership—will tax the traditional skills needed for successful diplomacy. So, too, will the current fragility of the nonproliferation treaty. The logic of nuclear competition does not require hostile intentions—just, alas, the consequences of uncertainty and insecurity. Moreover, the arms race or equilibrium will also depend in large part on the eventual balance between India and China (not even taking into account a potential Iranian nuclear threat). It will take a wise and restrained policy to avoid a renewed half century of nuclear competition—this time with space-based weapons, as well as those on land and water.

The Bush administration has tended to emphasize the need to preserve the country's military preponderance as the best way to navigate the uncertain shoals ahead. For the next presidential administration, the United States will continue to possess a commanding lead in military power and related technological capacities.[15] In the long run, such a lead must ebb. But that is not the preeminent source of vulnerability. Few political contenders at home really want to dismantle our arsenal imprudently. And, conversely, even were we to arm as extensively as the National Security Doctrine of October 2002 mandated, our security would not thereby be ensured. Indeed, such a program would in all likelihood just encourage others' armament programs and make the globe a more hazardous arena for international politics. As a more immediate constraint, the occupation of Iraq has made it clear that unless the United States is willing to reintroduce national service, the country is reaching the limits of relevant military resources—that is, not of the high-tech variety, but the simple number of soldiers recruited at home or hired abroad.

Just as important, there are political limitations to American interventionism. Niall Ferguson has charged that Americans suffer from attention-deficit disorder when it comes to assuming imperial responsibilities.[16] This critique may have some justification when it comes to carrying through on foreign aid or even military interventions in the Horn of Africa and elsewhere. But it certainly was not the case for the American commitment to defend Western Europe over four decades. Still, there are probably public limits to policy activism within the polity, as well. An electorate so evenly divided as the American might well abandon its toleration of an assertive foreign policy, just as it has begun to get uneasy over binding multilateral commitments to global warming, energy shortages, or possible new pandemics. But this does not imply a danger of isolationism. Critics of the Bush administration's testosterone-fueled policy have reminded voters that there was another alternative for American engagement without raising the specter of withdrawal without end. It was one that had motivated the country at an earlier moment of triumph right after World War II, when the country sought to leverage its power through international arrangements and institutions, not against them.[17]

Given the limits on traditional foreign policy interventionism and even on continuing military supremacy, will the United States, then, preserve its security through "soft power"? American soft power suggests a warm and fuzzy reassurance, but I do not think it has much relevance for our security. Joseph Nye offered the concept originally to argue that even if American military preponderance ebbed, the country's cultural and economic assets would ensure its leadership.[18] The appeal of our pop music, our continuing output of zany comedy and engaging television drama (*The Simpsons* and *The Sopranos*), technological inventiveness, and a strong commitment to scientific research, humanistic learning, and the arts are certainly desirable in their own right. They certainly will contribute to how the American republic will be remembered a millennium hence. How they relate to power is more problematic. Soft power cannot provide autonomy or ensure global leadership if hard power evaporates. Young Roman aristocrats visited Athens in the first century to soak up culture and philosophy, and the apostle Paul went to establish a bridgehead for Christianity, but the city was irrelevant as a power factor. There are signs, moreover, that our own soft-power assets—the power of the dollar as an international reserve currency, the preeminence of our universities and laboratories, the unique appeals of our entertainment industries—are losing their salience. As long as the reduction is relative and not absolute, such a development should be welcomed. Cultural resources should never have been conceived of as zero-sum.

All these developments suggest that to the degree that international politics persists along traditional lines, the United States will remain an influential, perhaps even hegemonic, actor—but, as hopefully even the most fervent celebrants of the American mission may come to understand, hardly an omnipotent one. I want the United States to play a responsible and important role in world affairs—we are too wealthy and too fortunate to stand aside, and for half a century between 1940 and 1990 we acted, I believe, as a force for global freedom, security, and welfare. But a beneficial American role will not be achieved by vaunting leadership, merely brandishing military technology, or clucking about how we are needed and how so many people might migrate here would we let them. (All of this quasi hubris, moreover, will seem even more bizarre if there were to be a real meltdown of international finance and a collapse of world asset prices. America is never at its best in depression diplomacy, so whatever scenarios are proposed must assume good times. A global economic crisis would mean that all bets are off.)

And thus our states, even the greatest of them, face a double set of challenges. On the one hand, we shall have to live with the old ones of Hobbesian territoriality or military insecurity, no longer produced by desires for annexations and enlargements but just for the maintenance of the status quo. At the same time we confront a new nonterritorial continuum of tensions generated by faith and inequality. All this suggests that the major challenges to global stability in the decades to come are not readily containable in the frameworks of international relations that governed them in the past century and perhaps even in the past three hundred years. If the profound sources of unrest arise from growing economic resentments and backlashes, from more zealous religious commitments, from the movement of migrants with all the social turmoil this brings, and from the unleashing of a higher general level of violence within weak or divided political communities, then we soon leave behind a world of fixed boundaries, territorial states, national and group rivalries. The balance of power presupposes stable reservoirs of power—bordered territories that can be filled and refilled with a measurable fluid of military assets and economic capital. But this carefully structured international order captures little of the tensions and the distress of the world's population. The issue is not the balance of power but the usability of power.

So we face the paradox: states are not the instrumentalities to deal with the transnational passions of religion and the reactions to market, but states are the instrumentality that we must rely on. What concrete suggestions follow from this diagnosis? There are no ready remedies for such deep-seated trends, but at least our country can signal new intentions.

First, insofar as economic inequality is at stake—domestic and global— American policy must signal that advancing equality remains a national and international priority. Pursuing this objective must start at home, but it also requires raising our derisory level of foreign economic aid. Of course, what we can supply is limited. The calls for a Marshall Plan here and there are not always relevant; the original European Recovery Program focused on an area that had great human capital and long industrial experience and that needed short-term assistance to overcome balance-of-payments constraints. Still, in those years the United States contributed an average of 1 to 2 percent per annum to reconstruction, about four or five times its current support. Skeptics cite the corruption that siphons off assistance and call for trade, not aid. But unless we are really prepared to open our markets to every producer, we should at least send help abroad. As for globalization, its champions and our policy makers must pay greater attention to promoting the institutions within which it takes place.

To my mind, Dani Rodrik at Harvard's Kennedy School of Government makes a persuasive case for pressing for the social safety networks that must accompany an open trade policy.[19] The international regulation sought should become a priority for our State Department, as well as for trade representatives. Trade policy and the advancement of liberalization should recognize that adverse consequences can also follow. Just as we assign an environmental impact statement to the development of physical plants, so we should consider assigning a formal equality impact statement (if only a range of probabilities) to negotiated trade arrangements.

Second, we must work to attenuate the passions of religion. The American experiment rested on pluralism and separation of political power from creed and faith. It has become fashionable to observe that Western Europe remains alone in its commitment to these secular values.[20] True, we cannot simply dictate secularist values to fundamentalists in general, Islamists in particular. We should make it feasible for moderates to achieve what European Christian Democracy accomplished after World War II, that is, to group a constituency of middle-class electors concerned with property and humane values. Turkey is obviously a key country in this strategy, and ultimately Iran will be as well. Constant harping that Islam has gone wrong or incorporates values fundamentally incompatible with the rule of law will not get us very far. Every religious tradition is divided between creedal hawks and doves; for those outside the respective faiths, it is important to encourage the doves. This means continuing dialogues with the moderates in any situation in which religious establishments offer a spectrum of opinion leaders. We should not be naive, either. To a great extent the general problem so far as Islamism is concerned will depend a great deal on the outcome of events dealing with Iranian nuclear ambitions, intra-Palestinian rivalries, and Israeli security perceptions. There has been more than one third rail in American politics, but it should be possible for courageous leadership to open security issues for discussion.

Foreign policy is a seamless web: the tough issues of security flow into the ambient concerns of religious passions and economic equality. But restoring America's prestige depends a great deal on signals sent and themes established. American policy makers must develop an imagination that takes us beyond the walls of separation now being erected at so many borders. Keeping deadly outbreaks at bay, whether avian flu or suicide bombing, does require watchfulness. But fortifying the frontier can only be a first response. The history of our era might be conceived as having opened with the fall of a wall in Berlin designed to keep people in, but it has continued with the construction of new walls, on the Rio Grande and across the West Bank, designed to keep people out. There is, unfortunately, logic to that cycle. The end of one fundamental ideological division created the opportunity for single-minded advocates to strengthen other cleavages, whether constructed around faith, gender, or economic fortune. Good fences don't make good neighbors, but we have settled for keeping out desperate ones. The failure of the Bush immigration reform package—precisely the most positive and generous response that the administration has offered in the face of global economic inequality—reveals that no consensus existed on going beyond strengthening the frontier. Foreign policy in the years to come must take us beyond building fences, which in any case will never be totally secure. Fences, after all, cannot address the externalities that arise from threats such as global warming. We have essentially left those tasks to NGOs and overtaxed UN missions. Indicatively, the founder of Médecins sans Frontières has become the foreign minister of a major state. In fact, an active post-Bush foreign policy must reclaim the tasks we have outsourced to the NGOs. Even as they claim the efforts of so many devoted activists willing to defer a career at Goldman or in a lucrative legal practice, and even as, as private citizens, we donate more to them, so our country must place its far greater public resources behind the same sorts of efforts.

Finally, American policy makers, journalists, and the interested public need to think about the societal presuppositions of democracy. It is commonplace to state that it fares best when constructed on the basis of a diffuse middle class. This hardly guarantees a favorable outcome; after all, Fascist regimes relied on a broad middle class, as well. Still, development efforts should aspire to such broad societal results and not simply the enrichment of local elites. And domestic policy should demonstrate for observers abroad that we are serious about these commitments across the board.

It is a liberal commonplace to plead for a greater regard for allies. Conservatives, indeed, have easy sport to show how often long-standing associates fail to support American priorities or just lack the strategic means. Their derision misses the point. Our allies help to structure a global milieu of economic and social stability. Europe in particular is building a unique form of political and economic association. It is cumbersome, undecided about how central it can be, and unsure about taking on security challenges outside Europe. It would be in Europe's own interest if the EU did increase its autonomous military capacity, not to challenge Washington but to seem more credible as an international actor. The contempt with which American policy makers spoke about Europe in 2001–2002 was not healthy for Europe or for the United States. Europe and North America are on the same side in the truly global conflicts: whether against terrorism, against the inequalities that breed massive popular resentment, or against environmental dangers, including contagious diseases. The United States and Europe are both conservative forces in the present global alignment of interests, compelled to hope that interests can still prevail against passions. The power that we should be constructing is that which inheres in institutions with authoritative legitimacy, not just national arsenals. This is at once a liberal and a conservative agenda: liberal in the sense that it must work to attenuate inequality and recognize the need for political initiatives to balance the lotteries inherent in the supposedly market distribution of goods but conservative in its efforts to avoid unrest and to promote stability by diminishing injustice.

None of this makes state power likely to wither away. Neither does it mean that NGOs will inherit the earth. It means only that balance-of-power coalitions seem increasingly irrelevant to much of what will preoccupy global politics during the coming years (assuming again that no large country simply runs amok). Still, states remain the fulcrums for creative political action. States and statesmen and political parties can still mobilize efforts to attenuate the privilege that seems to corrupt modern democracies and stack the deck against so many of the less advantaged at home and abroad. American leaders in the past have recognized this basic vulnerability and the potential for counteracting it: the greatest democratic statesman of the twentieth century, Franklin Roosevelt, called for "freedom from want" along with "freedom from fear." He envisioned it as a global policy, although he curbed his rhetoric and spoke only for the United States.[21] But it is time to revive his better instincts and his broader ambition.

Notes

1. Chalmers Johnson, "Blowback," *The Nation* (October 15, 2001), http://www.thenation.com/doc/20011015/Johnson.

2. I have described these historical arrangements in "Empires or Nations? 1918, 1945, 1989…" in *Three Postwar Eras in Comparison: Western Europe 1918–1945–1989*, ed. Carl Levy and Mark Roseman (Basingstoke and New York: Palgrave, 2002), 41–66; and "The Two Postwar Eras and the Conditions for Stability in Twentieth-Century Western Europe," *American Historical Review* 86, no. 2 (April 1981): 327–352, and "Reply": 363–367.

3. Pierre Hassner, "La revanche des passions," *Commentaire*, no. 110 (Summer 2005): 299–312 (see 304).

4. This strand of Enlightenment and post-Enlightenment thinking has been discussed by many, but it is worth recalling the work that helped bring it back to the attention of current commentators: Albert O. Hirschman, *The Passions and the Interests: Political Arguments for Capitalism before its Triumph* (Princeton, NJ: Princeton University Press, 1977).

5. On Islam and its dangers, see Gilles Kepel, *Jihad: The Trail of Political Islam*, trans. Anthony F. Roberts (Cambridge, MA: Harvard University Press, 2002). There was a subliterature that Islam (and the Middle Eastern communities) had somehow missed out on modernity. See Bernard Lewis,

What Went Wrong? The Clash between Islam and Modernity in the Middle East (New York: Perennial, 2003). A nuanced reading of Islamic impulses in the Iranian revolution is provided by Roy Mottahedeh, *The Mantle of the Prophet: Religion and Politics in Iran* (London: Chatto & Windus, 1986), and for a general sympathetic discussion, see Reza Aslan, *No God but God: The Origins, Evolution, and Future of Islam* (New York: Random House, 2005). Although it flies in the face of all my own training and impulses, my sense is that no religion can be judged on the basis of its texts alone—there is a point to the simplified quote: "*credo quia absurdum est.*"

6. Richard Kohl, ed., *Globalisation, Poverty and Inequality* (Paris: OECD, 2003). See also José Gabriel Palma, "Globalizing Inequality: 'Centrifugal' and 'Centripetal' Forces at Work," in *Flat World, Big Gaps: Economic Liberalization, Globalization, Poverty and Inequality*, ed. Jomo K. S. and Jacques Baudot (London: Zed Books, in association with the United Nations, 2007), 99–129. For revealing graphical presentations of the different aspects of globalization, see Marie-Francoise Durand et al., *Atlas de la mondialisation: Comprendre l'espace mondial contemporain*, new ed. (Paris: Presses de la Fondation Nationale des Sciences Politiques, 2007).

7. On the debate and its complexities, see Emma Aisbett's "Why Are the Critics So Convinced Globalization Is Bad for the Poor?" in *Globalization and Poverty*, ed. Ann Harrison (Chicago: University of Chicago Press, 2006), 33–75; also Donald R. Davis and Prachi Mishra, "Stolper-Samuelson Is Dead and Other Crimes of Both Theory and Data," in *Globalization and Poverty*, 87–109; and William Easterly, "Globalization, Poverty, and All That," in *Globalization and Poverty*, 109–142. See also David Woodward and Andrew Simms, "Growth Is Failing the Poor: The Unbalanced Distribution of the Benefits and Costs of Global Economic Growth," in *Flat World, Big Gaps*, 130–158.

8. See the chapter by Ethan Ligon, "Risk and the Evolution of Inequality in China in an Era of Globalization," and the probing critique by Shang-Jin Wei in *Globalization and Poverty*, 599–628.

9. John Weeks, "Inequality Trends in Some Developed OECD Countries"; also Heather Boushey and Christian E. Weller, "Unequal Fortunes, Unstable Households: Has Rising Inequality Contributed to Economic Troubles for [US] Households?" in *Flat World, Big Gaps*, 159–215.

10. W. B. Yeats, "A Prayer for My Daughter," in *Michael Robartes and the Dancer* (Dundrum, Ireland: Cuala Press, 1921).

11. So Stephen Krasner explained at a luncheon for the Bertelsmann-Austrian conference on Atlantic relations in Washington, D.C., in November 2006. For Krasner's own academic discussion of these issues, see his thoughtful (though unfortunately titled) *Sovereignty: Organized Hypocrisy* (Princeton, NJ: Princeton University Press, 1999).

12. Hannah Arendt, *The Origins of Totalitarianism*, new ed. with added prefaces (New York: Harcourt Brace & Company, 1973), 269–290.

13. Fareed Zakaria, *The Future of Freedom: Illiberal Democracy at Home and Abroad* (New York: Norton, 2004).

14. Robert Gilpin, *War and Change in World Politics* (New York: Cambridge University Press, 1981).

15. Barry R. Posen, "Command of the Commons: The Military Foundation of U.S. Hegemony," *International Security* 28, no. 1 (September 2003): 5–46.

16. Niall Ferguson, *Colossus: The Rise and Fall of the American Empire* (New York: Penguin, 2004).

17. See G. John Ikenberry's chapter in this volume and his book, *After Victory: Institutions, Strategic Restraint, and the Rebuilding of Order after Major Wars* (Princeton, NJ: Princeton University Press, 2001).

18. The most recent exposition is Joseph S. Nye, *Soft Power: The Key to Success in World Politics* (New York: Public Affairs, 2004).

19. Dani Rodrik, "How to Save Globalization from Its Cheerleaders," http://rodrik.typepad.com (accessed July 30, 2007). See also his "The Cheerleaders' Threat to Global Trade," *Financial Times*, March 27, 2007, available at http://www.ksg.harvard.edu/ksgnews/Features/opeds/032707_rodrik.html.

20. For profound explorations of Western secularism, see Talal Asad, *Formations of the Secular: Christianity, Islam, Modernity* (Stanford, CA: Stanford University Press, 2003). The argument about "the great separation" is most recently presented by Mark Lilla, "The Politics of God," *New York Times Magazine* (August 19, 2007): 28.

21. Elizabeth Borgwardt, *A New Deal for the World: America's Vision for Human Rights* (Cambridge, MA: Harvard University Press, 2005), 136.

FOUR

Liberal Order Building
G. John Ikenberry

I N THE TWENTY-FIRST century, America confronts a complex array of security challenges—diffuse, shifting, and uncertain. But it does not face the sort of singular geopolitical threat that it did with the Fascist and Communist powers of the last century. Indeed, compared with the dark days of the 1930s or the cold war, America lives in an extraordinarily benign security environment, and it possesses an extraordinary opportunity to shape its security environment for the long term. It is the dominant global power, unchecked by a coalition of balancing states or a superpower wielding a rival universalistic ideology. Most of the great powers are democracies and tied to the United States through formal alliances and informal partnerships. State power is ultimately based on sustained economic growth—and no major state today can modernize without integrating into the globalized capitalist system; that is, if you want to be a world power, you will need to join the World Trade Organization (WTO). What made the Fascist and Communist threats of the twentieth century so profound was not only the danger of territorial aggression but also the fact that these great power challengers embodied rival political-economic systems that could generate growth, attract global allies, and create counterbalancing geopolitical blocs. America has no such global challengers today.

The most serious threat to U.S. national security today is not a specific enemy but the erosion of the institutional foundations of the global order that the United States has commanded for half a century and through which it has pursued its interests and national security. America's leadership position and authority within the global system are in serious crisis—and this puts

American national security at risk. The grand strategy America needs to pursue in the years ahead is one aimed not at a particular threat but rather at restoring its role as the recognized and legitimate leader of the system and at rebuilding the institutions and partnerships on which this leadership position is based. America's global position is in crisis, but it is a crisis that is largely of its own making, and one that can be overcome in a way that leaves the United States in a stronger position to meet the diffuse, shifting, and uncertain threats of the twenty-first century.

The grand strategy I am proposing can be called "liberal order building." It is essentially a twenty-first-century version of the strategy that the United States pursued after World War II in the shadow of the cold war—a strategy that produced the liberal hegemonic order that has provided the framework for the Western and global system ever since. This is a strategy in which the United States leads the way in the creation and operation of a loose rule-based international order. The United States provides public goods and solves global collective action problems. American "rule" is established through the provisioning of international rules and institutions and its willingness to operate within them. American power is put in the service of an agreed-on system of Western-oriented global governance. American power is made acceptable to the world because it is embedded in these agreed-on rules and institutions. The system itself leverages resources and fosters cooperation that makes the actual functioning of the order one that solves problems, creates stability, and allows democracy and capitalism to flourish. Liberal order building is America's distinctive contribution to world politics—and it is a grand strategy that the country should return to in the post-Bush era.

The Bush administration did not embrace the logic of liberal hegemonic rule or support the rules and institutions on which it is based—and America is now paying the price in an extraordinary decline in its authority, credibility, prestige, and the ready support of other states. Along the way, the Bush administration has made America less rather than more secure, and its ruinous foreign policy is fast becoming an icon of grand strategic failure.

If America is smart and plays its foreign policy "cards" right, it is not fanciful to think that the United States can still be in twenty years at the center of a "one world" system defined in terms of open markets, democratic community, cooperative security, and rule-based order. This is a future that can be contrasted with less desirable alternatives that echo through the past—great power balancing orders, regional blocs, or bipolar rivalries. The United States should seek to consolidate a global order in which other countries bandwagon rather than balance against it—and in which it remains at the center of a prosperous and secure democratic-capitalist order that in turn provides the architecture and axis points around which the wider global system turns. But to reestablish this desired world order, the United States is going to need to make a radical break with Bush foreign policy and invest in re-creating the basic governance institutions of the system—investing in alliances, partnerships, multilateral institutions, special relationships, great power concerts, cooperative security pacts, and democratic security communities.

It is useful to distinguish between two types of grand strategies—positional and milieu oriented. A "positional" grand strategy is one in which a great power seeks to counter, undercut, contain, and limit the power and threats of a specific challenger state or group of states: Nazi Germany, imperial Japan, the Soviet bloc, and perhaps—in the future—Greater China. A "milieu" grand strategy is one in which a great power does not target a specific state but seeks to structure its general international environment in ways that are congenial with its long-term security. This might entail building the infrastructure of international cooperation, promoting trade and democracy in various regions of the world, or establishing partnerships that might be useful for various contingencies. The point I want to make is that under conditions of unipolarity, in a world of diffuse threats, and with pervasive uncertainty over what the specific security challenges will be in the future, this milieu-basic approach to grand strategy is needed.

This chapter makes five arguments. I start with an argument about the character of America's security environment in the decades to come. The United States does not confront a first-order security threat as it has in the past. It faces a variety of decentralized, complex, and deeply rooted threats. It does not face a singular threat—a great power or violent global movement—that deserves primacy in the organization of national security. The temptation is to prioritize the marshaling of American resources against a threat such as jihadist terrorism or rogue states, but this is both an intellectual and political mistake. If the world of the twenty-first century were a town, the security threats faced by its leading citizens would not be organized crime or a violent assault by a radical mob on city hall. It would be a breakdown of law enforcement and social services in the face of constantly changing and ultimately uncertain vagaries of criminality, nature, and circumstance.

Second, these more diffuse, shifting, and uncertain threats require a different sort of grand strategy than those aimed at countering a specific enemy such as a rival great power or a radical terrorist group. Rather, the United States needs to lead in the re-creation of the global architecture of governance, rebuilding its leadership position and the institutional frameworks through which it pursues its interests and cooperates with others to provide security. Above all, it needs to create resources and capacities for the collective confrontation of a wide array of dangers and challenges. That is, America needs a grand strategy of "multitasking"—creating shared capacities to respond to a wide variety of contingencies. In the twenty-first-century threat environment, a premium will be placed on mechanisms for collective action and sustained commitments to problem solving.

Third, America does have a legacy of liberal order building—it knows how to do it, and doing it in the past has made America strong and secure. It needs to rediscover and renew this strategy of liberal order building. During the decades after World War II, the United States did not just fight the cold war, but it also created a liberal international order of multilayered pacts and partnerships that served to open markets, bind democracies together, and create a transregional security community. The United States provided security, championed mutually agreed-on rules and institutions, and led in the management of an open world economy. In return, other states affiliated with and supported the United States as it led the larger order. It was an American-led hegemonic order with liberal characteristics. There is still no alternative model of international order that is better suited to American interests or stable global governance.

Fourth, American foreign policy in the past six years has severely eroded America's global position—and endangered its ability to lead and to facilitate collective action. This "crisis" of American authority is perhaps the most serious threat to the ability of the United States to secure itself in the decades ahead. The proximate cause of this crisis is the Bush administration's failure to operate within America's own postwar liberal hegemonic order. But there are deep shifts in the global system that make it harder for the United States to act as it did in the past—as a global provider of goods and a liberal hegemon willing to both restrain and commit itself. Unipolarity and the erosion of norms of state sovereignty—among other long-term shifts—make the American pursuit of a liberal order-building strategy both more difficult and more essential.

Fifth, the new agenda for liberal order building involves an array of efforts to strengthen and rebuild a global architecture. These initiatives include building a "protective infrastructure" for preventing and responding to socioeconomic catastrophe, renewing the cold war–era alliances, reforming the United Nations (UN), and creating new multilateral mechanisms for cooperation in East Asia and among democracies. In the background, the United States will need to renegotiate and renew its grand bargains with Europe and East Asia. In these bargains, the United States will need to signal a new willingness to restrain and commit its power, to accommodate rising states, and to operate within reconfigured and agreed-on global rules and institutions.

My point is that America needs to develop a post-post-9/11 grand strategy. It is not enough simply to fight the "global war on terror" (or GWOT). Instead, we need to return to basics—to a focus on the logic and organization of global order and governance. The United States does not need to fight an enemy so much as construct a political order that can function to protect the United States from lots of enemies and to solve collective action problems necessary to prevent the rise of new enemies. We do not need a GWOT 2.0. What we need is a PATC 2.0. PATC stands for *Present at the Creation*, which is the title of Dean Acheson's famous memoir in which he describes how he and his colleagues built the postwar American-led system. My point is that we need to think about international order building today with the same ambition and imagination as Acheson and other postwar architects did with PATC 1.0.

Threats, Challenges, and Opportunities

Grand strategy is, as Barry Posen argues, "a state's theory about how it can best cause security for itself."[1] As such, it is an exercise in public worrying about the future—and doing something about it. Looking into the future, what should America be most worried about? Grand strategy is a set of coordinated and sustained policies designed to address these prioritized national worries.

Some observers argue that American grand strategy should be organized around the confrontation with a specific enemy, as it was during the cold war. Jihadist terrorism, in particular, is offered as this premier global threat to which all else should be subordinated and directed. The Bush administration, of course, has made this the centerpiece of its grand strategy—describing a "long war" against terrorism, a generational struggle akin to the cold war. In the most evocative versions of this thesis, the United States is engaged in a war against "jihadist terrorism," "militant Islam," or "Islamofascists" who are the heirs of the Fascist and Communist threats of the past century—wielding a totalitarian political ideology and seeking our violent destruction. We face the prospect of a twilight war with an evil foe while Western civilization hangs in the balance.

But it is not altogether clear that fighting Islamic terrorism is the preeminent security challenge of the coming decades. Various are the threats that America faces. Global warming, health pandemics, nuclear proliferation, jihadist terrorism, energy scarcity—these and other dangers loom on the horizon. Any of these threats could endanger American lives and way of life either directly or indirectly by destabilizing the global system on which American security and prosperity depend. Pandemics and global warming are not threats wielded by human hands, but their consequences could be equally devastating. Highly infectious disease has the potential to kill millions of people. Global warming threatens to trigger waves of environmental migration and food shortages and to further destabilize weak and poor states around the world. The world is also on the cusp of a new round of nuclear proliferation, putting mankind's deadliest weapons in the hands of unstable and hostile states. Terrorist networks offer a new specter of nonstate transnational violence. The point is that none of these threats is, in itself, so singularly preeminent that it deserves to be the centerpiece of American grand strategy in the way that anti-Fascism and anti-Communism did in an earlier era.[2]

What is more, these various threats are interconnected, and it is the possibility of their interactive effects that multiplies the dangers. This point is stressed by Thomas Homer-Dixon: "It's the convergence of stresses that's especially treacherous and makes synchronous failure a possibility as never before. In coming years, our societies won't face one or two major challenges at once, as usually happened in the past. Instead, they'll face an alarming variety of problems—likely including oil shortages, climate change, economic instability, and megaterrorism—all at the same time." The danger is that several of these threats will materialize simultaneously and interact to generate greater violence and instability: "What happens, for example, if together or in quick succession the world has to deal with a sudden shift in climate that sharply cuts food production in Europe and Asia, a severe oil price increase that sends economies tumbling around the world, and a string of major terrorist attacks on several Western capital cities?"[3] The global order itself would be put at risk, as well as the foundations of American national security.

We can add to these worries the rise of China and, more generally, the rise of Asia. It is worth recalling that China was the preoccupation of the American national security community in the years before the September 11, 2001, terrorist attacks. China's rapid economic growth and assertive regional diplomacy are already transforming East Asia, and Beijing's geopolitical influence is growing. The United States has no experience managing a relationship with a country that is potentially its principal economic and security rival. It is unclear, and probably unknowable, how China's intentions and ambitions will evolve as it becomes more powerful. We do know, however, that the rise and decline of great powers—and the problem of "power transitions"—can trigger conflict, security competition, and war. The point here is that, in the long run, the way that China rises up in the world could have a more profound impact on American national security than incremental shifts up or down in the fortunes of international terrorist groups.[4]

The larger point is—and it is a critical assumption here—that today the United States confronts an unusually diverse and diffuse array of threats and challenges. When we try to imagine what the premier threat to the United States will be in 2015 or 2020, it is not easy to say with any confidence that it will be X, or Y, or Z. Moreover, even if we could identify X, or Y, or Z as the premier threat around which all others turn, it is very likely that it will be complex and interlinked with lots of other international moving parts. Global pandemics are connected to failed states, homeland security, international public health capacities, and so forth. Terrorism is related to the Middle East peace process, economic and political development, nonproliferation, intelligence cooperation, European social and immigration policy, and so forth. The rise of China is related to alliance cooperation, energy security, democracy promotion, the WTO, management of the world economy, and so forth. So again we are back to renewing and rebuilding the architecture of global governance and frameworks of cooperation to allow the United States to marshal resources and tackle problems along a wide and shifting spectrum of possibilities.

In a world of multiple threats and uncertainty about their relative significance in the decades to come, it is useful to think of grand strategy as an "investment" problem. Where do you invest your resources, build capacities, and take actions so as to maximize your ability to be positioned to confront tomorrow's unknowns? Grand strategy is about setting priorities, but it is also about diversifying risks and avoiding surprises.

This is where the pursuit of a milieu-based grand strategy is attractive. The objective is to shape the international environment to maximize your capacities to protect the nation from uncertain, diffuse, and shifting threats. You engage in liberal order building. This means investment in international cooperative frameworks—that is, rules, institutions, partnerships, networks, standby capacities, social knowledge, and so forth—in which the United States operates. To build international order is to increase the global stock of "social capital," which is the term Pierre Bourdieu, Robert Putnam, and others have used to define the actual and potential resources and capacities within a political community, manifest in and through its networks of social relations, that are available for solving collective problems. Taken together, liberal order building involves investing in the enhancement of global social capital so as to create capacities to solve problems that, left unattended, will threaten national security.

America and Liberal Order Building

To pursue a milieu strategy of liberal order building is to return to the type of grand strategy that America pursued in the 1940s and onward with great success. It is useful to recall the logic and accomplishments of this quintessentially American grand strategy. In fact, in the postwar era the United States did not just fight a global war against Soviet Communism. It also built a liberal international order. This order was not just the by-product of the pursuit of containment. It sprang from ideas and a logic of order that are deeply rooted in the American experience. It is an international order that generated power, wealth, stability, and security—all of which allowed the West to prevail in the cold war.

This postwar liberal order was built around a set of ideas, institutions, bargains, democratic community, and American hegemonic power. It is on this foundation that a renewed strategy of liberal order building must be based.

In comparison with the doctrine of containment, the ideas and policies of American postwar liberal order building were more diffuse and wide ranging. It was less obvious that the liberal order-building agenda was a "grand strategy" designed to advance American security interests. But in other respects it was the more enduring American project, one that was aimed at creating international order that would be open, stable, and friendly and that solved the problems of the 1930s—the economic breakdown and competing geopolitical blocs that paved the way for world war. The challenge was not merely to deter or contain the power of the Soviet Union but to lay the foundation for an international order that would allow the United States to thrive. This impulse—to build a stable and open international system that advantaged America—existed before, during, and after the cold war. Even at the moment when the cold war gathered force, the grand strategic interest in building such an order was appreciated. Indeed, one recalls that National Security Council Report 68 (NSC-68) laid out a doctrine of containment, but it also articulated a rationale for building a positive international order. The United States needs, it said, to "build a healthy international community," which "we would probably do even if there were no international threat." The United States needs a "world environment in which the American system can survive and flourish."[5]

The vision of an American-led liberal international order was expressed in a sequence of declarations and agreements. The first was the Atlantic Charter of 1941, which spelled out a view of what the Atlantic and the wider world order would look like if the Allies won the war. This agreement was followed by the Bretton Woods agreements of 1944, the Marshall Plan in 1947, and the Atlantic pact in 1949. Together these agreements provided a framework for a radical reorganization of relations among the Atlantic democracies. The emerging cold war gave this Western-oriented agenda some urgency, and the American Congress was more willing to provide resources and approve international agreements because of the threats of Communist expansion lurking on the horizon. But the vision of a new order among the Western democracies predated the cold war, and even if the Soviet Union had slipped into history, some sort of Western order—open, institutionalized, American-led—would have been built.

Between 1944 and 1951, American leaders engaged in the most intensive institution building the world had ever seen—global, regional, security, economic, and political. The UN, Bretton Woods, the General Agreement on Tariffs and Trade (GATT), the North Atlantic Treaty Organization (NATO), and the U.S.-Japan alliance were all launched. The United States undertook costly obligations to aid Greece and Turkey and reconstruct Western Europe. It helped rebuild the economies of Germany and Japan. It fought the Korean War, putting paid to America's hegemonic presence in East Asia. With the Atlantic Charter, the UN Charter, and the Universal Declaration of Human Rights, it articulated a new vision of a progressive international community. In all these ways, the United States took the lead in fashioning a world of multilateral rules, institutions, open markets, democratic community, and regional partnerships—and it put itself at the center of it all.[6]

This was an extraordinary and unprecedented undertaking for a major state. It marked the triumph of American internationalism after earlier post-1919 and interwar failures. It signaled the creation of a new type of international order, fusing together new forms of liberalism, internationalism, and national security. It heralded the beginning of the "long peace"—the longest period of modern history without war between the great powers. It laid the foundation for the greatest world economic boom in history. This liberal international order is in crisis today, and it needs to be reimagined and rebuilt. But in almost all important respects, we still live in the world created during these hyperactive postwar years of liberal international order building.

The core idea of this liberal international order was that the United States would need to actively shape its security environment, creating a stable, open, and friendly geopolitical space across Europe and Asia.[7] This required making commitments, building institutions, forging partnerships, acquiring clients, and providing liberal hegemonic leadership. In doing this, several ideas informed the substantive character of the emerging order. One idea was a basic commitment to economic openness among the regions. That is, capitalism would be organized internationally and not along national, regional, or imperial lines. In many ways, this is what World War II was fought over. Germany and Japan each built their states around the military domination of their respective regions, Soviet Russia was an imperial continental power, and Great Britain had the imperial preference system. American interests were deeply committed to an open world economy—and an open world economy would tie together friends and former enemies.

A second idea behind liberal international order was that the new arrangements would need to be managed through international institutions and agreements. This was certainly the view of the economic officials who gathered in Bretton Woods in 1944. Governments would need to play a more direct supervisory role in stabilizing and managing economic order. New forms of intergovernmental cooperation would need to be invented. The democratic countries would enmesh themselves in a dense array of intergovernmental networks and loose rule-based institutional relationships. In doing so, the United States committed itself to exercising power through these regional and global institutions. This was a great innovation in international order: the United States and its partners would create permanent governance institutions (ones that they themselves would dominate) to provide ongoing streams of cooperation needed to manage growing realms of complex interdependence.

A third idea was a progressive social bargain. If the United States and its partners were to uphold a global system of open markets, they would need to make commitments to economic growth, development, and social protections. This was the social bargain. There are losers in a system of open markets, but winners win more—so some of those winnings must be used for social protection and adjustment. Likewise, if the United States wants other countries to buy into this open order, it will need to help and support those states in establishing the sorts of Western social support structures that will allow for a stable and emerging democracy to coexist with open trade and investment.

Finally, there is the idea of cooperation security, or "security cobinding." In this liberal vision of international order, the United States will remain connected in close alliance with other democratic countries. NATO and the U.S.-Japan alliance are at the core of this alliance system, and these security pacts will be expanded and strengthened. This is a very important departure from past security arrangements—the United States would be connected to the other major democracies to create a single security system. Such a system would ensure that the democratic great powers would not go back to the dangerous game of strategy rivalry and power politics. It helped, of course, to have an emerging cold war to generate this cooperative security arrangement. But a security relationship between the United States and its allies was implicit in other elements of liberal order. A cooperative security order—embodied in formal alliance institutions—ensured that the power of the United States would be rendered more predictable. Power would be caged in institutions, thereby making American power more reliable and connected to Europe and East Asia.

With the end of the cold war, the American alliance system has seemed less vital to some people. What is forgotten, however, is that the postwar security pacts have always been about more than simply deterrence and containment of Soviet Communism. The alliances have also performed the function of providing "political architecture" for the policy community that bridges Europe, North America, and East Asia. The alliances provide mechanisms for each side to send signals of restraint and commitment. They provide institutional channels to "do business" across the advanced industrial world. They keep the United States engaged in Europe and East Asia, and they allow leaders in Europe and East Asia to be engaged in and connected to Washington.

In the background, this American-led order is built on two historic bargains that the United States has made with its European and East Asian partners. One is a realist bargain and grows out of cold war grand strategy. The United States provides its European partners with security protection and access to American markets, technology, and supplies within an open world economy. In return, these countries agree to be reliable partners who provide diplomatic, economic, and logistical support for the United States as it leads the wider Western postwar order. The result has been to tie America and its partners together—to make peace "indivisible" across the Atlantic and Pacific. Binding security ties also provide channels for consultation and joint decision making.

The other is a liberal bargain that addresses the uncertainties of American preeminent power. East Asian and European states agree to work with the United States and operate within an agreed-on political-economic system. In return, the United States opens itself up and binds itself to its partners. In effect, the United States builds an institutionalized coalition of partners and reinforces the stability of these long-term mutually beneficial relations by making itself more "user friendly"—that is, by playing by the rules and creating ongoing political processes with these other states that facilitate consultation and joint decision making. The United States makes its power safe for the world and, in return, Europe and East Asia—and the wider world—agree to live within this liberal international system. The institutional structure of the order provides mechanisms for conveying reassurance and signals of restraint and commitment on the part of the United States, embedding American hegemonic power inside of a community of democracies.

Out of these ideas, institutions, and bargains has come a liberal hegemonic order that has been at the center of world politics for over half a century. It is an order that is not simply organized around the decentralized cooperation of like-minded democracies—although it is premised on a convergence of interests and values among the democratic capitalist great powers. It is an engineered political order that reconciles power and hierarchy with cooperation and legitimacy.

The resulting order is liberal hegemony, not empire. It is a political order in which the United States is first among equals, but it is not an imperial system. The United States dominates the order, but that domination is made relatively acceptable to other states by the liberal features of this order: the United States supports and operates within an agreed-on array of rules and institutions; the United States legitimates its leadership through the provision of public goods; and other states in the order have access to and "voice opportunities" within it—that is, there are reciprocal processes of communication and influence.

The Crisis of American Liberal Hegemony

This postwar system of global governance—organized around a set of ideas, institutions, bargains, democratic community, and American hegemonic power—is now in trouble. So too is America's position within it. This is a problem because in a world of shifting, diffuse, and uncertain threats, the United States needs to lead and operate within a strengthened—rather than weakened—liberal order.

This liberal hegemonic order is in crisis in several ways. It is a crisis, most immediately, of America's global position as manifest in Bush administration foreign policy. The credibility, respect, and authority of the United States as the leader of the global system has been radically diminished in recent years.[8] America has a legitimacy problem. There is a basic disconnect between the way the Bush administration wants the world to be run and the way other states and peoples want the world to be run. This is the most visible aspect of the crisis. Moreover, the postwar institutions through which America has traditionally operated are in crisis, or at least they have become severely weakened in recent years. The UN, NATO, the International Monetary Fund (IMF), the World Bank, and even the WTO are all searching for missions and authority. The rise of new powers, particularly in Asia, is also putting pressure on these old postwar institutions to reform their membership and governance arrangements.[9] The institutional mechanisms of the system are not functioning very effectively or responding to emerging new demands. Finally, the deeper foundations of liberal international order have also been called into question. These are questions about how to reconcile rule-based order with a variety of new world historical developments—the rise of unipolarity, eroded state sovereignty, democratic legitimacy, and new sorts of security threats.

The immediate source of crisis is the Bush administration itself, which signaled from the beginning that it did not want to operate within the old postwar liberal order. This was signaled early in the administration by its resistance to a wide array of multilateral agreements, including the Kyoto Protocol on Climate Change, the Rome Statute of the International Criminal Court (ICC), the Germ Weapons Convention, and the Programme of

Action on Illicit Trade in Small and Light Arms. It also unilaterally with-drew from the 1970 Anti-Ballistic Missile (ABM) treaty, which many experts regard as the cornerstone of modern arms control agreements. Unilateralism, of course, is not a new feature of American foreign policy. In every histori-cal era, the United States has shown a willingness to reject treaties, violate rules, ignore allies, and use military force on its own. But many observers see today's unilateralism as practiced by the Bush administration as something much more sweeping—not an occasional ad hoc policy decision but a new strategic orientation, or what one pundit calls the "new unilateralism."[10]

The most systematic rejection of the old logic of liberal order came with the 2002 National Security Doctrine and the Iraq war, articulating a vision of America as a unipolar state positioned above and beyond the rules and insti-tutions of the global system, providing security and enforcing order. It was a strategy of global rule in which the United States would remain a military power in a class by itself, thereby "making destabilizing arms races pointless and limiting rivalry to trade and other pursuits."[11] American preeminent power would, in effect, put an end to five centuries of great power rivalry. In doing so, it would take the lead in identifying and attacking threats—preemptively if necessary. America was providing the ultimate global public good. In return, the United States would ask to be less encumbered by rules and institutions of the old order. It would not sign the land mine treaty because American troops were uniquely at risk in war zones around the world. It would not sign the ICC treaty because Americans would be uniquely at risk of political prosecutions. In effect, America would step forward and solve the problem of Hobbes—it would be the world's Leviathan.

But in the hands of the Bush administration, America was to become a conservative Leviathan. That is, the Bush architects of grand strategy brought a conservative discourse about order to the unipolar moment rather than the traditional liberal discourse. This is crucial. At the earlier moments of Ameri-can order building—after 1919, 1945, and 1989—American officials by and large invoked liberal ideas about order. These liberal ideas included, first, that the exercise of American power was consistent with, and indeed advanced by, strengthening the rule-based fabric of international community; second, that institutions and rules were integral tools of American power; and, third, that international legitimacy mattered in the conduct of U.S. foreign policy. As noted earlier, these ideas reinforced an American conviction that a loose mul-tilateral order was the best vehicle for the advancement of American interests. What the Bush administration did was introduce a conservative discourse on international order. These ideas included, first, that there really was no inter-national community that the United States had to build or adjust to; second, that rules and institutions were constraints on the United States; and, third, that legitimacy begins and ends at home—there is no "global test" for American foreign policy.[12]

The leading edge of this new conception of America's role and rule in the world concerned the use of force. The Bush administration's security doctrine was new and sweeping. The United States announced a right to use force anywhere in the world against "terrorists with global reach." It would do so largely outside the traditional alliance system through coalitions of the willing. The United States would take "anticipatory action" when it, by itself, determined that the use of force was necessary. Because these actions would be taken to oppose terrorists or overthrow despotic regimes, they would be self-legitimating. Countries were either "with us or against us"—or, as Bush announced, "no nation can be neutral in this conflict." Moreover, this new global security situation was essentially permanent—it was not just a temporary emergency. There could be no final victory or peace settlement in this new war, so there would be no return to normalcy.[13]

The point is that the Bush administration was, in effect, announcing unilaterally the new rules of the global security order. It was not seeking a new global consensus on the terms of international order and change, and it was not renegotiating old bargains. The United States was imposing the rules of the new global order, rules that would be ratified not by the support of others but by the lurking presence of American power. This grand strategic move was a more profound shift than is generally appreciated. The Bush administration was not simply acting "a little bit more unilaterally" than previous administrations. In rhetoric, doctrine, and ultimately in the Iraq war, the United States was articulating a new logic of global order. The old liberal hegemonic rules, institutions, and bargains were now quaint artifacts of an earlier and less threatening era.

In the background, longer term shifts in the global system provided the permissive circumstances for the Bush administration's big doctrinal move. The shift from cold war bipolarity to American unipolarity has triggered a geopolitical adjustment process that runs through the 1990s and continues today. Unipolarity has given the United States more discretionary resources—and without a peer competitor or a great power-balancing coalition arrayed around it, the external constraints on American action are reduced. But with the end of the cold war, other states are not so much dependent on the United States for protection, and a unifying common threat has been eliminated. So old bargains, alliance partnerships, and shared strategic visions are thrown into question. At the very least, the shift in power advantages in favor of the United States would help explain why it might want to renegotiate older rules and institutions.

But more profoundly, unipolarity may be creating conditions that reduce the willingness of the United States to support and operate within a loosely rule-based order. If America is less dependent on other states for its own security, then it has reduced incentives to tie itself to other states through restraints entailed in alliances and multilateral agreements. Incentives also increase for other states to free-ride on a unipolar America. Under these circumstances, the United States may indeed act unilaterally in ways it did not in the past—or, in the absence of willing partners, its own willingness to provide hegemonic leadership may decline.[14]

The erosion of international norms of state sovereignty is also putting pressure on the old liberal hegemonic order. This is the quiet revolution in world politics: the rise of rights within the international community to intervene within states to protect individuals against the abuses of their own governments. The contingent character of sovereignty was pushed further after 9/11 in the intervention in Afghanistan, in which outside military force, used to topple a regime that actively protected terrorist attackers, was seen as an acceptable act of self-defense. But the erosion of state sovereignty has not been accompanied by the rise of new norms about how sovereignty-transgressing interventions should proceed. The "international community" has the right to act inside troubled and threatening states—but who precisely is the international community? The problem is made worse by the rise of unipolarity. Only the United States really has the military power to engage systematically in large-scale uses of force around the world. The UN has no troops or military capacity of its own. The problem of establishing legitimate international authority grows.

The shift in the "security problem" away from great power war to transnational dangers such as terrorism, disease, and insecurity generated within weak states also compounds the problem of legitimate authority inherent in the rise of unipolarity. If intervention into the affairs of weak and hostile states in troubled regions of the world is the new security frontier, the problems of who speaks for the international community and of the establishment of legitimate rules on the use of force multiply. America's unipolar military capabilities are both in demand and deeply controversial.

So the rise of unipolarity brought with it a shift in the underlying logic of order and rule in world politics. In a bipolar or multipolar system, powerful states "rule" in the process of leading a coalition of states in balancing against other states. When the system shifts to unipolarity, this logic of rule disappears. Power is no longer based on balancing and equilibrium but on the predominance of one state. This is new and different—and potentially threatening to weaker and secondary states. As a result, the power of the leading state is thrown into the full light of day. Unipolar power itself becomes a "problem" in world politics. As John Lewis Gaddis argues, American power during the cold war was accepted by other states because there was "something worse" over the horizon.[15] With the rise of unipolarity, that "something worse" disappears.

American power and a functioning global governance system have become disconnected. In the past, the United States provided global "services"—such as security protection and support for open markets—that made other states willing to work with rather than resist American power. The public goods provision tended to make it worthwhile for these states to endure the day-to-day irritations of American foreign policy. But the trade-off seems to have shifted. Today, the United States appears to be providing fewer public goods, whereas at the same time the irritations associated with American dominance appear to be growing.

The New Agenda of Liberal Order Building

If American grand strategy is to be organized around liberal order building, what are the specific objectives, and what is the policy agenda?

As we have seen, there are several objectives that such a strategy might seek to accomplish. The first is to build a stronger "protective infrastructure" of international capacities to confront an array of shifting, diffuse, and uncertain threats and catastrophes—this is, in effect, creating an infrastructure of global social services. The second is the rebuilding of a system of cooperative security, reestablishing the primacy of America's alliances for strategic cooperation and the projection of force. The third is the reform of global institutions that support collective action and multilateral management of globalization—such as the UN and multilateral economic institutions—creating greater institutional capacities for international decision making and the provision of public goods. The fourth is to create new institutions and reform old ones so that rising states—particularly China, but also India and other emerging powers—can more easily be embedded in the existing global system rather than operating as dissatisfied revisionist states on the outside. Finally, through all these efforts, the United States needs to endeavor to reestablish its hegemonic legitimacy—a preeminent objective that must be pursued with policies and a doctrine that signal America's commitment to rule-based order.[16]

Given these goals, the agenda of institutional order building would include the following.

First, the United States needs to lead in the building of an enhanced "protective infrastructure" that helps prevent the emergence of threats and limits the damage if they do materialize.[17] Many of the threats mentioned earlier manifest as socioeconomic backwardness and failure that generate regional and international instability and conflict. These are the sorts of threats that are likely to arise with the coming of global warming and epidemic disease. What is needed here is institutional cooperation to strengthen the capacity of governments and the international community to prevent epidemics, food shortages, or mass migrations that create global upheaval—or to mitigate the effects of these upheavals if they, in fact, occur.

It is useful to think of a strengthened protective infrastructure as investment in global social services, much as cities and states invest in such services. It typically is money well spent. Education, health programs, shelters, social services—these are vital components of stable and well-functioning communities. The international system already has a great deal of this infrastructure—institutions and networks that promote cooperation over public health, refugees, and emergency aid. But in the twenty-first century, as the scale and scope of potential problems grow, investments in these preventive and management capacities will also need to grow. Early warning systems, protocols for emergency operations, standby capacities, and so forth—these are the stuff of a protective global infrastructure.

Second, the United States should recommit to and rebuild its security alliances. The idea would be to update the old bargains that lie behind these security pacts. In NATO—but also in the East Asia bilateral partnerships—the United States agrees to provide security protection to the other states and bring its partners into the process of decision making over the use of force. In return, these partners agree to work with the United States, providing manpower, logistics, and other types of support in wider theaters of action. The United States gives up some autonomy in strategic decision making—although it is a more informal than legally binding restraint—and in exchange it gets cooperation and political support. The United States also remains "first among equals" within these organizations, and it retains leadership of the unified military command. The updating of these alliance bargains would involve widening the regional or global missions in which the alliance operates and making new compromises over the distribution of formal rights and responsibilities.[18]

There are several reasons why the renewal of security partnerships is critical to liberal order building. One is that security alliances involve relatively well-defined, specific, and limited commitments, and this is attractive for both the leading military power and its partners. States know what they are getting into and what the limits are on their obligations and liabilities. Another is that alliances provide institutional mechanisms that allow accommodations for disparities of power among partners within the alliance. Alliances do not embody universal rules and norms that apply equally to all parties. NATO, at least, is a multilateral body with formal and informal rules and norms of operation that both accommodate the most powerful state and provides roles and rights for others. Another virtue of renewing the alliances is that they have been institutional bodies that are useful as "political architecture" across the advanced democratic world. The alliances provide channels of communication and joint decision making that spill over into the wider realms of international relations. They are also institutions with grand histories and records of accomplishment. The United States is a unipolar military power, but it still has incentives to share the costs of security protection and to find ways to legitimate the use of its power. The postwar alliances—renewed and reorganized—are an attractive tool for these purposes.

Robert Kagan has argued that to regain its lost legitimacy, the United States needs to return to its postwar bargain: giving some Europeans voice over American policy in exchange for their support. The United States, Kagan points out, "should try to fulfill its part of the transatlantic bargain by granting Europeans some influence over the exercise of its power—provided that, in return, Europeans wield that influence wisely."[19] This is the logic that informed American security cooperation with its European and East Asian partners during the cold war. It is a logic that can be renewed today to help make unipolarity more acceptable.

Third, the United States needs encompassing global institutions that foster and legitimate collective action. The first move here should be to reform the United Nations, starting with the expansion of the permanent membership on the Security Council. Several plans have been proposed. All of them entail new members—such as Germany, Japan, India, Brazil, South Africa, and others—and reformed voting procedures. Almost all of the candidates for permanent membership are mature or rising democracies. The goal, of course, is to make them stakeholders in the United Nations and thereby strengthen the primacy of the United Nations as a vehicle for global collective action. There really is no substitute for the legitimacy that the United Nations can offer to emergency actions—humanitarian interventions, economic sanctions, use of force against terrorists, and so forth. Public support in advanced democracies grows rapidly when their governments can stand behind a United Nations–sanctioned action.

The other step is to create a "concert of democracies." The idea would not be to establish a substitute body for the United Nations—which some advocates of a concert or league suggest—but simply to provide another international forum where democracies can discuss common goals and reinforce cooperation. Proposals exist for various types of groupings of democracies, some informal and consultative and others more formal and task oriented.[20]

The experience of the last century suggests that the United States is more likely to make institutional commitments and bind itself to other states if those countries are democracies. This is true for both practical and normative reasons. Because liberal democracies are governed by the rule of law and open to scrutiny, it is easier to establish the credibility of their promises and to develop long-term commitments. But the values and identities that democracies share also make it easier for them to affiliate and build cooperative relations. These shared identities were probably more strongly felt during the cold war when the United States was part of a larger "free world." Institutionalized cooperation between the United States and its European and East Asian partners is surely driven by shared interests, but it is reinforced by shared values and common principles of government. American leaders find it easier to rally domestic support for costly commitments and agreements abroad when the goal is to help other democracies and to strengthen the community of democracies.

Fourth, the process of order building must include the embedding of rising states. The rise of China—and Greater Asia—is perhaps the seminal drama of our time. In the decades to come, America's unipolar power will give way to a more bipolar, multipolar, or decentralized distribution of power. China will most likely be a dominant state, and the United States will need to yield to it in various ways. The national security question for America to ask today is: What sorts of investments in global institutional architecture do we want to make now so that the coming power shifts will adversely affect us the least? That is, what sorts of institutional arrangements do we want to have in place to protect our interests when we are less powerful? This is a sort of neo-Rawlsian question that should inform American strategic decision making.

The answer to this neo-Rawlsian question would seem to be twofold. One is that the United States should try to embed the foundations of the Western-oriented international system so deeply that China has overwhelming incentives to integrate into it rather than to oppose and overturn it. Those American strategists who fear a rising China the most should be ultra-ambitious liberal institution builders. The United States should compose its differences with Europe and renew joint commitments to alliance and multilateral global governance. The more that China faces not just the United States but a united West, the better. The more that China faces not just a united West but the entire Organization for Economic Cooperation and Development (OECD) world of capitalist democracies, the better. This is not to argue that China should face a grand counterbalancing alliance against it. Rather, China should face a complex and deeply integrated global system—one that is so encompassing and deeply entrenched that China essentially has no choice but to join it and seek to prosper within it. Indeed, the United States should take advantage of one of the great virtues of liberal hegemony, namely, that it is easy to join and hard to overturn. The layers of institutions and channels of access provide relatively easy entry points for China to join the existing international order.[21] Now is precisely the wrong historical moment for the United States to be uprooting and disassembling its own liberal hegemonic order.

In a version of this argument, Timothy Garten Ash has suggested that the United States and Europe have about twenty years more to control the levers of global governance before they will need to cede power to China and other rising states. His point is that the two Western powers need to take the long view, develop a common strategic vision, and redouble commitment to Atlantic cooperation.[22]

The second answer to the neo-Rawlsian question is to encourage the building of a regional East Asian security order that will provide a framework for managing the coming power shifts. The idea is not to block China's entry into the regional order but to help shape its terms, looking for opportunities to strike strategic bargains at various moments along the shifting power trajectories and encroaching geopolitical spheres. The big bargain that the United States will want to strike with China is this: to accommodate a rising China by offering it status and position within the regional order in return for Beijing's accepting and accommodating Washington's core strategic interests, which include remaining a dominant security provider within East Asia.

In striking this strategic bargain, the United States will also want to try to build multilateral institutional arrangements in East Asia that will tie down and bind China to the wider region. China has already grasped the utility of this strategy in recent years, and it is now actively seeking to reassure and co-opt its neighbors by offering to embed itself in regional institutions such as the Association of Southeast Asian Nations (ASEAN) Plus Three and the East Asia Summit. This is, of course, precisely what the United States did in the decades after World War II, building and operating within layers of regional and global economic, political, and security institutions—thereby making itself more predictable and approachable and reducing the incentives that other states would otherwise have to resist or undermine the United States by building countervailing coalitions.

The challenge for the United States is to encourage China to continue along this pathway, allaying worries about its growing power by binding itself to its neighbors and the region itself. But to do this, there will need to be a more formal and articulated regional security organization established into which China can integrate. Such an organization need not have the features of an alliance system—the countries in the region are not ready for this. But what is needed is a security organization that has at its center a treaty of nonaggression and mechanisms for periodic consultation.

Fifth and finally, a liberal internationalist "public philosophy" should be reclaimed. When American officials after World War II championed the building of a rule-based postwar order, they articulated a distinctive internationalist vision of order that has faded in recent decades. It was a vision that entailed a synthesis of liberal and realist ideas about economic and national security and the sources of stable and peaceful order. These ideas, drawn from the experiences in the 1940s with the New Deal and in the previous decades of war and depression, led American leaders to associate the national interest with the building of a managed and institutionalized global system. What is needed today is a renewed public philosophy of liberal internationalism that can inform American elites as they make trade-offs between sovereignty and institutional cooperation.

What American elites need to do today is recover this public philosophy of internationalism. The restraint and the commitment of U.S. power went hand in hand. Global rules and institutions advanced America's national interest rather than threatened it. The alternative public philosophies that circulate today—philosophies that champion American unilateralism and disentanglement from global rules and institutions—are not meeting with great success. So an opening exists for America's postwar vision of internationalism to be updated and rearticulated today.

Conclusion

In his memoir on American diplomacy at the end of the cold war, former Secretary of State James Baker recalled the thinking of his predecessors from the 1940s: "Men like Truman and Acheson were above all, though we sometimes forget it, institution builders. They created NATO and the other security organizations that eventually won the Cold War. They fostered the economic institutions...that brought unparalleled prosperity....At a time of similar opportunity and risk, I believed we should take a leaf from their book."[23] In proposing a post-Bush grand strategy of liberal order building, I am urging the return to this same global strategy, updated to the security environment of the twenty-first century.

The United States needs to plan for a future of sprawling and shifting threats. This means pursuing a milieu-based grand strategy, building international frameworks of cooperation to deal with multiple and evolving contingencies. To build a grand strategy around one threat is to miss the importance of the others, as well as to miss the dangerous connections between these threats. This is not to belittle the al Qaeda threat. But the point is that it is important for the United States to pull back and invest in the creation of an international environment to handle, well, come what may.

The good news is that the United States is fabulously good at pursuing a milieu-based grand strategy. The Bush administration sought a radical break with the postwar American approach to order but it failed—and failed spectacularly. It sought to construct global order around American unipolar rule, asserting new rights to use force while reducing the country's exposure to multilateral rules and institutions. America's strategic position has weakened as a result, and the institutions that have leveraged and legitimated its power have eroded. If America wants to remain at the center of an open world system—one that is friendly and cooperative and capable of generating collective action in pursuit of diverse and shifting security challenges—it will need to return to its tradition of liberal order building.

For the most part, the great powers in the modern era have pursued "positional" grand strategies. They have identified rivals and enemies and organized their foreign policy accordingly. Across the historical eras, the results have been various sorts of balances of power and imperial systems. Once in a while, a state can dare to ask slightly loftier questions about the organization of the international system. Here the questions are metaquestions about political order itself. These are essentially "constitutional" questions about the first principles and organizational logic of the global system. The great powers collectively addressed these questions after 1815, and the United States and its allies did it again after the world wars. Today, the United States can once again ask these constitutional-like questions. What sort of global governance order would the United States like to see in operation in, say, 2020 or 2030? If we are uncertain today about what precisely will worry us tomorrow, what sort of mechanisms of governance would we like to see established to deal with these unknowns? If all we know is that the security threats of tomorrow will be shifting, diffuse, and uncertain, we should want to create a flexible and capable political system that can meet and defeat a lot of complex threats.

We do know that growing globalization and the diffusion of technologies of violence will make it necessary to develop a complex protective infrastructure that will support global efforts at intelligence, monitoring, inspections, and enforcement. We will need the International Atomic Energy Agency on steroids. We also know that new states will be rising and wanting to share or compete for leadership, so there is an incentive today to get the rules and institutions embedded for the future. Under conditions of intensifying globalization, the opportunity costs of not coordinating national policies grow relative to the costs of lost autonomy associated with making binding agreements. So when we look into the future, we do know that there will be a growing premium attached to institutionalized forms of cooperation. The governance structures that pass for international politics today will need to be rebuilt and made much more complex and encompassing in the decades ahead.

Looking into this brave new world, the United States will find itself needing to share power and to rely in part on others to ensure its security. It will not be able to depend on unipolar power or airtight borders. To operate in this coming world, the United States will need—more than anything else—authority and respect as a global leader. It has lost that authority and respect in recent years. In committing itself to a grand strategy of liberal order building, it can begin the process of gaining it back.

Notes

1. Barry Posen, *Sources of Military Doctrine* (Ithaca, NY: Cornell University Press, 1983), 13.
2. This is our judgment in the Final Report of the Princeton Project on National Security. See G. John Ikenberry and Anne-Marie Slaughter, *Forging a World of Liberty under Law* (Princeton, NJ: Woodrow Wilson School of International and Public Affairs, 2006).
3. Thomas Homer-Dixon, *The Upside of Down: Catastrophe, Creativity, and the Renewal of Civilization* (Washington, DC: Island Press, 2006), 16–17.
4. This argument is advanced in Francis Fukuyama and G. John Ikenberry, "Report of the Grand Strategic Choices Working Group" (Princeton Project on National Security, Princeton University, 2005).
5. NSC-68 as published in Ernest May, ed., *American Cold War Strategy: Interpreting NSC-68* (New York: St. Martin's, 1993), 40.
6. I sketch this logic of liberal hegemony in G. John Ikenberry, *After Victory: Institutions, Strategic Restraint, and the Rebuilding of Order after Major War* (Princeton, NJ: Princeton University Press, 2001).
7. See Melvyn P. Leffler, *A Preponderance of Power: National Security, the Truman Administration, and the Cold War* (Stanford, CA: Stanford University Press, 1992), chapter 2.
8. Recent opinion polls from around the world reveal this changed reality. In a summary of these results, the report indicates: "A multinational poll finds that publics around the world reject the idea that the United States should play the role of preeminent world leader. Most publics say the United States plays the role of world policeman more than it should, fails to take their country's interests into account and cannot be trusted to act responsibly." The Chicago Council on Global Affairs and WorldPublicOpinion.org, "World Publics Reject U.S. Role as the World Leader" (April 18, 2007), http://www.thechicagocouncil.org/media_press_room_detail.php?press_release_id=62.
9. See G. John Ikenberry, "A Weakened World," *Prospect* (UK) (November 2005): 30–33.
10. Charles Krauthammer, "The New Unilateralism," *Washington Post*, June 8, 2001.
11. President George W. Bush, 2002 West Point commencement speech (June 1, 2002), http://www.whitehouse.gov/news/releases/2002/06/20020601-3.html.
12. G. John Ikenberry, "Why Bush Foreign Policy Fails," unpublished paper (2005).

13. These features of the Bush doctrine are discussed in Ian Shapiro, *Containment: Rebuilding a Strategy against Global Terror* (Princeton, NJ: Princeton University Press, 2007).

14. See Robert Jervis, "The Remaking of a Unipolar World," *Washington Quarterly* 29, no. 2 (2006): 7–19; and G. John Ikenberry, "Global Security Trap," *Democracy: A Journal of Ideas* 1, no. 2 (September 2006).

15. John Lewis Gaddis, *Surprise, Security and the American Experience* (Cambridge, MA: Harvard University Press, 2004), 66–67.

16. This section builds on Ikenberry and Slaughter, *Forging a World of Liberty under Law*. The case for global order built around "multi-multilateralism" is made in Francis Fukuyama, *America at the Crossroads: Democracy, Power, and the Neoconservative Legacy* (New Haven, CT: Yale University Press, 2007).

17. See Ikenberry and Slaughter, *Forging a World of Liberty under Law*, 10.

18. The case for renewal of NATO is made in Ikenberry and Slaughter, *Forging a World of Liberty under Law*.

19. Robert Kagan, "America's Crisis of Legitimacy," *Foreign Affairs* 83, no. 2 (March 2004): 86.

20. For proposals to create a concert of democracies, see Ikenberry and Slaughter, *Forging a World of Liberty under Law*; Ivo Daalder and James Lindsey, "Democracies of the World Unite," *The American Interest* (January–February 2007), http://www.the-american-interest.com/ai2/article.cfm?Id=219&MId=6; and Tod Lindberg, "The Treaty of the Democratic Peace," *Weekly Standard* (February 12, 2007): 19–24.

21. See G. John Ikenberry, "The Rise of China, Power Transitions, and Western Order," in *China's Ascent: Power, Security, and the Future of International Politics*, ed. Robert S. Ross and Zhu Feng (Ithaca, NY: Cornell University Press, 2008).

22. Timothy Garten Ash, *Free World: America, Europe, and the Surprising Future of the West* (New York: Random House, 2004).

23. James A. Baker, *The Politics of Diplomacy: Revolution, War, and Peace, 1989–1992* (New York: Putnam, 1995), 605–606.

FIVE

Boss of Bosses
James Kurth

E VER SINCE THE end of the cold war, the principal objective of U.S.
foreign policy has been the promotion of liberal democracies, free
markets, and open societies around the world. Insofar as national
security—which had been the principal foreign policy objective during the
cold war and before—was concerned, it had been assumed by both political
parties and by three successive administrations that it could be subsumed and
indeed best achieved under the more expansive objectives of democratization,
globalization, and universalization of human rights.

This foreign policy has achieved some great successes: most important, the
democratization of most of the post-Communist political systems of Eastern
Europe; the globalization of most of the post-Communist economies of East
Asia, including China and Vietnam; and the deepening of the democratization
and globalization of India. However, it has now reached the point of diminishing returns, or even of being rolled back, because of widespread reactions
and counterattacks, the most important by Islamism in the Muslim world and
populism in Latin America.

Moreover, insofar as democratization, globalization, and universalization
undermine the strength of states or indeed of any local authority imposing
law and order, they produce failed states and create the conditions in which
transnational terrorist networks and superempowered radical groups can
flourish, posing direct and grave threats to U.S. national security. In fact, this
situation has reached the point at which the United States is threatened, even
more than by rogue states, by rogue tribes, rogue religions, or even rogue

peoples (e.g., the Sunni Arabs in Iraq and the Pashtuns in Afghanistan and Pakistan).

The Threat from Nuclear Terrorism

The greatest single threat to the United States is the steadily growing potential of terrorist groups to acquire nuclear weapons and to use them to destroy one or more American cities, along with several hundred thousand American lives.[1] My view of the primacy of this threat is very similar to that of Stephen Van Evera in his chapter in this volume. The problem is enhanced because it has become very difficult to determine just who could be the source of such an attack and therefore who could be punished for it.[2] Professional specialists who deal with the conjunction of terrorist groups and nuclear weapons largely agree that a nuclear terrorist attack within the next decade or two is almost inevitable or, at least, that merely technical and bureaucratic means deployed by the U.S. government will not be sufficient to prevent it.

This threat of nuclear terrorism should wonderfully concentrate the mind of the United States and particularly of anyone who seeks to lead it. The Bush administration was preposterously and disastrously wrong when it equated al Qaeda and nuclear weapons with Saddam Hussein and Iraq. However, it was not wrong to worry about al Qaeda and nuclear weapons in the first place. As different as the next administration will be from the current one, it will have to worry about nuclear terrorism, too. If it does not, and if a nuclear terrorist attack does in fact occur on its watch, it will never be forgotten or forgiven by the American people. Its place in history will certainly be ensured.

Putting U.S. National Security First and Foremost

The time has come, therefore, to make national security once again the principal objective of U.S. foreign policy. This is the basic premise of this chapter. Moreover, the promotion of law and order around the world is the best way to achieve it. This may mean a willingness to accept and even promote, for example, political systems that are liberal but not democratic (liberal nondemocracies rather then illiberal democracies); economic systems with free trade but not free movement of capital or of labor (restrictions on short-term capital and on immigration); and social systems largely defined—and closed—by religious values, as long as these do not enable terrorists. The important thing from the perspective of U.S. national security is that some kind of strong state exist, one restrained by law while imposing order and one that the United

States and its allies can hold responsible for the actions of people and groups, particularly Islamist terrorists, who are operating on its territory.

This, regrettably but consequently, may also entail a willingness to accept some undemocratic political systems that nevertheless share with the United States the opposition to transnational terrorist groups (i.e., groups that may target them, as well as us). The most prominent examples are Russia and China. This will upset some Americans, particularly human rights groups. It may also entail a willingness to accept economic systems that restrict U.S. investment in particular sectors but that still share in the opposition to transnational terrorist groups. The most prominent example is again Russia. This will upset other Americans, particularly businesspeople in the international energy industry. As it happens, human rights activists are prominent in the Democratic Party, and energy businesspeople are prominent in the Republican Party.

However, as prominent as each of these two groups may be in its particular political party, neither is very prominent in the American public as a whole. And as much as the American public may value democracy, human rights, and free enterprise in the abstract, it values its own security a good deal more. Even today, most Americans have no objection to the often rough measures that the Russian or the Chinese authorities deploy against Islamist terrorists in their own countries (or even against, respectively, their Chechen and Uighur communities more generally).

Three Candidates for Security Threats

Of course, in recent years, foreign policy analysts have identified several different threats to U.S. national security. Indeed, there seem to be three different major candidates. As already stated, some analysts focus on the widening spread of transnational networks of Islamist terrorists and the increasing probability that these will acquire and use weapons of mass destruction against American cities; this will be the focus in this chapter. Islamist terrorists represent the most fundamental and potentially most catastrophic threat of all. However, some analysts focus instead on the rising economic and military power of China. An example is Robert Kagan in his chapter in this volume. Still others focus on the growing economic influence and continuing nuclear arsenal of Russia.

The last two plausible threats should be considered in any comprehensive analysis of U.S. national security, and I touch on them in my own account. However, the Chinese and Russian challenges are in many respects new versions of those that the United States has faced before, especially during the cold war. In regard to these powers, updated versions of the venerable cold war strategies of containment and deterrence can be adopted, although these can be softened by the opportunities for international economic cooperation that globalization has brought. It is the threat of transnational networks, nonstate actors, and superempowered groups, especially Islamist ones, that requires a new kind of American strategy. However, like the old strategies of containment and deterrence, this new strategy should be based on the existence of strong states.

A Tale of Three Problems and One Solution

The classical solution to the problem of order within a region or a world was, of course, empire—that is, one big Hobbesian Leviathan. Among the particular problems of disorder that empire addressed were three, each of them classical in its way. These were disorderly cities, turbulent frontiers, and civil wars. These problems once again beset the world today, and we often sum them up as the problem of "failed states."[3] There is plenty of evidence of these problems of disorder around the globe, especially within the Muslim world. Moreover, they provide an environment in which global networks of Islamist terrorists can flourish.

Of course, virtually everyone recognizes that empire, the classical solution to these classical problems, is not realistic in our own times. Consequently, as an alternative to one big Leviathan, some world-affairs experts have proposed a "sovereignty solution," that is, many little Leviathans.[4] Even this more modest proposal faces serious obstacles, however, because we now live in a world of many failed states, or even just weak states, which are not strong enough to deal with their problems of disorder. Francis Fukuyama, in his chapter in this volume and in other writings, deals with the importance of this matter in a thoughtful and sophisticated way.

The fundamental question of this chapter is thus posed: What is the prospect for constructing strong states and some resulting kind of global order where they do not now exist, especially within the Muslim world, where the three problems of disorder and the Islamist terrorist networks are so prevalent?[5] I consider the different prospects for several different regions of the world. I also propose a solution that is based on several big Leviathans—that is, not only the United States but also other great powers.

The Prospects for Strong, Liberal Democratic States

Because Americans and people in the West naturally would prefer that a strong state also be a democratic one, preferably a liberal democratic one—that Hobbes be combined with Locke and Jefferson—another prime question is, just where do the conditions now exist for the establishment of new, strong, and liberal democratic states? Actually, the prospects are rather bleak. It is a difficult enough task to consolidate the ten or so new democracies in post-Communist Eastern Europe and also a couple of recent democracies in East Asia. Another difficult but important task is to strengthen the immense but flawed democracy that is India. In areas beyond these three important but limited regions, however, there can be found few or none of the normal economic, social, and cultural prerequisites for a stable democracy, particularly a liberal democracy. This is regrettably the case in the three important regions of Latin America, China, and the Muslim world.

A Different Kind of Democratization: Illiberal Democracy in Latin America

Democratization might still have a promising future in Latin America. However, the form that democratization is most likely to take there will not be similar to the American one—that is, liberal democracy, complete with some kind of separation of powers, constitutionalism, rule of law, and minority rights. It is more likely to be what Fareed Zakaria has called "illiberal democracy," particularly populist democracy, marked perhaps by generally free elections but also by presidential dominance, pervasive executive discretion, and majority rule.[6]

Populist, or illiberal, democracy seems to be a natural political tendency and a perennial political system in much of Latin America. It has certainly returned in a big way in that region in the 2000s, replacing the more liberal-democratic regimes of the 1990s (which were often derided as imposing "neoliberalism" and "the Washington Consensus" on their citizens and on behalf of U.S. interests). The most extreme (and anti-American) versions of populism now rule in Venezuela and Bolivia, but some versions of populist democracy now prevail in Ecuador, Nicaragua, Argentina, Chile, and Uruguay. Populist movements also recently came close to electoral victory in Mexico and Peru. All in all, Latin America has been swept by a major wave of populist democracy in the past few years.

In the fullness of time, the recurring economic and social failures of populist democracy will probably discredit it, just as the failures of liberal democracy have recently discredited that political alternative. Some new (or renewed) system will then arise in Latin America, perhaps yet another variation on an authoritarian theme. But it will probably be at least a generation before we see a revival of the distinctively U.S. project of liberal democracy in Latin America.

If the prospects for additional democratic regimes are bleak, what about the prospects for additional liberal ones (i.e., systems that at least have some kind of rule of law, a strong civil society, and a generally free press, even if the government is not chosen in truly free elections)? After all, most Western European countries passed through this stage in the nineteenth century on their path from authoritarian monarchy to liberal democracy. We might call this stage *liberal undemocracy*. As it happens, there is indeed one very large country in which a phase of liberal undemocracy is a reasonable prospect: China. The extremely rapid economic development of China over the past two decades has produced a new, and extremely numerous, middle class and, like the classical European and American middle classes, the Chinese middle class is largely independent and certainly productive. For many practical purposes, the Chinese Communist Party has devolved economic decision making to a new and dynamic elite of entrepreneurs. Moreover, there is now a very well-educated, but also very sensible, professional sector. But entrepreneurs and professionals normally seek the legal and political stability and predictability that come with the expansion of the rule of law and constitutionalism. Historically, these two sectors have formed a strong constituency for liberal institutions, even if these institutions are not yet really democratic, and they do so in China today.

The Chinese entrepreneurs and professionals have become essential, indeed central, to China's developmental path, and the Communist regime understands and accepts this. Because of the vigorous push of these entrepreneurs and professionals for the rule of law and even constitutionalism, the prospects are good that China will move progressively, albeit in fits and starts, toward a more liberal regime. If so, China will follow along a path taken in earlier decades by other East Asian countries, in particular Japan, Taiwan, and South Korea. However, because of the vast size and diversity of China, full democracy itself would probably unleash a variety of centrifugal tendencies and secessionist movements. At least, this is what the Chinese Communist Party firmly believes. The road to democracy in China will be far more rocky and risky than it was in the much smaller and more homogeneous countries of Japan, Taiwan, and South Korea. Consequently, there will not be truly democratic institutions in China anytime soon, even though we may soon see some truly liberal institutions there—in short, liberal undemocracy.

Reviewing the regions or countries considered thus far, we have the following picture: the development of liberal democratic states in Eastern Europe and in India is progressing rather well, and these states also seem to be sufficiently strong ones. In Latin America, an area that poses a potential threat to the United States, the prospect is for democratic states, but not liberal ones. Conversely, in China, a country that poses another potential threat to the United States but of a very different kind, the prospect is for a liberal, but not a democratic, state.

The Muslim Crescent and the Islamist Threat

But what about that vast area that was once known as the third world, that is, the regions of Africa, the Middle East, Southwest Asia, and Southeast Asia? Looked at in another way—and with the exclusion of sub-Saharan Africa and with the inclusion of the former Soviet republics of Central Asia—this area comprises a vast crescent which includes almost all of the Muslim world, the very source of the growing Islamist threat. It is Islamism that represents the greatest threat to order in our own time, not only to global order but also to domestic order within any country with a Muslim population. This is the case even if that population is only a minority community, as in the West. Islamism is the source of a spreading, and potentially catastrophic, anarchy, bringing with it the prospect of a descent into a new barbarian Dark Age for much of the globe. Much of the vast Muslim world is the embodiment of the three particular problems that I have identified: disorderly cities, turbulent frontiers, and civil wars. And so we are driven to consider the proposed solution of constructing strong, sovereign states in the Muslim world.

What Kind of Strong State Is Feasible in the Muslim World?

The central problem thus is how to bring law and order to the Muslim world, how to build sovereign states throughout it that can be held responsible for their actions and for the actions of the people (including the Islamists) who live within them. Most of the countries in the vast Muslim crescent possess few or none of the normal prerequisites for democratic regimes or even for liberal ones. For the foreseeable future, their choice (and our choice for them) will be limited to either an authoritarian state or no state at all, be this condition called a failed state, a turbulent frontier, or simply anarchy.

The mere fact that a state is authoritarian is not enough to make it a strong state. It is true what the American promoters of democratization so often profess: established democracies with deep roots spread widely throughout the society, such as the democracies of the West, are usually the strongest states of all. An authoritarian state, to be a strong state, must be grounded in some kind of solid social base. It is best if that base is either a dominant economic class (ideally, a large middle class) or a majority ethnic group. Such a base will be especially enthusiastic about supporting the authoritarian state if it is repressing and containing some other economic class or ethnic group that threatens the dominant one. This was the case in much of Eastern Europe between the two world wars and in Franco's Spain after the Spanish Civil War.

In the Muslim world, however, even when efforts have been made to create authoritarian or even totalitarian states following some kind of European model (e.g., Abdel Nasser in Egypt from the 1950s to the 1960s and the Pahlavi shahs in Iran from the 1930s to the 1970s), the result has rarely been a truly strong state with roots in a deep social base. The only enduring success was that of Kemal Atatürk and his successors in Turkey in the 1920s and after.

However, the Ottoman Empire once ruled much of the Muslim world with a particular kind of authoritarian state that may be relevant there even today. This comprised a "ruling institution" run by the Ottoman Turks, who, in countries other than Turkey itself, were often a minority ethnic community ruling over several other minority ethnic communities. Under such conditions, there was no obvious solid social base for Ottoman rule, that is, no dominant middle class or majority ethnic group. The Ottomans had to use other means to support their rule and to strengthen their state. Among these were versions of the two famous imperial practices of indirect rule and divide and rule.

The European empires in the Muslim world often practiced a variation on the Ottoman system of rule. The British in Iraq, Jordan, and Egypt and the French in Syria, Lebanon, Tunisia, and Morocco established their own ruling institutions. These were usually based on a leading local minority ethnic community that assumed the coveted role of the "most loyal ally" of the imperial power. The loyal ethnic community, backed by the reliable aid and advice of the imperial power, then governed all of the other local ethnic groups. The loyal ally ruled directly, but the imperial power ruled indirectly. These were clear cases of indirect rule.

If the local ethnic community became strong enough to rule on its own, it would cease to be loyal. Conversely, if the community became too weak to govern effectively, it would require continuous and costly military intervention from the imperial power and would cease to be a useful ally. Ideally, the loyal ally had to be strong enough to rule directly but weak enough to be dependent on the imperial power. To keep the loyal ethnic community in just the right balance of capacity and dependence, of strength and weakness, required a great deal of intelligence—in every sense of the word—on the part of the imperial power, and particularly its officials on the local scene. More generally, these imperial officials understood their own versions of some classical American mottoes: (1) all politics is local and (2) think globally (or imperially) but act locally. If in real estate value is defined by location, location, location, in realpolitik, value must be defined by locality, locality, locality.

The local and loyal ethnic community often supplied the bulk of the actual troops for the imperial army in the country. These ethnic troops could be counted on to put down uprisings from other ethnic groups when it was necessary to do so. It was even better if the loyal ethnic community had something of a warrior tradition, that is, were what the British called a "martial people." In any event, the imperial formula of indirect rule always had to be joined with the even more fundamental and ancient imperial formula of divide and rule.

The Ottoman and European empires in the Muslim world are long gone, and the United States has manifestly failed to establish a new empire there. However, if it wants to bring the Muslim world into a global order, it too will have to adopt its own version of the two imperial formulas. In many Muslim countries, especially those with no majority ethnic community but several minority communities, the best state that the United States will be able to get is one that is constructed on the basis of indirect rule and divide and rule.

This dismal reality about much of the Muslim world is becoming all too evident as the United States struggles to find a solution to the challenge of Islamist insurgencies, particularly the ones in Iraq and Afghanistan. I therefore now turn to three special, but especially intense, contemporary problems of disorder in the Muslim world that pose serious threats to American national security. These are insurgency wars, suicide bombers, and rogue ethnic communities. With respect to the latter, I focus on the Pashtuns of Afghanistan and the Sunni Arabs of Iraq. I argue that the best way to deal with each of these problems is to work with some local ethnic community or communities and their own security forces, that is, to use some version of indirect rule and divide and rule.

The Problem of Insurgency Wars

During the past century or so, there have been many (about two dozen) major efforts by imperial or foreign powers to subdue an insurgency within some particular locality. Some of these counterinsurgency campaigns have been successful, most notably those undertaken by the United States in the Philippines in the 1900s and again in the 1950s; by the United States in Nicaragua, Haiti, and the Dominican Republic in the 1910s and 1920s and in El Salvador in the 1980s; and by Britain in Iraq in the 1920s, in Malaya in the 1940s and 1950s, and in Kenya in the 1950s. Other counterinsurgencies have been unsuccessful, most notably those undertaken by France in Indochina in the 1940s and 1950s and in Algeria in the 1950s and 1960s; by the United States in Indochina in the 1960s and 1970s; and by the Soviet Union in Afghanistan in the 1980s. And, of course, the U.S. counterinsurgency efforts in Iraq and Afghanistan thus far have been notoriously unsuccessful.

Military analysts have offered a variety of factors and conditions to explain why some counterinsurgencies have been successful and others have not. However, one factor notably absent or feeble in Iraq and Afghanistan has been essential in every successful case, and that is the active cooperation of local military, or at least militia forces, with the military forces of the foreign power. These local forces know the local people and their language, customs, and nuances. They can provide the equivalent of what in domestic U.S. law enforcement is known as community policing, and only they—not foreign troops—can do so.

There is another feature of local military forces that makes them essential for a successful counterinsurgency. Because they are local (and native and indigenous), everyone in the locality knows that they and the communities from which they come are not only on the scene now but also have been so in the past and will be so in the future. Their survival depends on making the counterinsurgency successful because they have no obvious place to escape to if it fails. In contrast, everyone in the locality (and in the foreign power) knows that the foreign military forces can always go home. Moreover, if the foreign power is a democratic one (especially one in our contemporary, postmodern era, with its high aversion to military casualties in a long war of attrition, which all counterinsurgencies are), everyone will know that eventually this foreign power will indeed bring its troops home. The insurgent forces will have many good reasons to believe that they will be able to outwait the foreign ones. A war of attrition (and, therefore, a counterinsurgency war) is a war of wills, and in a war of wills the side that must stay and fight will have more staying willpower than the side that can choose between staying put and going away. A counterinsurgency war, in other words, is an arena in which Albert Hirschman's famous analysis of "exit" versus "voice" fully applies.[7]

Consequently, in every successful counterinsurgency war, the foreign power has had to carry out a policy of localization. In the Vietnam War, the Nixon administration understood this, and "Vietnamization" was a centerpiece of its military strategy. In the Iraq war, the Bush administration keeps declaring that "when the Iraqi troops stand up, our troops can stand down," but the hoped-for Iraqi military forces have never come close to the efficacy that was obtained in that other grueling counterinsurgency war by the military forces of South Vietnam. (It is perhaps indicative of the great difficulty of the current challenge in Iraq that the Bush administration has almost never used the term "Iraqification" or anything like it.) As bad as conditions were in South Vietnam, there were at least a large number of soldiers there who identified with something called South Vietnam. In contrast, in Iraq the bulk of the local soldiers identify most not with something called Iraq but instead with their religious or ethnic community, that is, Shiites, Sunnis, or Kurds.

The Problem of Suicide Bombers

In recent years, insurgents have developed a new and formidable weapon: the suicide bomber. This tactic was not invented by Islamist insurgents (the Japanese kamikaze pilots were a famous predecessor, and the Tamil Liberation Front in Sri Lanka has made extensive use of it), but suicide bombing is now especially prevalent among Islamist terrorist groups. (In the 1980s, these groups were primarily Shiite and backed by Iran; in the 2000s, they are primarily Sunni and are parts of a widespread, transnational, even Internet-based, network.)

An especially cogent analysis of the causes and conditions that give rise to suicide bombing is offered by Robert Pape, a political scientist and military strategist at the University of Chicago.[8] Pape sees suicide bombing to be the product of two conditions. First, a foreign power is occupying a particular country with its military forces (or those foreign military forces are so near to the country that they constitute a continuous and pervasive threat of occupation). Prominent examples have been Israel in the West Bank and Gaza; India in Kashmir; and the United States in Lebanon (1982–1984), in Saudi Arabia (1990–2003), and now, of course, in Iraq. In the second condition, the foreign, occupying power is a democratic political system. These systems count public opinion as important, and suicide terrorism can have a large and visible impact on this public opinion. This feature is especially prominent in a postmodern, highly individualistic, and self-centered liberal democracy, such as those in much of the West today. The contrast with a premodern, highly communalist, honor-centered Muslim culture could not be greater. All suicide bombers come from very intense and dense communities; only these communities can create the very special incentives necessary for suicide bombing.

Pape's analysis clearly enhances the argument that under contemporary conditions a foreign military force engaged in counterinsurgency operations will find itself in a very unstable and even counterproductive situation. It therefore also enhances the argument that a foreign power (especially one that is a liberal democracy) will have to rely not only on strong local military forces but also on a strong local political authority (and in some situations even authoritarianism) that will essentially occupy its own country.

If the local military force and political authority are from the same community as that of the insurgent organization, then they are very likely to be able to acquire the intelligence information that is necessary to root out the insurgent's supporters within that community. This ability is especially relevant in regard to suicide bombing, because this tactic requires a substantial amount of community support.

Conversely, if the local military force and political authority are from a different community from that of the insurgent organization, they may not have the intelligence, but they very likely will have the will to root out (i.e., to ruthlessly devastate) that community and the insurgent's supporters within that community, which is both alien and a threat to them. This extreme version of the two formulas of indirect rule and divide and rule was used by the British in most of their successful counterinsurgencies, for example, enabling the Sunnis to repress the Shiites in Iraq in the 1920s, the Malays to repress the rural Chinese in Malaya in the 1950s, and several smaller tribes to repress the rural Kikuyu in Kenya in the 1950s.

The Problem of Rogue Ethnic Communities

In the past, therefore, there were particular ethnic communities which served as loyal allies of imperial powers in imposing order. However, there were also particular ethnic communities that always seemed to be in opposition to the imperial order or, indeed, to any order other than their own peculiar one. These were what the British called the "unruly peoples."

The most notorious of these unruly peoples—indeed, the British called them "ungovernable"—were the Pashtuns (then called the Pathans), who inhabited both the southern and eastern parts of Afghanistan and the Northwest Frontier Province of British India. And so the Pashtuns have remained, right down to the present day. We might now call them a rogue people. Indeed, it might be said that the Pashtuns still represent the ideal type, the classical example, of a rogue people.[9]

In the modern era, however, we have also witnessed the development of a second kind of rogue people. There are certain ethnic communities who once ruled over other ones in a modern society but who have recently been deposed from this rule and this role. In some cases, the deposed community was once even the local community, the "martial people," which an imperial power employed for its strategy of indirect rule. No longer a ruling and a martial people, and deeply resenting its loss, the community is now merely an "ex-ruling people."

The most notorious of these ex-ruling peoples are the Sunni Arabs of Iraq. For generations, this minority—but militant and martial—community ruled Iraq, first serving as the local rulers for the Ottomans, then for the British, and then, after 1958, for themselves. The Iraqi Sunni Arabs cannot imagine any role for themselves other than as a ruling people, and they will stop at nothing to regain that rule and role. We might now also call them a rogue people. Indeed, it might be said that the Iraqi Sunni Arabs today represent the ideal type of the modern kind of a rogue people.

And so we have the classical kind of rogue people best represented by the Pashtuns of Afghanistan and northwestern Pakistan and the modern kind best represented by the Sunni Arabs of Iraq. It seems that in the 2000s the cunning of history, and a diabolical cunning at that, has placed the United States into a long and grueling counterinsurgency war against both. Any discussion of an American strategy for global law and order will have to confront the brutal reality of these two rogue peoples.

THE CLASSICAL ROGUE PEOPLE: THE PASHTUNS OF AFGHANISTAN AND NORTHWESTERN PAKISTAN

The Pashtuns have always been a rogue people, at great cost to their neighboring ethnic communities (e.g., the Tajiks, the Uzbeks, the Hazaras, and the Punjabis). They are now also a rogue people at great cost to the rest of the world. The Pashtuns are virtually the only ethnic community in Afghanistan that supports the Taliban, and indeed virtually everyone in the Taliban is a Pashtun. It was, of course, the Taliban regime and therefore the Pashtun community that hosted and protected al Qaeda before the American invasion of Afghanistan in 2001, and it is the Pashtun community in the Northwest Frontier Province and the autonomous tribal areas of Pakistan that hosts and protects al Qaeda there today.

Like many close-knit ethnic or tribal communities, the Pashtuns have an intense sense of communal identity and almost no sense of an individual one. They also naturally have an intense sense of the communal identity, even the collective guilt, of their enemies. It is impossible to deal with the Pashtuns as if they were individuals, responding to calculations of individual benefits and costs. This is why, after more than six years, no one has ever stepped forward to turn in Osama bin Laden or Mullah Muhammed Omar (the leader of the Taliban), even though the United States has offered a $25 million reward for each. The only way to deal with the Pashtuns is the way they deal with themselves and with everyone else—as a community, one that is capable of collective guilt. Perhaps the best way for Americans to think about the Pashtun tribes on the Northwest Frontier of today would be the way the Americans of the late nineteenth century thought about the Apache and Comanche tribes on their own Southwest frontier at that time.

However, it is impossible for contemporary Americans—with their ideals of individualism, liberalism, and democracy at the very core of their own identity—to deal directly with the Pashtuns in such a communal and collective-guilt way. There are, however, other ethnic communities in Afghanistan (e.g., the Tajiks, the Uzbeks, and the Hazaras), and even in Pakistan, who have long been dominated or abused by the Pashtuns and who would be willing to do so, if this were allowed by the United States and the other North Atlantic Treaty Organization (NATO) countries now operating in Afghanistan. This would compose a new chapter in the long history of indirect rule and divide and rule.

Of course, to allow the local and historical adversaries of the Pashtuns to deal with them in the local, historical way and the way of the Pashtuns themselves would be repugnant to standards of human rights and universal justice. However, sometimes local, but generally held, conceptions of justice are more fitting to the local realities than are universal general ones. By putting the Pashtuns in their just place, these conceptions would also establish a new chapter in the history of global law and order.

THE MODERN ROGUE PEOPLE: THE SUNNI ARABS OF IRAQ

The Sunni Arabs long dominated and abused other ethnic communities in Iraq, particularly, of course, the Shiite Arabs and the Kurds, but they have always composed a minority of Iraq's population (now about 15–20 percent). Because of their long history of oppression and because of their support for the Islamist insurgency—an insurgency that certainly includes Shiites and Kurds among its targets—the Sunni Arabs have much to answer for, and they have laid the groundwork for a terrible civil war in Iraq.

Because the Sunni Arab minority was a rather small one, any regime composed by the Sunnis was especially authoritarian; the Sunni regime compensated for its especially small social base by employing unusually brutal methods against the Shiite and Kurdish communities. As Iraqi society underwent progressive modernization in the course of the twentieth century, the Shiites and the Kurds steadily acquired more of the economic and educational resources that enabled their political mobilization and organization. This largely explains why successive Sunni regimes had to become steadily more severe, leading to the brutal rule of the Baath Party and culminating in the genocidal regime of Saddam Hussein. Only by increasing pressure from above could the regime keep down the pressure from below coming from the increasingly mobilized Shiites and Kurds.

The Sunni leaders have repeatedly demonstrated their total lack of statesmanship or, indeed, of any sense of justice due to the Shiites and the Kurds. After the insurgent bombing of the major Shiite shrine in Samarra in February 2006, the Sunnis themselves should have apprehended the perpetrators and turned them over for justice, but they did not do so. Thus began a new and continuing quantum leap in the revenge cycle of Sunni-Shiite violence.

For many reasons—some based on American democratic ideals and some based on strategic calculations and economic interests involving the Sunni regimes of the Persian Gulf oil producers—the Bush administration has tried to co-opt or even appease the Sunnis. The result has been a continuing failure to subdue the Sunni insurgents in Iraq, including al Qaeda. However, in the southern and central regions of Iraq, including Baghdad, the Shiite militias and the Shiite-dominated units in the Iraqi army and police would have been willing and able to subdue them, if the United States had allowed it. Similarly, in the northern region of Iraq, including the cities of Kirkuk and Mosul, the Kurdish militias, already the equivalent of a Kurdish army, were willing and able to do the same. The long-term security of the United States would have been best protected if in 2003 and later the Bush administration had enabled the Shiite and Kurdish militaries to inflict a dramatic and decisive defeat on the Sunni insurgents and to bring about a profound and permanent demoralization of their Sunni supporters.

Instead, the success of the Sunni insurgents in Iraq is inspiring and energizing Sunni terrorists, particularly al Qaeda but also other Salifist networks around the world. The recent success of Hezbollah, a Shiite organization, in Lebanon is similarly inspiring and energizing Shiite extremists, particularly the Islamic regime of Iran, around the Middle East. In Iraq itself, both the al Qaeda Sunni insurgents and the Shiite militias now hate and oppose the U.S. military presence and the U.S. efforts to construct a unified and democratic nation in that torn and tormented country.

The solution to this dilemma and impending disaster in Iraq and elsewhere lies at the very heart of the problem—the hatred that possesses all Islamists, in both their Sunni and their Shiite versions. Of course, both Sunnis and Shiites hate America, but, as the escalating Sunni-Shiite mayhem in Iraq demonstrates, they hate each other even more. If the United States were to get out of their way, they would fall on each other in a maelstrom of ethnic cleansing and civil war, one which would be remembered by each for generations to come.

But U.S. troops cannot just get out of the war by a precipitous or timed withdrawal, as many Democratic politicians are now proposing. Islamists in general, and Osama bin Laden and al Qaeda in particular, are always pointing to past U.S. military retreats—Vietnam in 1975, Lebanon in 1984, and Somalia in 1993—as evidence that the American political will in a war will collapse after a few U.S. military fatalities and also as an encouragement to press on with more insurgencies and terrorism to push America out of the Muslim world. Another such retreat would therefore issue in more Islamist insurgencies and terrorist attacks. The United States should indeed leave Iraq, but not before it affects or allows, through Shiite and Kurdish forces, a dramatic and decisive defeat of the Sunni insurgents, a defeat so terrible that the Sunnis will never forget it and that demonstrates the unbearable cost and utter futility of the Sunni extremist and Salifist dream of establishing a united Muslim *umma* under the rule of a global Sunni Islamist caliphate.

As for the future role of the United States with respect to Iraq, it could continue to provide military assistance and diplomatic guidance to the Kurds. It would also have to encourage, with a variety of economic and diplomatic means, the long-run but natural separation of the Arab Shiites of Iraq from the Persian Shiites of Iran. At the end of the day and in the big picture, the role of the United States would become that of an "off-short balancer," balancing between Shiite Iraq and (Sunni) Kurdish Iraq and between Shiite Iran and Sunni Saudi Arabia. U.S. economic interests in a continuing flow of Persian Gulf oil to the global market would be preserved, and U.S. security interests in containing Iran would be enhanced. But the interests of more than 80 percent of the people of Iraq—that is, the Shiites and the Kurds—would be enhanced also. They would be the winners in the new order in that tormented country. The losers, of course, would be the Sunni Arabs of Iraq, who would have to pay, and pay big, for the sins of the cruel regimes which represented them in the past and of the cruel insurgents whom they support today.

The U.S. Superpower and the Three Great Powers: Russia, China, and India

In the world of the early twenty-first century, the United States is still the "sole superpower." However, it is also a world that still includes a few great powers, which are especially great in their immediate regions.

One of these great powers is Russia, which of course is much diminished in power since it was the Soviet Union. It still possesses, however, a massive nuclear arsenal, and it also possesses enormous oil and natural gas resources. Moreover, it remains highly influential in what it calls its "near abroad," particularly in the former Soviet and still authoritarian republics of Central Asia.

These countries, along with Azerbaijan, have Muslim populations. Moreover, Russia has a substantial Muslim population within Russia itself, and it has waged a particularly brutal and devastating counterinsurgency war in Chechnya. Overall, Russia has been confronting various transnational Islamist terrorist groups for almost three decades.

A second—now very obvious because it is rising so rapidly—great power is China. Everyone knows about, and many are astonished by, China's booming industrial growth and accompanying financial influence. Moreover, the

Chinese regime is deploying some of this economic strength to strengthen China's military, too.[10] And although China does not yet have a "near abroad" or neighboring sphere of influence equivalent to that of Russia in Central Asia, its government is using a sophisticated ensemble of "soft power" instruments to develop something like a sphere of influence in Southeast Asia.[11]

The threat that China faces from Islamist terrorists has thus far been much less deadly than that faced by Russia. However, China does have a problem with transnational Islamist terrorist groups operating within its Uighur population in Xinjiang, and in 2001 it formed the Shanghai Cooperation Organization with Russia and with Central Asian states to deal with these transnational networks.

China is also concerned about the threat that Islamist movements pose to the overseas Chinese communities living within largely Muslim Indonesia and Malaysia. Militant Islamists in these countries often violently attack the small (and richer) Chinese communities who are their neighbors. Finally, China is especially and increasingly concerned about potential Islamist terrorist attacks on the supply and flow of oil from Muslim countries, especially those along the vulnerable sea lanes of communication and commerce (SLOCS) in the Persian Gulf, the Arabian Sea, and the Strait of Malacca.[12]

A third, and also rising, great power is India. Although its economic and military growth is not as impressive as China's, it is still more impressive than that of any other power. Moreover, India is employing a variety of instruments to increase its influence in its neighbors across the Arabian Sea.[13]

With its vast Muslim population of 140 million, India has had ample and generally successful experience with the problem of maintaining law and order as it involves an internal Muslim community. And with an ongoing Islamist insurgency in Kashmir, it also has had ample and often painful experience with this problem, as it involves a sort of Indian "near abroad."

For the foreseeable future, therefore, the United States will have to deal with each of these three great—and often greatly annoying—powers. For its own vital interests—particularly its vital security interests—it had better deal with them in a sensible, realistic, and intelligent way.

Each of these three great powers is challenged by some kind of Islamist terrorist threat, and each sees this to be a major threat to its own vital security interests. Each of these powers, therefore, can be a natural ally of the United States as it tries to construct a system of global law and order. I agree very much with Stephen Van Evera, in his chapter in this volume, about the importance and feasibility of a concert of major powers and that the United States should adopt a "concert strategy" to bring this about. But this, in turn, will require the United States to prioritize its interests, to put the vital security goals of all Americans over the peripheral ideological and economic interests of particular American groups, such as human rights activists and a few businesspeople.

The Feasibility of a Grand Coalition of the United States and the Great Powers

In order to enhance its own national security, the United States can and should take the lead in constructing a grand coalition of great powers, a coalition united against transnational networks of Islamist terrorists and in support of a system of global law and order. It might reasonably be asked whether such a coalition or concert of the current great powers—which are now very suspicious of and competitive with each other—is actually practical. After all, there have been efforts to construct grand coalitions of the great powers before—most famously, the Concert of Europe after the Napoleonic wars—but they have always dissolved after a few years, and they sometimes have even ended in a war between the former members of the coalition (e.g., the Crimean War of 1853–1854). In his chapter in this volume, Robert Kagan argues strongly not only that competition between the great powers is inevitable but also that it should be the central focus of U.S. grand strategy.

My purpose in this chapter is not to construct a coalition that will be able to address the yet-unknown big international challenges in the remote future. I hope to address the biggest single challenge of today and for the next couple of decades, the steadily growing threat of nuclear terrorism. The particular conjuncture of international conditions in this era is favorable to the construction of a grand coalition composed of the United States, Russia, China, and India.

Any coalition of great powers must take into account and protect the vital national interests of each of its members, as each defines them. The United States sees itself as the only superpower and the only truly global power, and its leadership—in both the Republican and the Democratic parties—wants to keep it that way. This conception of vital U.S. interests is not going to change anytime soon.

The contemporary conceptions of the three great powers of their own vital interests are rather different. On the one hand, being great powers—China and India being rapidly rising ones—their conceptions are not limited to only their national territories. On the other hand, none of them sees itself as becoming a superpower and global power at any time in the next couple of decades. (This is in obvious contrast with the old Soviet Union.) Rather, each of these three powers sees itself as a regional power, wanting to construct a secure sphere of influence or near abroad composed of its neighbors (or at least of its less developed ones).

It appears to be a historical rule that all great powers, and especially rising ones, want to construct such a sphere of influence. The United States did so in the Caribbean and Central America after 1898. It eventually went on to construct secure spheres of influence in Latin America more generally, in Western Europe, and in East Asia, or at least to construct security alliances such as the Rio Pact (1947), NATO (1949), and a series of bilateral alliances with Asian countries. Indeed, it constructed something like a sphere of influence in so many regions that it became a truly global power.

For now, however, Russia, China, and India are more at the stage at which the United States was in the early twentieth century. They are therefore ready for a sort of grand bargain. If the United States allows them to order their own regions and spheres in particular, they will allow the United States to order the globe in general. In effect, if they can be regional hegemons, the United States can be the global hegemon. More crudely, the United States would be boss of all the bosses. And all the hegemons, all the bosses, would cooperate in putting down transnational Islamist terrorists and in constructing a global system of law and order.

At this point, historically minded readers will probably be reminded of President Franklin Roosevelt's conception near the end of World War II that the postwar world would be ordered by a concert of the four victorious great powers—the United States, the British Empire, the Soviet Union, and China. Roosevelt hoped that they would work together under U.S. leadership as "the four policemen" to put down the biggest threat to global order at the time, that is, military aggression.[14] Unfortunately, after 1945, the only powers big enough to undertake or promote military aggression were these four powers themselves, and it was too much to expect that they could effectively police each other. My own proposal is essentially composed of the contemporary heirs of these same four great powers—the United States; India, the "jewel in the crown" of the British Empire, taking that empire's place; Russia, taking the place of the Soviet Union (and Soviet empire); and China. This time, however, the four policemen have one external enemy—transnational Islamist terrorists—that they all oppose.

International Law as a Basis for Global Order

I have been discussing order a good deal, but what about law? The role of international law in the grand coalition of great powers is important, as it should constrain the actions of these powers in their respective spheres of influence.

In practice, great powers have periodically undertaken full-scale military interventions in client states within their spheres of influence. Since 1945, the United States has done this in the Dominican Republic (1965), Grenada (1983), Panama (1989), and Haiti (1994) and (though not fully in the U.S. sphere) Lebanon (1958 and 1962). The Soviet Union did so in East Germany (1953), Hungary (1956), and Czechoslovakia (1968) and (though not fully in the Soviet sphere) Afghanistan (1979). Each of these military interventions was judged by many international-law professionals (and by quite a few independent nations) to be a violation of international law, particularly of the solidly established international conventions against military aggression or the armed crossing of the borders of recognized sovereign states.

Knowing that its military intervention will contradict many interpretations of established international law, the United States has made elaborate efforts to find a basis in international law with which to legitimize it. The grounds it has used include an invitation to intervene made by a local authority (the more official the authority, the better) and authorization of the intervention by an international organization (the larger the organization, the better). It was successful in constructing a semblance of both of these elements in its four post-1945 interventions in the Caribbean and Central America. (In Lebanon, however, it only got the local invitation.) The Soviet Union was so impressed with this U.S. technique, especially as used in the Dominican intervention of 1965, that it also constructed a semblance of both elements in its invasion of Czechoslovakia in 1968. (In Afghanistan, it only got the local invitation.)

All of this established international law and extensive military history add up to the conclusion that the United States should itself follow, and that it should insist that the other coalition powers follow, this international law in the future. At minimum, some kind of international organization should authorize and legitimize any military intervention. This is part of the U.S. responsibility that would come with being the global hegemon of the regional hegemons. And if a coalition power (i.e., China and India) does not now have a congenial regional organization at hand to turn to for this purpose, it should get busy and create one.

The Implications for U.S. Defense Policy and Defense Spending

The American strategy of law and order which I have been discussing would mean major changes in U.S. defense policy and defense spending, especially from that of the Bush administration.

First, this strategy means that the U.S. military would not be expected to engage in counterinsurgency operations. The United States should avoid counterinsurgencies. When confronted with foreign insurgencies which the United States considers to be hostile to its interests, the U.S. military would at most engage in the training and the equipping of local militaries or militias. This was a successful U.S. policy in the Philippines in the 1950s and in El Salvador in the 1980s. It was also the concept of the Nixon doctrine of 1969, which was a generalization and formalization of the Vietnamization policy.

Consequently, the U.S. military would return to the expectation that it would be engaged only in conventional operations.[15] The past examples have been as varied as the Korean War (1950–1953) and the Gulf War (1991), and also military interventions in the Dominican Republic (1965), Grenada (1983), Panama (1989), Haiti (1994), Bosnia (1995), and Kosovo (1999). Each of these wars and interventions was conceived from the beginning to be a conventional operation, not a counterinsurgency one, and each was more or less a success in achieving its relatively limited and focused objective, which was defeating or deterring a hostile military force. (Although at the time of the intervention, some U.S. military analysts thought that some kind of insurgency might develop, e.g., in Haiti and in Bosnia.) This concept of limiting U.S. military operations to conventional ones was also implied in the Weinberger doctrine of 1984, which was a response to the failure of the U.S. military intervention in Lebanon in 1982–1984, and in its expanded version, which was the Powell doctrine of 1992. (David Kennedy, in his chapter in this volume, gives us a comprehensive account of the development of the Weinberger and Powell doctrines.)

The Revolution in Military Affairs and the Potential Enemies

The purpose of the U.S. military, therefore, would be to deter or fight other militaries. Indeed, the U.S. military would for the most part fight those enemies that only the United States had the will and the capability to fight; that is, it would provide the vital ingredient or the necessary condition (which is not the same as a sufficient condition) to defeat any particular enemy.

This strategy could very well entail a return to some aspects of the "Revolution in Military Affairs" (RMA), which was so much a topic of military discussion in the 1990s. (Kennedy also provides an informative discussion of the RMA.) The RMA has been largely discredited by the way that Defense Secretary Donald Rumsfeld carried it to arrogance and extremes in his "military transformation project" and then to irrelevance and failure in his Iraq war policy. However, continued development along the lines of the RMA could well be necessary in order to be able in the future to deter some potential "peer competitors" or to fight and defeat their militaries in some conventional war.

Who could be these potential peer competitors and conventional militaries? For the most part, they would be the very threats that some strategic analysts are pointing to now, that is, China and Russia. Under the new American strategy proposed here, the main purpose of the U.S. military would be to keep itself always in a state of superiority such that it would deter China and Russia from becoming threats to American security in the long run. In doing so, the United States would guide China and Russia to an alternative path, one that I have also proposed in this chapter: that is for each of them to maintain law and order at home and in its "near abroad" or recognized sphere of influence and not to expand its order beyond these recognized regions by engaging in military aggression.

Overall, this new American strategy would likely mean a return to something like the direction and the level of U.S. defense spending during the 1990s, that is, a focus on the continuing improvement of conventional capabilities while making full use of continuing developments in military technologies. It would certainly mean a reduction in the use of U.S. ground forces in combat operations, that is, in those "small wars" that always seem to grow into very big expenditures in money and in lives.

Boss of All the Bosses

When they turn their attention to world affairs, many Americans have a wide variety of interests—interests in the global economy, interests in universal human rights, interests in the security of particular favorite allies, and so forth. However, there is one fundamental and essential interest that all Americans share, and that is in national security. In our time, that means the establishment of a global regime of law and order.

The United States, and in particular the American state, cannot establish this regime on its own; there cannot be just one American Leviathan. Rather, the United States can take the lead in composing and orchestrating a grand concert of many Leviathans. Most of these will be strong states capable of imposing order on their own countries and their local areas. A few—most notably Russia, China, and India—can also do much to bring order to their own near abroad or spheres of influence. They would be regional hegemons, practicing their own versions of indirect rule and divide and rule. But the United States would be the global hegemon of all the other hegemons, the boss of all the bosses.

The United States can also be persistent (it would also have to be wise) in pressing the local strong states and even the regional hegemons to steadily add the rule of law to their particular forms of order. In doing so, they will be laying the foundations for adding a genuine civilization to their order, as well. The grand goal of American strategy should be a world of strong states, each ensuring for its people the benefits of order, law, and civilization—of life, liberty, and the pursuit of happiness. But the first of these—as it has always been and always will be—is order.

Notes

1. Graham Allison, *Nuclear Terrorism: The Ultimate Preventable Catastrophe* (New York: Owl Books/Henry Holt, 2004); Graham Allison, ed., "Confronting the Specter of Nuclear Terrorism," special issue, *Annals of the American Academy of Political and Social Science* (September 2006).

2. Matthew Phillips, "Uncertain Justice for Nuclear Terror: Deterrence of Anonymous Attacks through Attribution," *Orbis* 51, no. 3 (Summer 2007): 429–446.

3. These three problems are discussed, respectively, in three articles in a special section on "Civilization and Order" in *The American Interest* 2, no. 4 (March/April 2007): William H. McNeill, "Cities and Their Consequences": 5–12; Jakub Grygiel, "Empires and Barbarians": 13–22; and Steven R. David, "On Civil War": 23–32. I have discussed the problem of order and some of the themes in the present chapter in my own article, "Coming to Order," *The American Interest* 3, no. 1 (July/August 2007): 55–63.

4. Anna Simons et al., "The Sovereignty Solution," *The American Interest* 2, no. 4 (March/April 2007): 33–42.

5. For a systematic study of how to construct strong states, see Francis Fukuyama, *State-Building: Governance and World Order in the 21st Century* (Ithaca, NY: Cornell University Press, 2004).

6. Fareed Zakaria, *The Future of Freedom: Illiberal Democracy at Home and Abroad* (New York: Norton, 2003).

7. Albert O. Hirschman, *Exit, Voice, and Loyalty: Responses to Decline in Firms, Organizations, and States* (Cambridge, MA: Harvard University Press, 1970).

8. Robert A. Pape, *Dying to Win: The Strategic Logic of Suicide Terrorism* (New York: Random House, 2005).

9. Thomas H. Johnson and M. Chris Mason, "Understanding the Taliban and Insurgency in Afghanistan," *Orbis* 51, no. 1 (Winter 2007): 71–90; Vanni Cappelli, "The Alienated Frontier: Why the United States Can't Get Osama bin Laden," *Orbis* 49, no. 4 (Fall 2005): 713–729.

10. June Teufel Dreyer, "China's Power and Will: The PRC's Military Strengths and Grand Strategy," *Orbis* 51, no. 4 (Fall 2007): 651–664.

11. Joshua Kurlantzick, *Charm Offensive: How China's Soft Power Is Transforming the World* (New Haven, CT: Yale University Press, 2007); Toshi Yoshihara

and James R. Holmes, "China's Energy-Driven 'Soft Power,'" *Orbis* 52, no. 1 (Winter 2008): 123–137.

12. Andrew Erickson and Gabe Collins, "Beijing's Energy Security Strategy: The Significance of a Chinese State-Owned Tanker Fleet," *Orbis* 51, no. 4 (Fall 2007): 665–684; James Kurth, "The New Maritime Strategy: Peer Competitors, Rogue States and Transnational Insurgents," *Orbis* 51, no. 4 (Fall 2007): 585–600.

13. Harsh V. Pant, "A Fine Balance: India Walks a Tightrope between Iran and the United States," *Orbis* 51, no. 3 (Summer 2007): 495–509.

14. I am indebted to Melvyn P. Leffler for this comparison.

15. James Kurth, "Variations on the American Way of War," in *The Long War: A New History of U.S. National Security Policy since World War II*, ed. Andrew J. Bacevich (New York: Columbia University Press, 2007), 53–98.

SIX

Legitimacy and Competence
Samantha Power

PRESIDENT BUSH'S SUCCESSORS, whether Democrat or Republican, will not be able to recoup fully the global influence that the United States has lost since the turn of the century. Even if Iraq could be stabilized and U.S. troops withdrawn, it will not be possible to return to the unipolar 1990s. Nonetheless, the next president can make substantial headway in enhancing U.S. influence and security in the short and long term by doing four things: (1) taking stock of the altered twenty-first-century landscape; (2) improving U.S. intelligence-gathering and analysis and making a long-term, societywide commitment to understanding Islam; (3) enhancing U.S. legitimacy by ceasing practices that do not comport with international law, reckoning with recent blunders and injustices, and concretely improving human welfare abroad; and (4) strengthening U.S. resiliency by fortifying potential U.S. targets and thickening the domestic base for foreign policy, a base that has withered substantially since 9/11.

The Next President Must Recognize the World That We Have, Not the World We Wish We Had

Before the next president can pursue a tough, smart, and humane strategic vision, he or she must take stock of several tectonic shifts that have altered the global landscape: the erosion of U.S. influence, the rise of new powers, the heightened violence within and polarization with the Islamic world, and the borderlessness of contemporary threats.

First, U.S. influence has waned substantially since George W. Bush took office in 2001. The disproportionate military and economic might that this country had amassed by the 1990s lulled many Americans into a false sense of security: we measured power on an old-fashioned, twentieth-century abacus—according to unsurpassed military supremacy or gross domestic product (GDP). Even today, when hard power has decreased (due to military overstretch and lessened readiness, a demonstrable mismatch between U.S. military capabilities and the requirements of counterterrorism and counterinsurgency, and a burgeoning debt), the United States is still the world's dominant military and economic power. The U.S. military budget exceeds that of the next thirty powers combined, and the U.S. GDP trounces that of India and China combined.

But hard power is but one factor shaping America's ability to get what it wants—from U.S. allies, from U.S. competitors or rivals, and from U.S. foes. And what has become clear from the Bush administration's unsuccessful efforts to exert American will around the world (e.g., in Iraq, Iran, Israel/Palestine, or Darfur) is that actual influence stems from three elements: hard power, legitimacy, and competence. It goes without saying that the next president must restore U.S. hard power. He or she must also think far more about the other two elements of influence: other people's trust that the United States will use its power legitimately and other people's faith in U.S. competence—their relative confidence that the United States is capable of achieving what its leaders put their minds to.

Many U.S. actions carried out in the "global war on terror" have been seen as illegitimate because they have been carried out indiscriminately, unaccountably, and/or unilaterally. The most powerful economic and military power on earth will always be greeted skeptically or mistrusted by the court of global public opinion. But the Bush administration's policy choices have compounded this perception, which, in turn, has been a factor in undermining respect for the United States and lessening U.S. geopolitical influence.

The dips in hard power and legitimacy might not together suffice to reduce the U.S. ability to get what it wants internationally if not for the third factor: a loss of confidence in U.S. competence. Before the Iraq war and Hurricane Katrina, the United States was seen in distant corners of the earth as the country that did accomplish such feats as putting the man on the moon and giving the world antiretroviral AIDS medicines. Whatever non-Americans thought about of the morality of particular U.S. policies, even in the wake of Vietnam and Somalia, most foreigners assumed that when U.S. leaders set out to do something, U.S. decision makers and technicians would plan carefully and bring the required financial, political, and technological resources to bear. The Bush administration has undermined traditional U.S. hard power by stretching our armed forces and National Guard to their respective breaking points and by borrowing colossal sums of money. Its failures of planning and execution in Iraq have also made us look unprofessional and unprepared. The U.S. failure to protect its own citizens during the hurricane only compounds the impression of American incompetence.

It will not be enough for the next president to expand the size of the army and the marines, to extract U.S. forces in Iraq, to concentrate its resources on tackling the insurgency in Afghanistan, or to balance the budget if he or she does not concentrate on enhancing other people's perception that we use our power legitimately, as well as their perception that we use our power competently. In subsequent sections I recommend policy changes that could help the United States replenish its legitimacy and restore its reputation for competence.

Although U.S. policy choices are within U.S. control, many of the other twenty-first-century trends are not. A second major tectonic plate shift that the next president will face is the rise and greater assertiveness of new or resurgent powers. The most important of these ascendant powers is, of course, China. From North Korea to Darfur, it is clear that the days in which China concentrated on its economic ascent, forswearing an assertive geopolitical role, have passed.[1] It is increasingly using its veto on the United Nations (UN) Security Council and using its economic leverage in the developing world to get what it wants geopolitically. Russia and Venezuela, the new petro-authoritarian powers, are also becoming important global players, using their oil wealth as leverage to buy off or bully domestic opposition and to entice or dominate their neighbors.

The rise of these countries has given countries in the South growing confidence to stand up to those in the North. The Group of 77 (G-77) now includes 133 of the 192 countries in the UN, and its agenda frequently mirrors that of China. These countries refuse to sit back passively to receive Northern edicts within international bodies. Instead of simply venting in the General Assembly, they look for opportunities to build ties elsewhere and engage in an increasingly sophisticated balance of power politics. Suspicious of rich, Western countries, they exhibit a near reverence for sovereignty that Western governments thought had been banished by the carnage of the 1990s. The "southern revolt" is having three pronounced effects on international affairs: a diminishing number of voices speaking out on behalf of human rights in the international system; an assault on trade liberalization and globalization; and obstruction of the effort by developed countries to reform international bodies so that they are far better suited to meet twenty-first-century threats. A recent example of this came when the G-77 foiled meaningful UN management reform aimed at making the organization a more cost-efficient and nimble body.

The Middle East has long been the scene of violent conflict. But a third "new reality" is that the region will be the scene of multiple concurrent conflicts (Iraq, Fatah-Hamas, Israel-Palestine, Lebanese government–Hezbollah–Syria). Additionally, as the next president withdraws U.S. forces from Iraq, he or she will have to grapple with the looming possibility of a regional war that pits Sunni forces against Shia elements sponsored and armed by Iran. He or she will also have to deal with the humanitarian and strategic consequences of the conflicts already under way. The violence in the Middle East testifies to a growing, increasingly hostile division among and within societies between the religious and the secular; in their efforts to strengthen moderate, secular elements, U.S. policy makers have unwittingly undermined the domestic standing and credibility of the very pro-Western forces they sought to assist.

The fourth relevant feature of the future global landscape, which has been so long in coming that it has become almost cliché, is that the central foreign policy challenges faced by the next president will be transnational threats that will not confine themselves within borders, that cannot be managed by single or even like-minded coalitions of countries, and that cannot be vanquished with military force. Global warming and terrorism are the two most pressing of these challenges, both of which will require diverse stakeholders to overcome collective action problems and to allocate resources today for threats that may not metastasize for many years—a difficult domestic political sell.

Irrespective of who occupies the White House, mapping a national and international response to global warming will consume vast human, financial, and political capital. Terrorists and proliferators pose the gravest immediate dangers to the United States. Terrorists have gained in strength, numbers, and motive thanks to the past seven years of policy choices. The war and occupation in Iraq and the associated harms (torture, excessive force, extraordinary rendition, etc.) have caused demonstrable surges in anti-Americanism, and leaked classified intelligence indicates that terrorists have been able to recruit more widely as a result of recent U.S. policy choices.[2]

It is perhaps understandable that few presidential candidates have grappled head-on with these tectonic shifts or altered realities. Any mention of the decline of U.S. influence or the ascent of new powers provokes accusations of fatalism or a lack of patriotism. Republicans seem inclined to blame the current state of global affairs on Bush's quasi-revolutionary (and not at all conservative) agenda and his overreach. They seem to believe that a return to true conservatism can bring about the return of U.S. global domination. Democrats, too, generally blame Bush—for Iraq and for his policies of unilateralism and militarism. They seem to believe that getting out of Iraq and striking a more humble tone in international settings can bring about the return of global cooperation. But in January 2009 the next president is going to inherit a radically altered landscape from the one President Bush inherited in January 2001. Richard Clarke, the counterterrorism specialist who served under both Clinton and George W. Bush, has said that he felt senior officials in George H. W. Bush's administration had been "frozen in amber" during the 1990s, when the al Qaeda network was blossoming and executing its earlier attacks. Critics of President Bush have to be sure not to remain comparably frozen in time and to familiarize themselves with the realities of an altered global landscape.

In light of these tectonic plate shifts, what is the next president to do? I leave it to others in this volume to discuss what can be done to recoup U.S. hard power, and I devote the remainder of this chapter to the policies the United States can undertake to enhance its legitimacy (and its ability to attract others to its side), to improve its foreign policy performance (and its reputation for competence), and to strengthen its resiliency.

Enhancing Legitimacy

Legitimacy is difficult to measure and inherently subjective. Max Weber defined legitimacy as the willingness to adhere to international norms and institutions. John Locke framed legitimacy in terms of the consent of the governed. In order for laws to be legitimate, according to Locke, they needed to have been endorsed by a country's citizens. In the realm of international relations, countries have been seen to act legitimately when, for instance, they have received the consent of the UN Security Council for the use of military force, complied with international legal norms in the pursuit of security objectives, respected local cultural and religious norms in their diplomatic and military dealings, or demonstrated respect for alternative viewpoints. As the world has grown more polarized, the question of the legitimate use of power (and especially coercive force) has grown more divisive. Some of the arbiters of legitimacy, such as the UN Security Council, are themselves seen as illegitimate in many parts of the world owing to their outdatedness or perceived unrepresentativeness.

For all of this definitional fuzziness, legitimacy has become a touchstone phrase in international affairs. Even the U.S. military refers to it as a "force multiplier" in conflict. But one has to be careful not to overstate the importance of legitimacy, while also being sure not to exaggerate how easy it will be for the United States, still a global hyperpower, to be seen to be acting legitimately in its dealings abroad. Before discussing the ways the next president might restore at least some of the legitimacy that has been squandered, let me lay out some of my premises:

- Some anti-Americanism is incurable.
- Many Islamic militants who are prepared to take their own lives cannot be deterred or bargained with; they will have to be incapacitated in order to be prevented from causing large-scale loss of life.
- Positive attitudes toward the United States will, in the long term, strengthen the U.S. ability to diminish the local support and sanctuary for terrorists that is the sine qua non of their global reach.
- The very virulence of anti-Americanism reflects a disappointment in the United States and a residual appreciation for U.S. values. While China today offers internationalist mercantilist leadership, more is expected of the United States.
- The only thing more damaging for U.S. standing than foreign policy choices that are overtly indifferent to foreign life and welfare are those that are overtly indifferent *and* accompanied by rhetoric about American virtues and values.
- "Neutral" U.S. ties with other states are rarely feasible. U.S. bilateral ties will be interpreted as supporting or undermining a regime.
- In a globalized world in which inconsistencies among policies are given such prominent media exposure, it is increasingly difficult to take an a la carte approach to law and morality in our dealings with foreign nations. Even if full consistency in our foreign dealings is not achievable, we must minimize gross and systematic inconsistencies.
- What domestic constituents need and expect from the next president overlaps only partially with what global audiences will demand. This tension must be overcome, as both audiences matter to America's twenty-first-century security.
- A vibrant, self-critical, self-correcting democracy at home will do more to increase the success of U.S. diplomacy abroad than any rhetorical democracy-promotion strategy overseas.
- American deeds matter more than American words.

In order to recoup U.S. legitimacy, the next president will have to do something that presidents do not like to do. He or she will have to break with President Bush's policies dramatically. The next president will not simply be able to stand before the global public and announce, "I am not George Bush. Please like and trust America again, and please support us in our effort to combat the sources and effects of terrorism." He or she will have to undo many of the policies that contribute to the perception of the United States as a rogue nation *and* speak out publicly against the past harms inflicted and the past blunders made in America's name. Ending U.S. deviance from accepted international legal standards and public reckoning with past harms will meet significant domestic opposition and require courageous presidential leadership.

A Responsible Withdrawal from Iraq

Restoring U.S. legitimacy will entail not simply withdrawing from Iraq but withdrawing responsibly from Iraq. Some argue that an immediate withdrawal from Iraq is the only route to restoring U.S. legitimacy. But although I agree that withdrawal is necessary, one must acknowledge that, even in the broader Middle East, there is a deep ambivalence about a U.S. pullout. Four million Iraqis have been displaced by the violence there, two million of whom have fled into neighboring countries, destabilizing already fragile social, political, and sectarian balancing acts in Lebanon, Jordan, and Syria. If wholesale population movements or sectarian massacres followed a precipitous U.S. withdrawal, the damage would likely be felt for years to come. The Arab media's sustained coverage of events in Iraq means that, even absent further population flows in the region, the violence in Iraq will continue to be covered and blamed on the original U.S. invasion, suggesting that Washington will pay a price for bloodshed in Iraq long after its forces have departed.

As is true of every matter related to Iraq, there are no good options when it comes to withdrawal, but it is essential that U.S. decision makers make Iraqi welfare a centerpiece of any drawdown or withdrawal plan. Thus far, debates about Iraq have broken down into dismissals of bloodbath warnings by those who are pressing for withdrawal and bloodbath sirens by proponents of remaining in Iraq, unaccompanied by any account of how sectarian violence can be minimized—or sectarian healing brought about—by U.S. military forces. Offering and facilitating voluntary ethnic relocation must predate any U.S. withdrawal, as genocidal forces may well take advantage of any vacuum left by departing U.S. troops. The United States must work with other UN member states to create a war crimes commission or appoint a special rapporteur who can begin to take survivor testimonies about particular militia leaders or state actors who are behind the atrocities. U.S. officials should also try to deter widespread violence by threatening to make use of a residual counterterrorism quick reaction force to stop large-scale massacres of civilians. But those who talk of an over-the-horizon force are ignoring the stark reality that domestic opposition will preclude U.S. forces from being sent back to Iraq after the bulk of them have finally managed to leave. Whatever harm done to U.S. standing and security by the U.S. invasion, the damage done by the U.S. abandonment of Iraq will also be considerable.

The United States must also shoulder a far greater share of the burden currently being borne by Iraq's neighbors in caring for the Iraqi refugees who have managed to escape the country. In 2006, whereas Syria admitted one million Iraqis and Jordan accepted 750,000, the United States, whose invasion precipitated the displacement of Iraqis, let in just 202. (Ironically, in 2000, three years before the U.S. invasion, the United States admitted 3,145 Iraqis.) In 2007, although public pressure caused the State Department to announce that 7,000 asylum slots would be made available for Iraqis, fewer than 1,000 of those slots were filled by September, a national embarrassment. Only sustained presidential leadership will expedite the homeland security screening of candidates for asylum.

Generally, since 9/11 the number of refugees resettled in the United States has plummeted.[3] Resettlement from—and educational exchanges with—the Islamic world have been scaled back. At a time when 2.5 million African Muslims have been purged from their homes in Darfur, the United States has admitted no more than 3,000 Sudanese each year. This is a marked contrast with the cold war era, during which the United States bent over backwards to accommodate refugees fleeing Communism. Even today, it is astounding to note that refugees from countries connected with U.S. cold war policies continue to receive preferential treatment. In fiscal year 2006 refugees from Cuba and the former Soviet Union accounted for a whopping 50 percent of the total refugees admitted to the United States. In 2006, the same year 202 Iraqis were admitted, more than 17,000 refugees were resettled from Cuba.

Returning to International Law

Enhancing legitimacy will require improving U.S. compliance with international law. For both substantive and symbolic reasons, the next president must close Guantanamo Bay prison. Some 405 prisoners have already been released. An additional 375 remain there (including the "high value detainees" against whom significant evidence has been amassed). Many of the detainees have been held for five years without charge and without any ability to challenge the legality of their detention. All should receive counsel and face prompt, fair proceedings, rather than enduring the legal black hole. Some of the suspects in detention—such as Khalid Sheik Muhammed, a confessed terrorist who has been tortured while in U.S. custody, and those who have not committed any hostile acts against the United States but who articulate a clear intention to do so—present difficult legal challenges, but they are challenges that can be mastered by fairer, more expeditious, and more transparent proceedings.

The mere act of closing the prison and moving the detainees who are suspected to have engaged in terrorist-related crimes to another facility covered by law or extraditing them to prisons in their countries of origin would send an important signal around the world. The fact that one of Defense Secretary Robert Gates's first initiatives when he took over at the Pentagon was to try to close Guantanamo is but one testament to the national security imperative involved in what has often been improperly characterized merely as a civil liberties issue.

In many respects, although Guantanamo has become the global symbol of U.S. extralegal detention practices, it is the tip of the iceberg. Moving detainees will not cause Washington to be seen internationally overnight as a lawmaker and law enforcer rather than a lawbreaker. In order for this to happen, it will have to restore habeas corpus, the most vital Constitutional protection against the arbitrary exercise of executive power. (In September 2007 Senate Republicans defeated an effort led by Senators Patrick Leahy [D-Vt.] and Arlen Specter [R-Pa.] to hold a vote on restoring habeas rights to detainees.[4]) If Congress has not done so, the next president must also strike the provision from the Military Commissions Act that allows the use of coerced testimony and evidence obtained through cruel, inhuman, and degrading treatment if obtained before January 2006 and found "reliable" by a military judge. Again, absent congressional action, the president must put in place checks to ensure that detainees are not convicted—and eventually executed—on the basis of unreliable evidence obtained through torture.

Further, the next president must prohibit extraordinary rendition, explicitly renounce torture, and abolish secret prisons. General David Petraeus recently said in a memo to all his troops in Iraq: "Adherence to our values distinguishes us from our enemy. This fight depends on securing the population, which must understand that we, not our enemies, occupy the moral high ground."[5] The new *U.S. Army/Marine Corps Counterinsurgency Field Manual* argues the same point succinctly: "If you lose the moral high ground, you lose the war."[6] The policy must be clear and unambiguous, so that every U.S. intelligence official and military officer knows what the rules are. This means doing away with the novel distinctions between "enhanced interrogation techniques" and torture. U.S. military, civilian, and intelligence operatives' compliance with law and exposure to accountability and transparency will in the long run curb terrorist recruitment (which intelligence estimates believe has been aided by U.S. deviance from established global norms) and improve the likelihood that Americans in foreign custody will receive humane treatment.

In addition to those policy changes and choices, the next president will have to disassociate the new administration from its predecessor.[7] This disassociation can take many forms. But to implement any of them, the next president will have to resolve the trade-off between dueling imperatives: the traditional domestic imperative to close ranks behind one's predecessor and the global imperative to signal a clear break from practices that should again be considered "un-American." To make this palatable to the U.S. public, the administration will have to frame accountability as inextricably linked to security. Only by winning back respect will the United States limit the appeal of terrorists' rallying cries and convince allies to share the burden of defusing threats that by definition cannot be met alone. Recent public opinion polls indicate that Americans across the political spectrum are troubled by the United States' loss of standing, because of their fear that anti-Americanism will eventually affect U.S. security negatively. In addition, a majority of Americans now believe that the decision to go to war in Iraq was a mistake. These views should make it easier—but not at all easy—for the next president to sell any one of a number of measures that would show that he or she recognizes that history cannot simply be erased by a change in leadership.

The president can begin by appointing a 9/11-style independent, bipartisan investigation commission on U.S. detention and interrogation practices, so as to establish (and be seen to establish) real accountability regarding judicial responsibility for the criminal acts and the precise location and treatment of prisoners who have simply vanished. Coupled with this must be actual courtroom accountability. So far, although the Abu Ghraib scandal has cost the United States decades of goodwill inside and outside Iraq, only four low-ranking enlisted service members have been sentenced to imprisonment of more than a year.[8] Former defense secretary James Schlesinger was the only civilian investigator of sufficient rank to look into the abuses at Abu Ghraib, and when he issued his report and was asked by a reporter whether Defense Secretary Donald Rumsfeld should be forced to resign, his response was: "His resignation would be a boon to all of America's enemies and, consequently, I think it would be a misfortune if it were to take place."[9]

Senator Dianne Feinstein and other members of the Democratic Congress have tried to use congressional control over purse strings to force the closing of Guantanamo. But it has generally been seen in Democratic Party circles as "bad politics" to speak out against torture in this country. Joe Klein reported in his book *Politics Lost* that political consultant Bob Shrum carried out focus groups in advance of the three presidential debates to determine whether presidential candidate John Kerry should mention the events at Abu Ghraib in the debates. When the answer came back negative, according to Klein, Kerry stayed mute.

The next president will have to do something that few American presidents have done in history—apologize for the sins of a predecessor. Although such radical gestures are rare in U.S. history, the next American president will not get away with what other presidents have done in the past, which is to wish recent history away and hope that each new leader gets a blank slate on which to write his or her own history.

Retiring the "Global War on Terror" Frame

As has been pointed out by countless others, the "global war on terror" frame has been unhelpful and counterproductive. As al Qaeda steadily ratcheted up its attacks on U.S. targets throughout the 1990s (the first World Trade Center attack, the attacks on U.S. embassies in Kenya and Tanzania in 1998, the strike on the USS *Cole* in 2000, etc.), the Clinton administration attempted to neutralize the threat by channeling suspects through criminal processes. On taking office, senior officials within the Bush administration, who brought a conservative and distinctly statist agenda to their foreign policy, did not make the destruction of al Qaeda a priority. The terrorist attacks on 9/11 constituted a jarring blow to the system. Unlike traditional criminal acts, they resembled acts of war in that they deliberately struck the primary symbols of American military, economic, and political dominance—the Pentagon, the two World Trade Center towers, and, but for the courage of the passengers on the plane that crashed over Pennsylvania, the White House. Thus the al Qaeda strikes were experienced as a sophisticated, novel act of war against the United States. In addition, the al Qaeda attacks left U.S. planners with the impression that the "old" rules, old habits, and old systems were insufficient to meet the new threat. Clinton's criminal approach was ridiculed. And on September 20, 2001, in an address to Congress, Bush declared: "Our war on terror begins with al Qaeda, but it does not end there. It will not end until every terrorist group of global reach has been found, stopped and defeated."[10]

The phrase and the frame understandably caught on. After all, the threat that lay ahead was in fact "global"—terrorist cells were then estimated to be operational in more than 50 countries, terrorists move across borders, and stopping terrorism requires the cooperation of countries across the globe. And the deeds carried out were, in fact, acts of "terror." But the next president must do away with the "global war on terror" frame for several reasons.

First, the phrase and frame carry concrete policy implications. This is not always the case with the familiarly American "war on" phrasing, which is usually more metaphorical than real. When the United States declares a "war on drugs" or a "war on crime," the concept can be criticized because any reference to war suggests that the initiative will have a beginning, a middle, and an end, which, in the case of drug trafficking and crime, is unrealistic. The "war on terror" carries the similar implication that, in Bush's words, a "complete victory" is not only possible but, in fact, necessary. This leaves the country on a war footing that fuels war hysteria. It also licenses the executive branch to remove itself from traditional legal frameworks, taking advantage of the illusion that the legal derogations and war footing will be finite (even as Bush's National Security Strategy preamble reminds us that it will be a "global enterprise of uncertain duration").

But whereas in other contexts the use of the word *war* is largely metaphorical (we do not send the 82nd Airborne into downtown Detroit to combat crime), in the terrorism context the use of the word *war* seems to constitute not simply a framing device but also a strategic belief that war (i.e., ground and air invasions of other countries) is the tool the United States should use to neutralize terrorist threats. In the immediate wake of the 9/11 attacks, war was necessary, as Afghanistan's Taliban leader Mullah Omar refused to turn over bin Laden and invited an attack that UN Secretary General Kofi Annan, the Security Council, and even the General Assembly characterized as legitimate under the UN Charter. But although a war in Afghanistan was seen by most as an appropriate response to al Qaeda's attack, the war metaphor created space for the Bush administration to use its surging political capital to smuggle its preexisting, statist, anti–Saddam Hussein war agenda to the fore.

Bush has asserted often that the war on terror is "not a figure of speech" but, rather, is the "inescapable calling of our generation." "War" (at least traditional combat) is at best one tool among many that the United States must summon to prevent large-scale terrorist attacks. At worst—and Iraq offers a look at the worst—war is a blunt cudgel that, owing to the nature of the enemy, the slim U.S. appetite for casualties, and the likelihood of excesses by our own forces, can often do more to fuel or compound the threat than it does to neutralize it. U.S. intelligence officials and military commanders are on the record as believing that the operations used to kill or capture a single terrorist have often resulted in the creation of several new terrorists in his place.

Second, by branding the cause a "war" and the enemy "terror," one removes the opponent from the ranks of the criminal (which carries a stigma in all societies) to those of soldiers of war (who carry connotations of sacrifice and courage), enhancing the terrorist's cachet and political nobility, accentuating the image of self-sacrificing Davids taking up slingshots against rich and militarized Goliaths.

More significantly, lumping those hostile to the United States under a single banner of "terror" (grouping them by their means rather than their ends) unites unlike forces instead of dividing them, whereas a long-term strategy for reducing terrorism will entail employing divide-and-conquer tactics. We are making the mistake that John Foster Dulles made during the cold war when he deemed "Communism" a greater threat than the Soviet Union.[11] But then, eventually, the United States had the common sense to take advantage of the fissures among Communist countries. After initially lumping all "red menaces" together, it pried them apart, culminating in Nixon's opening to China.

British Secretary of State for International Development Hilary Benn put it best on April 16, 2007, when he said:

> In the UK, we do not use the phrase "war on terror" because we can't win by military means alone, and because this isn't us against one organized enemy with a clear identity and a coherent set of objectives.
>
> It is the vast majority of the people in the world—of all nationalities and faiths—against a small number of loose, shifting and disparate groups who have relatively little in common apart from their identification with others who share their distorted view of the world and their idea of being part of something bigger.
>
> What these groups want is to force their individual and narrow values on others, without dialogue, without debate, through violence. And by letting them feel part of something bigger, we give them strength.[12]

Improving U.S. Performance

Improving Intelligence and Disaggregating Threats

Neither the "Islamic world" nor "the West" is a monolithic bloc, as the virulent infighting within countries and communities reminds us. But many in the West are united by their fear and suspicion of the Islamic world, just as many Muslims share a deep suspicion of the United States specifically and of Western, capitalist, secular democracies more generally. In lieu of hyping a "clash of civilizations," U.S. policy makers must become knowledgeable about those societies in which such deep mistrust is being brewed. Not all grievances can or should be addressed, but it is essential that they be understood and that the diversity of faiths, commitments, and sensibilities be probed.

The next administration must vastly expand U.S. intelligence-gathering capabilities in the Islamic world, and it must differentiate among the multiple strands of Islam, of tribal groupings, and of inner- and intersectarian tension. If it stands any chance of taking advantage of the divisions among state and nonstate actors, it has to understand them. It must cease the practice of lumping together Hezbollah, which launches attacks inside Lebanon and is a Shiite Islamic movement; Hamas, which launches attacks inside Israel, is a Sunni Islamic movement, and has gained strength partly as a result of social service provision and anticorruption rhetoric; and al Qaeda, which strikes across the globe and has no identifiable social or political agenda of its own. The United States has thus far undertaken too many policies that have had the effect of uniting disparate forces. Just as the Israeli air strikes on Beirut in the summer of 2006 briefly united Sunni and Shia in the Middle East, so too the American war in Iraq, the refusal to negotiate at a high level with anybody branded "evil," and the seeming obliviousness to the distinctions among the ever-proliferating and splintering strands of jihadism has proven costly.[13]

It is not enough to refrain from policies that drive potential rivals together. The next administration must develop the organic capacity to step into "the enemy's" shoes. This requires making a multigenerational commitment to understanding Islam, to developing an entire cohort of Arabic-, Farsi-, and Urdu-speaking Americans, and to acquiring reliable human intelligence networks within hostile communities. Currently, as the foreword to the *U.S. Army/Marine Corps Counterinsurgency Field Manual* points out, more Americans serve in U.S. military marching bands than work in the U.S. foreign service.[14] Although the gigantic U.S. embassy in Iraq houses more than one thousand employees, no more than a dozen speak fluent Arabic.

Promoting Freedom from Fear and Want

The most effective way to enhance U.S. influence will be to undertake policies—bilaterally and within multilateral institutions—that bring benefits to citizens around the world. It is concrete performance more than democracy rhetoric that will win hearts and minds and enhance stability. The next president must work within international institutions to advance "human security"—physical and economic security, or what President Franklin Roosevelt once called freedom from fear and want. The United States has traditionally tended to speak out on behalf of "democracy" and freedom rather than on behalf of human security. This has translated into a regard for what some have called "electocracy." But creating the conditions in which people can cast ballots is not sufficient to maximize human dignity or strengthen a country's governing institutions, which are the best long-term guarantors of stability. Most people who vote in the developing world value the expression of their will, but they do so, crucially, as a way of putting in power people who have promised to rid their lives of corruption and violence and to bring them health care, education, and a full stomach.

The United States, which has more than doubled its foreign aid in the past five years, still ranks next to last among rich countries in the percentage of GDP it is willing to give away. As a leading member of a new "coalition of the concerned," the next president must commit the country to eliminating extreme poverty, narrowing the now grotesque inequality in the developing world, and ensuring that the poor have access to basic education and social services. Development work is less flashy than those scenes of Iraqis who waved their purple fingers, and the process can be exasperating because the scale of the challenge is so monumental, corruption so pervasive, and results inevitably incremental at best. It is unfortunate that it has taken the threat of terrorism to focus on the flaws in the international development regime. International organizations may not be able to supply reconstruction and development assistance or social services as nimbly as Hamas or Hezbollah, but the United States and international organizations can modernize their programs and make them more accountable and effective.

The international system has suffered from an egregious shortcoming since the end of the cold war. Despite sixteen years of complaints that postconflict or postautocratic societies lack policing and security enforcement capacity, and despite the recognition that trained, culturally ambidextrous police are almost impossible to mobilize in a timely fashion, instability has persisted and worsened because rogue elements have taken advantage of the recurrent policing vacuum. This is not a matter that the United States necessarily needs to take the lead in, but because it has a vested interest in seeing the gap filled, it should work with the two European countries, Italy and Germany, that have claimed responsibility for this issue. The United States should help garner prospective commitments, set up training missions, and mobilize a large and versatile cadre of police and police trainers.

Although they have become accustomed to bashing the United States in recent years, many rich countries have turned their backs on playing a prominent role themselves in securing the global commons. Most European governments are mute entirely when it comes to the carnage in Darfur or other civilian protection challenges. The Netherlands, Italy, and Canada are under substantial domestic pressure to withdraw their troops from Afghanistan. When it comes to UN peacekeeping around the world, Bangladesh currently deploys ten thousand more peacekeepers than does Denmark or even Canada, the country that prides itself on having invented UN peacekeeping. Regional heavyweights such as South Africa have not exerted meaningful leadership in shoring up failing states or in pressing for democratization on the African continent, which it considers its sphere of influence. In short, the muscle of responsibility in middle powers appears to have grown weak over the years for lack of use. European countries must be enlisted to exercise greater responsibility for maintaining international peace and security.

Strengthening U.S. Resiliency

Strengthening U.S. resiliency requires both reducing domestic liability in the event of a large-scale terrorist attack or natural disaster *and* thickening the domestic base for U.S. engagement abroad—a base that is withering as a result of recent overseas misadventures.

Mitigating the Consequences of Attacks or Disasters

The current approach to meeting twenty-first-century threats has been accompanied by rhetoric about "fighting them there so we don't have to fight them here." But it is inevitable that the United States will be targeted again at home. And despite the odds of this, adequate preparations have not been undertaken. It goes without saying that if a fraction of the resources poured into Iraq had been invested in homeland security preventive measures or, equally important, homeland security disaster response capacity, the United States would be a safer place. Despite placing the country on a "war footing," very few medical, public health, police, or other professionals are any more prepared today for a domestic strike than they were on September 10, 2001. The ongoing inadequate response to the Katrina disaster gave us a more recent preview of our incapacity to manage the economic and physical ramifications of the unexpected.

Taking on Special Interests That Can Undermine National Security

Washington is currently home to more than thirty-five thousand registered lobbying groups that spend more than $2 billion each per year.[15] These lobbies can skew foreign policy away from security needs. One familiar example: the $450 billion chemical industry has lobbied to keep the federal government from mandating security enhancements at the nation's chemical plants; thanks to the potent chemical lobby, the Environmental Protection Agency regulations are enforced by the industry itself.[16] The Chemical Security Act of 2001 sailed unanimously through the Senate Environment Committee but stalled on the Senate floor when seven of the senators who had originally supported it reversed their votes. In a letter to their colleagues, the senators (Inhofe, R-Okla.; Bond, R-Mo.; Specter, R-Pa.; Smith, R-N.H.; Voinovich, R-Ohio; Domenici, R-N.M.; Crapo, R-Idaho) wrote that they needed to "address concerns...that have arisen from scores of stakeholders upon thoughtful consideration of this legislation."[17] In an April 2003 interview on National Public Radio's *Morning Edition*, Al Martinez-Fonts, a top aide to Director of Homeland Security Tom Ridge, was asked: "Why do you think that it makes sense that the federal government told the airline industry, 'You've got to be safer, and here's how you're going to do it,' and why does it not make sense for the government to take that same role with, say, the chemical industry?" To this, Martinez-Fonts, who had just shortly before moved from JPMorgan Chase, replied: "Well, the answer is because September 11th happened, and they were airplanes that were rammed into buildings. I mean, it was not chemical plants that were blown up."[18]

Because the war in Iraq has consumed resources that might otherwise have been used to fortify infrastructure and improve training in the United States, it is worth looking at the role of special interests in American policy choices, where a correlation exists between campaign contributions and contracts awarded. In the first eighteen months after the Iraq invasion, the Center for Public Integrity conducted a review of war-related contracts.[19] Table 6.1 is a selection of the largest contracts and most notorious corporations.

In his "four freedoms" address, Franklin D. Roosevelt put it best: "We must especially beware of that small group of selfish men who would clip the wings of the American eagle in order to feather their own nests."[20] Yet despite the societywide awareness of this phenomenon and the growing evidence of its negative security ramifications, a candidate who will likely have spent as

TABLE 6.1   Contracts in Iraq and U.S. Campaign Contributions

Rank (total contract value)	Corporation	Total contract value (billions)	Rank (total campaign contributions among all contractors)	Total campaign contributions (billions)
1	Kellogg, Brown & Root	$11.43	7	$2.38
2	Parsons Corp.	$5.29	10	$1.40
3	Fluor Corp.	$3.75	5	$3.62
4	Washington Group, Intl.	$3.13	13	$1.18
5	Bechtel	$2.83	6	$3.31

much as $500 million winning the presidency will find it difficult to challenge the pernicious influence of money in politics. Yet it is essential that the president help build a bipartisan coalition in an effort to bring about meaningful campaign finance reform.

Thickening the Domestic Base for Foreign Policy

Domestic and foreign policy conversations tend to happen separately, but the stovepiping is not sustainable in the twenty-first century. In the same way the war in Iraq has reduced the resources available for education and health care spending in this country, so, too, an alienated public will undermine the ability of U.S. foreign policy makers to achieve their aims. Gone are the days when gray-haired statesmen could simply make decisions and then inform the American people of policies that they had already put in motion.

Each of the central foreign policy and human rights challenges—helping shore up failing states, increasing rule of law assistance, embedding the United States in international frameworks (and retrieving international standing), minimizing the harmful impact of special interests, reducing U.S. energy dependence, transforming our ties with abusive regimes in the Middle East, and curbing global warming—will require the support of large segments of the American people. Such tasks will impose costs on taxpayers, require us to surrender sovereignty, necessitate difficult conversations with the American farmer, and mandate changes in our driving habits.

Making America safer will not require just the support of the American people. It will necessitate American sacrifice. In a January 2007 interview with Jim Lehrer, President Bush was asked why he had not asked more Americans to "sacrifice something," and he said, "Well, you know, I think a lot of people are in this fight. I mean, they sacrifice peace of mind when they see the terrible images of violence on TV every night."[21] Almost all of us are living our lives as we did before September 11, 2001. The dollar does not go as far, and we are inconvenienced at airports. But *we* can hardly be said to be at war.

Building a base for a different kind of foreign policy will require building a base for foreign policy as a whole. Today only 27 percent of Americans carry passports.[22] A November 2005 Pew poll found that 42 percent of Americans believe that the United States "should mind its own business internationally." A 2006 survey from the Chicago Council on Global Affairs found that only 10 percent of Americans agree that "as the sole remaining superpower the United States should continue to be the preeminent leader in solving world problems." More than one million U.S. soldiers have spent time in Iraq; many are already on their third or fourth tours. But because of the end of the draft, as David Kennedy argues in his chapter, only a narrow segment of society is carrying a disproportionate share of the national security burden. This matters not merely because it is morally wrong to make one class of people pay the price for our elected officials' bad judgments. It also matters because it allows most Americans to feel immune from the consequences of American foreign policy.

One veteran of the U.S. war in Iraq recently described his unit's being so distraught over the vulnerability of their Humvees that they commissioned Iraqis to weld large slabs of iron onto the Humvee doors as an ad hoc solution.[23] But the greater weight on the doors caused the hinges to break, and the unit ended up patrolling in Humvees that had no doors at all. In a recent op-ed the veteran asked, "if American shipyards were able to cut the time for completing cargo ships from one year to one day during World War II, how is it possible that our factories, had they worked round the clock, could not have produced the armored Humvees we needed?" Leaving the American people behind, he argued, "is akin to a football coach keeping his offensive line on the bench. No matter how gifted his quarterback, no matter how talented his running backs and receivers, his team will have no chance to win."[24]

After the attack on Pearl Harbor the American people accepted higher taxes and gasoline rationing. Car manufacturers worked round the clock to produce the planes, tanks, and trucks needed for soldiers. Textile mills ran double shifts to fill orders for uniforms. Local communities organized aluminum scrap and rubber drives to save vital raw materials. More than 15 million men and women (out of a population of 135 million) served in the military, and three-quarters of them went overseas. The next generation of Americans must spend time in countries in which U.S. decision making is leaving its stamp. Government, businesses, educational institutions, law firms, hospitals, and the like should team up to sponsor and organize educational exchange programs, international volunteering initiatives, and short-term midcareer secondments to aid development and reconstruction abroad. This is a crucial prerequisite to gaining domestic political buy-in—and to spurring domestic political accountability.

When Harry S Truman introduced the Marshall Plan to Congress, he did not simply assume that Americans would understand that human security and national security were linked. Indeed, he knew that the Republican-controlled Congress was skeptical about throwing money into what members called a European "sinkhole." The European powers, opponents of the Marshall Plan argued, were incapable of remaining at peace. But Truman launched a sophisticated sales campaign, and he drew on the grassroots efforts of ex-Undersecretary of State Dean Acheson. He established a "Committee for the Marshall Plan," which sent chief executive officers, academics, labor organizers, civic leaders, and clergymen to champion the plan across the country.[25]

As the public mood shifted, Congress decided to authorize the $13 billion program that gave grants and loans to seventeen countries. A comparable effort is going to be required if public support is going to be garnered for the measures proposed herein. And because of the disenchantment with George W. Bush's foreign policy, it will be more challenging to mobilize this base.

Conclusion

Criticizing the calamities of the past seven years of American foreign policy has become too easy. And such criticisms do not themselves improve our approach to combating terrorist threats that do in fact loom large—larger, in fact, because of Bush's mistakes. The challenge now is to accept the fact that although George W. Bush hyped the threat, it does not mean that dangers do not exist. Rather, we must urgently set about reversing the harm done to the nation's standing and security by enhancing U.S. legitimacy; by highlighting the moral difference between the United States and Islamic terrorists; by improving U.S. intelligence; by working with international institutions to deliver tangible human security dividends; and by ensuring that the United States can withstand attacks at home and garner the domestic support it needs for long-term efforts to meet transnational threats.

Notes

1. According to the Center for Arms Control and Non-Proliferation, China's military expenditures grew from $62.5 billion in 2004 to $122 billion in 2006; for a defense of China's increase in military budget, see Xu Guangyu, "What's Behind Increase in the Military Budget," *China Daily* (March 15, 2007), http://www.chinadaily.com.cn/china/2007–03/15/content_828342.htm. The authoritative *Military Balance*, published annually by the International Institute for Strategic Studies in London, estimates that China's military spending has increased nearly 300 percent in the past decade, from 1.08 percent of its GDP in 1995 to 1.55 percent in 2005; see Stephen Fidler, "Beijing Spends More on Defense than It Claims," *Financial Times*, May 25, 2006. By contrast, the United States spends 3.9 percent of its GDP on defense, and the U.S. economy is more than five times as large as China's. The U.S. military budget will officially grow by nearly 24 percent (or $100 billion), from $522 billion in fiscal year 2007 to $622 billion in fiscal year 2008. The U.S. figures from the Center for Arms Control and Non-Proliferation include the Department of Defense budget plus supplementals for Iraq and Afghanistan. See Travis Sharp, "The Bucks Never Stop: Iraq and Afghanistan War Costs Continue to Soar," Center for Arms Control and Non-Proliferation, Military Budget and Oversight

Program (August 2007), http://www.armscontrolcenter.org/assets/pdfs/bucks_never_stop.pdf; see also Michael Elliot, "China Takes on the World," *Time* (January 11, 2007): 34.

2. The leaked National Intelligence Estimate, "Trends in Global Terrorism: Implications for the United States," completed in April 2006, was the first official appraisal of global terrorism since the Iraq war began, and it represented the consensus view of the sixteen disparate U.S. intelligence services. As the *New York Times* put it: "An opening section of the report, 'Indicators of the Spread of the Global Jihadist Movement,' cites the Iraq war as a reason for the diffusion of jihad ideology.... The estimate concludes that the radical Islamic movement has expanded from a core of al Qaeda operatives and affiliated groups to include a new class of 'self-generating' cells inspired by al Qaeda's leadership but without any direct connection to Osama bin Laden or his top lieutenants. It also examines how the Internet has helped spread jihadist ideology, and how cyberspace has become a haven for terrorist operatives who no longer have geographical refuges in countries like Afghanistan." See Mark Mazzetti, "Spy Agencies Say Iraq War Worsens Terrorism Threat," *New York Times*, September 24, 2006.

3. A staggering 207,000 refugees were admitted in 1980, as Washington agreed to shoulder part of the burden of the Vietnamese boat people. In 1999, that figure totaled around 85,000, whereas—thanks in large measure to the 2001 Patriot Act's expansion of the definition of terrorist, the 2005 REAL ID Act's expansion of the definition of "nondesignated" terrorist organization, and the broad prohibition on "material support," which has barred such people as persecuted ethnic Karen fighters in Burma and physicians in Colombia and Nepal forced to provide medical care to the terrorist groups—the number of refugees admitted in 2006 fell to 32,000. Nobody can be admitted who has committed "an act that the actor knows, or reasonably should know, affords material support" to anybody who plans a terrorist act. The material-support restriction summarily excludes persons who are armed abroad with no regard for the cause for which they armed and excludes persons (e.g., physicians and nurses) who have helped those persons who have been armed. The laws have resulted in such exclusions that Ellen Sauerbrey, assistant secretary of the Bureau of Population, Refugees, and Migration, noted last year: "We now estimate that, as a result of this issue, we will fall short by some 12,000 of 54,000 admissions for which we were funded. Many are now being disqualified because of their resistance activities to oppressive governments or because they have been coerced to provide 'material support' to their persecutors. In order to preserve our country's well-deserved reputation for fairness and generosity, we will continue to address this issue at the highest levels of government until we arrive at a just resolution." See Ellen Sauerbrey, "The U.S. Commitment to Refugee Protection and Assistance; Humanitarian and Strategic Imperative," remarks to Heritage Foundation (June 20, 2006), http://www.state.gov/g/prm/rls/2006/68116.htm.

4. On September 20, 2007, the Leahy-Specter amendment to restore habeas corpus was defeated by a vote of 56 to 43. See the Congressional Record at http://thomas.loc.gov/cgi-bin/bdquery/z?d110:SP2022:.

5. David H. Petraeus, "Commanding General David H. Petraeus' Letter about Values" (May 10, 2007), http://www.globalsecurity.org/military/library/policy/army/other/petraeus_values-msg_torture070510.htm.

6. John A. Nagl, David H. Petraeus, and Sarah Sewell, *The U.S. Army/Marine Corps Counterinsurgency Field Manual* (Chicago: University of Chicago Press, 2007).

7. The rare exception was the congressionally driven apology President George H. W. Bush gave in 1990 to the descendants of Japanese Americans who had been imprisoned by President Franklin D. Roosevelt. The apology came about after a long struggle. Over twenty days in 1981, the congressionally established Commission on Wartime Relocation and Internment of Civilians reviewed Roosevelt's infamous Executive Order 9066, calling more than 750 witnesses (the interned, government officials, historians, etc.) to examine the circumstances giving rise to the order, as well as the impact of the implementation of it. On the commission's recommendation, HR 442 was finally signed into law, providing for individual payments of $20,000 to each surviving internee and a $1.25 billion education fund. The first nine payments were made in Washington, D.C., on October 9, 1990. Accompanying the payments that went to some sixty thousand survivors of those interned was a letter of apology from President George H. W. Bush: "A monetary sum and words alone cannot restore lost years or erase painful memories; neither can they fully convey our Nation's resolve to rectify injustice and to uphold the rights of individuals. We can never fully right the wrongs of the past. But we can take a clear stand for justice and recognize that serious injustices were done to Japanese Americans during World War II. In enacting a law calling for restitution and offering a sincere apology, your fellow Americans have, in a very real sense, renewed their traditional commitment to the ideals of freedom, equality, and justice. You and your family have our best wishes for the future." However, whereas the Japanese Americans were U.S. citizens or legal residents, all but a few of the detainees apprehended around the world in counterterrorism or counterinsurgency operations are not.

8. Incredibly, the U.S. military was going to send Sgt. Santos Cardona, an Abu Ghraib dog handler convicted of dereliction of duty and aggravated assault, back to Iraq in November 2006. Cardona was fined, given a reduction in rank, and sentenced to ninety days' hard labor in May 2006. Public outrage and media coverage drew unfavorable attention to the reassignment, and the Pentagon then announced Cardona's redeployment to Iraq was being "evaluated." See Adam Zagorin, "An Abu Ghraib Offender's Return to Iraq Is Stopped," *Time* (November 2, 2006), http://www.time.com/time/world/article/0,8599,1554326,00.html.

9. "Report: Abu Ghraib Was 'Animal House' at Night," CNN.com (August 25, 2004), http://www.cnn.com/2004/US/08/24/abughraib.report/index.html. Asked again in December, Schlesinger reiterated his opposition to Rumsfeld's

resignation, saying, "They would rejoice in the caves in which al-Qaida leaders hide; that our enemies in the Middle East would rejoice. He has become a symbol of American steadfastness, and I think that that would be tragedy if he were to be removed." See "Under Fire," *PBS NewsHour* (December 20, 2004), http://www.pbs.org/newshour/bb/white_house/july-dec04/rumsfeld_12-20.html.

10. President George W. Bush, "Address to a Joint Session of Congress and the American People" (September 20, 2001).

11. See Ian Shapiro, *Containment: Rebuilding a Strategy for Global Terror* (Princeton, NJ: Princeton University Press, 2007).

12. "Where Does Development Fit in Foreign Policy?" Speech by Secretary of State Hilary Benn, New York (April 16, 2007), http://www.dfid.gov.uk/news/files/Speeches/foreign-policy-april07.asp.

13. The Israeli strikes brought about a unity rarely seen within Islam. In Cairo, for instance, the *New York Times* reported crowds pouring out of a Sunni mosque in Cairo, carrying posters of Sheik Nasrallah and chanting, "Oh, Sunni! Oh, Shiite! Let's fight the Jews.... The Jews and the Americans are killing our brothers in Lebanon." John Kifner, "Israel Is Powerful, Yes. But Not So Invincible," *New York Times*, July 30, 2006.

14. Nagl, Petraeus, and Sewell, *U.S. Army/Marine Corps Counterinsurgency Field Manual*.

15. Tim Hartford, "There's Not Enough Money in Politics," Slate.com, April 1, 2006.

16. Some fifteen thousand facilities in the United States produce, use, or store "more than threshold" amounts of one or more of 140 toxic or flammable chemicals which the federal government has identified as posing the greatest risk to human health if released into the air. Of these chemical facilities, 123 around the nation have toxic "worst case" scenarios in which more than a million people in the surrounding area could be at risk of exposure to a cloud of toxic gas if a release occurred. General Accounting Office, *Homeland Security: Voluntary Initiatives Are Under Way at Chemical Facilities, but the Extent of Security Preparedness Is Unknown* (March 2003): 1.

17. "Dear Colleague" letter entitled "The Chemical Security Act Misses the Mark" signed by Senators James Inhofe (R-Okla.), "Kit" Bond (R-Mo.), Arlen Specter (R-Pa.), Bob Smith (R-N.H.), George Voinovich (R-Ohio), Pete Domenici (R-N.M.), and Mike Crapo (R-Idaho) (September 10, 2002), quoted in Niaz Dorry and Nityanand Jayaraman, "Chemical Industry vs. Public Interest: Redefining the Public Debate on Chemical Security," The No More Bhopals Alliance (June 2004), http://www.come-clean.org/pdfs/security.pdf. The U.S. Senate passed the Homeland Security Department Act on November 19, 2002, but did not include any chemical industry security provision. On January 14, 2003, Senator Jon Corzine (D-N.J.) tried to reintroduce his chemical security bill (there was a companion bill in the House), but the bills were not included in the final version of the comprehensive Homeland Security Act. In April 2007 the Bush administration announced new security requirements for the

country's high-risk chemical plants, but the federal rules did not set a timetable for changes or require specific measures. They also left it up to homeland security officials to decide which plants qualified as high risk. Senate Democrats complained that the administration was attempting to undercut state laws that were tougher on the chemical industry.

18. "Profile: Lobbying by Chemical Industry Groups against the Corzine Chemical Security Bill," *NPR Morning Edition*, April 15, 2003.

19. The full list of contractors ranked by contract value compiled by the Center for Public Integrity can be viewed at http://www.publicintegrity.org/wow/resources.aspx?act=total; the full list of contractors ranked by campaign contributions can be viewed at http://www.publicintegrity.org/wow/resources.aspx?act=contrib.

20. Franklin Delano Roosevelt, "Franklin Roosevelt's Annual Address to Congress" (January 6, 1941), http://millercenter.virginia.edu/scripps/digitalarchive/speeches/spe_1941_0106_roosevelt.

21. George W. Bush, interview on *NewsHour* (January 16, 2007), http://www.pbs.org/newshour/bb/white_house/jan-june07/bush_01–16.html.

22. Jane L. Levere, "Scrambling to Get Hold of a U.S. Passport," *New York Times*, January 23, 2007.

23. See Joseph Kearns Goodwin, "Unmobilized for War," *Boston Globe*, April 6, 2007.

24. Quoted in ibid.

25. See Greg Behrman, *The Most Noble Adventure: The Marshall Plan and the Time When America Helped Save Europe* (New York: Free Press, 2007).

SEVEN

Two Concepts of Sovereignty
David M. Kennedy

ERRORISM IS NEITHER the least nor the greatest of the threats facing the United States. Containing the terrorist virus and the rogue and failed states that incubate it is surely an urgent task. But it is far more important that America itself cease acting like a rogue state, one that repeatedly disrupts the fabric of international society, sometimes cavalierly, sometimes violently—and does so in large measure because a kind of Caesarism has infected the American body politic, rendering its leaders ever more enamored of military solutions and ever less accountable to the will of the American people.

The most important tasks for American foreign policy today are two: to rebuild the nation's role and reputation as a lawful and legitimate leader in the global community and to restore the American people's ownership of the purpose, efficacy, and justice of their country's continuing international engagement.

Much is at stake here. From its founding, the United States aspired both to revolutionize the international order and to be a beacon of democracy—the fabled "city on the hill" that has inspired Americans from John Winthrop to Ronald Reagan. It took nearly two centuries for the nation to muster the means to begin transforming the international system, and Americans are still struggling to sustain a democracy worthy of their own highest ideals—not least with respect to the conduct of foreign policy. But should the world lose what is left of its confidence in American leadership, and should a disillusioned American public retreat to a sour and wary isolationism, not only will the war against terror fail but so also will the entire edifice of the international order that the Founders dreamed of and that three generations of Americans have labored since World War II to make a reality.

To those tasks, abroad and at home alike, a restored respect for the principle of sovereignty is essential. Recent American behavior has grotesquely distorted the nation's historic legacy with respect to sovereignty in the international arena, even while threatening to betray the very principles of representative government, rooted in the sovereignty of the people, which have long defined American nationhood.

All discussion of the international dimension of sovereignty begins with the Peace of Westphalia, signed at Münster in 1648. Reflecting its origins in the wars of the Reformation that the Westphalian peace concluded, its essential logic was captured in the famous dictum, *cuius regio, eius religio* ("whose rule, his religion"). The confessional—and, by easy extension, the political—character of a state was henceforward to be regarded as a matter of exclusively internal concern. Only states that themselves breached the Westphalian rules were rightfully liable to sanctions and reprisal.

The diplomatists at Münster defined the norms that guided international behavior for centuries thereafter. Their work can be summarized as a form of syllogism: all states have the right to self-determination; all states are equal; therefore, no state has the right to intervene unbidden in the affairs of another.

When Britain's North American colonies struck for their independence in 1776 they at once invoked Westphalian principles and bid them defiance. The Declaration of Independence pronounced the Americans to be "one people" with the consequent right to self-determination. It announced their "separate and equal station" among the powers of the earth. On those familiar Westphalian grounds it justified their determination to throw off the British yoke and "dissolve the political bonds which have connected them with another." Yet in the very act of declaring their independence, the American revolutionaries also radically qualified the meaning of "self-determination" when they advanced the claim that only certain kinds of sovereign power could be regarded as fully legitimate.

Thomas Paine's *Common Sense* is conventionally credited with convincing the American colonists that their true cause was independence, rather than reconciliation with Britain—not least because without independence they could not hope for foreign assistance. Paine could thus be said to have drafted the foundational document of American foreign policy, a document that also, and not incidentally, championed the broader principles of anticolonialism, antimercantilism, and free trade.

But it is well to remember that *Common Sense* begins with a treatise on the nature of government, proceeds to an assault on the "Royal Brute of Britain" as a way of discrediting all monarchies, and eloquently anticipates Thomas Jefferson's declaration that the only lawful states are those that derive "their just powers from the consent of the governed."

Thus at its birth the United States did not just champion the core tenets of what would come to be known as the Manchesterian agenda for economic liberalism. It also infused its diplomacy with a radical political ideology that looked to the creation of a *novus ordo secolorum* in the international sphere, as well as in the domestic. From the outset, that potent compound constituted an integral component of America's national identity. As Robert Kagan has recently written, "American foreign policy, as a result, would...have a revolutionary quality."[1]

The United States has ever after pursued foreign policies that in some measure pay respect to those principles. But the true genius of American diplomacy has consisted in its capacity to balance its transformative dreams with countervailing considerations of capacity, cost, and feasibility—and with judicious regard for Westphalian definitions of sovereignty. When American diplomacy has been most effective is when it has tempered ideology with interest, aspiration with practicality, and universalistic yearnings with frank acknowledgment of nationalist particularities. That kind of realistic moderation, not bravura utopian posturing or uncritical ideological literalism, is urgently needed now.

Soon after America achieved its independence, Edmund Burke pointed out the menace of unbridled ideology in the foreign policies of the French revolutionaries. "We are in a war of a peculiar nature," Burke wrote of Britain's confrontation with France in 1796. "We are at war with a system, which, by its essence, is inimical to all other Governments....It is with an armed doctrine, that we are at war," one that Burke correctly understood was inherently subversive of the extant international order, precisely because it ruptured the Westphalian distinction between a state's internal complexion and its international standing. With the perpetrators of this "violent breach of the community of Europe," Burke concluded, there could be no negotiation nor diplomacy, no truck nor commerce, but only armed confrontation with whatever means available.[2]

The Americans were then still an upstart people, struggling to establish their authority over a remote part of the western Atlantic littoral. But in the fullness of time, when its influence would reach to the farthest corners of the planet, how would the United States pursue its transformative agenda? Would it galvanize the animosity of the globe by becoming the vehicle of an implacable "armed doctrine" of the sort that Burke denounced? Would it rely on sword and swagger or pen and persuasion to achieve its goals?

Throughout the nineteenth century, the United States remained a peripheral, isolated country preoccupied with subduing vast tracts of the North American continent and little engaged elsewhere. In the Old World chanceries where the great game of geopolitics was played, the United States simply did not matter. As late as 1890, the U.S. Army ranked fourteenth in size, after Bulgaria's. All but uniquely among modern industrialized societies, America's foreign trade accounted for barely 10 percent of gross national product at century's end, and even that decidedly modest share was trending downward. Not until 1893 did Congress adopt standard diplomatic practice and authorize the rank of ambassador for American representatives to foreign governments. In 1900 the Department of State in Washington counted a mere ninety-one employees. These were not the attributes of a great or even a middling power. America's ability to transform the received international order still hovered uncertainly beyond the horizon of some indefinite tomorrow.[3]

But as the dawn of the twentieth century approached, the United States was no longer so easy to ignore. It had grown to be the second most populous country in the Western world, save only Russia. It boasted the world's largest rail network. It was the leading producer of wheat, coal, iron, steel, and electricity. It annually posted robust surpluses on its international trade account and would soon command the world's largest pool of investment capital. It launched a modern steel navy surpassed in battle-line strength only by Germany's and Britain's. The Spanish-American War in 1898 and the subsequent annexation of Puerto Rico and the Philippine Islands dramatically announced that the United States had acquired the capacity to project its power well beyond North America.

Yet, though the fact that the Americans now wielded immense *potential* strength to work their will in the world was evident, when, if ever, and how, if at all, would that potential be realized? And what, exactly, did they will? Those questions excited intense discussion in the twentieth century's opening decades, a discussion with resonant echoes in our own time.

Anti-imperialists such as Mark Twain advocated a return to traditional isolationism. Realpolitikers such as Theodore Roosevelt urged the country to shed the isolationist illusions nurtured by the peculiarities of its historical development and start behaving like a conventional great power, with gusto and without apology. But Woodrow Wilson, whose ideas would eventually triumph, believed that those same peculiarities had fashioned for Americans a lever with which they could move the world.

"What are we going to do with the influence and power of this great nation?" Wilson asked in a Fourth of July address at Philadelphia's Independence Hall in 1914. "Are we going to play the old role of using that power for our aggrandizement and material benefit only?"[4]

Just six days earlier, in distant Sarajevo, two rounds from a Serbian nationalist's pistol had heralded the outbreak of the Great War, a bloody global upheaval that provided Wilson with a grand opportunity to answer his own pregnant queries. He did not so much invent the diplomatic principles that came to be known as "Wilsonianism" as discover them—in the legacy of the Revolutionary era. The aspirations of the Founders illuminated the entirety of Wilson's diplomatic program. His proposals, he said, constituted "no breach in either our traditions or our policy, but a fulfillment, rather, of all that we have professed or striven for." On presenting the Treaty of Versailles to the Senate in 1919, he declared: "It is of this that we dreamed at our birth." And like the American founders, Wilson understood the difference between ideological aspiration and concrete historical possibilities. Like them, he carefully fitted his ideas to the circumstances he confronted. In the process he articulated the major principles that would come to guide American foreign policy in the last half of the twentieth century—the season of its greatest triumph.[5]

Perhaps the most famous distillation of Wilson's thinking is to be found in his War Address of April 2, 1917, when he said that "the world must be made safe for democracy."[6] Ever after, that maxim and the entire Wilsonian scheme it is thought to represent have been derided as hopelessly idealistic and impractical. The famed historian and diplomat George F. Kennan excoriated Wilson for "the colossal conceit of thinking that you could suddenly make international life over into what you believed to be your own image."[7]

That is a formidable criticism, but it is misdirected at Wilson, and at the Founders, too. Properly understood, Wilson's simple declarative sentence—"The world must be made safe for democracy"—deserves to be recognized as an invaluable lodestar for the guidance of American foreign policy today. And Wilson, though often and unfairly maligned, deserves to be celebrated as the intellectual godfather of America's most successful foreign policies.

Wilson recognized more clearly than many of his contemporaries the cardinal facts of the modern era: that the world now bristled with dangers that no single state could hope to contain on its own, even as it shimmered with prospects that could be seized only by states acting together. And although the United States might be secure for the moment in its own domains and in its political institutions, it had acquired global interests and liabilities. It inhabited a world of qualitatively different opportunities and threats from anything the Founders could have imagined—opportunities generated by the gathering momentum of the Industrial Revolution and the spread of liberal ideas, threats incubated by emerging technologies of wholesale destruction and the ravening appetites of newly powerful nation-states in Asia, as well as Europe.

Making such a world safe for democracy required more than rhetorical grandstanding, more than the comforting counsels of isolation—and more than taking the inherited international order as given and conducting the business of great-power diplomacy as usual. It required, rather, active engagement with other states in ongoing efforts to muzzle the dogs of war, suppress weapons of mass destruction, and raise both standards of living and international interdependence through economic liberalization. Most urgently, it required the creation of new institutions that would import into the international arena at least a modicum of the rule of law that obtained in well-ordered national polities.

Wilson elaborated on his views in the famed Fourteen Points Address of January 8, 1918. At its heart lay three simple propositions. The first two, advocating self-determination and free trade, would have been easily recognizable to Paine and Jefferson, not to mention Adam Smith, David Ricardo, and Wilson's heroes, Richard Cobden and John Bright. But the third, proposing the creation of a League of Nations, appeared to be something altogether new. Yet for all the League's seeming novelty, Wilson's own conception of its highest purposes honored a traditional Westphalian objective: "affording mutual guarantees of political independence and territorial integrity to great and small states alike."[8] To be sure, Wilson proposed to secure that conventional end by innovative means: the creation of a permanent international forum with many of the features of a global legislature. But the challenge that the League posed to received Westphalian principles has frequently been exaggerated. The League is best understood not as a revolutionary challenge to the inherited international order but as an evolutionary adaptation of venerable principles to modern circumstances. Respect for sovereignty was of its essence. It aimed above all to protect the territorial and political integrity of individual states. Only states could be members. All action required unanimous consent by the member states of the League Council. Lacking an armed force of its own, the League depended entirely on its member states, especially the great powers, for enforcement of its provisions.

Nor did Wilson propose a wholesale cession of American sovereignty to the new body. As Wilson saw it, the choice for America was clear. It could either become a reliable international citizen or retreat into isolationism. Wilson, in effect, was offering a kind of grand bargain: the United States would abjure its historic isolationism and agree to play a continuously engaged international role—but only if the rules of the extant international system were altered in accordance with American wishes.

The changes Wilson proposed may have been potentially radical in the long term, but they were decidedly modest in the immediate term. They anticipated neither a new American imperium nor a sudden, wrenching redefinition of the existing international regime but a gradual, step-by-modest-step progression toward the ultimate goals of multilateral collaboration to achieve collective security and international order—and perhaps, in its turn, widening democratization, too.

The ironic result of this hopeful initiative is well known. For Wilson's purposes, the war ended too soon—before he had the Allied governments firmly in his financial grip, before American arms could make a decisive military contribution to victory, and while the major European states, despite the war's ravages, retained considerable economic and political resilience. Wilson consequently held a weak hand at the Paris peace negotiations, and, as it happened, an even weaker hand at home. His Old World counterparts largely frustrated his wishes for a nonpunitive "peace without victory" and thus sowed the seeds of a greater conflict to come. The U.S. Senate blocked American membership in the League, which dithered along ineffectually for the next two decades, until World War II effectively extinguished it. Having failed to transform the international system, the United States slumped back into a smug and self-righteous isolation. It demobilized its army, scrapped much of its navy, capped immigration for the first time in its history, enacted record-high tariff barriers, and formally legislated no fewer than five "Neutrality Acts" in the war-breeding decade of the 1930s.

So Wilsonianism was stillborn at the end of the Great War, with consequences that helped spawn the global Great Depression of the 1930s and led ultimately to the even more destructive Second World War. But when the United States emerged from that latter struggle wielding might unimaginable to Wilson and the Founders alike, the story was dramatically different. Understanding the nature of that pivotal historical moment is essential to comprehending the character of the international regime that flowed from it, why that regime was so successful, and how much it matters that it is now at risk.

America's power at the end of World War II, both absolute and relative, was breathtaking in its scale and sweep. It was exponentially greater than what Wilson possessed in 1918, exceeding even the dimensions of America's allegedly "hyperpower" status at the twentieth century's end. The United States had a monopoly, albeit one that proved short-lived, on nuclear weapons. It floated the world's largest navy and had built a massive long-range strategic air arm. It commanded more than half the planet's manufacturing capacity and a like share of merchant shipping bottoms. It held most of the world's gold stocks and foreign currency reserves. It was the leading petroleum producer and exporter. Thanks to the dispensations of geography, the United States boasted the only intact large-scale advanced industrial economy on the globe—indeed, thanks to the Roosevelt administration's decision to fight a war of machines, not men, an economy that the war had robustly (and singularly) invigorated. The war had meanwhile devastated all other belligerents, including even America's fellow victors, the Soviet Union and the United Kingdom. Winston Churchill thus spoke a truth as profound as it was simple when he declared on the day after Japan's decision to surrender in August 1945 that "the United States stand at this moment at the summit of the world."[9]

A notable cohort of American leaders now at last gave their answer to the question that Wilson had posed at the outset of World War I. They determined to use "the influence and power of this great nation" in ways that finally set in train the transformation of which Americans had dreamed for nearly two centuries. They affected nothing less than what John Ikenberry rightly calls "America's distinctive contribution to world politics."[10]

On the occasion of the first gathering of the United Nations (UN) in San Francisco on April 16, 1945, President Harry S Truman used words that could have been Wilson's—or Jefferson's or Paine's: "The responsibility of great states is to serve and not to dominate the world."[11] And although it is undeniable that the United States continued to pursue what Wilson had scorned as its own "aggrandizement and material benefit" (considerations never absent from American foreign policy, nor should they be), what is most remarkable is the way that Washington exerted itself to build what the Norwegian scholar Geir Lundestad has called an "empire by invitation."[12] That unconventional "empire" paid great deference to the inherited norms of Westphalian sovereignty even while artfully modifying them. It did not peremptorily compel the subordination of others but rather provided incentives—and resources—for their willing participation. Its architects knew, as Robert Kagan says elsewhere in this volume, that "predominance is not the same thing as omnipotence."[13] They appreciated that this was the moment to use America's unrivaled power to shape an international order that would, among other things, provide a hedge against the inevitable moment when America's power was less.

Ikenberry's chapter in this volume catalogues the array of institutions created in that transmogrifying end-of-war moment: the UN, with its headquarters welcomed on the soil of America's principal city; the International Monetary Fund (IMF), designed to stabilize international exchange rates and encourage fiscal discipline; the International Bank for Reconstruction and Development, better known as the World Bank, to finance postwar reconstruction and foster worldwide economic growth; and the General Agreement on Tariffs and Trade (GATT), which would later morph into the World Trade Organization (WTO), to reduce tariff barriers and liberalize world commerce.[14] Given the innovative character of those institutions, it is worth emphasizing that, again, membership in all of them was limited to states; participating states, particularly large and powerful ones such as the United States, ceded to the new organizations only modest and marginal elements of their own sovereignty, a price willingly paid to secure the benefits of order and reciprocity. The UN in particular, held in check by the veto power of each of the five permanent members of the Security Council, could not at all plausibly be described as an incipient "world government." (Indeed, it had intellectual antecedents in John C. Calhoun's fanciful concept of a "concurrent majority," which was designed to frustrate the exercise of power, not facilitate it.)

The post–World War II order was a historically conditioned but easily recognizable descendant of the centuries-old Westphalian system. It remained committed to preserving the political and territorial integrity of all states and to facilitating their peaceful relations with one another.

And yet the framework of cooperation that constituted that order began subtly, incrementally, to fulfill the Founders' promise of a new world order, one that would be densely populated by transnational institutions and accords that would breed new norms of interstate behavior. The Marshall Plan, announced in 1947, offered further assistance for the rebuilding of Europe and strongly catalyzed the process that eventually yielded the European Union (EU). The North Atlantic Treaty Organization (NATO), formed in 1949, provided strong security guarantees for Western Europe throughout the cold war and sustained the framework of peace that made the maturation of the EU possible. (It also eventually empowered the EU, in turn, to challenge America's own sovereign prerogatives—for example, when European regulators in 2001 barred the merger of two American firms, General Electric and Honeywell: this was a dramatic instance of grudging but eventually gracious submission by the United States to the rule of an international entity it had helped to create.) The International Atomic Energy Agency (IAEA), dating from 1957, played a major if not always fully successful role in limiting nuclear proliferation. The Nuremberg and Tokyo war crimes trials, along with the UN Declarations on Human Rights and on Genocide (a word coined in this intellectually and institutionally fecund era), established at least a minimal basis in international law for superseding a state's sovereign authority in the face of egregious crimes against humanity—though those precedents proved feeble prophylaxis against the likes of Pol Pot, Slobodan Milŏsević, or the murderous predators of Rwanda and Darfur.

Most of those institutions are now more than half a century old—a long life span in the history of international regimes. Many, perhaps all, need substantial reform, of the sort that Kofi Annan tried to effect in his final years as UN secretary general. In a world awash in liquidity, it is at least arguable that the IMF, as well as the World Bank, may have become redundant organizations. And it is self-evident that even this impressive matrix of institutions is ill suited to the task of extinguishing radical Islamist terrorism. But institutions suited to that purpose can arise only on the foundations of mutual trust that a half century of multilateral life engendered—and that the policies of the last several years have put in grave jeopardy.

Whatever their limitations, for nearly three generations those institutions sustained a remarkable passage in the world's history. They constituted the major pillars underlying an international economic expansion of unprecedented reach. So large were its dimensions that by the twentieth century's end another new word had been coined to describe it: globalization. They underwrote the advance of self-determination and democracy, as well. The colonial powers withdrew from Africa and Asia; the Soviet empire disintegrated; and open, contested elections became the norm in countries that had not seen them in generations, if ever. Security was enhanced, too. No *grand guerre* erupted on anything remotely approximating the scales of the two world wars. Barbarous, bloody Europe was pacified after centuries of conflict—itself a historic accomplishment sufficient to distinguish the age.

In this same era Americans enjoyed economic prosperity and personal security to a degree unmatched even in their enviably felicitous history: nearly doubling the size of the middle class in a single generation (as measured by the incidence of home ownership); finding the confidence and courage at last to make racial equality a legally enforceable reality; lengthening life-spans, raising living standards, lifting educational levels, and widening the spectrum of opportunity for tens of millions of citizens. As international regimes go, the post–World War II era, despite the chronic tensions of the cold war and even the tragedy of Vietnam, was on the whole a laudably successful affair.

This brief historical rehearsal points to the following conclusions:

- Americans aspired to transform the international order from the moment of their birth, long evincing little interest in foreign policies that aimed for anything less.
- In Woodrow Wilson they found a leader who translated their yearnings into a concrete plan for international action, which nevertheless failed to be implemented.
- The conclusion of World War II provided the opportunity at last for the United States to build an impressive latticework of multilateral institutions promoting economic growth and political security. That project substantially modified but did not abandon Westphalian conceptions of sovereignty.
- The post–World War II era is the only extended period in the republic's more than two centuries of existence when it consistently played a responsible international role, a role that is now at risk.
- The American public's support for that role was contingent on the perception that American policy comported with the experience and

values of the American people, the ultimate sovereign authority in the American polity—and with their active engagement in the foreign-policy-making process.

- International support for that role depended on the perception that American policy respected the core principles of national sovereignty as understood in the Westphalian schema.
- The international order shaped by those several institutions brought measurably large benefits to Americans and to many other peoples as well. It would be folly to abandon that order or to let it slide into irretrievable disrepair.

In short, the key to the success of American policy in the post–World War II half century was that it honored inherited notions of sovereignty both internationally and at home. The United States became not a traditional imperial power but a *hegemon*, a word whose Greek roots denote a guide, or a leader—and leadership has been well defined as a relationship between consenting adults, not an arrangement between a capricious master and sullen vassals, nor, as discussed later in this chapter, between a president and a public manipulated into apathy or irrelevance.

Here is where the full meaning of Wilson's call that "the world must be made safe for democracy" becomes clear and compelling. Wilson tempered his diplomatic ideals with a highly pragmatic comprehension of the nature of the modern world and both the promise and the danger it held. He shrewdly calculated the reach, as well as the limits, of American power. Perhaps most important, he was keenly attentive to what kind of foreign policy the American public would reliably support.

Wilson asked only that the world be made safe for democracy, not that the entire world be made democratic. He would have gagged on the Bush administration's sweeping assertions that there is but "a single sustainable model for national success: freedom, democracy, and free enterprise" and that the primary goal of American policy is "to bring the hope of democracy, development, free markets, and free trade to every corner of the world."[15]

Wilson also understood the danger of seeking even laudable goals unilaterally in the modern world—a danger amply illustrated by a preemptive war against Iraq that ignored the depth of Iraqi tribalism and the tenacity of Iraq's sovereign pride. The same war has alienated even traditionally reliable allies such as the core members of NATO and may convince states in the Middle Eastern region and well beyond that they must contemplate heroic measures, including the acquisition of nuclear arms, to defend themselves against the prospect of American intervention.

The damage done by this willful trashing of Wilson's legacy has yet to be fully calculated. Future historians will take its measure not only in the worldwide surge of anti-American sentiment but also in the palpable erosion of trust in the very multinational institutions—including NATO, the UN, the IMF, the World Bank, and the WTO—that the United States itself so painstakingly nurtured over many decades. In an era awakening to the global dimensions of environmental degradation, the fungibility of employment across national frontiers, massive international migrant and refugee flows, the unprecedented scale of international capital transactions, the contagious volatility of credit markets, and the planetary menace of nuclear proliferation, not to mention the worldwide threat of terrorism, that erosion threatens to deny the world the very tools it needs most to manage the ever more interdependent global order. And it leaves all nations, conspicuously including the United States, markedly less secure.

George W. Bush has proved to be Woodrow Wilson on steroids, a grotesquely exaggerated and pridefully assertive version of the original, undisturbed by doubt, uninformed by history, unchecked by a feel for the cussedness and complexity of the world, unconstrained by considerations of the finitude of American power, unconcerned with the receptivity of others to America's self-defined civilizing mission, and, perhaps most ominously, uninhibited by the will of the American people. We and the world will be a long time repairing the damage done by his reckless Caesarism.

Woodrow Wilson himself was too much the historian, too sensitive to the plurality and stubbornness of cultures and the vagaries of circumstance, too wary of his countrymen's commitment to international engagement, too familiar with the annals of failed utopias, to posit a single sustainable model for anything. And he was too much the child of his Presbyterian forebears to believe that man's agency on Earth, even the full and righteous potency of the United States—perhaps *especially* the full and righteous potency of a self-anointed redeemer nation such as the United States—was up to the task of bending history's course at will. That was a task for the Almighty, not for mere mortals.

Remembering those Wilsonian tenets of restraint, the United States should put at the heart of its foreign policy the principle of *consent*—a principle that underlies all definitions of sovereignty and that is as important to democratic diplomacy as it is to democracy's essence. To adopt a maxim of Theodore Roosevelt's, Washington should sheathe the big stick and do more talking—about its willingness to engage and lead once again in institutions such as the UN, the IMF, and the World Bank, and, yes, the International Criminal Court, the Biological Weapons Convention, the Doha Round of trade liberalization talks, and the Kyoto Protocol. America should aim to update and strengthen the carefully constructed framework of multilateral institutions and practices that has served so well for so long. Diplomacy should seek consent where it is most likely to be forthcoming, among the democracies that already share America's values and with whom the United States has a history of consequential cooperation. That means Europe, Japan, our North and South American neighbors, and such other societies as care to join in the project of protecting the sphere of democracy. As Francis Fukuyama suggests, American policy should channel China's rising might to constructive ends by taking advantage of Beijing's interest in engaging with international institutions such as the UN and the WTO. That interest is sure to fade if those institutions do not remain robust and attractive, and a China willingly bound to multilateral norms is surely preferable to a China willfully asserting itself unilaterally. (Indeed, this is precisely the way much of the world currently feels about the United States.) As Woodrow Wilson urged, others can be given incentives to join in this grand enterprise and can be rewarded for doing so; indeed, the cost of not joining can be made painfully prohibitive. But as Wilson also knew, the United States must abandon the fatuous notion that it can single-handedly extend the frontiers of freedom by *force majeure*.

Those reflections bring us to the second dimension of this discussion of sovereignty, particularly as it concerns the role of military force in American foreign policy. As retired British general Rupert Smith has recently argued, it is not simply force but the *utility of force* that matters. And as the fiasco in Iraq conclusively demonstrates, for the creation of democratic cultures in which democratic values and practices have little or no organic history of their own, traditional forms of military force have limited utility indeed.[16] Smith makes a strong case that conventional military force may have outlived its usefulness altogether—even while, in what history may judge to be an acridly bitter irony, the Bush administration has yielded to the delusion that military force equals national power and made such force the principal instrument of its foreign policy. The results have been catastrophic in the Middle East and have led to the neglect of other and more appropriate instruments of the national purpose. How did this sorry situation come to pass?

The disutility of the current U.S. military force structure owes in no small measure to the neglect of the fundamental principle that the consent of the governed is the only legitimate basis for political power. When it comes to the conduct of foreign policy, particularly its military dimensions, the American people today have unwittingly lost much of their sovereign authority. This lamentable circumstance results principally from technological developments that have contrived to give the United States an armed force that has many of the characteristics of a mercenary army—or, to be more precise, characteristics that have largely decoupled its use from the informed consent and participation of the citizenry and thereby tempted the political leadership to treat it as if it were a mercenary force. It has been rightly said that since 2003 the armed forces have been at war, whereas the nation has not.

The etymology of *mercenary* is rooted in the Latin term *mercari*, "to trade," or "to exchange." So what are the terms of trade between American civil society and the military organization that fights in its name and on its behalf? What is the relation of service to citizenship? Most important, what is the relation of America's current force structure to foreign-policy decision making?

Our forebears had ready answers to those questions. From the time of the ancient Greeks through the American Revolutionary War and well into the twentieth century, the obligation to bear arms and the privileges of citizenship were intimately linked. In republics from Aristotle's Athens to Thomas Jefferson's Virginia and beyond, to be a full citizen was to stand ready to shoulder arms. It was their respect for the political consequences of that link between service and citizenship that made the Founders so committed to militias and so anxious about standing armies, which Samuel Adams warned were "always dangerous to the liberties of the people." African Americans understood that linkage in the Civil War, and again in both world wars, when they demanded combat assignments as a means to advance their claims to full citizenship rights. For more than two millennia, the tradition of the citizen-soldier served to strengthen civic engagement and promote individual liberty. Most important, it helped to underwrite political accountability when it came to the supremely consequential matter of making war.

In the United States today that tradition has been dangerously compromised. No American is now obligated to military service. Very few Americans will ever serve in uniform. Even fewer will actually taste battle. And fewer than ever of those who do serve come from the more favored ranks of American society.

A comparison with a prior generation's war will serve to illuminate both the scale and the danger of this novel situation.

In World War II, the United States took some sixteen million men and several thousand women into service, the great majority of them draftees. What is more, it mobilized the economic, social, and psychological resources of the society down to the last factory, railcar, victory garden, and classroom. This was a "total war." It compelled the participation of all citizens, exacted the last full measure of devotion from 405,399 citizen-soldiers, and required an enormous commitment of the society's energies to secure the ultimate victory.

Today's military, in contrast, numbers just 1.4 million active personnel, with nearly 900,000 more in the reserves—in a country whose population has more than doubled since 1945. Relative to population, today's active-duty military establishment is about 4 percent the size of the force that won World War II. And in today's behemoth, $13 trillion American economy, the total military budget of more than $500 billion (including the supplemental appropriations for the conflicts in Afghanistan and Iraq) amounts to little more than 4 percent of gross domestic product (GDP). That is less than half the rate of military expenditure relative to GDP at the height of the cold war. In World War II that rate was more than 40 percent—a greater than tenfold difference in the relative incidence of the military's wartime claim on American society's material resources.

Yet this relatively small and relatively inexpensive force is at the same time the most potent military establishment the world has ever seen. I say "relatively inexpensive" advisedly. The absolute numbers tell a different story. American defense expenditures, even at 4 percent of GDP, are greater than the sum of all other nations' military budgets combined—a calculation that testifies as much to the scale of the U.S. economy as it does to Washington's current conception of the relation of the military to America's security needs and foreign policy priorities.[17]

Today's American military, in short, is at once exceptionally lean and extraordinarily lethal. It displays what might be called a compound asymmetry: it is far larger in its destructive capacity than any potential rival yet far smaller with respect to the American population and economy than at any time since the onset of World War II. For those very reasons, it has become the instrument of choice in the conduct of American foreign policy, even though it is demonstrably the wrong instrument for the job at hand. We have contrived to create a situation akin to what Jefferson feared about Napoleon Bonaparte, whom he described as having transferred the destinies of the republic from the civil to the military arm. As a result, the United States can be said to have waged in Iraq the wrong war, at the wrong time, in the wrong place, with the wrong enemy, using the wrong strategic doctrine, and with a force that is wrongly trained, equipped, and configured.

The United States can make war today while putting at risk precious few of its sons and daughters, and only those who go willingly into harm's way. History's most powerful fighting force can now be sent into battle in the name of a society that scarcely breaks a sweat when it does so. And unlike virtually all previous societies in history, the United States today can inflict prodigious damage on others while not appreciably perturbing its civilian economy. We have, in short, evolved a uniquely American way of war that does not ask, *precisely because it does not require,* any large-scale personal or material contributions from the citizens in whose name war is waged. Paradoxically, what the military historian Andrew Bacevich has called the "new American militarism" has given rise to what might be called the "new American isolationism"—if by that we mean popular disengagement from the conduct of foreign affairs.

Some may celebrate these developments as triumphs of the soldierly art or as testimony to American wealth, know-how, and technological prowess. But the present force structure also presents a seductive temptation to engage in the kind of military adventurism that the Founders feared was among the greatest dangers of standing armies. Leaders in the past, however, had somehow to sustain a broad public consensus to support the *levée en masse* and the huge drafts on economic resources that made such armies possible. Imagine how Napoleon, the incarnation of Burke's "armed doctrine," might have envied a twenty-first-century leader who shared his transformative aspirations but who deployed a compact, low-cost, highly effective force that substantially liberated him from the constraints of available manpower and finite *matériel* that ultimately frustrated the French emperor's ambition to remake the world.

This danger-laden situation traces its origins to the Vietnam era. Seeking to dampen the rising tide of anti–Vietnam War protests, President Richard Nixon in the closing weeks of the 1968 presidential campaign announced his intention to end the draft. Accordingly, in 1973 the Selective Service System stopped conscripting young men, and the United States adopted an all-volunteer force. With the winding down of the Vietnam War, that force also shrank from forty to just sixteen army divisions by the time Nixon left office in 1974. Today's army numbers eighteen divisions, ten active and eight reserve, down from twenty-eight divisions at the time of the first Gulf War in 1991. Additionally, the Marine Corps has one reserve and three active divisions. (The Army fielded ninety divisions in World War II; the Marines, six.)

Vietnam's influence on civil-military relations went much deeper. Nixon's last Army chief of staff, General Creighton Abrams, a veteran of both World War II and the Vietnam War, was among those members of the officer corps deeply disillusioned with the way the military had been used—or misused—in the Vietnam episode. To prevent what he regarded as the mistakes of Vietnam from being repeated, Abrams devised the "Total-Force Doctrine." Its goal was to structure the armed forces in such a way that they could not easily be deployed in the absence of strong and sustainable public support—something that Abrams and others believed had been disastrously missing in Vietnam. Abrams's means to that end was to create a force structure that tightly integrated both active and reserve components, transforming the latter from a strategic reserve to be mobilized only in major emergencies to an operational reserve regularly supporting and closely interdigitated with the active-duty military.

The reserves, of course, are always less costly to maintain than the active forces. But configuring the overall force so that it was inextricably dependent on the reserves served a political far more than a fiscal purpose. Reserve units are typically composed of somewhat older men and women with deeper roots and responsibilities in civil society than the typical eighteen-year-old draftee of the Vietnam or World War II eras. Abrams hoped that with his total-force structure in place, political leaders would hesitate to undertake a major deployment that would necessarily be deeply disruptive to countless communities—unless they were certain of solid and durable public support. In effect, Abrams's doctrine was intended to raise the threshold for presidential demonstration of a genuine threat to national security, to compel careful presidential cultivation of a broad, sustainable consensus on the nature and urgency of that threat, and to require the exhaustion of all other means of addressing the threat as prerequisites for military deployment.

The Abrams Doctrine thus amounted to a kind of extraconstitutional restraint on the president's freedom of action as commander in chief. Its legislative counterpart was the War Powers Act of 1973, also aimed at restricting the president's ability to commit troops without due deliberation. The act passed over President Nixon's veto. No subsequent president has recognized its constitutionality. Underlying the War Powers Act, in turn, is the constitutional provision (Article I, Section 8, paragraph 11) giving Congress the power to declare war. Here it might be noted that Congress has formally exercised that power only five times in more than two centuries—whereas the number of overseas military engagements that might fairly be called "war" is many times larger: no fewer than 234 between 1798 and 1993, according to a Congressional Research Service study, and conspicuously including in recent decades Korea, Vietnam, Grenada, Panama, Somalia, Afghanistan, and Iraq.[18] That record, as well as the inconclusive confrontation between Congress and the president in 2007 over Iraq war financing, suggests a chronically deficient constitutional mechanism for bringing democratic practices effectively to bear on the decision to wage war.

Ronald Reagan's defense secretary, Caspar Weinberger, reinforced Abrams's effort to insulate the military from ill-considered political decisions. The precipitating factor in this instance was not Vietnam but Lebanon, to which the Reagan administration had sent troops over the objections of the Pentagon and the Joint Chiefs. On October 23, 1983, some 241 Marines died in a suicide attack on their Beirut barracks. Weinberger thereupon laid down a set of principles governing military deployment. What became known as the "Weinberger Doctrine" was Doric in its simplicity:

- The United States should not commit forces to combat unless the vital national interests of the United States or its allies are involved.

- If we decide it is necessary to put combat troops into a given situation, we should do so wholeheartedly and with the clear intention of winning.
- We should have clearly defined political and military objectives.
- The relationship between our objectives and the forces we have committed—their size, composition, and disposition—must be continually reassessed and adjusted if necessary.
- Before the United States commits combat forces abroad, there must be some reasonable assurance that we will have the support of the American people and their elected representatives in Congress. This support cannot be achieved unless we are candid in making clear the threats we face; the support cannot be sustained without continuing and close consultation.
- The commitment of U.S. forces to combat should be a last resort.[19]

Some seven years later, in the context of the first Gulf War, then-chairman of the Joint Chiefs of Staff General Colin Powell glossed the Weinberger Doctrine—and managed thereby to substitute his own name for Weinberger's in popular perception of it—by adding the criteria of "overwhelming force" and a viable "exit strategy" for any prospective deployment. Powell also invoked the Beirut bombing:

> We must not, for example, send military forces into a crisis with an unclear mission they cannot accomplish—such as we did when we sent the U.S. Marines into Lebanon in 1983. We inserted those proud warriors into the middle of a five-faction civil war complete with terrorists, hostage-takers, and a dozen spies in every camp and said, "Gentlemen, be a buffer." The results were 241 dead Marines and Navy personnel killed and U.S. withdrawal from the troubled area.[20]

Contrary to many ill-informed stereotypes about the bloodthirstiness of a so-called warrior class, these various doctrines—Abrams's, Weinberger's, and Powell's—did not seek primarily to provide rationales for doing battle. They were intended instead as formulas for avoiding war if at all possible, and they relied on citizen engagement to do so. Like the Total-Force Doctrine that preceded and informed them, the Weinberger Doctrine and the Powell Doctrine grew out of persistent anxiety on the part of senior military leaders that they lived in a world in which it was too easy for their political masters to head for the gun case rather than the conference table; too easy to evade democratic deliberation; too easy to behave irresponsibly, even recklessly; too easy to commit the armed forces to action in the absence of clearly compelling reasons, a well-defined mission, and—especially—the reliable, properly informed approval of the citizenry. These were counsels of prudence and responsibility, intended to induce caution and consensus building when confronting the fateful decision to make war.

Those counsels relied on mechanisms that were both cumbersome and constitutionally contested. It is not too much to say that they had about them the air of almost desperate contrivance. Then, in the decade following the first Gulf War in 1991, a stunning technological development further weakened these already frail inhibitions on the decision to take up arms. That development was the RMA, or the "Revolution in Military Affairs."

There have been many revolutions in military affairs, from the introduction of gunpowder in the Middle Ages to the twentieth century's invention of "Blitzkrieg" and strategic bombing and the advent of nuclear weapons, all of which fundamentally redefined strategic, as well as tactical, doctrines and the very character—even the very purpose—of warfare. But this newest RMA is notable for the speed with which it has worked its effects, its intimate relation to parallel developments in civil society, and the lack of public understanding of its implications, especially concerning the role of military force in the conduct of foreign policy.

The RMA was foreshadowed in the 1980s in the writings of Albert Wohlstetter, long an influential theorist of nuclear war at the RAND Corporation, later a professor at the University of Chicago (where his students included Paul Wolfowitz, destined to become a principal architect of the Iraq intervention). Wohlstetter stressed the factor of accuracy in determining force composition and war-fighting doctrine. He argued that a tenfold improvement in accuracy was roughly equivalent to a thousandfold increase in sheer explosive power. By extension, a hundredfold increase in accuracy multiplied destructive potential by a factor of one million.

The Pentagon's Office of Net Assessment energetically pursued the implications of that alluring calculus, seeking to capitalize militarily on the information and computer revolutions that were transforming the civilian sector. Especially important were impressive advances in VLSI (very large-scale integration) technologies, enabling dramatic upgrading of stealth, standoff, and unmanned weapons, all-weather and all-terrain fighting capacities, space-based networking, joint-force integration, miniaturization, range, endurance, speed, and, above all, precision, precision, precision.

The RMA's first fruits were evident in the 1991 Gulf War, when news coverage headlined the advent of "smart" air-launched weapons. But the first Gulf War is best understood as the "final mission" of a force that had been configured to fight a conventional land battle against Warsaw Pact adversaries in Central Europe. "Smart bombs" accounted for only about 10 percent of the ordnance used in that conflict. The decisive action was General Norman Schwarzkopf's Blitzkrieg-like armored flanking attack against the Iraqi army, a classic World War II–era maneuver, mimicking the German run around the Maginot Line in May 1940 or Patton's great sweep to Argentan in August 1944.

By one calculation, in World War II it took 108 aircraft, dropping 648 bombs, to destroy a single target. In contrast, during the 2001 campaign in Afghanistan, the first large-scale demonstration of the consequences of the RMA, 38 aircraft demolished 159 targets in one night. By the time of the invasion of Iraq in 2003, when smart munitions accounted for nearly 90 percent of the American arsenal, the implications of accuracy as a "force multiplier" proved to be spectacular. The RMA was conclusively shown to have vastly amplified the firepower and fighting effectiveness of the individual soldier, sailor, or airman. It was now possible to field a dramatically smaller force capable of wreaking much greater destruction than the lumbering, terrain-bound, largely sightless armies that had clashed on battlefields since time immemorial.

These several developments—political, fiscal, and especially technological—have converged to yield the downsized, affordable, and impressively efficient military establishment we now have.

The compact all-volunteer force made possible by the RMA can be seen as a triumph of American ingenuity. But it has also incubated a grave threat to the cardinal values of political accountability and responsible decision making that the Founders, as well as Creighton Abrams, Caspar Weinberger, and Colin Powell, were trying to bolster. The RMA has thoroughly vitiated the intended effect of the Total-Force Doctrine by making possible the downscaling of the armed forces to such a degree that only relatively small numbers of the willing—or the desperate—need serve and that even the call-up of the reserves does not have an appreciable impact on civilian society. Exploiting that logic, Secretary of Defense Donald Rumsfeld sought to drive the last spike in the coffin of the Abrams Doctrine with a policy of "rebalancing" the military to make the active force wholly independent of the reserves.

It cannot be healthy for a democracy to let something as important as war making grow so far removed from broad popular participation and the strictest possible political accountability. That is why the war-making power was constitutionally lodged in the legislative branch in the first place. Our current situation makes some literally life-or-death matters too easy—such as the violent coercion of other societies and the resort to military solutions on the assumption that they will be swifter, more cheaply bought, and more conclusive than what could be accomplished by the more vexatious and tedious process of diplomacy.

A democratic society should make demands on its citizens when they are asked to engage with issues of life and death. To be sure, the RMA has made obsolete the kind of huge citizen-army that fought in World War II, but if we are to honor the concept of popular sovereignty in the critical area of foreign—and especially military—policy, we are in need of some mechanism to ensure that the civilian and military sectors do not become dangerously separate spheres and to ensure that America makes war only after due deliberation and democratic assent.

There is no silver bullet here, no single reform that will resolve the chronic dilemma of balancing the values of flexibility in national defense with democratic deliberation. Even with the draft in place during the decades of the cold war, the United States engaged in military contests of dubious worth, conspicuously including Vietnam. But some reforms, especially if taken together, may go some modest but meaningful way toward inducing more caution about resorting to force, raising the threshold level at which the military option is chosen, and encouraging more reliance on the "soft power" instruments that are such impressive but recently underutilized weapons in America's national security arsenal.

Restoring universal *liability* to military service by means of a lottery is one means to that end. Exposure to the low-probability prospect of obligatory military service may not have the same power to concentrate the mind as facing the proverbial firing squad, but it will go some way toward increasing citizen awareness and public engagement in the shaping and use of military force. Though robust cultural norms argue against it, perhaps a program of obligatory national service, in which military duty is one among several options, may prove another way to focus the citizenry's attention on the implications of using force.

Restoring Creighton Abrams's Total-Force Doctrine is yet another such means to that end. As the National Security Advisory Group warned in 2006:

> It is imperative that our armed forces remain structured so as to preserve the essential link between the military and the body politic—to ensure that any President must mobilize substantial numbers of America's "citizen soldiers" in order to go to war. Maintaining this link—and the accountability it brings—was the original intent of the Abrams Doctrine in creating the All Volunteer Force, and it should remain a fundamental design principle of the U.S. armed forces.[21]

The restoration of Reserve Officer Training Corps (ROTC) programs to the several elite college campuses that do not have academically accredited ROTC instruction and that resist allowing military recruiters on campus would be still another means to the important end of citizen engagement in military affairs. Many institutions severed their ties with ROTC in the Vietnam era. But today those restrictive policies serve to ensure that our self-proclaimed best universities, which pride themselves on training the next generation's leaders, will have minimal influence on the leadership of a hugely important American institution, the U.S. armed forces. Why is that a good idea?

One further note about the separation of civilian and military spheres: Andrew Bacevich reports that in 2000, minorities composed 42 percent of the Army's enlistments, and that whereas 46 percent of the civilian population has had at least some college education, only 6.5 percent of the eighteen- to twenty-four-year-olds in the military's enlisted ranks have ever seen the inside of a college classroom.[22] So not only is today's military remarkably small in relation to the overall structure of civil society—a "minority" institution, as it were—but it is also disproportionately composed of racial, ethnic, and socio-economic minorities. Whoever they are, and for whatever reasons they enlist, they surely do not make up the kind of citizen-army that the United States fielded two generations ago—its members drawn from all ranks of society, without respect to background or privilege or education, and mobilized on such a scale that civilian society's deep and reliable consent to the use of that force was absolutely necessary.

Here is another asymmetry of worrisome proportions. A hugely preponderant majority of Americans with no risk whatsoever of exposure to military service has, in effect, hired some of the least advantaged of their fellow countrymen to do some of the nation's most dangerous business while the majority goes on with its own affairs unbloodied and undistracted. Meanwhile, evidence suggests that the military is becoming an increasingly self-perpetuating institution, its ranks disproportionately filled with recruits from families that already have a military connection.

It would be a gross exaggeration to suggest that the cultural divide between soldiers and civilians in the United States today augurs the emergence of an American equivalent of the Freikorps or Fasci di Combattimento, the disillusioned World War I–era veterans' groups that helped bring Adolf Hitler and Benito Mussolini to power. But the widening gap that separates those who serve from those who do not—while some of our most prestigious universities remain insulated from the officer corps—can only exacerbate the social tensions that already threaten our national comity. Here is one more reason to worry about the longer term implications of maintaining an all-volunteer "rebalanced" force—not to mention the wisdom of continuing to ban ROTC.

American Caesarism mocks the nation's own most cherished ideals and gravely menaces the stability of the international order. The widening separation of the military from civil society in the United States was among the factors that enabled the Bush administration to wage a dubious war of choice in Iraq. That war has not only failed on the ground but has also inflicted massive collateral damage on the entire structure of the multilateral order that the United States itself so laboriously pioneered.

American diplomacy has historically achieved its most notable successes when it has respected the principle of sovereignty in both its traditional senses—as it applies to relations among states and to relations between state and citizen. For the United States to have a national security policy that is both effective and legitimate that policy must respect the sovereignty of other nations and the sovereignty of the American people alike. In the age of terror, those considerations may seem to lack immediacy and drama. But the time of terror is the most urgent of times to focus on fundamentals as well as on the lessons of experience. In the long run, only policies that are perceived to be legitimate, by Americans themselves and by others, can hope to be workable. And legitimacy is a matter of constraint and collaboration abroad and informed consent at home. If there is any truth at all in the venerable maxim that democratic societies are peaceable societies, then the way to peace—and to restoration of the liberal international system that served so much of the world so well for so long—is for more democratically guaranteed political accountability in America, including an armed force that is democratically recruited.

Notes

1. Robert Kagan, *Dangerous Nation: America's Place in the World from its Earliest Days to the Dawn of the 20th Century* (New York: Knopf, 2006), 40.
2. Edmund Burke, "First Letter on a Regicide Peace," in *Empire and Community: Edmund Burke's Writings and Speeches on International Relations*, ed. David P. Fidler and Jennifer M. Welsh (Boulder, CO: Westview Press, 1999), 295.
3. David M. Kennedy, *Over Here: The First World War and American Society*, rev. ed. (New York: Oxford University Press, 2004), 376–378.
4. Arthur S. Link, ed., *The Papers of Woodrow Wilson* (Princeton, NJ: Princeton University Press, 1966–1994), 30:251.
5. Ibid., 40:534–539; 61:436.
6. Ibid., 41:525.
7. George Kennan, *American Diplomacy, 1900–1950* (Chicago: University of Chicago Press, 1951), 95.
8. Link, *The Papers of Woodrow Wilson*, 45:536.
9. David Cannadine, ed., *Blood, Toil, Tears and Sweat: The Speeches of Winston Churchill* (Boston: Houghton Mifflin, 1989), 282.
10. See G. John Ikenberry's chapter in this volume.
11. Quoted in Elizabeth Borgwardt, *A New Deal for the World: America's Vision for Human Rights* (Cambridge, MA: Harvard University Press, 2005), 180.
12. Geir Lundestad, "Empire by Invitation? The United States and Western Europe, 1945–1952," *Journal of Peace Research* 23, no. 3 (1986).
13. See Robert Kagan's chapter in this volume.
14. See Ikenberry's chapter in this volume.

15. *The National Security Strategy of the United States of America* (Washington, DC: The White House, 2002).

16. Rupert Smith, *The Utility of Force: The Art of Warfare in the Modern World* (London: Allen Lane, 2005).

17. See, for example, Condoleezza Rice, "Promoting the National Interest," *Foreign Affairs* 79, no. 1 (January/February 2000): 45; and *National Security Strategy* (2002).

18. Ellen C. Collier, *Instances of Use of United States Forces Abroad, 1798–1993* (Washington, DC: Congressional Research Service, October 7, 1993), http://www.history.navy.mil/wars/foabroad.htm.

19. Caspar W. Weinberger, "The Uses of Military Power," remarks before the National Press Club, Washington, D.C. (November 28, 1984), http://www.afa .org/magazine/jan2004/military_power.pdf. Of course, Congress has on several occasions passed legislation authorizing the president to use military force, as in the notorious Tonkin Gulf Resolution in 1964 and the Iraq War Resolution in 2002. But, strictly speaking, these actions have fallen considerably short of formal declarations of war.

20. Colin L. Powell, "U.S. Forces: Challenges Ahead," *Foreign Affairs* 71, no. 5 (Winter 1992/1993): 32.

21. The National Security Advisory Group II, *The U.S. Military: Under Strain and at Risk* (January 2006), 18. See http://merln.ndu.edu/merln/mipal/reports/US_ Military_Under_Strain_and_at_Risk.pdf.

22. Andrew Bacevich, *The New American Militarism: How Americans Are Seduced by War* (New York: Oxford University Press, 2005), 28. For an interesting discussion of the changing strategies employed to recruit the all-volunteer force, see Beth Bailey, "The Army in the Marketplace: Recruiting an All-Volunteer Force," *The Journal of American History* 94, no. 1 (June 2007): 47.

EIGHT

A Shackled Hegemon

Barry Eichengreen
and Douglas A. Irwin

I N MANY AREAS of foreign policy, the Bush doctrine marks a break with the approaches of earlier administrations. At first glance this seems true of the Bush administration's foreign economic policy, as well. President Bush and his advisers brought to Washington a powerful ideology, that of limited government, to inform and shape policy decisions. This noninterventionist, free-market approach had led candidate Bush to campaign as a supporter of free trade. It led his inner circle to conclude that intervening in the foreign exchange market, however acceptable for Europe or Japan, was inappropriate for the United States. Bush and his advisers opposed using government influence and taxpayer money to intervene in emerging markets suffering financial crises. They were skeptical that government largesse could be an agent of change in less developed countries.

But there was little opportunity to pursue this ambitious vision once the 9/11 attacks intervened. The idea that government should be limited rested uncomfortably with this reminder of the paramount responsibility of any administration for national security. The wish to limit discretionary trade policy and foreign aid butted up against the realization that these could be valuable devices for supporting allies in the war on terrorism. The fallout from 9/11 meant that a tremendous amount of U.S. Treasury resources were diverted toward terrorism-related issues such as the economic and financial reconstruction of Iraq. Rather than striving for a more focused International Monetary Fund (IMF), the administration pushed to make the institution responsible for rooting out terrorist-related money laundering.

Even had the 9/11 attacks not occurred, attempts to fundamentally reshape U.S. foreign economic policy would have had to overcome powerful interests and long-standing structures. Multilateral trade agreements could be easily stymied by other countries. Free trade could antagonize special interests on whose support reelection prospects depended, forcing domestic concessions to protectionism. Leaving emerging market economies such as Turkey or Argentina to their financial fate might have negative repercussions for the region or destabilize global financial markets. Denying foreign aid to countries with weak governments could contribute to the further breakdown of their economic and political systems and render them breeding grounds for terrorism.

The constraints of the international financial system and the pressure of powerful lobbies forced the Bush administration, now having to maneuver in the policy arena, to adopt a more pragmatic tone. The existence of such structures as the World Trade Organization (WTO), which constrains the president's trade policy-making options, and international capital markets, which have too much destabilizing capacity to simply be left to their own devices, required the administration to modify or abandon the more radical elements of its agenda.

Reflecting these constraints, actual policies differed less from those of earlier presidents than the administration's rhetoric would have led one to suppose. Whereas political scientists and diplomatic historians are apt to see the Bush presidency as a distinctive epoch in American foreign policy, we argue that there has been no Bush doctrine in international economic policy.

This argument leads us to expect that there will be continuities with future policy as well. Neither the new foreign policy concerns created by 9/11 nor long-standing structural constraints on international economic policy making will go away. They will similarly prevent the next administration from undertaking radical changes to U.S. foreign economic policy—much as they have constrained the administration of George W. Bush. Many of the challenges facing the next president are not new—trade negotiations with other countries, the large current account deficit, economic frictions with China—but levers for dealing with them will be limited.

Indeed, the next administration will have less room for maneuver than the Bush administration had when it came into office. With trade negotiations deadlocked at the WTO and the domestic consensus in favor of trade liberalization in tatters, the next administration is unlikely to have grandiose plans for trade policy. With the United States dependent on foreign capital inflows to finance its current account deficit and the IMF less powerful and relevant today than it was a decade ago, the next administration will not be in a strong position to promote reform of the international economic institutions. And the U.S. economy remains just as vulnerable to an oil price shock and an abrupt change in international capital flows as it was five or ten years ago. The next administration is likely to have to manage current difficulties within the existing policy framework rather than being in a position to propose new policies or institutions to deal with the changing world.

This chapter lays out the constraints that will affect the conduct of the next administration's international economic policy. We begin by reviewing how the ambitious plans of the Bush administration in the areas of international trade and finance were scaled back as a result of the pitfalls and roadblocks that it encountered. We then turn to the specific international economic policy challenges that will confront the next administration. We show how it, too, will face similar constraints that will limit its ability to influence events to its liking.

Trade Policy

In the field of trade policy, the Bush administration has behaved like almost every other post–World War II presidential administration: it linked trade policies to broader foreign policy goals, supported the multilateral trading system's goal of reducing trade barriers, and sought trade negotiating powers from Congress to conclude trade agreements with other countries. Also like previous administrations, the Bush administration made exceptions to this approach by giving temporary trade protection to politically influential sectors, such as steel and agriculture. Thus, although some policy details have diverged from previous experience, particularly the energetic pursuit of bilateral free-trade agreements, the Bush administration does not stand out as being markedly different in its trade policy; policy continuities dwarf discontinuities.

The current trade-policy framework was established by the Reciprocal Trade Agreements Act (RTAA) of 1934. The RTAA came into existence during the Franklin D. Roosevelt administration at a time when world trade had collapsed due to protectionism and the Great Depression.[1] Under the RTAA, Congress delegated some of its constitutional powers over trade policy to the executive branch, allowing it to negotiate agreements with other countries. Under this authority, the United States helped create the General Agreement on Tariffs and Trade (GATT) in 1947, which became the WTO in 1995. Multilateral trade agreements were initially infused with an important bipartisan foreign policy rationale: the strengthening of Western Europe and the fight against Communism.[2] A bipartisan consensus on the importance of open trade policies meant that Congress rarely allowed the trade negotiating authority of the RTAA to lapse.

This framework has left presidential administrations little scope for developing distinctive trade policies. Every president since Franklin Roosevelt has believed that the open world trading system and trade liberalization are fundamentally in America's economic and foreign policy interests. Every president has sought congressional authority to negotiate trade agreements that would open up foreign markets to U.S. exports in exchange for a reduction in U.S. trade barriers. And every president has bowed to political considerations by accommodating the protectionist demands of domestic interest groups affected by foreign competition.[3] But without a strong foreign policy rationale, as has been the case in the post–cold war era, persuading Congress to embrace policies to open trade has been difficult.

Indeed, the tragic events of 9/11 gave a jump start to world trade negotiations. After the attack, other countries rallied around the United States and sought to ensure that world trade would be kept open and free despite the terrorist attacks by supporting the Bush administration's efforts to launch the Doha Round of WTO trade negotiations in 2001. The Bush administration then enlisted the "war on terror" as part of the push to gain trade promotion authority (TPA) from the U.S. Congress. Just nine days after 9/11, U.S. trade representative Robert Zoellick published an op-ed in which he argued:

> Economic strength—at home and abroad—is the foundation of America's hard and soft power. Earlier enemies learned that America is the arsenal of democracy; today's enemies will learn that America is the economic engine for freedom, opportunity and development. To that end, U.S. leadership in promoting the international economic and trading system is vital. Trade is about more than economic efficiency. It promotes the values at the heart of this protracted struggle.... Congress needs to enact U.S. trade promotion authority so America can negotiate agreements that advance the causes of openness, development and growth. It is a sad irony that just as the old world of bipolar blocs faded into history and the new world of globalization fast-forwarded, the United States let its trade promotion authority lapse [in 1995].[4]

These efforts helped persuade Congress to enact TPA in 2002.

Yet, in the subsequent six years, the Doha Round failed to come close to a successful conclusion. WTO negotiations operate on the basis of consensus, meaning that a few large countries or a group of smaller countries can block agreement. The reluctance of member countries of the Organization for Economic Cooperation and Development (OECD) to reduce agricultural subsidies and of developing countries to open their markets to foreign competition has made the conclusion of the Doha Round seemingly impossible.[5] Since 2001, many ministerial meetings have ended and deadlines have passed without agreement.

Given the difficulties of reaching an agreement at the WTO, Zoellick was not content to wait for the slowest countries to agree to open up markets. He endorsed the doctrine of "competitive liberalization," in which the United States would bypass the WTO and pursue bilateral and regional trade agreements as a way of putting pressure on other reluctant reformers in the world trading system.[6] He explained:

> We will promote free trade globally, regionally and bilaterally, while rebuilding support at home. By moving forward on multiple fronts, the United States can exert its leverage for openness, create a new competition in liberalization, target the needs of developing countries, and create a fresh political dynamic by putting free trade onto the offensive.... To multiply the likelihood of success, the United States is also invigorating a drive for regional and bilateral free-trade agreements (FTAs). These agreements can foster powerful links among commerce, economic reform, development, investment, security and free societies.... The United States is combining this building-block approach to free trade with a clear commitment to reducing global barriers to trade through the WTO. By using the leverage of the American economy's size and attractiveness to stimulate competition for openness, we will move the world closer toward the goal of comprehensive free trade.[7]

Prior to the Bush administration, the United States had signed just a few FTAs: the U.S.-Israel FTA in 1985, the U.S.-Canada FTA in 1989, the North American Free Trade Agreement (NAFTA) in 1993, and the U.S.-Jordan FTA in 2001 (signed by Bush but initiated by the Clinton administration). In a break from past practice, Zoellick aggressively increased the number of bilateral negotiations pursued by the United States. He concluded agreements with Australia, Chile, Singapore, and five Central American countries (Costa Rica, El Salvador, Guatemala, Honduras, and Nicaragua) that eventually became known as CAFTA-DR (Central American Free Trade Agreement with the Dominican Republic). Negotiations were also undertaken with Morocco, Bahrain, four Andean countries (Colombia, Peru, Ecuador, and Bolivia), and five nations in southern Africa, as well as Panama, Malaysia, Thailand, and South Korea.[8]

The domestic problem raised by FTAs is that they force Congress to vote frequently on trade bills, which most members find uncomfortable given that the domestic politics of trade focuses on workers who might potentially lose their jobs as a result of imports. Some FTAs (Australia, Singapore, Morocco, and Bahrain) were uncontroversial and passed through Congress easily, whereas others (CAFTA-DR, Oman) encountered stiff opposition and required much arm twisting to ensure passage. The partisan nature of these trade votes gives individual members of Congress an incentive to keep their positions ambiguous until they obtain some other political favor from the president in exchange for their votes.

Yet even the distinctive Bush turn toward bilateral FTAs was brought to a halt with the Democratic capture of Congress in the 2006 midterm elections. Democrats tend to be more skeptical of measures to expand trade and have resisted FTAs—particularly with developing countries—that they believe should include stronger labor and environmental provisions, if they should be pursued at all. They allowed the president's TPA to expire in June 2007 without any commitment to renew it.

Hence, there have been two backlashes against Bush's agenda: foreign (reluctance of other countries to liberalize) and domestic (reluctance of Congress to pass trade agreements). This resistance is likely to persist and constrain future administrations.

Monetary and Financial Policies

In keeping with its free-market, free-trade rhetoric, the Bush administration came to office skeptical of activist international financial policies, such as IMF bailouts in emerging market financial crises, foreign exchange intervention, and World Bank development assistance. In 2000 candidate Bush made critical remarks about how the Clinton administration had repeatedly run to the rescue of crisis countries. Administration officials were skeptical about the efficiency and intentions of a European-led bureaucracy such as the IMF. They signaled that the Bush administration would not engage in bailouts and would seek significant reforms of the IMF and the World Bank.

In fact, Treasury Secretary Paul O'Neill and his undersecretary for international affairs, John Taylor, had complex views of the bailout question. In a 1998 interview (which remained obscure so long as Taylor was a member of the Stanford University faculty but which gained notoriety once he was nominated to be under secretary), Taylor had echoed the views of his mentor George Shultz that the world would be better off without the IMF. O'Neill was known for the observation that the IMF was "associated with failure" and that its resort to international rescues had been "too frequent."[9] But the two Treasury officials were pragmatic. O'Neill had praised the Clinton administration's 1995 bailout of Mexico in his confirmation hearings. If there was a problem, O'Neill believed that smart, hardworking officials could solve it. Taylor, for his part, was anxious to avoid precipitous action that might roil the markets.

The first test of the Bush administration's approach to foreign monetary and financial affairs was the crisis in Argentina. Argentina had an enormous program with the IMF, but when Bush took office there had been three years of economic stagnation, reflecting domestic problems compounded by devaluation in neighboring Brazil. Argentine voters and foreign bondholders were losing patience, raising the specter that a combination of political backlash and capital flight might bring both the government and the financial system tumbling down.

This would have been an appropriate time for the IMF and the U.S. government to signal that no more assistance would be extended, forcing Argentina to restructure its debts and to put in place wage and exchange rate policies to make for a more flexible economy. The country would have been forced to address the domestic roots of its mess. Investors would have learned that indiscriminate lending had costs.

The golden opportunity to make this point was in the summer of 2001, when the Argentine government leaked to the press that the IMF would not only accelerate disbursal of the $1.25 billion to be paid out at the end of the second quarter, assuming satisfactory performance, but also augment its program. This not being the way the IMF normally operates—it is not typically forced into additional lending by public announcements from the borrower, especially when there are very limited prospects of success—this occasion would have been a fine time to pull the plug. But the State Department worried about the consequences of failing to support a fledgling South American democracy. Taylor worried that forcing Argentina to restructure could undermine investor confidence in the debts of other emerging markets and damage the banks and investment funds that had built their portfolios on conventional assumptions about U.S. and IMF policy. O'Neill believed that money was leverage and that with sufficient leverage the United States could force reforms of Argentine policy. In the White House, R. Glenn Hubbard, chairman of the president's Council of Economic Advisers, and Lawrence Lindsey (head of the National Economic Council) were skeptical of the merits of forbearance. With the economists divided, the arguments of the State Department tipped the balance. Thus the United States agreed to disbursal of the $1.25 billion already committed subject to meeting performance criteria. It agreed to consider augmenting the program by an additional $8 billion.

O'Neill was impressed by the contrast between how companies and countries dealt with debt sustainability problems. Corporations could restructure under the protection of the bankruptcy court. The burden was shared by the creditors, with not even bondholders with seniority being immune. Its finances having been reorganized in orderly fashion, the enterprise could continue as a viable entity. The problem was that there existed no analogous procedure for countries, a situation that forced the IMF to lend and gave rise to moral hazard. O'Neill was not alone in this observation. The analogy with Chapter 11 bankruptcy had been made in academic circles.[10] Similar ideas had circulated within the Fund. But O'Neill's insistence on results made these abstract ideas very real.

The scheme eventually designed was for $3 billion of the $8 billion of new IMF credits extended to Argentina to be used for an orderly, market-based debt restructuring. But how it would work was never specified. In fact, the reason for expecting that earmarking $3 billion of IMF assistance for this purpose should have significantly changed creditors' calculus is unclear. Three billion dollars was a drop in the bucket when gauged against Argentina's $95 billion of debt to private creditors, especially when one recalls that the IMF's $3 billion was not free money; Argentina would have to pay it back. Nothing would be changed simply by replacing $3 billion of private debt with $3 billion of official debt, which was the implication of using the earmarked funds to retire outstanding obligations. And there was no obvious way that the earmarked funds could be leveraged beyond that. In effect, locking up more than a third of the IMF's $8 billion in this way only limited the liquidity of its assistance. It diminished the credibility of the IMF program, given that observers had not the slightest idea of the content of this $3 billion restructuring-related initiative. In all, this affair did not enhance the reputation of either the Treasury or the Fund.

The importance of debt restructuring and Argentina during the administration's first two years in office was matched by the importance of external imbalances during the subsequent period. The United States' current account deficit rose from $413 billion in 2000 to roughly $800 billion in 2005, expanding to an unprecedented 6 percent of U.S. gross domestic product (GDP). Among economists, explanations for the U.S. deficit included low U.S. savings, reflecting the Bush tax cuts of 2001 and the run-up first of high-tech stocks and then of real estate values; high U.S. investment, responding to the attractions of a flexible U.S. economy; high foreign saving, mainly in Asia, reflecting the underdevelopment of markets in consumer credit and social safety nets; and depressed foreign investment, reflecting the slow pace at which the East Asian economies recovered from their financial crisis.[11] In the public mind and those of politicians, however, there was no question but that China was at the center of the equation. The emergence of China was the most dramatic international economic event of this period; the Chinese economy was fully 50 percent larger in 2005 than in 2000, and the country's exports nearly doubled over the period. U.S. producers of manufactures seemingly could not compete with Chinese exporters who paid their labor only a fraction of American wages.

Thus the Bush Treasury and the U.S. trade representative had to contend with the threat of protectionist sanctions, notably in the form of a bill by Senator Charles Schumer (D-N.Y.) that, in the absence of an initiative to allow the renminbi to appreciate, would have slapped a 27.5 percent tariff on imports from China. But to do so would have cast doubt on the U.S. commitment to a rules-based WTO and jeopardized prospects for getting the Doha Round back on track (discussed earlier), not to mention risking Chinese cooperation on North Korea. To their credit, Secretary John Snow and his colleagues instead urged China to allow more currency flexibility on the assumption that a flexible renminbi would appreciate and thereby cut the bilateral Chinese-U.S. surplus. From the summer of 2003, the Treasury pressed the case for renminbi adjustment in public statements and bilateral discussions with Chinese officials. The administration asked Schumer and Congress to wait for it to produce results.

The question was whether it would. The Chinese were reluctant to adjust the exchange rate, their policies of export-led growth depending, in the dominant view, on the maintenance of a stable and competitively valued currency. Since the late 1970s the legitimacy of the regime had depended on its ability to deliver the goods, and since the mid-1990s this had meant, in practice, delivering them to the United States. Social stability hinged on creating millions of additional jobs in urban manufacturing annually, something with which a sharp appreciation and sharp slowdown in export growth were not compatible. And simply revaluing the renminbi might have little effect on the U.S. deficit if other countries did not go along.

Finally, it was not clear that American tactics were well designed for getting the Chinese to move. U.S. officials pushed for free floating rather than offering to settle for a transitional revaluation. They spoke of the desirability of a "market-determined exchange rate," reflecting uncertainty about the extent of the renminbi's undervaluation and their preference for shunning intervention in foreign exchange markets. But China, lacking deep and liquid markets and hedging instruments for banks and firms, was in no position to let its currency float freely. This "market-determined exchange rate" rhetoric seemingly asked them to do the impossible. In any case, focusing on the renminbi exchange rate made little sense insofar as what was needed was a package of policy changes (increased spending on infrastructure and public services, the development of financial markets and a social safety net, and increased domestic demand to soften the impact of lower net exports) and parity adjustments not just by China but by a range of U.S. trading partners. Nor was the United States in a position to offer anything in return other than avoidance of punitive tariffs. Finally, it was not clear that the Chinese would react favorably to badgering.

There are multiple explanations, then, for the fact that direct pressure produced little other than Chinese statements of willingness to move to a more flexible exchange rate "eventually." In early 2005 the administration switched tactics from public pressure to private diplomacy; from exclusive focus on the exchange rate to the need for a coordinated set of Chinese policy adjustments (developing financial markets, augmenting the social safety net, and getting state-owned enterprises to pay dividends); and from preoccupation with the bilateral relationship to encouraging China to become a "responsible stakeholder" in multilateral institutions in which international economic policy outcomes were shaped. This last tactic was the culmination of a long journey for an administration that had come to office with attitudes that ranged from disdain to outright hostility toward the IMF and the World Bank but that now sought to enlist them as vehicles for advancing its foreign economic policy.

Robert Zoellick invoked this responsible-stakeholder rhetoric both publicly and privately. Henry Kissinger, Brent Scowcroft, and William Rhodes were briefed by the Treasury Department and enlisted to carry the message to Beijing. The fact that, aside from Rhodes (the senior vice chairman of Citigroup), these individuals were not financial specialists pointed to the fact that the administration sought to encourage China to assume more responsibility for the operation of the international system generally and not just for the problem of imbalances. But even from this narrowly financial perspective, the new approach paid dividends: the Chinese revalued the renminbi by 2.1 percent on July 21, 2005, and announced that henceforth it would be allowed to fluctuate more freely.

Movements in the currency were still tightly controlled by the People's Bank, resulting in little further appreciation and explosive growth in the Chinese surplus through the first half of 2007. Still, this could be advertised as a down payment. Snow's successor, Henry Paulson, continued to press the Chinese for greater currency flexibility and appreciation. On his inaugural trip to China as treasury secretary in September 2006, Paulson met with the party secretary of fast-growing Zhenjang Province and dined with the central bank governor, himself a well-known proponent of flexibility. Paulson thus sought to reframe the debate as one not between the United States and China but between pro- and antiliberalization forces in both countries.

To redirect attention away from the bilateral imbalance and to further encourage China to assume greater responsibility for the problems of the international system, the Bush administration reluctantly embraced the IMF's multilateral consultations initiative, announced in the spring of 2006. The idea was that, with the IMF providing projections and serving as honest broker, and with Europe, Japan, and Saudi Arabia (as a representative of the oil-exporting surplus countries) also at the table, it was more likely that the major players could agree on a coordinated package of policy adjustments to increase the likelihood of a smooth unwinding of global imbalances. In particular, the onus would not be on China alone to offset any compression of U.S. demand; with China, Europe, Japan, and the oil exporters expanding demand simultaneously, there would be less need for sharp adjustments by any one economy. This was also a way of cloaking U.S. demands in multilateral cloth and lending international legitimacy to the country's call for Chinese adjustment. The IMF—not the Treasury through its semiannual report on exchange rate manipulation—would be responsible for determining whether currencies such as the renminbi were significantly undervalued. There is an obvious parallel to the Bush administration's initial reluctance to deal with Saddam Hussein through the United Nations and its subsequent efforts to enlist the UN in Iraq.

The administration understood, however, that the multilateral consultation was a two-edged sword. Allowing the IMF to become adjudicator of exchange rates and external imbalances was fine and good except when the Fund concluded that the U.S. deficit was unsustainable and the dollar would have to fall significantly. Convening a multilateral consultation inevitably raised the question of what the United States would bring to the table. Other countries unanimously identified low U.S. savings as contributing to the imbalances problem. Raising taxes or even just sunsetting the Bush tax cuts of 2001–2002 were obvious ways of raising public saving, but there was reluctance to do so on ideological and practical political grounds. Sharper increases in interest rates might encourage private saving, but this grew less attractive as the U.S. expansion entered its late stages. Not surprisingly, when the results of the first consultation were released in April 2007, they turned out to be weak soup. The U.S. government acknowledged the desirability of cutting its budget deficit and raising household savings but without committing to any new policies designed to do so. China acknowledged the desirability of greater exchange rate flexibility, as it had in the past, without committing to any actual changes in policy.

By early 2007, the trade-weighted value of the dollar had fallen by 17 percent since the beginning of 2002. Demand had begun picking up in Europe and Japan, and there were some signs that the U.S. deficit had peaked, leading the IMF to back off the issue. The problem was that China had allowed the renminbi to appreciate by only a cumulative 7 percent against the greenback, placing most of the burden on other countries that were forced to absorb the bulk of the adjustment and rendering them reluctant to do more. Thus it was important for the soft-landing scenario that in early 2007 the Chinese authorities indicated a willingness to contemplate greater flexibility if the country's external surplus continued to grow.[12] Precisely what this means and whether it will support a smooth unwinding of global imbalances remain to be seen. If it does, the administration's approach of relying on words rather than deeds—avoiding both trade conflicts with China and measures that would have interfered with U.S. expansion—will have been vindicated.

By the administration's second term, then, there had developed an appreciation of the advantages of attempting to advance U.S. foreign monetary and financial interests through the IMF rather than relying exclusively on bilateral initiatives.[13] Working through the Fund was a way of depersonalizing and depoliticizing the international debate over policy adjustments. More strikingly, the administration evidently realized that the United States could more effectively advance its interests within the Fund only by agreeing to boost the representation of emerging markets. The institution would be seen as a legitimate venue for policy debate and action, it realized, only if rapidly growing countries were adequately represented in terms of quotas (which determined voting rights) and seats on the executive board. The U.S. government led the charge for governance reform at the Fund starting in 2004. The summer of 2006 saw agreement on a 1.8 percent quota increase for four egregiously underrepresented emerging markets—China, Korea, Turkey, and Mexico—and on the principle of a more comprehensive quota revision designed to reflect changes in the global economic landscape, to be completed by September 2008, in which the U.S. quota would not be increased. This was a turnaround for an administration initially so hostile to the Fund—again demonstrating how the United States is constrained by the existing international financial architecture.

This brings us to World Bank reform. One can readily imagine that George W. Bush himself was no fan of indiscriminate assistance for poor countries, which he likened to welfare. Secretary O'Neill insisted that the aid apparatus needed to be overhauled before being given more money. The world had spent "trillions of dollars [on development] and there's damn little to show for it," he complained, implying that the Bank was inefficient and poorly run.[14] O'Neill complained that World Bank president James Wolfensohn had no second in command and that the institution lacked priorities. It did not have adequate systems for assessing results.

John Taylor writes that he was sympathetic to the goal of poverty reduction.[15] Like O'Neill, he pushed for more measurement of results. He urged that the World Bank focus on its core competency, namely measures to reduce poverty in the poorest countries; that it "graduate" middle-income countries such as Brazil and Turkey that now enjoyed access to capital markets. And he pushed for shifting from loans to grants to avoid burdening poor countries with still more debt-servicing obligations. To the extent that the reflow of interest from earlier loans allowed the Bank to lend more, it was simply double-counting the transfers made to poor countries—adding new loans to its list of achievements without subtracting the repayments. Eventually, Taylor concluded in favor of forgiving the debts of the poorest countries.[16]

Bush rolled out his plan for replacing loans with grants in a speech on the eve of the Group of Eight (G8) Summit in Genoa in July 2001. The result was a tug-of-war between the Bush administration on one side and on the other its European counterparts and Bank staff, which suspected the administration of using these proposals as cover for scaling back the Bank. The Europeans opposed graduating middle-income countries because this meant limiting Bank involvement in many parts of the world. They opposed shifting from loans to grants because, in the absence of new resources, there would be no money for new loans unless previous recipients paid back what they had borrowed.

At this point came the September 11 attacks on the World Trade Center. Soon after the attacks, Wolfensohn began emphasizing the contribution of the Bank's antipoverty mission to the administration's war on terror. He spoke with National Security Council chair Condoleezza Rice and ramped up Bank missions in the strategic region around Afghanistan. O'Neill resisted calls from Britain and suggestions from Wolfensohn to back these initiatives with increased aid flows, insisting that the Bank first demonstrate that it could put more money to good use.

But O'Neill's influence was in decline, and the argument that foreign aid was more than an act of altruism—that it was now a mechanism for enhancing the national security—was compelling in the wake of 9/11.[17] In the spring of 2002, the Bush administration performed a U-turn. At the Monterrey summit it promised an extra $5 billion in aid over three years (later changed to an extra $5 billion a year indefinitely). Evidently, Wolfensohn's line that Bank assistance was critical to the war on terror trumped O'Neill's skepticism. This was the origin of the Millennium Challenge Corporation (MCC), an administration initiative to tilt aid toward countries that met sixteen benchmarks of good governance and policy.

The problem was the difficulty of finding countries and projects that satisfied these conditions. It was as if lending would be limited to countries that had removed the fundamental obstacles to growth and development—thereby rendering development assistance redundant.[18] The underlying ideas may be appealing—that only countries with reasonably strong controls and policies can make productive use of additional grants in aid—but the result has been to limit disbursements to a trickle. Other initiatives have produced greater results; these include the Emergency Plan for AIDS Relief in Africa (Pepfar) and paying more attention to such problems as malaria. Thus, no matter how much the administration may have wanted to get out of the "welfare for poor countries" business, the realities and constraints were too complex.

Nor was the war on terror an unmitigated blessing for the World Bank. In the summer of 2003, the United States pushed Wolfensohn and the Bank to lend to Iraq. Snow called for this publicly. Taylor requested that the Bank pledge billions in loans to Iraq's budget. Wolfensohn objected that there was no recognized government (no government that had been recognized by a UN resolution) to which to lend. It is hard to see how this initiative could have done anything but undermine the administration's emphasis on lending only to countries with efficient governments.

Against this background, the nomination of Paul Wolfowitz to succeed James Wolfensohn as president of the Bank proved controversial. Wolfowitz incited controversy for his campaign against corruption and graft. To be sure, this emphasis was consistent with earlier administration attacks on the Bank: Secretary O'Neill had pointed to these and other problems when criticizing the Bank's inefficiency, and control of corruption had been one of the sixteen indicators enumerated by the MCC. And Wolfensohn had already highlighted the corruption issue during his tenure. But it became controversial once Wolfowitz charged his personal advisers, Americans with Republican Party ties, with heading up the program and failed to develop an open process and transparent criteria. Bank staff referred to an atmosphere of suspicion and criticized program administrators for their failure to consult. Countries such as South Africa complained that the anticorruption agenda threatened to compromise the Bank's key mission of poverty reduction. Once this spat went public, the development committee of governmental overseers of the Bank insisted on revisions in the anticorruption paper.

That said, there were achievements. The Bank strengthened its systems to measure the results of its programs. European opposition to substituting grants for loans was partially overcome. The decision that 21 percent of International Development Association (IDA) funds would be used for grants was a compromise between European insistence on using no more than 10 percent of Bank resources in this way and the administration's opening bid of 50 percent. There was agreement on the U.S. proposal to forgive the IDA debt of the poorest countries over initial European objections that this would further limit World Bank resources. To make this palatable, the administration agreed to increase its funding for IDA and tabled its proposal to graduate middle-income countries.

Agenda for the Next Administration

Given our thesis that U.S. foreign economic policy is significantly constrained by existing interests and inherited structures, we suspect that the agenda of the next administration will again be dominated by familiar issues and that its options will be similarly limited. The next administration, like its predecessors, will confront WTO ministerial meetings (on a two-year cycle), domestic farm bills (on a five-year cycle), protectionist pressures from particular industries (trade law enforcement), and the desire to renew its negotiating authority. It will have some latitude in how it responds, but it will have to respect the existence of long-standing U.S. government policies on these issues. These positions are based on the view that America's economic engagement with the world is in the national economic and foreign policy interest.

The next administration will inherit many unresolved issues from the Bush administration. One notable unresolved matter is the loss of trade promotion authority and the fate of the Doha Round. Although administration officials had hoped for an "early harvest" from the Doha Round, they were powerless to produce such a result without a willingness on the part of the EU to compromise on its agricultural subsidies and of India and Brazil to agree on market opening. With a divided WTO membership of 150 countries, reaching any agreement has proven difficult and will continue to be so.[19] There is little that a new administration can do about this situation, even if it wanted to.

Deadlock at the multilateral level is nothing new. A more important problem is the increasingly sour domestic political environment for trade. Here, a constellation of factors portends a long pause in activist U.S. trade policies geared toward trade liberalization.[20] The incoming president is likely to lack trade promotion authority. Although trade negotiations can conceivably take place even if the president does not have such authority from Congress, U.S. negotiators will lack credibility with their foreign counterparts, and those negotiations will lack a sense of urgency without it.

The next administration will almost certainly want trade promotion authority as an arrow in its quiver, so the question is whether Congress can be persuaded to go along. Congress has become increasingly hostile to protrade measures: the trade agenda has been complicated by fears about offshoring of American service jobs, by growing concerns about income inequality and the distribution of the gains from globalization, and by the large bilateral trade deficit with China. These issues may affect many administrations to come. Each defies easy solution.

An unfortunate characteristic of the Bush years has been sharply divisive, partisan congressional votes on TPA and various FTAs. The Bush administration did not seriously attempt to build a domestic consensus in favor of open trade but pushed through its legislative initiatives by the brute force of marginal votes. A domestic consensus on trade might be restored with greater social insurance measures to help those adversely affected by imports or by coupling trade agreements with stronger labor and environmental provisions, as many Democrats propose. The catch is that a move by Congress to require meaningful labor and environmental standards in trade agreements will be greeted with suspicion, if not outright hostility, by developing countries. They have resented Western demands for such standards in the past, viewing such requirements as merely providing an additional avenue for the United States and other developed countries to close their markets.

Because of domestic discontent on trade, it is easy to imagine a new U.S. president simply deciding that it is not worth spending political capital on pushing for new trade initiatives. If such initiatives encounter domestic resistance and lack a compelling foreign policy rationale, trade could easily be put on the back burner. The United States could enter a long period of disengagement on trade.

All this portends a long pause in activist U.S. policies geared toward trade liberalization. At best, this would mean that the status quo remains intact. Ongoing technological change and foreign investment will continue to bring the world's economies closer together. Continued drift in or even collapse of the Doha Round could mean a missed opportunity, but nothing more. Even if it encounters stiff domestic resistance to trade-expansion policies, the next administration almost certainly will not seek to withdraw from the WTO. And the rules and procedures of the WTO will continue to constrain domestic trade policy.

The greater risk is that, without forward progress on trade, past gains from liberalization will be whittled away as countries backslide on previous commitments. If the domestic political climate for trade liberalization deteriorates further, with greater domestic income inequality and job losses becoming linked in the public mind to factors emanating from the world economy, Congress may be tempted to enact antitrade protectionist legislation. Although most presidents would be expected to veto such legislation, containing such pressures would still be a formidable challenge.

And if legislation should be enacted that seriously violates America's commitments under the WTO, the United States could not only face retaliation from abroad but also trigger a weakening of WTO commitments by other countries, leading to a general unraveling of the open multilateral system of world trade. Although the large economic stakes make a full-blown trade war seem unlikely, a gradual breakdown in the WTO disciplines would take many years to repair and could have grave economic consequences for the United States. Thus the next president may end up playing defense against Congress rather than pursuing an offensive trade policy with other countries.

As other chapters in this book have discussed, some of the most difficult challenges for American foreign policy are located in the Middle East. Because of its dependence on imported oil, America is tied to the region in a way in which it is not tied to other areas of the world, such as South America. Although every president since Richard Nixon has made statements about the need to reduce America's dependence, none has actually taken serious steps to encourage alternative energy sources. As a result, although the amount of energy needed to produce a dollar's worth of GDP has fallen considerably since the 1970s, the U.S. economy remains at risk of an oil price shock. Even worse, the huge revenues associated with Middle Eastern oil exports create the problem of vast financial resources falling into the hands of extremist regimes, resources with which they could purchase weapons of mass destruction or fund terrorist campaigns across the world. The domestic solution—higher taxes on the consumption of fossil fuels— may seem obvious to economists, but it has yet to find a strong political constituency.

A long-term goal of the United States has been to enable the countries of the Middle East to diversify their economies away from oil and to generate economic growth that brings about shared prosperity for all citizens in the region. The Bush administration has proposed free-trade agreements in the greater Middle East as one means to this end. The hope is that opening up a repressed Middle Eastern economy to the world will unleash beneficial economic, as well as societal, changes. But the administration has found few willing partners. Countries such as Saudi Arabia, Syria, and Iran have relatively closed societies and oppressive political systems and are not hospitable to the rough-and-tumble of foreign investment.[21] Thus there are severe constraints on what American power can do to help the economies of the Middle East. Even if the United States believes that improved economic performance in the Middle East will reduce the threat of terrorism, it lacks the capability of doing so without a willingness on the part of those countries to bring about change.

America's continuing large current account deficit and ongoing dependence on foreign central banks for financing will continue to be a source of vulnerability going forward. The fact that critical financing is provided by the central banks and governments of countries such as China and Saudi Arabia means that anything that upsets U.S. relations with these countries could upset the U.S. economy, as well. In turn, this gives foreign governments a lever with which to demonstrate their displeasure with U.S. foreign policy.

Imagine a conflict with China over Taiwan or Saudi displeasure over U.S. policy in the Middle East. If these countries curtail their ongoing accumulation of dollars and shift the composition of their reserve portfolios away from dollars in favor of, say, euros, the dollar will fall sharply, and the U.S. current account deficit will have to be compressed. The mechanism would be higher inflation that leads the Federal Reserve to raise interest rates and, quite possibly, a recession. This is not to argue that American foreign policy will be dictated by foreign financial leverage over the U.S. economy but to suggest that this additional source of dependence will complicate the efforts of the next administrations to pursue an independent foreign policy.

More generally, the country's external deficit and dependence on foreign finance heightens economic risks. One can equally imagine that foreign central banks, seeing the U.S. external deficit as unsustainable, might shift out of dollars in order to avoid capital losses on their reserve portfolios. In the longer run, a chronically weak dollar will encourage foreign central banks, governments, and corporations to consider alternatives to the dollar as the medium in which to hold reserves, to price petroleum, to invoice trade, and so forth. Estimates of the value to the United States of the dollar's international currency status vary, but the country clearly will be no better off when that status is history.

Following the 2004 presidential election, there was an opportunity to address these vulnerabilities. With the economy expanding strongly it would have been possible to pursue what is politely referred to inside the Beltway as "revenue enhancement" to address the problem of public dissaving. But more than seven years into the expansion, growth has slowed as the economy has come to operate close to full capacity. In turn, this constrains economic policy options. Tax increases run the risk of interrupting growth. The next administration will inherit from the campaign a mandate to provide universal health care and to reform the alternative minimum tax, along with other familiar spending pressures; so the idea that it will be able to solve the twin deficits problem with expenditure discipline is naive. Winding down U.S. involvement in Iraq will create fiscal savings, but military and homeland security-related spending is not a plausible source of budgetary economies overall. The window for proactive adjustment having closed, the next administration will have little choice but to hope for the best. It will have to pray that foreign financing for the U.S. current account continues to flow while the dollar declines smoothly, stimulating exports, and that the absence of capital gains on housing will encourage more saving by American households. Crossing one's fingers and hoping for the best is not an attractive position for a new administration to find itself in, but such is the inheritance.

An orderly adjustment that limits U.S. external vulnerabilities would be facilitated by rebalancing of demand in Asia. If U.S. spending has to decline relative to U.S. output, Asian spending should rise relative to Asian output to avoid compressing global demand and depressing global growth. This is largely an issue involving China.[22] A strategy for dealing with that country will be high on the foreign economic policy agenda of any future administration. Experience suggests that "China-bashing" is unlikely to produce the desired reforms; we suspect that a continuation of the Paulson strategy of gently encouraging reformist interests in the country has greater prospects of success. There may also be some scope for playing "good cop, bad cop" by warning that if China fails to reduce dependence on exports and to stimulate domestic demand, the administration may be unable to contain protectionist sentiment in Congress.[23] That said, the effectiveness of U.S. pressure for Chinese policy adjustments will be limited by what Lawrence Summers has dubbed "the balance of financial terror." China can always push back against aggressive pressure by selling some of its U.S. treasury bonds or simply slowing their rate of accumulation. This suggests that pressure for policy adjustments in China can be more effectively applied by a coalition of like-minded countries.

This brings us to the next administration's relations with the multilateral financial institutions. The Bush administration came into office suspicious of the IMF and the World Bank and sought to address economic and financial issues with other countries primarily through bilateral channels. Its economic relations with China, not unlike its experience in Iraq, demonstrate the limitations of going it alone. In addition to bilateral means, the administration tried to address the China problem through the IMF's multilateral consultations initiative and by encouraging support for the Fund's authority to identify misaligned exchange rates. The Bush Treasury accepted the idea of a modest reduction in the U.S. quota share as its contribution to a larger package of reforms designed to enhance the legitimacy of the institution. It rethought its initial hostility toward foreign aid by agreeing to the Monterrey Consensus. The next administration will almost certainly continue down this road.

But American relations with the Bretton Woods institutions, like the country's relationship to the UN, remain uneasy. The next administration will have more fences to mend, particularly in the wake of the Wolfowitz affair. Here the decision to nominate Robert Zoellick to replace Wolfowitz, however qualified Zoellick may have been as an individual, was an opportunity lost. By insisting on its historical privilege to nominate the president of the World Bank, the Bush administration did nothing to enhance the perceived legitimacy of the institution among emerging markets. It encouraged European governments to argue that sauce for the goose was sauce for the gander and that they had the right to nominate the successor to Rodrigo de Rato as managing director of the IMF. The idea that the United States can work through these institutions to advance global economic prosperity and stability and, not incidentally, its own foreign economic policy agenda, presumes that these institutions have legitimacy and are taken seriously elsewhere in the world.[24] An illegitimate leadership selection process increasingly undermines this presumption. Why, for example, should China accept the IMF as a legitimate umpire for exchange rates when it has no real say in the appointment of that institution's director? A simple and effective initiative for the next administration would thus be to announce, on taking office, that it would not seek to nominate Zoellick's successor when his term expires and that it expects similar concessions of Europe.

Conclusion

Our analysis of the Bush administration's international economic policies stresses continuities with rather than breaks from its predecessors. In trade policy, the administration sought to push a free-trade agenda, but often found it difficult to avoid the use of protectionist measures—just like its predecessors. In financial policy, the administration forswore bailouts of financially distressed developing countries yet ultimately yielded to the perceived necessity of lending assistance—just like its predecessors. Not unlike previous executives, President Bush assumed a stance of benign neglect of the country's current account deficit.

We see the next administration grappling with the same problems under the same political and policy constraints. The challenges facing it will be broadly similar to those that beset the Bush administration when it took office: deadlock at the WTO, the difficulty of encouraging European Union agricultural reform, trade tensions with China, the risk of a disorderly unwinding of the U.S. current account deficit, and ongoing World Bank and IMF reform. The nature of U.S. interests and the structure of international institutions and U.S. policy making suggest that there will be few sharp breaks in policy, partisan differences notwithstanding. The institutions and interests in which the policy-making process is embedded shape outcomes too powerfully for any other forecast to be credible.

Acknowledgment

We thank Glenn Hubbard, Phil Levy, Will Melick, and Ted Truman for helpful comments on earlier drafts of this chapter.

Notes

1. Douglas A. Irwin, "From Smoot Hawley to Reciprocal Trade Agreements: Changing the Course of U.S. Trade Policy in the 1930s," in *The Defining Moment: The Great Depression and the American Economy*, ed. Michael Bordo, Claudia Goldin, and Eugene White (Chicago: University of Chicago Press, 1998), 325–352.

2. The logic was straightforward: the expansion of world trade would promote economic recovery in Western Europe and secure the foundations of democracy, thereby enabling those countries to resist Soviet Communism, and thus promote the national security interests of the United States. Similarly, Bush repeatedly made the case that free trade is an uplifting policy that not only would spread prosperity and hope to places in which both were in short supply but also would ultimately lead to political freedom. "Free trade is also a proven strategy for building global prosperity and adding to the momentum of political freedom.... And greater freedom for commerce across the borders eventually leads to greater freedom for citizens within the borders." Bush's remarks at signing of the Trade Act of 2002 (August 6, 2002), http://www.whitehouse .gov/news/releases/2002/08/20020806-4.html.

3. The WTO now provides an important constraint on the use of such discretionary protection. The Bush administration imposed safeguard duties on imported steel in March 2002, but after the EU and others won their case against the tariffs in the WTO dispute settlement system, the administration removed the tariffs in December 2003. Robert Read, "The Political Economy of Trade Protection: The Determinants and Welfare Impact of the 2002 U.S. Emergency Steel Safeguard Measures," *World Economy* 28 (2005): 1119–1137.

4. Robert Zoellick, "Countering Terror with Trade," *Washington Post*, September 20, 2001.

5. For a sharp analysis of the WTO's difficulties, see Paul Collier, "Why the WTO Is Deadlocked, and What to Do about It," *World Economy* 29 (2006): 1423–1449.

6. The term *competitive liberalization* was first used by C. Fred Bergsten, "Competitive Liberalization and Global Free Trade: A Vision for the Early 21st Century" (working paper no. 96-15, Institute for International Economics, 1996), to describe the process of Asian trade liberalization during the early 1990s and was adopted by Zoellick as a description of his approach.

7. Robert Zoellick, "Unleashing the Trade Winds: A Building Block Approach," *The Economist* (December 7, 2002).

8. The shift toward more bilateral and regional trade agreements has received mixed reviews from economists. Some tend to support the nondiscriminatory most-favored-nation principles of the GATT and WTO and believe that multilateral negotiations are the only way to deal with the troublesome issue of agricultural and export subsidies; see Jagdish Bhagwati and Arvind Panagariya, *The Economics of Preferential Trade Agreements* (Washington, DC: AEI Press, 1996). Proponents of FTAs argue that they are a useful alternative if the

multilateral option is not viable, given the difficulties of reaching an agreement at the WTO. According to the proponents, the FTA, or "like-minded country" approach, bypasses the holdup problem at the WTO and is likely to create more trade than it diverts, and hence it may put pressure on reluctant trade reformers to change their approaches.

9. Paul Blustein, *And the Money Kept Rolling In (and Out)* (New York: Public Affairs, 2005), 118.

10. A comprehensive account of the prehistory is found in Kenneth Rogoff and Jeromin Zettelmeyer, "Early Ideas on Sovereign Bankruptcy: A Survey," *IMF Staff Papers* 49 (2002): 471–507.

11. The problem of low U.S. savings is discussed by Nouriel Roubini and Brad Setser, "The U.S. as a Net Debtor: The Sustainability of the U.S. External Imbalances" (unpublished manuscript, Stern School of Business, New York University, 2004). On high U.S. investment, see Richard Cooper, "U.S. Deficit: It Is Not Only Sustainable, It Is Logical," *Financial Times*, October 31, 2004; on high foreign saving, see Ben Bernanke, "The Global Savings Glut and the U.S. Current Account Deficit," Sandridge Lecture, Virginia Association of Economics (March 10, 2005), http://www.federalreserve.gov/boarddocs/speeches/2005/200503102/; on depressed foreign investment, see Raghuram Rajan, "Perspectives on Global Imbalances" (January 23, 2006), http://www.imf.org.

12. See, inter alia, Bloomberg News, "China Says It May Be Flexible with Yuan," *New York Times*, January 8, 2007.

13. Again, it is not hard to see an analogy with other forms of foreign policy and with the evolution of the administration's attitude toward the UN.

14. Quoted in Sebastian Mallaby, *The World's Banker: A Story of Failed States, Financial Crises, and the Wealth and Poverty of Nations* (New York: Penguin, 2004), 289.

15. John B. Taylor, *Global Financial Warriors* (New York: Norton, 2007), chapter 5.

16. In formulating this agenda, Taylor was influenced by the Meltzer Commission, which had considered World Bank, as well as IMF, reform. Its report had called for curtailing Bank operations in middle-income countries and for replacing loans with grants; Meltzer knew both O'Neill and Taylor and once had an office on the same corridor as Lawrence Lindsey and R. Glenn Hubbard at the American Enterprise Institute. Taylor cites the Meltzer report in his book when discussing the need for World Bank reform; Taylor, *Global Financial Warriors*, 135.

17. This idea was explicitly incorporated into successive national security strategies. It was also the motivation behind Secretary Rice's "transformational diplomacy" push.

18. The administration addressed this problem by creating threshold program agreements, or contracts, between the U.S. government and a country that provide for financial assistance to help improve a low score on one of the MCC's sixteen policy indicators.

19. Multilateral trade negotiations are notoriously slow to complete. The Kennedy Round took three years (1964–1967); the Tokyo Round took six years (1973–1979); and the Uruguay Round took seven years to finish (1986–1993).

20. Even if an internationalist Democrat similar to Bill Clinton succeeds in taking the White House, economic nationalism is rampant among congressional Democrats, potentially blocking any action on trade. Such Democratic divisions are not new; the Roosevelt administration was deeply divided between liberal internationalists such as Secretary of State Cordell Hull and other economic nationalist New Dealers who thought that trade liberalization would undermine domestic price supports and other measures that sought to ensure full employment. Hull battled long and hard to ensure that his views became established administration policy.

21. Bessma Momani, "A Middle East Free Trade Area: Economic Interdependence and Peace Considered," *World Economy* 30, no. 11 (November 2007): 1682–1700.

22. Other emerging Asian countries (South Korea, Thailand, and the Philippines) have allowed their currencies to appreciate against the dollar and have already moved their current accounts toward balance. The two other emerging Asian economies in strong surplus, Singapore and Hong Kong, are too small to have a first-order impact on global imbalances. One nonemerging Asian economy, Japan, is also in strong surplus, though its high debt and lethargic growth leave little room for monetary or fiscal measures to stimulate spending.

23. Of course, a president who had campaigned in favor of anti-China trade measures could not credibly adopt this posture.

24. U.S. support for quota increases for egregiously underrepresented emerging markets and the Treasury's commitment to ensuring that the United States would not demand a quota increase itself as part of this process can be seen as recognition of this fact.

NINE

Soft Talk, Big Stick
Francis Fukuyama

THERE ARE FOUR broad approaches that U.S. foreign policy can take in the post-Bush era. America can talk loudly and carry a big stick (the policy of Bush's first term); talk loudly and carry a small stick (where Bush's second term has ended up); talk softly and carry a big stick; or talk softly and carry a small stick. Some observers from diverse points in the ideological spectrum, from Pat Buchanan to Barry Posen and John Mearsheimer, have argued for the latter, whereby the United States largely retreats from the Middle East and takes a much narrower view of its national interests.

My own preference, which I elaborate in this chapter, is for talking softly and carrying a big stick. I do not believe that the United States can seriously disengage from many parts of the world, though it will surely have to get out of Iraq over time and diminish its overall footprint in the Middle East. The Bush administration greatly overplayed the role of "benevolent hegemon," overestimating the degree to which the rest of the world would accept the legitimacy of American leadership and its unilateral use of power. But the fact of the matter remains that there are a number of global public goods that will be significantly undersupplied if the United States does not remain heavily engaged in world politics, from maintenance of an open international trading order to sea lane security to environmental protection and disease control to humanitarian assistance and, yes, a world in which democracy and human rights are observed. Existing international institutions are important for facilitating international collective action, but at this stage in history they are far too weak and ineffective to supply these public goods. In the past, they have worked much better in concert with strong support from the

United States, and indeed many (such as the Bretton Woods institutions or the World Trade Organization [WTO]) have been created only with American leadership.

The reasons for preferring a strongly engaged United States are both practical and moral. The current globalized international system is one that the United States played a large role in creating and from which it benefits enormously. To give one example, American living standards would not be nearly so high as they are now were it not for the willingness of foreign countries to hold large reserves of American dollars. Although current global financial imbalances have been much commented on and are in the long run unsustainable, the fact of the matter is that the United States is in a mutual suicide pact with China and other holders of U.S. currency reserves. Neither we nor they can unilaterally extricate ourselves from the relationship of mutual dependence without risking huge economic losses.

The second reason for continued involvement is moral. The United States, as the world's richest and most powerful country, cannot, in my view, simply stand aside when countries are faced with famine, poverty, or dictatorship. There are, of course, many dangers to unbridled moralism in international politics, particularly when undertaken by a global hegemonic power. Countries with the ability to protect the weak have an obligation to do so, and not simply because the United Nations (UN) says so.

The exercise of American power will continue to be necessary and inevitable, but it can be done in a much more indirect and nuanced fashion. By talking loudly and carrying a big stick, the United States under President Bush has fostered a high degree of anti-Americanism throughout the world and stimulated opponents everywhere to think about how to constrain and limit U.S. influence. We need to back out of this dead end, not by disengaging in a wholesale way but by exercising forms of power other than hard military power and by using international institutions to shape incentives globally over the long term.

There is no overarching concept such as containment that would define a global American strategy. One problem of these large doctrines is that they are not very helpful in defining policy toward regions of lesser strategic interest; such places tend to get shoehorned into the grand concept as lesser included cases. There are today two major theaters of strategic importance to the United States, the greater Middle East and East Asia, each having very different characteristics and requiring different strategic approaches. But the United States has interests as well in such places as Latin America and Africa, neither of which can be subsumed under policies appropriate for the Middle East or Asia. I discuss what a big-stick, soft-talk strategy looks like for each.

The Greater Middle East

The general context for thinking about any overall foreign policy for the United States after the Bush administration is a recognition of the ways in which international relations themselves have changed at the beginning of the twenty-first century.

International relations in the twentieth century were dominated by such strong states as imperial and Nazi Germany, imperial Japan, the former Soviet Union, and the European colonial powers, all of whom could command a monopoly of force (though not necessarily a legitimate one) over their own territories.[1] In this state-centric world, conventional military power was indeed useful: it could be used to undermine the will of those at the top of the state hierarchy; when they admitted defeat, you had peace. This kind of world continues to exist in the global north and in the rapidly developing parts of East Asia (this subject is covered in the next section).

The United States was very well suited to play in such a world, given its margin of superiority in virtually all aspects of conventional military power. The United States alone spends as much on its military establishment as virtually the whole rest of the world combined. Yet it is worth pondering why it is that after five years of effort, thousands of American lives, and over a trillion dollars of outlays, it has not succeeded in pacifying a small country of some twenty-four million people called Iraq, much less leading it to anything that looks remotely like a successful democracy. Israel's huge margin of conventional superiority failed to achieve the ambitious transformational goals it set for itself in the war with Hezbollah in the summer of 2006; Ethiopia replicated this experience by successfully invading Somalia and then getting bogged down in an urban insurgency in Mogadishu.

The reason that conventional military power has been of so little use has to do with the fact that the band of instability that runs from North Africa through the Middle East, Africa, and Central Asia is characterized by numerous weak and sometimes failed states and by transnational actors that are able to move fluidly across international borders, abetted by the same technological capabilities that produced globalization. States such as Afghanistan, Pakistan, Iraq, Lebanon, Somalia, Palestine, and a host of others are not able to exercise sovereign control over their territories, ceding power and influence to terrorist groups such as al Qaeda, to political parties-cum-militias such as Hezbollah in Lebanon, or to the different ethnic and sectarian parties and factions elsewhere.

This situation is clearly disorienting to people accustomed to the state-centric world of the past century. In an article written after the Lebanon war of 2006, Henry Kissinger asserted that "Hezbollah is, in fact, a metastasization of the al-Qaeda pattern. It acts openly as a state within a state....A non-state entity on the soil of a state, with all the attributes of a state and backed by the major regional power, is a new phenomenon in international relations."[2] This pattern is only *relatively* new: it has been emerging for a good fifteen years now, as anyone following recent African politics understands all too well.[3] Such normally astute observers as Kissinger and the Bush administration are the ones that have been slow to recognize this new reality, with disastrous results. In the wake of the September 11 attacks, many officials in the administration simply could not believe that they could have been organized by a nonstate actor, leading them to their fateful search for a state sponsor in Baghdad. They are having a similar problem today in seeing Hezbollah as anything but a tool of Tehran.

In this world of weak states, transnational militias, and terrorist groups, conventional military power is much less useful than it was in the twentieth-century world of strong states. American military doctrine has emphasized the use of overwhelming force, applied suddenly and decisively, to defeat the enemy. But in a world in which insurgents and militias are deployed invisibly among civilian populations, overwhelming force is almost always counterproductive: it alienates precisely those people who have to make a break with the hard-core fighters and deny them the ability to operate freely. The kind of counterinsurgency campaign that is needed to defeat them puts political ahead of military goals and emphasizes hearts and minds over shock and awe.

The fact that we are dealing with a weak-state world in the Middle East, Africa, and Central Asia has several broad foreign policy implications. Traditional realism is not going to work here. Realism presumes the existence of centralized and competent states. But in a world of weak states and transnational nonstate actors, it is inevitable that U.S. policy will have to reach into the insides of states for solutions to certain problems. Despite the allergy to nation building that Americans have contracted as a result of our Iraq experience, they will have to develop tools for nation builders in the future. Without them, there will be no long-term solution to problems in Palestine, Lebanon, Somalia, Afghanistan, and elsewhere. A hearts-and-minds campaign cannot rely on power and arms-length state-to-state relations alone; it must also pay careful attention to questions of legitimacy and justice.

Nor is it clear that aggressive democracy promotion of the sort preached, at least rhetorically, by the Bush administration and its neoconservative backers will work, either. The Iraq fiasco has greatly deepened anti-Americanism in many parts of the world and tainted the democracy project as a tool of U.S. foreign policy, leading to pushback and countervailing strategies that have for the time greatly diminished the prospects of further democratic gains.

The kind of policy that will be needed to operate in this weak-state world will therefore need to be a hybrid. It will periodically require the use of hard power against hard-core enemies of the United States and its friends and allies; it will draw on various soft-power instruments to promote better governance and political development in turbulent parts of the world; and it will have to be flexible in its choice of friends and causes to support.

The War on Terrorism

Since the 9/11 attacks, President Bush has consistently overstated the seriousness and stakes involved in the conflict with al Qaeda and other jihadist groups (a.k.a. the "war on terrorism"). He has compared this struggle to the world wars and the cold war; in doing so, he has justified a huge American overreaction involving preventive war and torture that has ensured that the threat becomes a self-fulfilling prophecy. The next president has to learn to speak about the threat in a more balanced way and devise a very different and much less militarized strategy for dealing with it.

The fundamental problem in assessing the jihadist threat has to do with assigning the proper probabilities to terrorists' getting hold of either biological or nuclear weapons and using them against the United States. If one could somehow imagine a world in which such weapons of mass destruction (WMDs) did not exist, then the jihadism would clearly be a threat to the stability of regional allies but not a strategic threat to the United States itself.[4] Were terrorists to plant car bombs in U.S. cities or bring down transatlantic jetliners, we would face a serious security problem, but not one out of the range of experience of any number of other democracies during the cold war era. It rises to something more than that because of the continuing possibility of mass casualty attacks against the United States.

If one holds the view that many of the world's more than one billion Muslims hate the United States for what it is rather than for what it does, are motivated by a deep-seated religious fanaticism, and have the incentive and potential means for causing America catastrophic harm, then one might consider a wide range of rather extreme countermeasures. But this picture of the threat is, in my view, very overstated. The United States is deeply unpopular in many parts of the Muslim world today not because Muslims "hate freedom" but because they do not like our foreign policy. There is a lot of evidence that the vast majority of people in Muslim countries actually like American society, but they are deeply offended by the occupation of Iraq and our lack of sympathy for the Palestinians. The United States no longer inspires admiration for its concern for democracy and human rights but rather scorn for its hypocrisy in light of Abu Ghraib and Guantanamo.

The idea that we have not been attacked in America since 9/11 because we are fighting them "over there" is nonsensical because it assumes that there is an inelastic supply of terrorists globally. The use of the word *terrorism* by the Bush administration has also been deliberately misleading. We call an Iraqi nationalist who plants a bomb targeting American soldiers on Iraqi soil a terrorist just as much as a jihadist who attacks American civilians on American soil. America's occupation of a major Arab country is in itself a huge source of terrorist recruitment and serves to destabilize the whole region. Terrorism would not end if we withdrew from Iraq, but at the margin it would fall substantially.

There are a small and growing number of much more extremist Islamists who would dislike the United States regardless of what we do. But the number of people with the motive and potential means to carry out mass casualty attacks against the United States is probably closer to the hundreds than to the hundreds of millions. The blowback from the invasion will continue to dog us for many years to come, as it has already done in Lebanon with the insurgency mounted by the Fatah al-Islam group. This means that the objective of any sensible counterterrorism strategy should not be to think about the struggle as World War IV,[5] to be fought with conventional military power and overwhelming force, but rather as a global counterinsurgency campaign in which the political goal of winning hearts and minds among potential terrorist sympathizers should be at the center of U.S. strategy. On an ongoing basis, the strategy will look more like a police and intelligence operation, as well as a matter for defense and homeland security, than a war.

Part of the strategy must involve reconstructing state authority so that we can deal with coherent political interlocutors. We have been trying to do this unsuccessfully in Iraq and Afghanistan; Lebanon and the Palestinian Authority are other places in which long-term political solutions are not possible without stronger states. The problem here is that there is no technology for state building; it is an inherently political process, one in which outside powers have limited scope for influence. This requires on the one hand a certain amount of selectivity regarding where we undertake state-building projects and, on the other hand, emphasis on state-building strategies that adequately recognize the importance of local ownership—something we have not focused on in the past.[6]

Democracy, Development, and the Rule of Law

In the wake of Iraq and President Bush's rhetorical emphasis on democracy promotion, there has been a backlash both in public and elite opinion against it. In my view, the traditional emphasis on democracy promotion as an important component of U.S. foreign policy is appropriate. It is in line with American values; it commands broad support and, indeed, builds consensus in favor of international engagement on the part of the American public; and for the most part it serves American security interests.

The means by which we promote democracy are, of course, very important, and it is certainly possible to argue for greater prudence in means. To say that the United States should promote democracy does not mean that it should at all times and places put idealistic goals ahead of other types of national interests or that it should use military force in pursuit of these goals. Indeed, the United States has *never* made democracy promotion the overriding goal of its foreign policy, including under the Bush administration.

There are very few realists so hard core as to say that the United States should show *no* concern for democracy and human rights; rather, the more sophisticated arguments concern sequencing. State building, creation of a liberal rule of law, and democracy are conceptually different phases of political development, which in most European countries occurred in a sequence that was separated by decades, if not centuries. State building and creation of a rule of law are more critical for economic development than is democracy. Jack Snyder and Edward Mansfield have argued that democratization's early phases pose special dangers of promoting nationalism and illiberal politics.[7] Authors from Samuel Huntington to Fareed Zakaria have consequently argued that U.S. policy ought to focus on broad governance agenda and delay pushing for democracy until a higher level of economic development has been achieved.[8] This "authoritarian transition" has been followed by a number of countries, such as South Korea, Taiwan, and Chile, and is often recommended as a model for U.S. policy in such regions as the Middle East.

There is no question that liberal authoritarianism has worked quite successfully to promote economic development in such places as Singapore, and even less liberal versions of it, such as that of China, have piled up impressive economic growth rates. If these countries should eventually follow the Korean and Taiwanese paths toward a broadening of political participation, it is not obvious that an earlier democratic transition would clearly have brought about a better long-term result. In addition, there are specific instances (primarily in postconflict-failed state settings) in which outside pressure for early elections has arguably resulted not in the emergence of democratic political parties but rather in the locking in place of the same groups responsible for the original conflict.[9]

As Tom Carothers has recently pointed out, however, there are a number of problems with the sequencing strategy.[10] First, in most parts of the world it is very difficult to find liberal, developmentally minded authoritarians on which such a strategy can be built. Developing countries from Africa to the Middle East and Latin America have more commonly been characterized by authoritarian governments that are corrupt, incompetent, or self-serving.

The vast majority of liberal or developmentally minded authoritarian regimes or leaders are clustered in East Asia, for reasons that probably have roots in the region's Confucian culture. This means, in practice, that in most of the world, exactly the same groups want both liberal rule of law *and* democracy; it is simply not an option for the United States to promote the former and delay the latter.

A further problem with the sequencing strategy is that it presumes that the United States and other foreign powers can somehow control democratic transitions, holding back pressure for democratic elections while pushing for rule of law and good governance. This vastly overestimates the degree of control outsiders have over democratic transitions. Democratic transitions are driven by domestic actors who want accountable government; the United States and other external donors do not control the timing or extent of domestic pressures for democratization.

The real trade-offs come in regions such as the Middle East, in which America's closest strategic allies are such autocracies as Saudi Arabia, Jordan, Morocco, and Egypt. The Bush administration has made the general argument that the deep root cause of terrorism and Islamist radicalism is the region's lack of democracy and that promoting democracy is therefore one route to solving the terrorist threat. Natan Sharansky has made the argument that the Oslo peace process was fatally flawed because the United States and Israel relied on Yasser Arafat's authoritarian Fatah as an interlocutor instead of pressing for democracy in Palestine prior to peace negotiations.[11] Prior to the invasion of Iraq, some observers similarly hoped that a democratic Iraq would be a strategic partner of the United States and recognize Israel. By this view, democracy, security, and peace with Israel all went hand in hand.

It is quite clear in retrospect that this interpretation of the sources of Arab radicalism was too simplistic. The deep sources of terrorism are much more complex than a lack of Middle Eastern democracy. One can argue, in fact, that it is precisely the modernization process that produces terrorism and that more democracy is likely to worsen the terrorism problem, at least in the short run.[12] Many of the Iraqis who went to the polls in the various elections of 2005 were Shiites who wanted not liberal democracy but Shiite power and who have subsequently worked to establish an Iranian-style Islamic republic in areas under their control. The winners of democratic elections elsewhere in the region tend to be profoundly illiberal Islamist groups who are also more hostile to America's ally Israel than are the authoritarian governments they would like to displace. The political tide in the Middle East is not running in favor of pro-Western liberal opposition groups. In addition, America's authoritarian allies such as Hosni Mubarak of Egypt and Pervez Musharraf of Pakistan have been quite clever at sidelining liberal opponents in ways that heighten the threat from the Islamist opposition. The assertion of President Bush's second inaugural address that there is no necessary trade-off between American security interests and its idealistic goals would thus seem to be wrong.

The appropriate policy in response to this political landscape needs to be a graduated one that takes account of individual cases. There are some countries, such as Saudi Arabia, in which there is no realistic democratic alternative to the current authoritarian leadership or in which likely alternatives would clearly be worse from a strategic perspective. In these cases, sticking with authoritarian allies is the lesser of two evils. Although quiet pressure on Egypt to liberalize might be appropriate, provoking a major showdown to strong-arm Cairo into permitting free and fair elections is not likely to work. On the other hand, General Pervez Musharraf in Pakistan has undermined his own legitimacy to the point that he himself has become a source of instability. In the wake of former prime minister Benazir Bhutto's assassination, it is not clear who might emerge as a democratic alternative to military rule, but it is not at all obvious that Pakistan faces a stark choice between dictatorship and radical Islamism. An open election in Pakistan risks further gains by Islamist parties, but there are also a middle-class electorate and many who do not want to see Pakistan follow an anti-Western course.

Hamas in Gaza represents a more difficult case because it is not only illiberal but also committed to the destruction of America's ally Israel. The strategic problem here is whether it is better to have this group on the inside of a long-term peace and Palestinian state-building process or outside of it trying to block it. Hamas represents a significant part of the Palestinian electorate and the party will continue to be an important part of Palestinian politics regardless of whether the United States and Israel choose to deal with it. A strong argument can be made that it is better to accept Hamas's participation in a government in hopes that its goals will moderate over time. It is, in any event, difficult to see how basing American and Israeli policy on a corrupt Fatah government, as in the past, will be the basis for long-term progress either toward peace or toward the development of a legitimate interlocutor in the Palestinian Authority.

Foreign Policy as Social Work

Back in the first term of the Clinton administration, Michael Mandelbaum wrote an article in *Foreign Affairs* attacking the Democratic administration's early emphasis on humanitarian intervention in countries of marginal importance to core U.S. security interests, under the title "Foreign Policy as Social

Work."[13] This article reflects a common perception on the part of foreign policy specialists, particularly those of a realist bent, that hard power and security are the coin of the realm in international politics and that a focus on softer issues such as development, humanitarian assistance, and the like is a distraction and a misuse of American resources and influence. Whereas the United States has been consistently committed to promoting political democracy as part of its foreign policy, its commitment to promoting social development, particularly in such sectors as education and health, has been much spottier. Indeed, the United States, through international financial institutions, often supported cutbacks in social spending in the name of fiscal discipline under the so-called Washington Consensus. In this respect, foreign policy reflected the priorities of U.S. politics during the shift to the right that began with the election of Ronald Reagan, when domestic American social programs themselves came under attack.

It is not clear that this dismissive attitude toward a social agenda in U.S. foreign policy remains appropriate, however, in light of the post-Iraq struggle for hearts and minds around the world. What many openly anti-American forces around the world have in common, including Hezbollah in Lebanon, Hamas in Gaza, Mahmoud Ahmadinejad in Iran, the Muslim Brotherhood in Egypt, and Hugo Chávez in Venezuela, is an active social agenda. All of these organizations or leaders appeal to poor or marginalized constituencies by directly offering such social services as schools, clinics, and the like. Indeed, many of the radical groups that were democratically elected received support more for their social agendas than for their anti-American foreign policy stands.

What the United States has had to offer, by contrast, either directly through its aid programs or on the part of democratic political parties that it supports, has tended to be a combination of political democracy and the hope of trade-driven economic growth. There is absolutely nothing wrong with this agenda; democracy is a good thing in itself, and trade under the right circumstances can be an engine for economic development. The problem, however, is that this agenda tends to appeal to better educated middle-class voters rather than the poor in many developing societies. Although individual countries such as Chile and Jordan have benefited from free-trade agreements with the United States, such agreements are often hard to negotiate, and their impact is either small or delayed in ways that mitigate the political credit that the United States receives in return.

In many respects, much of the growth of radical Islamism in the Middle East can be traced to the failure of social policy on the part of ostensible U.S. allies such as Mubarak's Egypt or Pakistan under both civilian and military leaders. Parents would be much less likely to send their children to Islamist madrassas if the public education systems in these countries delivered good services. Similarly in Latin America, the old elites in such countries as Venezuela, Ecuador, and Bolivia failed to deliver on programs for the poor and marginalized, particularly the indigenous communities in the Andean countries. This failure then paved the way for populist demagogues such as Chávez or representatives of indigenous groups such as Evo Morales to come to power.

The United States is obviously not in a position to solve the deeply embedded problems of poverty and inequality in developing countries. It is not in a position to outbid local leaders who seek to provide social services to their constituents. Nor would it be desirable for the United States to advocate a return to the old socialist agenda of ever-increasing social spending and labor market regulation. But it is also very difficult to compete politically with populist leaders if the United States and its local democratic allies have nothing to offer in the social arena and indeed fail to even acknowledge the problems of poverty and marginalization in their political rhetoric.

Part of the problem is that social policy has not been of interest to most policy makers, especially those concerned with international affairs, for at least the past generation. Since the conservative Reagan-Thatcher revolutions of the 1980s and 1990s, the thrust of a lot of public policy has been, again, to cut back on social spending and welfare states. Many economists would argue that the best way to fight poverty is through rapid economic growth rather than through targeted social programs. In this, they are right: fast-growing countries such as China and Vietnam have reduced poverty dramatically through sustained growth. But many countries are simply not going to be able to achieve growth rates like those of the high performers in East Asia, and in the meantime they face serious political demands for more direct approaches to poverty. And in this realm, there has been relatively little new thinking on how to handle social policy better—that is, how to deliver basic social services such as education and health care in an equitable fashion but also in ways that do not bust budgets, create dependence and expanding entitlements, and return countries to conditions of permanent fiscal crisis.

There are, fortunately, existing new ideas that have some hope of addressing problems of poverty in ways compatible with economic growth. Back in the 1990s, for example, Mexico began a conditional cash transfer (CCT) program called *Progresa* under which low-income families would receive a direct stipend on the condition that they either send their school-age children to school or, if they were pregnant mothers, receive prenatal care. The program was carefully designed by a group of economists and had built into it facilities for statistically measuring the impact of the CCTs. The program proved both successful and popular and was greatly expanded under President Vicente Fox under the title *Oportunidades*. Since then, CCTs have been widely copied throughout Latin America and other parts of the developing world. The largest by far is the *Bolsa Família* in Brazil, which today reaches some fifteen million poor Brazilians and by some accounts has had a measurable effect in lowering Brazil's notoriously high Gini coefficient.[14]

How better to integrate innovative social programs into U.S. foreign policy is an issue that requires a long and separate analysis that would be inappropriate here. There are large problems in the mechanisms the United States employs for delivering development assistance, and repeated efforts to fix U.S. foreign assistance over the years do not make one optimistic about the prospects of doing this in the short term. The required change has to begin at a conceptual level, however. U.S. leaders have to learn to listen better to what people want from their governments and from the United States and not simply preach to them about what they should want. There is no reason to abandon the democracy/free trade agenda, but it needs to be broadened to include at least a rhetorical concern for the poor and politically excluded, who up to now have not been prime audiences for U.S. foreign policy.

Implementing a Soft-Power Approach

The different aspects of a new U.S. foreign policy converge in many ways, requiring a focus on democracy, development, hearts and minds, and an indirect use of force. Implementing this policy will not require new budget resources. Indeed, the overall military budget should fall substantially once the United States begins to disengage from Iraq. What is needed, rather, is a restructuring of the U.S. government to be able to project soft power and accomplish nation building better the next time around.

The United States wants to promote democracy and development as ends in themselves, but also to build goodwill among audiences that have been alienated by events since the Iraq war. Ironically, the best way to do this is not to slap a "made in U.S.A." sticker on all American aid and democracy-promotion programs but, rather, to distance them from U.S. foreign policy. It is, of course, not possible to do this completely. But trends over recent years that have sought, for example, to subordinate democracy promotion and development assistance to the authority of the State Department are a step in the wrong direction. If they are to produce goodwill for the United States, they need to be deinstrumentalized as means to the end of fighting terrorism and promoting U.S. strategic interests.

The most obvious way to do this is by implementing an organizational separation between the U.S. State and Defense departments on the one hand and those parts of the U.S. government tasked with democracy promotion and economic development on the other. The most logical step would be to create an independent, cabinet-level "Department of Development" modeled on the British Department for International Development (DfID) or the development ministries of any number of Western governments. This department would take over those long-term development functions of the current U.S. Agency for International Development both on the democracy and governance side and on the side of economic support. Those programs that are specifically meant to support U.S. foreign policy goals, such as Endowment for Middle East Truth (EMET) or aid to Israel and Egypt, can be left under the purview of the State Department.

I have elsewhere suggested a second separation, between this new Department of Development and a new or revamped agency that would make grants directly to foreign civil society organizations, as the National Endowment for Democracy does currently.[15] The logic is the same: the more organizational independence this agency has, the less its assistance will be freighted with association with U.S. grand strategy. In the end, a complete separation will not be either possible or desirable. Foreign governments and publics will understand that resources are coming from the same place—the U.S. taxpayer—and the latter will be called on to be generous in funding activities that do not always have direct links to U.S. security interests. But the principle of separation remains an important one.

A further necessary institutional innovation is the creation of an independent office to handle postconflict reconstruction and nation building. In the aftermath of the Iraq planning failure, there were many suggestions as to how to better organize nation-building functions within the U.S. government, leading in 2005 to the formation of an office of the Coordinator for Reconstruction and Stabilization (S/CRS) in the Department of State. Unfortunately, this office was never adequately funded and was hostage to the interagency rivalries over control of postconflict operations with the Pentagon. A similar function needs to be located outside of any of the big-line agencies in the U.S. government, but in a crisis it needs to be given adequate authority by the president to draw on resources and resolve interagency conflicts.[16]

Neither democracy promotion, development assistance, nor postconflict reconstruction should be thought of as wholly independent American activities. America's European allies and Japan, as well as a host of newer democracies, all engage cooperatively in these initiatives. In the case of the countries of the European Union, overall support for democracy promotion and development is substantially higher on a per capita basis than it is for the United States. A further way of delinking these activities from American foreign policy is to pursue them to a greater extent through multilateral organizations. This could happen in a number of ways, from increasing annual U.S. contributions

to organizations such as the World Bank and the UN Development Programme to proposing entirely new multilateral fora for certain development-
related functions (e.g., creating a permanent offshore trusteeship to hold and
manage public monies for countries subject to high levels of corruption). One
idea suggested by any number of observers is to get around the legitimacy
problems of the UN by creating a democratic caucus within the UN General
Assembly, by beefing up the existing Community of Democracies, or by creating an entirely new organization whose members would have to meet certain democracy and rule-of-law criteria to join. Such an organization would
include a large number of developing-country democracies and so would look
less like a rich nations' club, the way the North Atlantic Treaty Organization
(NATO) currently does. It might not in the first instance be able to organize
armed interventions, but it could certainly serve as a platform for promoting
democracy in different parts of the world.

Part of the trick to talking softly while carrying a big stick is for the United
States to shape global outcomes without it being obvious that that is what we
are trying to do. In the post-1945 period, the United States did this by setting
up a series of multilateral institutions, many of which have survived to this
day. Multilateralism is not an aim in itself. It is a way of buying institutionalized support from like-minded countries and of writing the United States into
the larger structure of global decision making.

China and Asia

Although there are some weak states in Asia, this region is characterized to a
much larger degree than the greater Middle East by strong and indeed rising
nation-states. This means that conventional American military power is much
more usable, as are many of the traditional tools of classical balance-of-power
diplomacy. Here, the problem will be a familiar one that has a number of
historical precedents: the entry of a new and rapidly rising great power into
the regional state system. This happened after the unification of Germany in
the late nineteenth century (with bad results) and with the rise of the United
States as a global maritime power (with better results). John Mearsheimer has
argued that these sorts of relative shifts in power often lead to conflict, and
he has predicted conflict between the United States and China. But there is
no inevitability to this happening, regardless of what international-relations
theory purportedly tells us, and one of the objectives of U.S. policy toward
this region will be to prove him wrong.

A rising China poses some new challenges for U.S. foreign policy precisely because it is complex and multidimensional. Earlier challenges in the

twentieth century, such as Nazi Germany, imperial Japan, and the former Soviet Union, were in a sense easier to deal with. These earlier adversaries were all territorially aggressive, had unlimited aims (at least in the case of Germany and the former Soviet Union), and were willing to use force to achieve their international ambitions. China is a different kind of power. It is in many ways playing by Western rules: its growth is powered by market capitalism, it has begun to engage international institutions such as the UN and the WTO, and it presumably does not have unlimited ideological or territorial ambitions. There is also a large area of shared interest in terms of trade and investment interdependence between China and potential strategic competitors such as the United States and Japan.

If we assume that China will remain on its current economic and military growth path over the next two decades, surpassing Japan in absolute gross domestic product (GDP) and developing power projection capabilities that could challenge U.S. military predominance in Asia, what will Chinese goals be, and to what extent will Chinese ambitions be compatible with U.S. interests? It is certainly easy to imagine scenarios in which U.S.-Chinese conflict occurs, such as an unprovoked Chinese effort to conquer Taiwan or military aggression against other neighbors such as Korea or Japan. But is it possible to imagine the United States accommodating a rising China, much as Britain accommodated a rising United States at the beginning of the twentieth century? The latter, after all, is the most notable recent example of a major power shift not producing great power conflict.

Even raising the British example suggests limits to the analogy. The United States and Britain shared a common ethnicity, culture, and historical tradition; the latter could look with equanimity on the growth of U.S. power because it saw America as broadly supportive of its global interests. China might approach this status if it underwent a democratic revolution and became a developed liberal democracy, which is what many observers have been hoping for as the solution to the rising China problem. But even a democratic China will be quite different culturally from the United States and is likely to be nationalistic in many ways. In any event, we cannot count on democratic change happening. We need to plan strategically, then, on a rising China that will continue to be Communist, authoritarian, and nationalistic. What, then, will be Chinese ambitions?

The first answer is not simply that we do not know but that the Chinese themselves do not know. There is a plurality of views within China. Part of the society is highly Westernized and seeks to integrate into the broader East Asian and world community; part is highly nationalistic; and ideology continues to drive the Chinese Communist Party, whose legitimacy remains contested. Many observers have pointed out that whatever a country's ambitions are at a given point, they change and become more expansive with increasing national power. But economic growth will strengthen other voices in the country, as well, and it is not possible to predict how the resulting political struggle will turn out.

There are, however, some boundaries that we can put around likely outcomes; once these are established, we need to define red lines in the space between them for future Chinese behavior that will trigger different U.S. responses. On the one hand, it seems unlikely now that China will ever develop global ambitions on the scale of Nazi Germany or the former Soviet Union. It is hard to see China, for example, sending aid, arms, and advisory missions to help convert regimes in Latin America or Africa to its form of government. China is involved in a large number of territorial disputes with virtually all of its neighbors, but there is no reason to think that, beyond these, it wants to annex neighboring countries outright the way Nazi Germany did.

On the other hand, it seems very unlikely that a China that has become a superpower peer of the United States will not want to change many aspects of the international system. The United States currently exerts tremendous influence over global politics—through the direct exercise of power (e.g., military intervention in Afghanistan and Iraq), through its alliances, through its influence over international institutions (the International Monetary Fund, the World Bank, and the WTO), through the economic impact of its multinational corporations, and through various soft-power mechanisms in the social and cultural realms. The Chinese tolerate and in some cases participate in some of these U.S.-backed institutions (e.g., the WTO), but they resent other aspects of the current global order (e.g., American criticism of its human rights practices). It is inconceivable that as a superpower China will not want to change many of these practices and structure a world more to its liking.

Institutional Architectures for East Asia

There are two broad ways of meeting this twenty- to thirty-year challenge. The first would be to try to hold on to our hegemonic position for as long as possible, maintaining our own margin of superiority and trying to delay and constrain China's rise to the degree possible. The second approach is to accede to China's rise as gracefully as possible, recognizing that we can do little to stop it over the long run. We would nonetheless want to put in place as many institutional constraints as possible now while we are relatively strong, in the hopes that they will make China's future behavior more predictable. I strongly prefer the latter policy, but I elaborate both at greater length.

The value of American leadership and the importance of maintaining it as an end in itself is accepted by many Americans. There is actually less difference between the Clinton and Bush administrations on this subject than many people (particularly Democrats) would like to admit. It was not George W. Bush but Bill Clinton's secretary of state, Madeleine Albright, who called the United States the "indispensable nation" on the grounds that the United States could "see farther" than other nations.

The most explicit statement making hegemony an objective was the first leaked version of the Defense Planning Guidance for Fiscal Years 1994–1999 (written in 1992), which stated:

> Our first objective is to prevent the re-emergence of a new rival, either on the territory of the former Soviet Union or elsewhere, that poses a threat on the order of that posed formerly by the Soviet Union.... First, the U.S. must show the leadership necessary to establish and protect a new order that holds the promise of convincing potential competitors that they need not aspire to a greater role or pursue a more aggressive posture to protect their legitimate interests. Second, in the non-defense areas, we must account sufficiently for the interests of the advanced industrial nations to discourage them from challenging our leadership or seeking to overturn the established political and economic order. Finally, we must maintain the mechanisms for deterring potential competitors from even aspiring to a larger regional or global role.[17]

But it is not at all clear how the United States would have implemented a long-term primacy policy in the face of a rising China had the first version of the Defense Planning Guidance been adopted as official U.S. policy. Isolation, sanctions, and preventive war seem to work poorly, even when used against relatively small countries such as Cuba or Iraq. They are out of the question in dealing with large peer competitors who achieve that status through sustained economic growth, as China and India are doing. The U.S. defense budget appears to be the primary policy lever that would be used to achieve this end; the thinking of some advocates of hegemony seems to have been to keep the margin of U.S. military superiority so great that no other country would even contemplate the costs of trying to catch up. Apart from the long-term costs this would impose on the United States, it is not clear that preemptive arms racing can be made to work. Despite the huge increases in American defense spending that have occurred since 9/11, the Chinese have nonetheless invested in rapid force modernization in ways that are already changing the balance of power in the Taiwan Strait. (That is not to say that the United States cannot or should not be concerned with the military balance in East Asia, only that it is not possible to deter other powers from ever trying to challenge American supremacy.)

A more realistic interpretation of an American primacy policy vis-à-vis China is something that looks like the containment strategy used against the former Soviet Union. The United States would seek to create formal military and political alliances with like-minded states threatened by growing Chinese power and push back at Chinese efforts to extend its power and influence into other parts of the globe. Because many current Chinese initiatives in other parts of the world are economic, this might mean conducting a form of economic warfare by trying to persuade American friends and allies not to cut trade or investment deals with China, by setting up alternative trade blocs to those favored by China, and the like. This would mean, inevitably, that East Asia would be organized into competing pro- and anti-Chinese camps, with the United States and Japan providing leadership for the latter.

The second option for a long-term strategy toward China is to assume that China will rise whether we like it or not and that the goal of U.S. strategy is make sure that the fewest core American interests are compromised in the process.[18] We would assume that the United States would lose some of its current freedom of action and that China's wishes would have to be taken more seriously. Obviously, we would want China's rise to be peaceful (i.e., no forcible annexation of Taiwan), and we would want to preserve as many of our interests and prerogatives, as well as those of our friends and allies, as possible. We would generally want China's behavior to be as predictable as possible and constrained by as many international rules and norms as possible. The emergence of democracy and a strong rule of law within China would be one possible source of constraint, but one that we cannot count on. Absent democracy, China would of course continue to be constrained by power: China would be a peer competitor, but not a hegemonic power itself; India would also be a great power, and Japan, although weaker vis-à-vis China, would still be a major player in Asia. China would still be heavily interdependent with other parts of the world, including its Asian neighbors and the United States. But we would in addition want China accustomed to following a set of international norms with respect to trade, investment, use of force, and the like through engagement with a series of overlapping multilateral institutions in which the United States and Japan were participants.

The difference between these two long-term strategic choices with regard to China and East Asia revolves around which kind of international institutional architecture we put into place in the near term. The fundamental design choice concerns whether these institutions exclude China and are designed to meet a long-term Chinese military threat or whether they include China and are meant to make Chinese behavior more predictable. There are a number of possible alternatives emerging today:

- Lay the foundations for a multilateral democratic alliance whose ultimate purpose is to contain China (a Chinese NATO).
- As an economic variant of this, create an East Asian economic community with membership criteria sufficiently stringent in terms of governance to exclude China.
- Revitalize the current Washington-centered hub-and-spoke system based on the United States–Japan alliance and oppose the formation of any new multilateral organizations that do not include the United States.
- Create a new Five Power Organization growing out of the Six Party Talks.
- Try to revitalize existing broad multilateral institutions such as the Asia-Pacific Economic Cooperation (APEC) and the Association of Southeast Asian Nations (ASEAN) Regional Forum (ARF).
- Encourage existing trends toward Asian multilateralism such as ASEAN Plus Three, even if they exclude the United States, as a means of reintegrating Japan into East Asia.

The first and second of these options are today neither possible nor desirable; the only country in the region that would sign up for such an alliance is Japan, and its short-term impact would be to polarize the region prematurely. Revitalization of broad organizations such as APEC and the ARF also do not seem very promising, given the diluted character of their membership. A targeted Northeast Asian security organization would be more promising as a means of regularizing military-to-military contacts between Japan, China, and Korea.

These choices are not necessarily mutually exclusive; it might be possible for a time to quietly strengthen America's bilateral military ties with countries potentially threatened by China while at the same time promoting inclusive institutions that seek to rope China into a broader normative order. This is essentially a hedging strategy; we cannot know ahead of time how a powerful China will act, and so we need to keep our options open with regard to future developments. It is also where the Bush administration has ended up, not by design but for lack of better ideas. It is also possible to combine Japanese engagement with pan-Asian organizations such as ASEAN Plus Three with a continued strong United States–Japan alliance, the former being a means of effecting better Japanese-Chinese-Korean cooperation.

A new administration, however, needs to think through the institutional question afresh. Do we want to join with Japan in the construction of a honeycomblike structure of overlapping bilateral security agreements whose ultimate purpose is to link countries threatened by China? Or do we want to build up a more inclusive set of institutions that seek to commit China to rules regarding trade and investment, governance, environmental protection, and the like? In my view, the first strategy risks prematurely polarizing Asia into pro- and anti-Chinese camps and makes Chinese hostility a self-fulfilling prophecy. As noted earlier, there is considerable indeterminacy to Chinese long-term intentions at this point. International institutions will not permanently bind them to certain modes of behavior, but they can help socialize Chinese elites and support those who are more internationalist in orientation.

The Rest of the World

As noted at the beginning of this chapter, one of the problems with designing a coherent global strategy is that American policy makers are then tempted to try to fit all parts of the world under one rubric, even if that rubric does not apply in all cases. Thus the cold war played out as a bilateral United States–Soviet struggle in Latin America and Africa, turning nationalist, class, and ethnic struggles into ones over ideology. A similar temptation exists today: with the creation of an Africa Command, the United States is beginning to subsume parts of East Africa into the global war on terrorism. This leads to conflicts in U.S. priorities: Ethiopia's Meles Zenawi had been sharply criticized for his authoritarian behavior after the elections of 2005, but he returned to the good graces of the United States by signing up as a U.S. ally in the struggle against al Qaeda and by invading Somalia at the end of 2006. It is not clear, however, that the United States has powerful strategic interests in many parts of the world or that the war on terror is in fact global.

Latin America is a case in point. Venezuela's Hugo Chávez is an open admirer of Cuba's Castro, and in the years since his first election in 1998 he has been steadily centralizing power in his own hands. He has bought weapons from Russia and Belarus, established ties with Iran, and used his oil money to support a series of left-wing, anti-American actors in the region. Despite his overt hostility to the United States, however, it is not clear how much of a threat Chávez presents to American strategic interests. Although he has tried to destabilize countries such as Peru and Colombia that are friendly to the United States, there has been a regional counterreaction to Chávez that has limited the extent of his influence. A U.S.-organized effort to sanction and isolate him will simply play into his hands, as did the "ambivalent" position of the United States during the attempted coup against him in 2004.

America's real priorities in Latin America are to see the successful economic and democratic development of countries in the region. The region has been the scene of a morality play in which different developmental models have struggled against one another and in which the model promoted by the United States during the 1990s has seen unfortunate setbacks in the past decade. But for all of the talk about a new turn to the left in Latin America, democratic, market-oriented policies have made important advances, particularly in the larger countries such as Mexico and Brazil. The latter are emerging as important players in the global economy, as well as being sources of immigrants into the United States. Washington has had a tendency to pay attention to Latin America only when there was instability or a chance of left-wing forces coming to power; small countries in Central America and the Caribbean attracted much more attention than they were inherently worth. A far better strategy would be for the United States to emphasize the region's success stories rather than its problem cases, seeing it through the lens of development rather than in strategic terms. A shift toward this kind of policy was already evident in the second term of the Bush administration; when the president finally got around to making a tour of Latin America in 2006, he wisely talked about the problems of poverty and exclusion and failed to mention Hugo Chávez—an important symbolic shift from policy toward the region in his first term.

Conclusion

The Bush doctrine was characterized by the use of preventive war as a means of dealing with rogue state proliferation and terrorism, by a unilateral approach to intervention and general disdain for international organizations, and by the use of democracy as a tool for achieving American national security objectives. These policies produced the fiasco of the Iraq war, and an inevitable reaction has set in. In some sense, the reaction was already embedded in the policies of the administration's second term, when policies became more multilateral and somewhat less reliant on a quick resort to force. But clearly, once President Bush is history, a much deeper and prolonged reaction will set in. The question is how much retrenchment will occur and in what direction.

While he was a candidate for president in 2000, George W. Bush argued in favor of a more humble foreign policy. In light of what has happened since, many Americans, I suspect, yearn for more American humility across the board; however, that can take a number of forms. A more radical rethinking of America's role in the world, which would have us withdraw from much of the Middle East and from our alliance commitments in Europe and Asia, has been suggested by some, even before the Iraq war.[19] This means not just ending our presence in Iraq but pulling away from globalization as well: many opponents of an overly militarized foreign policy also oppose offshoring and the exposure of American workers to low-wage competition from foreign countries.

At this stage in our history, I do not think that we should simply dismiss these arguments under such various labels as isolationism, protectionism, or defeatism. A serious case can be made that many of the threats we currently face are self-generated. Nor is it clear that hegemonic global power is good for American institutions or politics. The American regime is founded on the idea that unchecked power, even if democratically legitimated, is dangerous; and yet in the international sphere, we have been happy to tell the rest of the world to simply "trust us" to do the right thing. One does not want a world with more abusive or tyrannical great powers in it, but a more multipolar world would force the United States to exert a greater degree of prudence in its use of power.

That power, however, is a reality, and although a more multipolar world may come to exist in another generation, it is still a long way off. This is why, in my view, the "talk softly and carry a small stick" visions of American foreign policy are not realistic: we cannot wish away our dominance of the global economy, the dependence of various friends and allies on our military power, or the fact that American power continues to provide predictability in international relations in many parts of the world. A transition out of this role will create large uncertainties unless it is carefully negotiated, and in many instances it will simply not be believable.

So my particular version of a more humble policy is not the abjuring of a significant international role for the United States but a much greater sense of the limits of American power, and particularly conventional military force, in shaping outcomes around the world. Over the years, some of the most important forms of American power have been its example and its moral standing, and it is precisely to recover those that I think we need a change in course. Neither Bismarck's Germany after unification nor China today could fool themselves that they were not powerful and threatening to many around them. But they did focus on reducing the sense of threat their neighbors felt in an effort to forestall the formation of hostile coalitions against them. Doing this more effectively requires not demanding things of others but listening to what they want and, in some way, being able to accommodate them.

Notes

1. This reflects, of course, Max Weber's classic definition of a state.
2. Henry Kissinger, "After Lebanon," *Washington Post*, September 13, 2006.
3. For an excellent overview of weak state politics in Africa, see William Reno, *Warlord Politics and African States* (Boulder, CO: Lynne Rienner, 1999).
4. It is true that the 9/11 attacks did not involve WMDs and had an arguably strategic impact on the United States. However, the likelihood of a terrorist group pulling off a similarly spectacular operation without WMDs is much lower today than it was on September 10, 2001.

5. See Norman Podhoretz, *World War IV: The Long Struggle against Islamofascism* (New York: Doubleday, 2007).

6. See Francis Fukuyama, *State-Building: Governance and World Order in the 21st Century* (Ithaca, NY: Cornell University Press, 2004).

7. Jack Snyder, *From Voting to Violence: Democratization and Nationalist Conflict* (New York: Norton, 2000); and Jack Snyder and Edward D. Mansfield, *Electing to Fight: Why Emerging Democracies Go to War* (Cambridge, MA: MIT Press, 2007).

8. Samuel P. Huntington, *Political Order in Changing Societies* (New Haven, CT: Yale University Press, 1968); Fareed Zakaria, *The Future of Freedom: Illiberal Democracy at Home and Abroad* (New York: Norton, 2003).

9. Krishan Kumar, *Postconflict Elections, Democratization, and International Assistance* (Boulder, CO: Lynne Rienner, 1998).

10. Thomas Carothers, "The 'Sequencing' Fallacy," *Journal of Democracy* 18, no.1 (January 2007): 12–27.

11. Natan Sharansky, *The Case for Democracy: The Power of Freedom to Overcome Tyranny and Terror* (Green Forest, AR: Balfour Books, 2006).

12. Francis Fukuyama, "Identity, Immigration, and Liberal Democracy," *Journal of Democracy* 17, no. 2 (April 2006): 5–20.

13. Michael Mandelbaum, "Foreign Policy as Social Work," *Foreign Affairs* 75, no. 1 (January/February 1996): 16–32.

14. Other CCT programs include the *Red de Proteccion Social* program in Nicaragua and the *Programa de Asignaciones Familiares* in Honduras.

15. See Francis Fukuyama and Michael McFaul, *Should Democracy Be Promoted or Demoted?* Report, The Stanley Foundation (June 2007), http://www.stanleyfoundation.org/publications/other/FukuyMcFaul07.pdf.

16. For a fuller discussion, see *Nation-Building: Beyond Afghanistan and Iraq*, ed. Francis Fukuyama (Baltimore: Johns Hopkins University Press, 2005).

17. Quoted in Patrick E. Tyler, "Pentagon's Document Outlines Ways to Thwart Challenges to Primacy of America," *New York Times*, March 8, 1992. Due to the outcry caused by this leak, this passage was expunged from the document finally released.

18. This was the framework for the China policy outlined by Deputy Secretary of State Robert Zoellick. See Robert Zoellick, "Whither China: From Membership to Responsibility?" Remarks before the National Committee on United States–China Relations, New York (September 21, 2005), http://www.state.gov/s/d/former/zoellick/rem/53682.htm.

19. See, for example, Eugene Gholz and Daryl G. Press, "Come Home, America: The Strategy of Restraint in the Face of Temptation," *International Security* 21, no. 4 (Spring 1997): 5–48; Chalmers Johnson, *Blowback: The Costs and Consequences of American Empire*, 2nd ed. (New York: Owl Books, 2004); Patrick Buchanan, *A Republic, Not an Empire: Reclaiming America's Destiny* (New York: Regnery, 2002); and Andrew J. Bacevich, *American Empire: The Realities and Consequences of U.S. Diplomacy* (Cambridge, MA: Harvard University Press, 2002).

TEN

The Problem of Conjecture
Niall Ferguson

Perhaps the deepest problem is the problem of conjecture in foreign policy....Each political leader has the choice between making the assessment which requires the least effort or making an assessment which requires more effort. If he makes the assessment that requires least effort, then as time goes on it may turn out that he was wrong and then he will have to pay a heavy price. If he acts on the basis of a guess, he will never be able to prove that his effort was necessary, but he may save himself a great deal of grief later on....If he acts early, he cannot know whether it was necessary. If he waits, he may be lucky or he may be unlucky. It is a terrible dilemma.

"Decision Making in a Nuclear World," Henry Kissinger Papers,
Library of Congress

I T IS NOW nearly six years since President Bush promulgated what has become known as "the Bush doctrine." The seminal document, published above the president's signature twelve months after the terrorist attacks of September 11, 2001, and titled *National Security Strategy of the United States of America*, argued that because "deliverable weapons of mass destruction in the hands of a terror network or murderous dictator...constitute as grave a threat as can be imagined," the president as commander in chief should, at his discretion, "act preemptively" to forestall or prevent any such threat. "As a matter of common sense and self-defense," the president stated, the United States would "act against such emerging threats before they are fully formed" and before they reached America's borders.[1] The *National Security*

Strategy asserted not only the principle of preemption but also the principle of unilateralism. "While the United States will constantly strive to enlist the support of the international community," the document declared, "we will not hesitate to act alone, if necessary."[2] At the time and subsequently, the two principles of preemption and unilateralism were widely criticized as dangerous novelties in American foreign policy.[3] Other aspects of the *National Security Strategy* were rather less controversial, notably the stated intentions "to bring the hope of democracy, development, free markets, and free trade to every corner of the world" and to "stand firmly for...the rule of law; limits on the absolute power of the state; free speech; freedom of worship; equal justice; respect for women; religious and ethnic tolerance; and respect for private property."[4] In many ways, however, this plan to export American-style economic and political institutions—"to extend the benefits of freedom across the globe"—was the most ambitious and perilous element of the Bush doctrine.

In my book *Colossus: The Rise and Fall of the American Empire*, I argued that the Bush doctrine was in some ways less radical than its critics claimed.[5] Far from being a revolutionary departure, the idea that preemptive action might be legitimate in the face of a mortal threat had been asserted by more than one president during the cold war and had been assumed by them all.[6] The radical aspect of the Bush doctrine was not so much its theory as its practice. It became clear even before the invasion of Iraq in 2003 that the White House intended to use the doctrine of preemption to justify overthrowing certain "rogue regimes" suspected of complicity with terrorists and establishing American-style democracies in their places. In an earlier book, I had already expressed some doubts as to how far the United States had the economic, military, and political capabilities to make a success of what was an implicitly imperial undertaking.[7] Unlike many critics of the Bush administration, however, I did not dismiss the administration's project as morally wrong or misconceived. Rather, I argued that there were indeed a number of regimes around the world that were likely to cease sponsoring terrorism, acquiring nuclear weapons, or abusing their own populations only as a result of effective and enduring foreign intervention. I was also confident that the United States had the ability to overthrow some (though not all) of these regimes. My qualms related to the ability of the United States successfully to execute the radical economic and political transformations that were, from the outset, an integral part of the Bush doctrine.

My central argument was that three deficits reduced significantly the likelihood of American success in Iraq (and indeed in Afghanistan, where intervention was retaliatory, not preemptive). These were the financial deficit (the fiscal and current account imbalances, which have made the United States increasingly dependent on foreign capital); the manpower deficit (which places a low ceiling on the number of combat-effective troops available for overseas deployment); and the attention deficit (which inclines American voters and legislators to lose patience with foreign interventions within a period of two to four years—long before success is likely to have been attained). Those arguments have been in considerable measure vindicated. However, I overlooked the importance of a fourth deficit: the legitimacy deficit (which has widened as international support for U.S. policy has collapsed). In what follows, I review the roles played by the four deficits in constraining U.S. foreign policy, suggesting that they will constrain President Bush's successor even more than they have constrained Bush himself.

But this is not merely a variation on an earlier theme. I also ask how far the Bush doctrine was conceptually flawed in ways that I had not appreciated at the time I wrote *Colossus*. In particular, I show that the political rewards to be garnered by a policy of preemption are bound to be low, even when the policy is successful. As a prophylactic against the relatively low-probability threat of an attack by terrorists armed with Iraqi weapons of mass destruction (WMDs), the overthrow of Saddam Hussein was always likely to be an expensive and ultimately unpopular prescription. Looking ahead, I reflect on the much more serious threats that the Iraq debacle is obscuring: the descent of the Greater Middle East into a large-scale war; the disintegration of the system of nuclear nonproliferation; the escalating competition between developed and emerging economies over scarce raw materials; and the deepening crisis in the system of multilateral trade liberalization. I question whether preemption, unilateralism, and the effort "to extend the benefits of freedom across the globe" constitute a viable or effective response to any of these. I conclude with some reflections on the kind of national security strategy that the next president ought to adopt. A first constructive step, I suggest, would be the abandonment of all three of the key tenets of the Bush *National Security Strategy*.

"*Nervi belli pecunia infinita*," as Cicero observed more than two thousand years ago: the sinews of war are limitless money. The Bush doctrine certainly presupposed abundant financial resources for American foreign policy. Preemption implied, as we have seen, more than one overseas war. Unilateralism implied that the United States might have to pay for these wars itself (which had not been the case in the first Gulf War). The wider goals of "extending the benefits of freedom" implied additional costs beyond the narrowly military costs of regime change. The *National Security Strategy* of 2002 also pledged to "build defenses against ballistic missiles and other means of delivery," to "build better, more integrated intelligence capabilities to provide timely, accurate information on threats, wherever they may emerge," and to "transform our military forces to ensure our ability to conduct rapid and precise operations to achieve decisive results."[8] This transformation was, in fact, already under way, having been made a priority at the Pentagon by Defense Secretary Donald Rumsfeld almost from the day of his appointment. The question he and his advisers were addressing on the eve of the 9/11 attacks was how best to "maintain U.S. predominance." The most conservative option they discussed—"full spectrum response"—envisaged an increase in defense spending to "4.5 per cent of GDP during build-up [3–5 years] and 4 per cent steady-state...indefinitely." The most radical option—"break out"—appears to have appealed to Rumsfeld more, as it implied "speed, agility, responsiveness and innovation" and a downsizing of the existing military establishment. But the "affordability" of this option was "unclear."[9]

We now have a more precise idea of the cost of the "break out" unleashed by the Bush doctrine. Contrary to the claims made by the administration in 2003, this has been an expensive enterprise. According to the Congressional Budget Office (CBO), the total amount that the United States spent on the war on terror between September 2001 and February 2007 was $503 billion. To this figure should be added the amounts the administration has subsequently requested, giving a total cost by mid-2007 of $746 billion. However, the Nobel Prize–winning economist Joseph Stiglitz has argued that, taking account of costs not captured in budgetary figures and assuming that the United States will still be in Iraq until 2017, the final cost of the war could rise as high as $3.2 trillion.[10] This is fully twice the maximum cost projected by the Yale economist William Nordhaus in December 2002 ($1.6 trillion), which at that time seemed wildly exaggerated.[11] There can no longer be any serious debate that it would have been cheaper to continue the pre-2003 policy of containing Saddam Hussein's regime with a combination of airpower, sanctions, and weapons inspections.[12]

At one level, to be sure, even $3.2 trillion is a sum that the United States can afford. The American economy is enormous: in terms of gross domestic product (GDP) in current dollars, it is two and a half times bigger than the next largest economy in the world and almost as large as the six other members of the Group of Seven combined. And, compared with the cold war, the war on terror has been cheap in relative terms. Between 1959 and 1989, U.S. defense spending averaged 6.9 percent of GDP. Since President Bush entered the White House, it has risen from 3 percent to a peak of just 4 percent. On the basis of the growth estimates used by the CBO, even Stiglitz's $3.2 trillion, spread over fifteen years, works out at just 1.3 percent of GDP. The key question, however, is how far such levels of military expenditure can be sustained over the longer term. The most important of the American deficits may prove to be the financial deficit, precisely because it shows every sign of growing and constraining U.S. foreign policy much more in the near future than it has in the past.

The critical point is that growth in the United States has become heavily reliant on the accumulation of debt by both the public sector and the household sector. Since becoming president, George W. Bush has presided over a significant rise in the size of the federal debt. The gross federal debt is fast approaching 9 trillion, around 60 percent larger than it was when he entered the White House.[13] According to the CBO, the debt will keep on growing over the next five years, swelling by an additional half trillion dollars.[14] The drivers of the post-2000 increase in debt have in fact been fourfold: not only increased military spending but also reduced revenues during the 2001 recession, generous tax cuts for higher income groups, and increased expenditure on welfare at home.[15] How big a burden does this represent? If one excludes bonds and bills in the possession of government agencies, such as the Social Security trust fund, the debt held by private investors falls to around $5 trillion. That works out at around 36 percent of GDP, a major increase relative to 1981, when it was below 25 percent, but still modest compared with the aftermath of World War II, when it exceeded 100 percent. What is more, the CBO forecasts that the debt-to-GDP ratio will actually decline in the decade ahead to perhaps as little as 20 percent.[16] By historical standards, this is not an especially heavy debt burden. At its peaks, at the end of the Napoleonic wars and World War II, the British national debt exceeded 250 percent of GDP.[17] Compared with the last English-speaking empire to bestride the earth, the United States is not especially leveraged. The trouble is that the officially stated borrowings of the federal government are only a small part of the U.S. debt problem.

For it is not just government's debt that has grown large of late. Ordinary American households, too, have gone on a borrowing spree of unprecedented magnitude. U.S. household credit market debt has risen from just above 45 percent of GDP in the early 1980s to above 70 percent in recent years. Since 2000, the value of U.S. home mortgage debt has more than doubled, from $4.8 trillion to $9.7 trillion. Consumer credit debt has risen from $1.7 trillion to $2.4 trillion.[18] Not only do Americans borrow as never before, but they also engage in remarkably little offsetting saving. The remarkable resilience of American consumer spending in the past fifteen years was based partly on a collapse in the personal savings rate from around 7.5 percent of income to below zero. The aggregate national saving rate, which includes the public sector and corporations, averaged 13 percent in the 1960s. In 2005 it was just 2.1 percent. For demographic reasons, however, Americans need to be saving more than this.[19] According to the United Nations' medium set of projections, the share of the American population that is age sixty-five or over will rise from 12 percent to nearly 21 percent over the next forty-five years.[20] Already, Social Security, Medicare, and Medicaid benefits consume half of federal tax revenues. That proportion is bound to rise, not only because the number of retirees is going up but also because the costs of Medicare are out of control.[21] These figures imply that the federal government has much larger unfunded liabilities than official data imply. Subtracting the present value of all projected future government expenditures—including debt service payments—from the present value of all projected future government receipts, economists Jagadeesh Gokhale and Kent Smetters found a discrepancy of around $66 trillion.[22] That is roughly seven times the size of the gross federal debt as officially stated.

The appetite of American households and politicians for debt has an inevitable and strategically significant corollary, as it exceeds the ability of U.S. corporations to save. The United States has become the world's biggest international debtor, increasing its reliance on foreign lenders to unprecedented heights. In nearly every year since 1992, the gap between the amount of goods and services the United States exports and the amount it imports has grown wider. In 2006 the current account deficit—which is largely a trade deficit—was more than 6 percent of GDP, nearly double its peak in the mid-1980s. The result has been a rapid accumulation of foreign debt. The estimated net international investment position of the United States—the difference between the overseas assets owned by Americans and the American assets owned by foreigners—has declined from a modest positive balance of around 5 percent of GDP in the mid-1980s to a huge net debt of minus 20 percent today.[23] What this means is that foreigners, notably Asian central banks, as well as Middle Eastern sovereign wealth funds, are accumulating large claims on the future output of the United States.[24] Foreign ownership of the federal debt passed the halfway mark in June 2004. Two-fifths of corporate bonds are now in foreign hands, as is 19 percent of the U.S. stock market.[25]

Unlike a Latin American economy, of course, the United States retains the right to reduce the value of its debts to foreigners by debasing the unit of account, which is the U.S. dollar. Steep depreciations have certainly happened before. Between March 1985 and April 1988, the dollar depreciated by more than 40 percent in terms of the currencies of America's trading partners. A comparable slide may conceivably be under way now; indeed, the real trade-weighted exchange rate declined by 22 percent between February 2002 and August 2007. As a financial exit strategy, dollar depreciation has much to recommend it. American exports would regain their competitiveness overseas, whereas foreign creditors would find their dollar assets suddenly worth less in terms of their own currencies. However, an increase in the dollar price of

American imports could stoke U.S. inflation. True, "core" inflation (which excludes the cost of energy and housing) has fluctuated at around the 2 percent level since President Bush entered the White House. Inflation expectations have also been relatively stable. But if that were to change—for example, as a belated response to the steep rise in energy prices since 2000—the Federal Reserve might find itself in a precarious position. It should be remembered that before the onset of the financial crisis in August 2007 the Federal Funds target rate had risen more than fivefold from its nadir of 1 percent in 2003–2004.

The true significance of higher interest rates has only recently begun to be apparent. The first debtors to be affected were households with adjustable rate mortgages (ARMs), particularly those in the "subprime" segment of the housing market. As their two-year teaser rates began to expire, these borrowers found their monthly repayments rising by as much as 50 percent.[26] By August 2007 the level of defaults and foreclosures was sufficient to trigger a crisis in the markets for asset-backed bonds, asset-backed commercial paper, and collateralized debt obligations, as large proportions of these were secured on subprime mortgages. The enforced return of securitized debt to banks' balance sheets seems certain to cause a general tightening of credit conditions, with unforeseeable but certainly negative macroeconomic consequences. The second category of debtor that is vulnerable to higher short-term rates is none other than the federal government itself. The protracted decline of long-term interest rates since the 1980s was a boon for an indebted government. The cost of servicing the federal debt actually declined from 3.2 percent of GDP in 1990 to 1.5 percent in 2005, even as the absolute size of the debt soared.[27] But that decline was achieved partly thanks to the term structure of the debt; the relatively short duration of the bonds issued by the Treasury allowed the government to take maximum advantage of falling rates. At the end of 2006, for example, fully a third of the federal debt had a maturity of less than one year, and the average maturity of the entire debt was just fifty-seven months (down from seventy-four months at the end of 2000).[28] This term structure was beneficial so long as interest rates were heading downward. But with the rise in rates between 2003 and mid-2007, substantial slices of the federal debt had to be refinanced at a higher cost.

Viewed from a strictly macroeconomic perspective, today's "global imbalances" may be correctable via dollar weakness and slower growth. From the point of view of national security, they are more problematic. Fluctuating debt-servicing costs and slowing growth are almost certain to translate into a squeeze on discretionary expenditure. It is not without significance that expenditure on social security has consistently exceeded expenditure on national security in every year of the Bush administration. The difference between the two is that most social security spending is not discretionary but mandated by legislation. By contrast, expenditure on the military can more easily be cut by Congress.

It is at least arguable, in short, that the Bush doctrine is simply not affordable over the medium term—a somewhat serious vulnerability in what was billed (for a time at least) as "the long war." Yet even if a policy of regular overseas military intervention were affordable in the years to come, the United States would still struggle to achieve its objectives because of a chronic shortage of combat-effective manpower. This is the second of the four deficits that will constrain the next president.

It might have been thought that 300 million Americans would be enough to rule the world—or at least a couple of medium-sized "failed states." The population of Iraq is 27 million, that of Afghanistan 31 million. Less than a century ago, before World War I, the population of Britain was 46 million, barely 2.5 percent of humanity at that time, yet the British were able to govern a vast empire that encompassed an additional 375 million people, more than a fifth of the world's population. So why cannot 300 million Americans control fewer than 58 million foreigners? Part of the answer is simply that, considering the size of the U.S. population and the Pentagon's vast budget, the American military is a remarkably small operation when it comes to putting "boots on the ground." There are today approximately 75 million American men aged between 15 and 49. In 2004, however, the total number of Department of Defense personnel on active duty was 1,427,000, substantially fewer than the country's two-million-strong prison population. The number of military personnel on active duty in all overseas theaters is currently less a quarter of a million, roughly 0.1 percent of the American population. When Britain was the global colossus in the 1880s, that proportion was six times higher. Put differently, the number of troops deployed in Iraq today is roughly the same number that Britain had to send to the same country to defeat an insurgency in 1920. But the population of Iraq has increased by a factor of roughly ten in the intervening period. In 1920, when the British successfully quelled an insurgency in Iraq, there were roughly twenty-three Iraqis for every British soldier. Today, in the midst of an American troop "surge," there are approximately 169 Iraqis for every American soldier. What is more, those Iraqis are better fed, better educated, better armed, and better "connected" (thanks to cheap mobile telephony) than their counterparts eighty-seven years ago.

In some ways, this manpower deficit is itself a function of what I have called the American "attention deficit disorder"—namely, the tendency of the U.S. electorate quite rapidly to lose interest in difficult overseas conflicts. When British Prime Minister Tony Blair addressed a joint session of Congress in July 2003, he conjured up a vivid image of the parochial American: "In some small corner of this vast country, out in Nevada or Idaho...there's a guy getting on with his life, perfectly happily, minding his own business, saying to you, the political leaders of this country, 'Why me, and why us, and why America?'" Blair's answer—"because destiny put you in this place in history in this moment in time, and the task is yours to do"—has not convinced most Americans.[29] As a people, the citizens of the United States are famously uninterested in the world outside their own vast country. A poll conducted on behalf of *National Geographic* in 2006 found that 63 percent of Americans between the ages of 18 and 24 could not find Iraq on a map, and 75 percent could locate neither Israel nor Iran.[30] Asked by Gallup in July 2006 whether "the U.S. should mind its own business internationally and let other countries get along as best as they can on their own," nearly half of Americans (46 percent) said it should—compared with just 20 percent forty years ago. Since September 2005, a majority of Americans have said that it was a mistake for the United States to go into Iraq. According to recent Gallup polls, 62 percent of Americans believe it was "not worth going to war"; 71 percent believe that "things are going moderately or very badly" for the United States in Iraq; and 59 percent believe that a timetable should be set for withdrawing U.S. troops from the country.[31]

The speed with which the public lost confidence in the administration's Iraq policy, needless to say, was a function of more than mere parochialism. Support might have been less ephemeral if WMDs had been found in Iraq, as their alleged existence furnished the casus belli. Nevertheless, it was not difficult to predict in 2003 that public enthusiasm would wane within two to four years. Quite apart from any innate attention-deficit disorder, American political culture is subject to the relentless pressures of the electoral cycle. Though public disillusionment over Iraq was already detectable in November 2004, it had not penetrated the Republican "base" sufficiently to affect the outcome of the presidential election of that year. Two years later, by contrast, it unquestionably played an important part in the Democrats' victory in the midterm elections.

Part of the reason that Americans have lost faith in the Iraq adventure is its extreme unpopularity abroad. "Why do they hate us?" is a question often raised by the American media. Unfortunately, being hated is what happens to dominant empires. It comes—sometimes literally—with the territory. But who hates Americans the most? Where is the Bush doctrine's "legitimacy deficit" biggest? It might be expected that it would be in countries that the United States has recently attacked or threatened to attack. Americans themselves have a clear idea about who their principal enemies are. Asked by Gallup earlier this year to name the "greatest enemy" of the United States today, 26 percent of those polled named Iran, 21 percent named Iraq, and 18 percent named North Korea—a noteworthy success for George W. Bush's concept of the "axis of evil," as only 8 percent had named Iran and only 2 percent North Korea six years before. Are those feelings of antagonism reciprocated? Up to a point. According to a poll by Gallup's Center for Muslim Studies, 52 percent of Iranians have an unfavorable view of the United States. But that figure is down from 63 percent in 2001, and it is significantly lower than the degree of antipathy toward the United States felt in Jordan, Pakistan, and Saudi Arabia. Two-thirds of Jordanians and Pakistanis and a staggering 79 percent of Saudis have a negative view of the United States. Sentiment has also turned hostile in Lebanon, where 59 percent of people have an unfavorable opinion of the United States, compared with just 41 percent a year ago. No fewer than 84 percent of Lebanese Shiites say they have a very unfavorable view of the United States.[32]

These figures suggest a paradox in the Muslim world. It is not America's enemies who hate the United States most. It is people in countries that are supposed to be America's friends, if not allies. Nor is that the only paradox. The Gallup poll (which surveyed ten thousand Muslims in ten different countries) also revealed that the wealthier and better educated Muslims are, the more likely they are to be politically radical, debunking the notion that anti-Western sentiment is an expression of deprivation. Even more perplexingly, Islamists are more supportive of democracy than are Muslim moderates. In short, those who imagined that the Middle East could be stabilized with a mixture of economic and political reform—including the author of the *National Security Strategy*—could not have been more wrong. The richer people get, the more they favor radical Islamism. And they see democracy as a way of putting the radicals into power.

The paradox of unfriendly allies is not confined to the Middle East. Anti-Americanism is nothing new in European politics, to be sure, particularly on the Left. But the current mood of disapproval extends to traditionally pro-American constituencies. Back in 1999, 83 percent of British people surveyed by the State Department Office of Research said they had a favorable opinion of the United States. But by 2007, according to the Pew Global Attitudes Project, that proportion had fallen to 51 percent. Indeed, British respondents to the Pew surveys now give higher favorability ratings to Germany and Japan than to the United States—a remarkable transformation in attitudes, given the notorious British tendency to look back both nostalgically and unforgivingly to World War II. It is also very striking that Britons polled by Pew in 2006 regarded the U.S. presence in Iraq as a bigger threat to world peace than Iran or North Korea (a view that was shared by respondents in France, Spain, Russia, India, China, and throughout the Middle East). Nor is Britain the only disillusioned ally. Perhaps not surprisingly, two-thirds of Americans believe that their country's foreign policy considers the interests of others. But this view is shared by only 38 percent of Germans and 19 percent of Canadians. More than two-thirds of Germans surveyed in 2004 believed that American leaders willfully lied about Saddam Hussein's weapons of mass destruction prior to the previous year's invasion, and a remarkable 60 percent expressed the view that America's true motive was "to control Mideast oil." Nearly half (47 percent) said it was "to dominate the world."[33] The truly poignant fact is that when Americans themselves are asked to rate foreign countries, they express the most favorable views of none other than Britain, Germany, and Canada. Back in the 1990s, Madeleine Albright pompously called the United States "the indispensable nation." Today it seems to have become the indefensible nation, even in the eyes of its supposed friends.

The facile explanation for the Bush doctrine's legitimacy deficit—at home, as well as abroad—is the incompetence of the present administration, handicapped as it has been by a combination of delusion, ignorance, and obstinacy. According to Bob Woodward, Bush once complained bitterly about the difficulty of finding a reliable Iraqi to lead the new democratic government in Baghdad. "Where's George Washington?" he exclaimed to his chief of staff, Andy Card. "Where's Thomas Jefferson? Where's John Adams, for crying out loud?"[34] This is a question many Americans have been asking about their own leadership, as the debacle of Bush's second term has unfolded. By January 2007, only a minority of Americans can have been persuaded by their president's televised assertions that the war in Iraq was "the decisive ideological struggle of our time" and that "the most realistic way to protect the American people" was "by advancing liberty across a troubled region." Having asserted the right of the United States to act preemptively against potential threats, President Bush has appeared impotent to prevent the two remaining members of his "axis of evil"—North Korea and Iran—from, respectively, testing and building weapons of mass destruction. The administration that once rode roughshod over the United Nations now has to engage in horse trading on the Security Council in the hope that tighter sanctions will deter the Iranians from following the North Korean example. The U.S. ambassador in Iraq has even been reduced to holding direct talks about the security situation with his Iranian counterpart, a belated vindication of the recommendations put forward in 2006 by the Iraq Study Group.[35]

Yet it would be a mistake to conclude that merely by being more competent a new president could somehow close the American legitimacy deficit. The deficits of American power are structural, not merely the results of mistakes by one misguided administration. A new president needs to recognize, in a way that President Bush did not, the limitations these deficits impose. They are not likely to diminish in the years ahead. In addition, however, Bush's successor needs to identify the fundamental misconception that underpinned the *National Security Strategy* of 2002. "History," declared President Bush in that document, "will judge harshly those who saw this coming danger but failed to act."[36] Yet it may judge even more harshly those who acted preemptively and appeared to fail. Gratifying though it is to heap opprobrium on the administration for its ineptitude, critics would do well to consider a more profound conceptual defect of the Bush doctrine itself, for which no excellence of execution could have compensated. It relates to the fundamental problem that confronts any democratically elected strategist, as identified more than forty years ago by Henry Kissinger: "the problem of conjecture."

The rationale for a policy of preemption was quite explicit in Bush's *National Security Strategy* of 2002: it was to prevent a terrorist organization, with or without the assistance of a rogue regime, from acquiring WMDs and using them to perpetrate a "super 9/11." The nightmare was "catastrophic technologies in the hands of the embittered few":

> Traditional concepts of deterrence will not work against a terrorist enemy whose avowed tactics are wanton destruction and the targeting of innocents; whose so-called soldiers seek martyrdom in death and whose most potent protection is statelessness. The overlap between states that sponsor terror and those that pursue WMD compels us to action.[37]

There is, of course, a clear logical argument in favor of acting to avert a catastrophe—whether it be a nuclear, biological, or chemical terrorist attack, or an asteroid's striking the earth—no matter how low its probability.[38] Yet there is also a serious danger that we misjudge the probabilities of such catastrophes and take preemptive actions that are at best futile and at worst positively harmful to our security. This is precisely the mistake the Bush administration made. "Even if there's only a one percent chance of the unimaginable becoming true," Vice President Dick Cheney told Central Intelligence Agency and National Security Agency officials in November 2001, "act as though it's a certainty. It's not about our analysis, or finding a preponderance of evidence. It's about our response."[39] There is, however, a world of difference between a probability of 1 percent and a certainty of 100 percent.

Viewed retrospectively, terrorism is very clearly not the principal threat to the lives of ordinary Americans. In all, 48,071 people lost their lives in transport accidents in 2003, vastly more than were killed by terrorists in 2001. The average American's lifetime risk of dying as a result of a transport accident is around 1 in 78. His or her risk of dying as a result of a violent assault by a firearm is 1 in 314. His or her risk of dying as a result of war is 1 in 267,719.[40] Americans, in short, are vastly more likely to kill themselves—more often accidentally than deliberately—than to be killed by terrorists. They are more threatened by their diets and by their driving than they are by al Qaeda. Yet when asked in 2007 to name the "most important problem facing the United States," 22 percent cited the war in Iraq and 8 percent terrorism—the same proportion that named the health care system. If it is lives that need to be saved, resources would surely be better spent on a system of universal health insurance than on the forcible export of "freedom."

Another way of considering the problem of terrorism is to compare it with the problem of natural disasters such as Hurricane Katrina. The direct costs of the terrorist attacks of 9/11 have been estimated at $27 billion, excluding unknowable indirect losses due to deferred investment decisions and lower growth. Viewed from the perspective of the insurance (and reinsurance) industry, the losses arising from 9/11 were in the region of $30–50 billion.[41] The losses due to Katrina were of a similar order of magnitude: around $38 billion. But natural disasters are much more frequent than really big terrorist attacks. Overall, between 1984 and 2004, the inflation-adjusted losses in the United States due to terrorism amounted to $24 billion; the losses due to natural disasters in the same period were $188 billion.[42] If it is property that needs to be protected, federal resources would be better spent on improved flood defenses and storm warning systems. Perhaps resources might also be better spent on combating climate change. After all, there is at least some evidence that the incidence of meteorological disasters is rising as a result of global warming, whereas the trend in the number if not the magnitude of international terrorist incidents—as well as in human conflict generally— would appear to be downward.[43]

The conventional response is that another, bigger terrorist attack—such as a nuclear explosion in a major city—would render such calculations obsolete. Yet, leaving aside the extreme difficulty of causing a nuclear explosion as compared with hijacking and crashing planes, there is a need for caution. Having been completely caught out by some random event, we human beings are wonderfully good at retrospectively "predicting" it and then prospectively exaggerating the likelihood of its happening again. The truth is that 9/11 was what Nassim Taleb calls a "black swan," a term derived from what philosophers call the problem of induction.[44] For a variety of reasons, not least the tendency of economists and others to assume that most things conform to the normal distribution, or "bell curve," we have a tendency, *ex ante*, to regard low-probability disasters as virtually zero-probability events. But the statistical distributions of earthquakes, financial crises, and wars are not like those of human heights or weights, which cluster around the mean value. They obey a quite different set of rules (sometimes known as fractal distribution, or "power laws"). In each case, when you plot a chart, there is much less clustering around the average, and there are many more data points at the extremes. Compared with the standard bell curve, these curves have "fat tails" at each end; there are more really big (and really small) quakes, crashes, and wars than the normal distribution would lead you to expect.[45] The same is almost certainly true of terrorist acts (and, interestingly, of insurgency-type wars).[46] If one were to plot all the international terrorist incidents that have taken place in the world in the past quarter-century according to the number of people killed, there would be a surprisingly large number of very lethal attacks and, at the other end of the chart, a comparably large number of damp squibs in which no one received so much as a scratch. In the nearly forty years between 1968 and the present, 6 percent of recorded terrorist incidents accounted for nearly half (46 percent) of fatalities attributable to international terrorism. But 3 percent of incidents killed no one at all. In only one month since records began to be kept—September 2001—has international terrorism killed more than three thousand people. The next most dangerous month, October 2002, claimed fewer than four hundred lives.

Since Thucydides, historians have sought to endow low-probability calamities with commensurately large causes. Generations of scholars toiled in this way to explain the origins of great upheavals such as the French Revolution or World War I, constructing elegant narrative chains of causes and effects stretching back decades before the events themselves. Ambitious journalists today do the same for 9/11; Lawrence Wright's *The Looming Tower* traces the origins of the terrorist attacks of 2001 back to the execution of Sayyid Qutb, the Islamist writer who inspired the Muslim Brotherhood, in 1966.[47] There is something suspect about this procedure, however, for these causal chains were quite invisible to contemporaries, to whom 9/11, like the outbreak of World War I, came as a bolt from the blue. The point is that there were numerous Balkan crises before 1914 that did not lead to Armageddon.[48] In the same way, there were numerous attempts by al Qaeda to hit American targets that were far less devastating than 9/11—enough, indeed, to enable a number of commentators (including myself) to predict a much bigger attack at some unspecified future date.[49] Only in retrospect, however, did these earlier crises appear to be harbingers of the most lethal terrorist attack in history.

On the other hand, having been caught out once, we err if we swing to the other extreme by proceeding, ex post facto, to exaggerate the probability of another, similar disaster (hence Vice President Cheney's equation of 1 percent with 100 percent). This does not matter greatly if the cost of prophylaxis against another "black swan" is relatively cheap. But the same is not true if the cost is high. Knowing that world wars can happen roughly twice a century is like knowing that a college student can run amok roughly once a decade. It does not allow you to predict which diplomatic or personality crisis will be the lethal one. And if you cannot do that, prophylaxis can become very expensive.

Not all depressed students can be incarcerated preemptively to eliminate the tiny risk that one of them may be the next Cho Seung-Hui, the student who murdered thirty-two people on the campus of Virginia Tech in April 2007. In the same way, not all rogue regimes can be overthrown preemptively to eliminate the risk that one of them may equip al Qaeda with WMDs. In a democracy, as President Bush has learned, no policy maker will be rewarded for writing that kind of prescription. Acting preemptively to stop bad things from happening will not make you popular, precisely because the cost of prophylaxis will always have to be paid. If the treatment fails, you will be blamed. But if the treatment is successful, you will not be thanked, precisely because the bad things will not happen.

On Bush's watch, let it not be forgotten, there has not been another 9/11. And Saddam Hussein will never again aspire to own WMDs, much less (if the idea had ever crossed his mind) to give them to al Qaeda. For all we know, there may even be some connection between the absence of another 9/11 and the ongoing conflict in Iraq. Perhaps, as some neoconservatives suggested in 2004, Iraq really has acted as a kind of "honey trap" for would-be terrorists, absorbing violent energies that might otherwise have been directed against the American homeland. At the very least, some credit must surely be due to the administration for tightening up domestic security after 2001. But is anybody grateful for these putative successes of the national security strategy? On the contrary: President Bush's approval rating touched a nadir of 29 percent in July 2007, a level not seen by a second-term president since Richard Nixon. The logic is sadly inexorable. Not even Bush himself can be certain that his strategy of preemption deserves the credit for nonevents. As we have seen, however, everyone can be certain that his strategy does deserve the blame for the increase in defense expenditure, the loss of around four thousand American service personnel, and the decline in the international standing of the United States.

Herein lies the essential flaw of the Bush doctrine—a fatal flaw that even the most perfect implementation could not have overcome. There is a complete asymmetry in the rewards conferred on politicians for retaliation as compared with preemption. Retaliation is nearly always popular and can be carried out with considerable ferocity and at considerable cost. But preemption is doomed to be unpopular. Its success can never be proven. And its failure is far more costly than the consequences of mere negligence. Were another major terrorist attack to happen now—which can never be ruled out—President Bush would surely overtake Richard Nixon, and perhaps all other previous occupants of the White House, in the unpopularity stakes. With one voice, the world's media would declare that administration's policy had worsened the very disease it had purported to cure.

So what is to be done? The first thing a new president must do is to abandon all three of the key pillars of Bush's national security strategy: preemption, unilateralism, and cryptoimperialism ("extending the benefits of freedom across the globe"). Because of the various deficits I have already described, the United States can neither afford nor sustain numerous overseas interventions, especially when these enjoy the backing of nothing more than ad hoc "coalitions of the willing" and when their duration is almost certain to exceed four years. At the same time, President Bush's successor needs to jettison the assumption, which was fundamental to the Bush doctrine, that the biggest threat to the United States today is posed by terrorist organizations armed with WMDs. It is not. At least four more pressing problems suggest themselves.

1. *The imminent descent of the Greater Middle East into a large-scale conflagration.* At the time of writing, debate on U.S. strategy is tightly focused on how quickly the United States can wind down its involvement in Iraq and on whether or not neighboring countries can be persuaded to help stabilize it. But what if it is Iraq that destabilizes its neighbors? Currently, between one and three thousand civilians are dying every month in Iraq, the majority of them victims of the bitter sectarian violence between Sunnis and Shias that has flared up since the overthrow of Saddam. Iraq, however, is not the only Middle Eastern state to have a mixed population of Sunnis, Shias, and other religious groups. There are substantial numbers of Shias in Bahrain, Kuwait, Lebanon, Saudi Arabia, Syria, Turkey, and Yemen (to say nothing of Afghanistan and Azerbaijan). Even predominantly Shiite Iran has its Sunni minority, the persecuted Ahwazis who live in the strategically vital southwestern province of Khuzestan.[50] Ironically, the world is not facing the "clash of civilizations" predicted by Samuel Huntington in 1993, which pitted the West against Islam, but a clash within Islamic civilization. We must take very seriously the risk that the Greater Middle East could become in our time what Eastern Europe was in the 1940s or Central Africa in the 1990s: a lethal zone of conflict.[51]

2. *The breakdown of the system of nuclear nonproliferation.* Meanwhile, the principal beneficiary of the overthrow of Saddam—Iran—is proceeding more or less brazenly with a program of uranium enrichment designed ultimately to produce weapons-grade fissile material. In a recent lecture at Harvard, the Nobel Prize–winning economist and nuclear theorist Thomas Schelling argued that three things had prevented nuclear weapons from being used in anger

over the past sixty years: the Nonproliferation Treaty, the informal taboo on their use, and the fear of retaliation. That was the reason the bomb was not dropped during the Korean War, and that was the reason both superpowers invested heavily in conventional forces in Europe, which would have been redundant in a nuclear exchange. Nuclear weapons give their possessors influence, Schelling concluded, precisely through not being used.[52] Yet these calculations may no longer be valid. First, on the eve of its fortieth birthday, the Nonproliferation Treaty is beginning to look like a dying, if not a dead, letter. Israel, India, and Pakistan did not sign it; North Korea withdrew from it; and Iran is now almost certainly in breach of it. Second, the taboo on the use of nuclear weapons and the fear of retaliation are more likely to be overcome the more powers possess nuclear weapons. We may be moving toward a world of multiple mini-cold wars, with pairs of nuclear powers eyeball to eyeball in nearly every region, as is already the case in South Asia. Japan could quite quickly acquire nuclear weapons if it felt insufficiently protected by the United States against China. The key cold war of the future, however, would be the one in the Middle East, with Israel on one side and Iran on the other.

3. *Intensifying competition between the world's major economies for raw materials, including energy sources, and export markets.* The race to acquire nuclear energy makes sense in a world of finite fossil fuel supplies. Yet with the rapid growth of the world economy, led by breakneck industrialization in Asia, the demand for traditional energy sources is growing faster than the supply of nuclear and "renewable" energy. As the consumption of oil, natural gas, and coal rises—to say nothing of the many other commodities consumed by a modern economy—so the potential for new conflicts grows. Russia has for some time been flexing its muscles as one of the world's leading energy exporters. High oil and gas revenues are also enriching regimes that have a record of financing Islamic extremism. China, meanwhile, is seeking to establish economic ties with African commodity exporters regardless of their human rights records. The "resource curse," whereby political development is hampered by plentiful natural resources, is a more potent curse when commodity prices are high. Paradoxically, Iraq's oil wealth may well become one of the drivers of that country's disintegration as the rival ethnic groups compete for what they see as their rightful shares. Perhaps the biggest difference between pulling out of Vietnam and pulling out of Iraq is that the latter accounts for 10 percent of proved global oil reserves.[53]

4. *The potential unraveling of the system of multilateral trade negotiation.* Finally, it is easily forgotten that the momentum toward a comprehensive agreement on world trade has largely been lost, to the extent that the completion of the Doha Round now seems a remote prospect. Increasingly, the trend is toward bilateral or subregional trade agreements, which tend to advantage the bigger players while reducing the aggregate global benefits of freer trade. This may seem a prosaic point, but it should not be dismissed as such when there are so many protectionist measures before the U.S. Congress that aim at penalizing China for alleged currency manipulation. Quite what protectionist legislation would do to the delicate equilibrium of Sino-American relations is not easy to predict, but it would surely have some impact on the reserve policy of the People's Bank of China.

The common theme that links these four problems is that they can be effectively addressed only within the framework of international institutions established after World War II and centered on the United Nations. In particular, more effort needs to be made to revive the credibility and effectiveness of the UN Security Council, the International Atomic Energy Agency, and the World Trade Organization. Fortunately for the next president, these are institutions that were in large measure created by the United States. They are therefore institutions in which its interests are well represented. Those who recommend radical reform of the Security Council should reflect more deeply on this point. In a recent work, G. John Ikenberry and Anne-Marie Slaughter endorsed the proposal of the UN's own High Level Panel that Brazil, Germany, India, Japan, and two African states—presumably the most populous, Egypt and Nigeria—should be invited to join the Security Council as permanent members without a veto. They also called for the abolition of all the existing veto rights "for resolutions authorizing direct action in response to a crisis." Instead, they argue, such resolutions should require only a "supermajority" vote of "perhaps three quarters of voting members."[54] Such a Security Council would certainly represent a much larger proportion of the world's population (55 percent as opposed to the current 29 percent). On the other hand, were these proposals to be adopted, it would be possible to construct a supermajority without the United States and its most dependable ally, the United Kingdom. Being outvoted on resolutions for "direct action" would scarcely endear an already little-loved institution to American voters. Indeed, it is hard to think of a reform of the international system that would be less in the American national interest.

The new president should therefore seek to exploit the inbuilt advantage the United States enjoys in most international institutions to reassert America's commitment to the ideals of Woodrow Wilson and Franklin Roosevelt. Yet there is another aspect of their legacy that should also be revived: the primacy of retaliation over preemption. When Wilson was elected president, the probability that imperial Germany would sink American merchant ships and offer a military alliance to Mexico was infinitely small. When Roosevelt entered the White House, the probability that imperial Japan would try to wipe out the U.S. Pacific fleet was equally tiny. Had either president adopted a policy of preemption, designed to destroy German submarines or Japanese aircraft carriers before they could be used against the United States, they would have been thought quite mad, wise though these policies might now seem with the benefit of hindsight. As was true of the attacks of September 11, 2001, the sinking of the *Lusitania* and the raid on Pearl Harbor were true surprises—or, in Taleb's terminology, "black swans"—which were extremely hard to foresee.[55] Trying to preempt them would not have been a rational policy choice. Success would not have been appreciated; the cost of the prophylaxis would almost certainly have been deemed excessive.

Not every president suffers a nasty surprise, it is true. Nevertheless, the next president should act on the assumption that black swans do exist. She or he must also acknowledge how difficult even the most astute human being finds it to overcome the distortions imposed on cognition by heuristics and biases. We are not, as a species, especially good at assigning probabilities to future threats. We underestimate the frequency of "black swans." Experiments show that we all too readily succumb to such cognitive traps as the fallacy of conjunction, confirmation bias, contamination effects, the affect heuristic, scope neglect, overconfidence in calibration, and bystander apathy.[56] That is the reason the next president's security strategy should be crafted in the light of all the existing or potential threats that confront the United States, and not just the one threat ("deliverable weapons of mass destruction in the hands of a terror network or murderous dictator") that the *National Security Strategy* of 2002 purported to address. The spread of conflict in the Middle East, the proliferation of nuclear weapons, the chase for commodities, and the return of protectionism—the dangers associated with these trends may be harder to visualize than a nuclear explosion in New York, but they also have a much higher probability. Given the finite resources at the president's disposal, in terms of finance, military manpower, public support, and international legitimacy, there is an urgent need to construct a diversified and well-hedged strategic portfolio.

As we have seen, Kissinger's "problem of conjecture" remains the essential dilemma that confronts any new commander in chief. By underestimating a nascent threat, the line of least resistance may prove costly in the end. The bolder course of preemption may go unrewarded precisely because it prevents that threat from being realized. But when resources are limited, when threats are myriad, and when cognition is imperfect, discretion may be the better part of valor. The lesson of the Bush era, and of the ignominious fate of the Bush doctrine, is that, when one is given the choice between "the assessment which requires the least effort [and]…an assessment which requires more effort," sometimes the former is the right one to pick.

Notes

1. *The National Security Strategy of the United States of America* (Washington, DC: The White House, 2002), 4.
2. Ibid., 12.
3. See, for example, Ivan Eland, *The Empire Has No Clothes: U.S. Foreign Policy Exposed* (Oakland, CA: Independent Institute, 2004), 205.
4. *National Security Strategy*, 4, 9.
5. Niall Ferguson, *Colossus: The Rise and Fall of the American Empire* (New York: Penguin, 2004), 152f.
6. The point was first made in Melvyn P. Leffler, "9/11 and the Past and the Future of American Foreign Policy," *International Affairs* 79, no. 5 (October 2003): 1045–1063. See also Colin S. Gray, *The Implications of Preemptive and Preventive War Doctrines: A Reconsideration*, Strategic Studies Institute monograph (July 2007).
7. Niall Ferguson, *Empire: The Rise and Demise of the British World Order and the Lessons for Global Power* (New York: Basic Books, 2003), 368ff.
8. *National Security Strategy*, 20.
9. "Strategies for Maintaining U.S. Predominance," OSD/NA Summer Study (August 1, 2001).
10. Joseph E. Stiglitz and Linda J. Bilmes, *The Three Trillion Dollar War: The True Cost of the Iraq Conflict* (New York: Norton, 2008).
11. William D. Nordhaus, "Iraq: The Economic Consequences of War," *New York Review of Books* 49, no. 19 (December 5, 2002). The White House initially projected the cost of the war at $100–200 billion. Increased Iraqi oil revenues were supposed to cover much of this outlay.
12. For an attempt to argue the contrary, see Steven J. Davis, Kevin M. Murphy, and Robert H. Topel, "War in Iraq versus Containment" (NBER working paper 12092, March 2006).
13. Chairman of the Council of Economic Advisers, *Economic Report of the President 2007* (Washington, DC), table B-78, http://www.gpoaccess.gov/eop/tables07.html.
14. Congressional Budget Office, *Baseline Budget Projections, 2007–2017* (Washington, DC, 2007), http://www.cbo.gov/budget/budproj.pdf.
15. Robert D. Hormats, *The Price of Liberty: Paying for America's Wars* (New York: Times Books/Henry Holt, 2007), 271–299.

16. Congressional Budget Office, *Baseline Budget Projections, 2007–2017*.

17. Data provided by Professor Charles Goodhart of the London School of Economics and the Bank of England.

18. Federal Reserve Board, *Flow of Funds Accounts of the United States: Debt Growth, Borrowing and Debt Outstanding Tables* (Washington, DC, September 17, 2007), http://www.federalreserve.gov/releases/z1/current/z1r-2.pdf.

19. For a contrary view, see Richard N. Cooper, "Understanding Global Imbalances" (working paper, Harvard University Economics Department, 2006), http://www.economics.harvard.edu/faculty/cooper/papers/frbb.rev.pdf.

20. Niall Ferguson and Laurence J. Kotlikoff, "A New New Deal," *New Republic*, August 15, 2005.

21. Further details in Laurence J. Kotlikoff and Scott Burns, *The Coming Generational Storm: What You Need to Know about America's Economic Future* (Boston: MIT Press, 2004). See also Peter G. Peterson, *Running on Empty: How the Democratic and Republican Parties Are Bankrupting Our Future and What Americans Can Do about It* (New York: Farrar, Straus, & Giroux, 2004).

22. Jagadeesh Gokhale and Kent Smetters, "Fiscal and Generational Imbalances: New Budget Measures for New Budget Priorities" (policy discussion paper, The Federal Reserve Bank of Cleveland, March 2002). See most recently their paper "Measuring Social Security's Financial Problems" (NBER working paper 11060, January 2005), http://www.nber.org.

23. Chairman of the Council of Economic Advisers, *Economic Report of the President 2007*, table B-107.

24. George Magnus, "The New Silk Road," UBS Investment Research (February 2006).

25. Data from Bridgewater Daily Observations, http://www.bwater.com.

26. Jonathan R. Laing, "Coming Home to Roost," *Barron's*, February 17, 2006.

27. Congressional Budget Office, *Baseline Budget Projections, 2007–2017*, http://frwebgate.access.gpo.gov/cgi-bin/multidb.cgi.

28. Chairman of the Council of Economic Advisers, *Economic Report of the President 2007*, table B-88.

29. "Blair's Address to a Joint Session of Congress," *New York Times*, July 17, 2003.

30. "Young Americans Geographically Illiterate: Survey Suggests," National Geographic News (May 2, 2006), http://news.nationalgeographic.com/news/2006/05/0502_060502_geography.html.

31. The Gallup Poll, *Gallup's Pulse of Democracy: The War in Iraq*, http://www.galluppoll.com/content/default.aspx?ci=1633.

32. Lydia Saad, "'Axis of Evil' Countries Dominate U.S. Perceptions of Greatest Enemy," Gallup News Service (February 22, 2007), http://www.galluppoll.com/content/?ci=26653&pg=1; data on the opinions of the Muslim world from Gallup World Poll, http://www.gallupworldpoll.com/analyses/?r=5098.

33. All data from http://pewglobal.org/reports/.

34. Bob Woodward, *State of Denial: Bush at War, Part III* (New York: Simon & Schuster, 2006).

35. Kirk Semple, "In Rare Talks, U.S. and Iran Discuss Iraq," *New York Times*, May 28, 2007. For the Iraq Study Group, see James A. Baker III and Lee H. Hamilton, with Lawrence S. Eagleburger, Vernon E. Jordan, Jr., Edwin Meese III, Sandra Day O'Connor, Leon E. Panetta, William J. Perry, Charles S. Robb, and Alan K. Simpson, *The Iraq Study Group Report* (Vintage Books: New York, 2006).

36. *National Security Strategy*, 4.

37. Ibid., 15.

38. Richard A. Posner, *Catastrophe: Risk and Response* (Oxford, UK: Oxford University Press, 2004), especially 73–84.

39. Quoted in Ron Suskind, *The One Percent Doctrine: Deep Inside America's Pursuit of Its Enemies since 9/11* (New York: Simon & Schuster, 2007).

40. National Safety Council, "What Are the Odds of Dying?" http://www.nsc.org/lrs/statinfo/odds.htm.

41. Robert Looney, "Economic Costs to the United States Stemming from the 9/11 Attacks," *Strategic Insights* I, no. 6 (August 2002).

42. "Assessing the Damage," *Economist* (September 15, 2005).

43. The statistics are highly problematic, particularly since the discontinuation of the State Department's annual publication, *Patterns of Global Terrorism*; see Francis Rheinheimer and Chris Weatherly, "Terrorism Statistics Flawed," *Center for Defense Information* (April 12, 2006). Different series are available online from the Memorial Institute for the Prevention of Terrorism (MIPT) and the Worldwide Incidents Tracking System (WITS). A widely used data set can be found in Edward F. Mickolus and Susan L. Simmons, *Terrorism, 2002–2004*, 3 vols. (Westport, CT: Greenwood, 2005).

44. Suppose you have spent all your life in the Northern Hemisphere and have only ever seen white swans. You might very well conclude (inductively) that all swans are white. But take a trip to Australia, where swans are black, and your theory will collapse. A "black swan" is therefore anything that seems to us, on the basis of our limited experience, to be impossible.

45. Nassim Nicholas Taleb, *The Black Swan: The Impact of the Highly Improbable* (London: Penguin/Allen Lane, 2007).

46. Neil F. Johnson, Mike Spagat, Jorge A. Restrepo, Oscar Becerra, Juan Camilo Bohórquez, Nicolas Suárez, Elvira Maria Restrepo, and Roberto Zarama, "Universal Patterns Underlying Ongoing Wars and Terrorism" (2006), http://xxx.lanl.gov/abs/physics/0605035.

47. Lawrence Wright, *The Looming Tower: Al-Qaeda and the Road to 9/11* (New York: Knopf, 2006).

48. Niall Ferguson, "Political Risk and the International Bond Market between the 1848 Revolution and the Outbreak of the First World War," *Economic History Review* 59, no. 1 (February 2006): 70–112.

49. Niall Ferguson, *The Cash Nexus: Money and Power in the Modern World, 1700–2000* (New York: Basic Books, 2001), 412.

50. See, in general, Vali Nasr, *The Shia Revival: How Conflicts within Islam Will Shape the Future* (New York: Norton, 2006).

51. Niall Ferguson, "The Next War of the World," *Foreign Affairs* 85, no. 5 (September/October 2006): 61–74.

52. Thomas Schelling, "An Astonishing Sixty Years," Weatherhead Center, Harvard University (March 2, 2006).

53. BP Global, "Statistical Review of World Energy" (June 2005), http://www.bp.com/statisticalreview.

54. See, for example, G. John Ikenberry and Anne-Marie Slaughter, *Forging a World of Liberty under Law: U.S. National Security in the 21st Century: The Final Report of the Princeton Project on International Security* (Princeton, NJ: Princeton University Press, 2006).

55. For a somewhat different view, see John Lewis Gaddis, *Surprise, Security, and the American Experience: The Joanna Jackson Goldman Memorial Lectures on American Civilization and Government* (Cambridge, MA: Harvard University Press, 2005).

56. Eliezer Yudkowsky, "Cognitive Biases Potentially Affecting Judgment of Global Risks," in *Global Catastrophic Risks*, ed. Nick Bostrom and Milan Cirkovic (New York: Oxford University Press, 2008).

ELEVEN

Dilemmas of Strategy
Melvyn P. Leffler
and Jeffrey W. Legro

AMERICA'S CRYSTAL BALL on strategy is murky.[1] Officials in the next administration will face a complex world, will receive conflicting advice, and will need to mobilize domestic support for their policies.[2] They must nonetheless act, most likely without the convenience of a single threat such as the Soviet Union during the cold war or terrorism in the immediate aftermath of the 9/11 attacks. In this conclusion, our aims are to highlight the decisive issues of consensus and contention that resonate across the chapters. We seek to delineate the trade-offs involved in making choices, and we hope to illuminate the national security dilemmas that any administration must grapple with as the United States helps to shape, and is shaped by, the next stage in world politics.

Foundations of Strategy Consensus

There are certainly important differences among the authors. Yet along very crucial dimensions—perhaps distinctly American dimensions—shared beliefs unite their blueprints. And these ideas appear to accord with American public opinion. Equally notable, they have backing in the broader world. The efficacy of any policy necessarily depends on audiences at home and abroad; therefore, the basis for a feasible strategy may be at hand. The beliefs that seem to be shared by all the authors can be summarized as leadership, preponderance, freedom, economic openness, and collaboration.

The contributors agree that the United States should be a leader in the international system. True, they dispute what kind of leader the country should be and what particular tasks are required in such a role. Yet not a single one of the experts is calling for disengagement from the international arena.

They accept Madeleine Albright's description of the United States as "the indispensable nation." That is, they understand that the world is faced by collective action problems. Such problems take many governments to solve, but all are hesitant to try to do so because the costs are high and the benefits are not easily withheld from those who do nothing. In such situations, it helps to have a lead country to encourage contributions and discourage free riding.[3] Were the United States to pull its support from the International Monetary Fund (IMF), the Nuclear Nonproliferation Treaty (NPT), the policing of sea lanes, and the stabilization of Europe and Asia with no replacements at hand, there would be a collapse of, or grievous harm done to, the effective functioning of the international system.

This consensus among experts on U.S. leadership might appear at odds with popular U.S. opinion. By a margin of 75 to 22 percent, polls indicate that the public rejects the United States' playing the role of a "world policeman" that enforces international law and fights aggression.[4] Only 10 percent of the public accepts the proposition that the United States "should continue to be the preeminent world leader in solving international problems."[5] Yet U.S. opinion is not isolationist; only 12 percent believe that the country should withdraw from most efforts to address international problems. It appears that Americans do believe (75 percent) that the U.S. should do its share to solve problems (see figure 11.1). They, however, do not want to carry all the costs; Americans want U.S. hegemony to be Dutch treat.

Opinion abroad also does not want the United States to be the sole decider. In fourteen countries surveyed from around the world, minorities of respondents, usually less than 10 percent, believe that the United States "should continue to be the preeminent world leader in solving international problems." Majorities, or near majorities, thought the United States "should do its share in efforts to solve problems in cooperation with other countries."[6] What is not clear is whether other countries would be willing to assume more of the responsibility and financial burdens of international collective action should the United States step back from a leadership role.[7]

The key unresolved issue, then, is how to reconcile the experts' preference for leadership with the public's hesitancy to get stuck with the bill. Put differently, it remains unclear how much the financial burden of U.S. leadership can

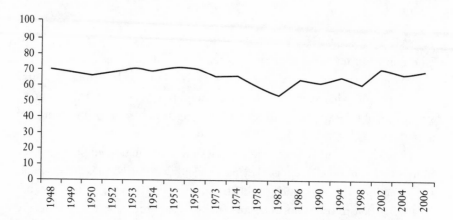

FIGURE 11.1 Percentage of Americans Who Think It Best That the United States Take an Active Part in World Affairs. *Source*: Chicago Council on Global Affairs Public Opinion Study (2006), http://www.worldpublicopinion.org/pipa/articles/brunitedstatescanadara/256.php?nid=&id=&pnt=256&lb=brusc.

be shared with others while still avoiding collective action problems in which nothing gets done in such areas as managing debt crises, combating global terrorism, dealing with climate change, protecting sea lanes, and responding to global pandemics.

Preponderance

Our contributors may disagree on how U.S. military capabilities should be configured and how military power should be exercised, but they concur that the United States should retain its military dominance (see figure 11.2). They believe that superior U.S. military power and technology enable the United States to deal with major conflicts should they arise, deter the use of force by others, and buttress U.S. influence in the international system.

None of the contributors proposes to reduce military spending significantly or wants to allow U.S. superiority to erode, even though several of them criticize the degree of U.S. military dominance and wonder about the utility of military force. The use of overwhelming conventional power against insurgents, Francis Fukuyama argues, is almost always counterproductive; overwhelming power, insists David M. Kennedy, tempts the United States to disrespect other nations' sovereignty and alienates public opinion abroad. Likewise, G. John Ikenberry worries that U.S. unipolarity invites unilateral action and discourages participation in a collaborative multinational order. Most of the contributors would agree that even though power is needed, it should be exercised subtly.

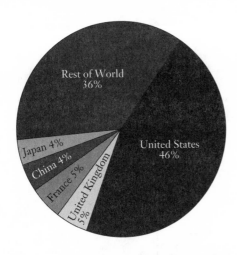

FIGURE 11.2 World Military Expenditure, 2006. *Source*: "Fifteen Major Spender Countries in 2006," Stockholm International Peace Research Institute (2007).

The support for preponderance reflects a long-standing bipartisan consensus. In his 2002 *National Security Strategy*, President George W. Bush declared, "It is time to reaffirm the essential role of American military strength. We must build and maintain our defenses beyond challenge"; and in 2006 he reasserted that "we must maintain a military without peer."[8] Such claims are not simply limited to the president or to Republicans. Democratic presidents have also consistently asserted that the United States should "remain the strongest of all nations."[9] Fifty-five percent of Americans today agree that maintaining military superiority is an important goal, and 53 percent believe that the United States should retain the majority of its overseas military bases.[10]

Right now the cost of preponderance in terms of military spending and development (as opposed to the growing burden of military operations and casualties) does not appear burdensome to the U.S. economy. Gross domestic product (GDP) has risen at a healthy pace during the defense buildup of the past six years, and military spending as a percentage of gross national product (GNP) is not out of line with historic levels, as seen in figure 11.3.

Yet as Niall Ferguson and Barry Eichengreen and Douglas A. Irwin point out, the United States is increasingly becoming a debtor nation. Debt will squeeze defense spending as the costs of Social Security and Medicare balloon in the years ahead with the aging of the baby boomers. If the ultimate source of U.S. preponderance—that is, the relative strength of the U.S. economy—continues to shrink (see figure 11.4), and if the United States becomes increasingly indebted to creditors abroad, there may be pressure to cut military spending in order to deal with the underlying issues that are eroding the nation's competitive position in the international economy.[11]

Preponderance is the issue on which international opinion is least supportive, though attitudes vary widely, often depending on whether

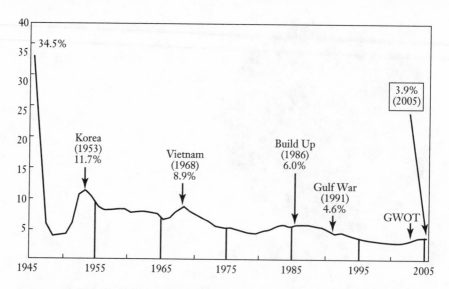

FIGURE 11.3 U.S. Defense Budget as a Percentage of GDP. *Source*: U.S. Department of Defense, "FY 2007 Department of Defense Budget," briefing slides, February 6, 2006, p. 25, www.defenselink.mil/news/Feb2006/d20060206slides.pdf.

FIGURE 11.4 Share of World GDP, 1820–2001. *Source*: Angus Maddison, "The World Economy: Historical Statistics," OECD, 2003, http://runningofthebulls.typepad.com/toros_running_of_the_bull/images/world_gdp.gif.

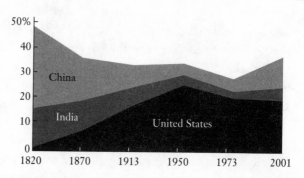

a country is closely allied with the United States or not. With regard to whether the United States should have fewer, the same number of, or more long-term overseas military bases, a majority in Argentina, France, Palestine, Ukraine, and China voted for fewer. In Poland, the Philippines, Israel, and Armenia, a majority voted for either the same number or more.[12] In nine of thirteen countries, more people saw the prospect of China's economy equaling that of the United States as mostly positive than as mostly negative. The four countries in which greater numbers saw it as negative were the United States, France, India, and Russia.[13] So there is skepticism abroad on U.S. preponderance, but how other countries react to it may also depend on who is rising to eclipse it.

Most people who live in stable democracies see political freedom as desirable. President Bush has emphasized that human rights, liberty, and justice are protected best in democracies. All our authors would agree—all other things being equal—that promoting democracy and protecting human rights are valued objectives. Even skeptics of democratization, such as James Kurth, see the spread of freedom and the improvement of human rights as goals ultimately worth seeking.

Charles S. Maier, Samantha Power, and Fukuyama, however, are skeptical that electoral democracy is the best means to further U.S. values because it can serve radical ends and often does little to meet the basic needs of people. But they do want to improve human rights, nurture civil society, spread freedom, and reduce poverty and inequality. These goals are not just morally desirable; depending on circumstances, they can also contribute to stability in the international system ("democracies do not fight one another"[14]) and enhance U.S. influence (democracies are thought to be more likely to side with the United States than other types of regimes).[15] The authors, of course, do disagree on how best to spread democracy, a topic we will revisit.

Internationally, many countries support democratization in principle. Even some of the most authoritarian opponents of the United States give lip service to democracy. Chinese officials, for example, do not reject political democracy. Their position is quite different from the Soviet Union's during the cold war (which preferred "economic democracy" and the "dictatorship of the proletariat"). Beijing's leaders, however, believe that a rapid transition to democracy would destabilize the country. They say they want to liberalize slowly in order to maintain order and expand the economy. There is reason to be skeptical that Chinese Communist officials would ever relinquish power, but it is also true that China has slowly liberalized—with fits and starts—since the beginning of Deng Xiaoping's reforms in the late 1970s.[16] The norm of democracy has spread internationally, and this should be a welcome development for U.S. foreign policy.

Economic Openness

Most studies of U.S. security policy focus largely on its political-military aspects, not on economic policy. In the preceding chapters, our contributors mainly embrace an open capitalist global economic order. No author champions greater protection for U.S. markets or a withdrawal from the global economic system. Indeed, Ikenberry, Ferguson, and Eichengreen and Irwin identify a liberal or open economic order as one of the United

States' most important interests. Maier and Power thoughtfully criticize the results of globalization, but they still seem to support an open international order with social safeguards that protect the poor and close the income inequality gap.

The premise of openness is widely shared in U.S. political culture even as Americans sometimes seek protection. It is based on the notion that the country and the world have prospered under an open system; that a closed system led to the collapse of democracies and the onset of World War II; that open trade among Western countries helped them to thrive and succeed in the cold war; and that the emergence of new economies (South Korea, China, India, etc.) has depended on an open system that not only raises U.S. welfare but also enhances global well-being.

It is notable that criticism of the Bush doctrine has largely avoided economic policy; in fact, Bush economic policy has largely been a continuation of the Clinton strategy. As Eichengreen and Irwin point out, it is the same basic policy that has prevailed since at least 1945. Bush has largely followed the multilateral stance of his predecessors, sometimes using bilateral agreements to liberalize further the global regime of openness governed by the World Trade Organization (WTO). The next president is likely to pursue a similar course, though he or she may employ a different rhetorical style and implement complementary policies to assist workers hurt by global competition and to protect against damage to the environment.

Openness has a good deal of support internationally, as well. Majorities in many countries around the world believe that increasing global economic ties is desirable (see figure 11.5). The challenge is that open trade may have somewhat less popular support in the United States than elsewhere, as seen in table 11.1 (on page 258).

Americans do support free trade in general, but they have reservations about the distribution of benefits in the United States between rich and poor, and they worry about its implications for the environment. Our contributors, however, barely discuss the potential downside of openness. Openness can erode U.S. global advantages in education and technology, comparative advantages that have long sustained U.S. economic vibrancy. Arthur Stein calls this the "hegemon's dilemma": in order to protect its dominant position in the world order, the United States faces a choice between protectionist practices that could destabilize that very system or openness that may atrophy its leading position in an increasingly competitive international economic order.[17]

The experts writing in this volume clearly opt for continuing support of an open world order, but perhaps because they do not see decline as inevitable

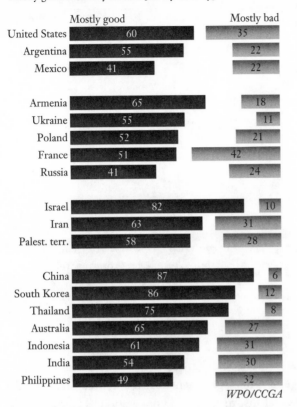

Views of Globalization

... Do you believe that globalization, especially the increasing connections of our economy with others around the world, is mostly good or mostly bad for [survey country]?

Mostly good — Mostly bad

Country	Mostly good	Mostly bad
United States	60	35
Argentina	55	22
Mexico	41	22
Armenia	65	18
Ukraine	55	11
Poland	52	21
France	51	42
Russia	41	24
Israel	82	10
Iran	63	31
Palest. terr.	58	28
China	87	6
South Korea	86	12
Thailand	75	8
Australia	65	27
Indonesia	61	31
India	54	30
Philippines	49	32

WPO/CCGA

FIGURE 11.5 International Opinion on Globalization and Trade. *Source*: Chicago Council on Global Affairs (April 2007), http://www .worldpublicopinion .org/pipa/articles/ btglobalizationtradera/ 349.php?nid=&id=&pnt =349&lb=btgl.

or even likely. Previous warnings of U.S. decline in the face of a rising Soviet Union or Japan proved wrong, and perhaps the ingenuity of American entrepreneurs, the ambitions of millions of immigrants, and the hardworking ethos of American labor will enable the United States to overcome the challenges that accompany international economic openness. It is significant that all our contributors assume that an open international economic order is a good thing.

International Collaboration

Should the United States pursue the unilateralism that so many attribute to the Bush doctrine or adopt more multilateralism in its foreign affairs? Are "coalitions of the willing" suitable for the future, or should the United States seek more formalized relationships and reinvigorate international institutions?

TABLE 11.1   U.S. Opinion on the Impact of Free Trade Agreements on...

	Sept. 1997	Sept. 2001	Dec. 2003	July 2004	Oct. 2005	Dec. 2006
The country						
Good thing	47	49	34	47	44	44
Bad thing	30	29	33	34	34	35
Don't know	23	22	33	19	22	21
	100	100	100	100	100	100
Your personal financial situation						
Helped	—	—	27	34	—	35
Hurt	—	—	38	41	—	36
Neither/Don't know	—	—	35	25	—	29
			100	100		100

Source: "Free Trade Agreements Get a Mixed Review," Pew Research Center for the People and the Press (December 19, 2006), http://people-press.org/reports/display .php3?ReportID=299.

One might think that these would be questions of debate among the authors, but they are in remarkable agreement that the United States needs to embrace more multilateral institutionalized cooperation. Their schemes vary significantly in the types of cooperation they propose and the degree to which they want to commit the United States, ranging from Robert Kagan's strengthened traditional alliances to Stephen Van Evera's call for a global concert. We return to these significant disputes on how to pursue collaboration later. But here it is worth underscoring that no one is saying that the United States should go it alone or that it should go about its business without hearing and accommodating the desires of others to a much greater degree than has been the case in recent years. Indeed, they suggest that U.S. leaders should go out of their way to build and solidify relationships, rules, and organizations in a variety of areas, including global order, security, economics, health, and the environment. Almost all believe that greater U.S. respect for international law would serve American interests.

The views of the experts receive strong support from U.S. public opinion. In polls in recent years, majorities of respondents, sometimes often large majorities, think that the United States should work more closely with allies

(91 percent), take into greater account the views and interests of other countries (90 percent), and deal with problems such as terrorism and the environment by working through international institutions (69 percent) and that strengthening the United Nations (UN) should be an important U.S. foreign policy goal (79 percent).[18]

Would other countries welcome U.S. cooperative efforts? There is reason here for some concern, as discussed further later. In ten of fourteen countries polled recently, a majority of respondents did not trust the United States to act responsibly. In five out of seven countries they believe that the United States does not take into account their interests in making policy. But in a large number of countries polled, majorities want the United States to cooperate more in dealing with the world's problems.[19] Public opinion is not policy. Yet these numbers suggest some basis for expecting that U.S. efforts at multilateralism could be reciprocated.

Surprisingly, then, our contributors do possess shared premises that provide a likely basis for future national security strategy. They support U.S. leadership in world affairs, military preponderance, the spread of political freedom, economic openness, and more collaboration and/or multilateral institution building with key partners abroad.

Disagreements over Strategy

Although there is much that the contributors agree on, they part company on a number of key issues that will be central to formulating a coherent foreign policy. They disagree on the landscape of international affairs; they assess threats differently; and they argue over the importance of "legitimacy," the utility of coercive power, the right approach to democratization, and the value and configuration of international institutions.

The Future of World Politics

The starting point of any analysis of foreign policy has to be the landscape of the international system. Will the future be different from the past? Is war obsolete? Are states withering away? Can globalization continue? Our authors sometimes offer sharply different portraits of the evolving world.

This is clear at the outset of the volume when one contrasts the views of Van Evera and Kagan. Van Evera sees a world in which prior U.S. concerns about a dominant power achieving geopolitical hegemony in Eurasia are no longer relevant. China is the most plausible candidate, but even it is an unlikely aggressive expander. China is not going to conquer other major industrial centers; nationalism and nuclear weapons make territorial aggression less likely than ever before, says Van Evera. He sees a dramatic break with the past: weapons of mass destruction, terrorism, climate change, and global viruses now present a threat to all, and in doing so offer an opportunity for cooperation that is unprecedented in modern history. Kagan, in contrast, predicts "the return of history"—the reemergence of great power competition. In his view, there can be no shared morality among Russia, China, and the United States that would allow for Van Evera's harmony. Conflict, not collaboration, is the likely scenario.

If Kagan's view encompasses a world of continuity, other authors portray a radical break in the ordering principles of the international system. They question the longevity of the nation-state and the norm of sovereignty. If the world used to be composed of discrete political units, each controlling its own boundaries and polities, the future may be much messier. Maier, for example, sees a global system that is "a more fluid aggregate of communities, sometimes local, sometimes contained within particular countries, but increasingly transnational and unbordered." It is a world of interconnected societies not amenable to traditional state-to-state diplomatic actions.

Others see the decline of sovereignty as a defining trait of the emerging international order. For Fukuyama this is occurring not everywhere, but mainly in "a band of instability that runs from North Africa through the Middle East, Africa, and Central Asia." In this region, weak states are the rule and transnational nonstate actors are powerful. Foreign policy, therefore, cannot operate on a "state-to-state" basis; it must reach inside states, argues Kurth. He says that restoring sovereignty is the key to order in such areas. Because empire is no longer a viable option, order requires that states be made viable. Governments must be empowered to assert control over their polities, and they must be held accountable for undesirable behavior within their territorial boundaries and in the global arena.

For Ikenberry, order is also the defining problem of the future, but the issue is less a particular area of the world than it is a deficit in the rules of the international system itself. He sees many challenges ahead for the United States that can be successfully addressed only by a new global compact—a liberal order—that only the United States can lead.

A number of authors share Ikenberry's premise that the future hinges on what the United States can or cannot do, that the American Goliath will by its very actions define world politics. Kennedy, for example, sees the decline of sovereignty and the prevalence of force in the global arena as (in part) a product of the United States' own choices—ones that can be reversed. Similarly, Power believes that a defining trait of world politics is the decline of U.S. competence and legitimacy, changes that have affected its ability as the key global player to provide order. She argues that if the United States makes different choices in the future, legitimacy and order are possible.

Others are skeptical of the possibility for a global order or of the United States' ability to bring it about through its own actions. Kagan allows little room for such a broad community in his portrait of a dog-eat-dog world of competitive states. Eichengreen and Irwin also doubt that the United States will be able to reform old institutions or start new ones, given the constraints on U.S. international economic policy. In effect, Gulliver has already been bound.

Threats and Opportunities

Based on the preceding, it is not surprising that the contributors emphasize different threats and opportunities ahead. And, similarly, they often differ on the appropriate response. Policy makers, however, must assign priorities to the dangers they face. Not all challenges and responses can be fully pursued at the same time without undercutting other efforts or exceeding the organizational and financial capabilities of the nation. And so threats must be ranked in some fashion.

The Bush administration identified terrorism as the overwhelming danger facing the United States and made it the centerpiece of its security strategy, followed by a secondary focus on "rogue states" and the spread of nuclear weapons. The *9/11 Commission Report* confirmed this orientation, stating that "countering terrorism has become, beyond any doubt, the top national security priority for the United States."[20]

Many of our contributors disagree. Some do view terrorism as a major challenge, though they are quick to specify, as does Van Evera, that it is terrorists with nuclear weapons or, as Kurth argues, those inspired by a noncooperative ideology (i.e., radical Islam) who are the overriding threat to U.S. national security. Ferguson, in contrast, maintains that the United States is being distracted by the possibility of nuclear terrorism, that it is unlikely and that actions taken to prevent it worsen the situation.

As summarized in table 11.2, most other contributors also point to challenges other than terrorism: the return of great power politics, the fragility of the global economic system, the divide between democracies and autocracies, the rise of religious fanaticism, the magnitude of inequality, mounting U.S. debt, the growth of Chinese power, the instability in the periphery, the fragility of the international economy, the erosion of liberal international institutions, and the rogue use of U.S. power and the attendant loss of U.S. legitimacy. Some of these analyses of the threats—and the proposed policies to deal with them—are compatible, but many of them are not.

TABLE 11.2 Threats and Priorities

Author(s)	Main threat	Proposed response
Eichengreen and Irwin	Collapse of the world economic system; U.S. deficits	Hope for the best; restore commitments to international institutions
Ferguson	U.S. debt; Middle East instability; nuclear proliferation; resource competition; crisis of multilateral trade	Abandon Bush doctrine; revive international institutions; avoid focus on another terrorist attack like 9/11
Fukuyama	State failure; rising powers	Focus on state building and international engagement
Ikenberry	Erosion of global order	Restore U.S. legitimacy and rebuild institutions
Kagan	Great power competition; rise of autocracies; radical Islam	Maintain dominance; promote democracy
Kennedy	U.S. disrespect for sovereignty and lack of domestic check on use of force	Return to principle of consent; engage and lead international institutions; draft by lottery
Kurth	Disorder; nuclear terrorism	Form grand coalition with Russia, China, India; impose order
Maier	Inequality and religious zealotry	Increase foreign aid and support of nongovernmental organizations; require an equality check on trade deals; support religious moderates
Power	Decline of U.S. legitimacy and competence	Support intelligence reform; promote social aid; respect international law; apologize; restrict special interests; educate domestic base
Van Evera	Nuclear terrorism; climate change; global health	Build a global concert; redirect resources from old geopolitical scenarios to new threats

For example, if terrorism is *the* challenge to U.S. security, it will mean that Washington will pay less attention to other threats, such as the growth of Chinese power or U.S. domestic economic problems. This inattention to other threats has been one of the criticisms of the Bush doctrine, and U.S. leaders will have to resolve the trade-offs in the future. Obviously, the country will have to deal with all potential menaces, but it will nonetheless face tough choices in terms of allocating resources to deal with different demands. Should the United States fund forces that deter and fight conventional military conflicts, or should it develop conflict-prevention and nation-building capabilities? Should it devote more of its budget to foreign aid or to retraining U.S. workers to compete in the global economy? Should the United States spend more on developing the Chinese-language skills of its intelligence analysts or on Arabic or Persian speakers?

A second dilemma involves the need to establish order in areas of the world in which there is none versus the need for the United States to show fidelity to its values. In the former case, an emphasis on order may involve cutting deals with unsavory governments (ones that are anything but democratic) or not intervening when groups within other countries maintain order through repressive violence. Or it could involve bending domestic principles of justice to deal with terrorist or other challenges abroad. In this view, rendition or the use of extraordinary prisons (such as those at Guantanamo Bay) may seem necessary.

Kurth favors the maintenance of order and would support at least some of those measures. Power, in contrast, sees the need for the United States to match its deeds to its values in order to reestablish legitimacy. America's rhetorical emphasis on democracy, human rights, and political equality, she insists, must be reflected in action. For her, order follows from influence that is based not on coercion but on legitimacy. For Kurth, coercive control as the "boss of bosses" is more critical.

These are starkly different approaches to security, and they cannot be pursued simultaneously. Which one is best hinges on some judgment of relative efficacy. Could the United States really cooperate effectively with China and Russia to maintain order? Would those countries operate in ways acceptable to the U.S. public? Or would less hypocrisy on the part of the United States by adhering more closely to domestic values lead to a growth of credibility that would make international cooperation easier, as Power asserts? Both argue their positions persuasively, and the trade-offs and judgments are dauntingly difficult to make.

The different plans call for varying types of security investments, not all of which can be accommodated at the same time. For example, the "get your financial house in order" message of Eichengreen and Irwin does not fit easily, as Ferguson suggests, with the military prescriptions of Kagan. In the short term, so long as foreign purchases of U.S. bonds and securities continue, the trade-offs are less severe, but should investors flee the dollar, the choices will become much more difficult.

Likewise, if the United States is to undertake major initiatives to shore up failed states or to reduce international inequality or to build new international institutions, it will have to allocate significant resources to accomplish these tasks. Such resources will have to come from domestic spending, from new taxes, or, most likely, from the defense budget. Again, it means making choices, assigning priorities, and placing bets on one path or another.

Even rejecting the need to rank threats comes with a significant risk. Ikenberry's suggestion that the United States avoid planning for any specific danger—that is, allowing for many contingencies and responding as events demand—may mean not being well prepared for any challenge, thus allowing them to metastasize into something truly overwhelming. Yet if the United States focuses on a single scenario, it may leave itself unprepared to deal with contingencies outside of its purview, as was the case in the years before the 9/11 attacks when terrorism was pushed to the side by a lingering cold war mentality—if the 9/11 *Commission Report* is accurate. The balance must be somewhere between those two extremes: preparing very well for a single threat or being somewhat prepared for many threats. The optimal point is by no means obvious.

Finally, readers should consider the threats that receive little attention in the chapters. Only Van Evera and Power point to global warming as worthy of mention, and they do so only in passing. Aside from the economists (Irwin and Eichengreen) and one of the economic historians (Ferguson), none of the experts points to fading U.S. competitiveness or financial strength or its deficits as a cause for concern. Nuclear proliferation is not seen by anyone—except so far as it involves terrorists—as the most pressing issue. Surprisingly, given the soaring price of petroleum over the past few years, energy is also relatively ignored, except for brief mention in two chapters. Finally, the fraying of transatlantic relations between the United States and Western Europe is not a focus of any analysis (Ikenberry and Maier are partial exceptions) and is disregarded in most of the chapters. Such oversights do not reflect ignorance but, instead, the attempts of contributors to assign priorities in a world of many challenges. That their judgment does not spotlight these last few areas may reflect a collective wisdom or, more worrisome, a blinding bias.

International Legitimacy and Pushback

A significant debate exists among our contributors over the nature and importance of the rise of anti-Americanism and the decline of U.S. legitimacy in world politics. All our authors recognize that world opinion toward the

United States has grown sour since 2002.[21] What is less clear is whether, how, and how much that affects the efficacy of U.S. actions in the world. Does it impede the American ability to provide for its own well-being?

After 9/11, the attitude of the Bush administration was that world opinion was not crucial to American effectiveness. In an age in which the United States towered over other countries in terms of its combined economic, military, and political capabilities, what others thought of the United States did not seem consequential. Vice President Richard Cheney believed that when other governments recognized that they could not thwart U.S. action, they would rally to the American cause. He believed the United States could create its own realities.[22]

Kagan argues that other nations will react negatively to the United States regardless of what it does; this outcome, he claims, is the inevitable result of the preponderance of U.S. power. He stresses, however, that despite U.S. assertiveness in recent years, states have not countered as strongly as expected; there has been no formal "balancing" in terms of alliances with a specifically anti-American purpose or an arms buildup to offset U.S. power. Yes, other powers are hedging against the United States, but that is largely the result of changes in relative international power as they begin to catch up with the hegemon.[23]

Other contributors are much less sanguine. They believe that U.S. standing in the world has declined markedly and that it matters. Power, for example, asserts that in waging its war on terrorism the Bush administration has undermined U.S. legitimacy by contradicting U.S. values. Likewise, the advantages derived from the U.S. reputation for competence have been sacrificed in the aftermath of the Bush administration's performance in Iraq and in dealing with Hurricane Katrina. Kennedy similarly believes that the United States has lost international leverage by violating norms of sovereignty valued by others. Fukuyama also contends that the Bush administration overplayed its hand in Iraq, spoke too arrogantly, and triggered a blowback that has made U.S. diplomacy more difficult than it need be. These authors believe that the United States is losing the advantages it should derive from its attractive standard of living, its democratic values, and its free political system.[24]

Their advice for restoring U.S. legitimacy follows from these judgments. They suggest strategies that include apologizing for past violations, respecting others' sovereignty, adhering more closely to international law, lowering the American international profile, and listening to others. Many contributors, including the diverse group of Fukuyama, Ikenberry, Maier, and Power, say that to improve its legitimacy, the United States must do more to meet basic human needs: reducing hunger, providing clean water, mitigating inequality, and enhancing heath care. Their plans focus on different aspects of legitimacy, but they basically assert that it is better to be loved, respected, and competent than it is to be feared.

Which view, then, is right? Kagan points to the electoral victories of conservative pro-American governments as evidence that U.S. deeds have produced no lasting harm. It seems, however, that those same governments were elected less on the basis of opinion about the United States than on other issues more closely related to their domestic economic and social affairs.

The critics, on the other hand, seem correct in arguing that legitimacy is an issue in international politics and that the United States has lost prestige as a result of its violating its own principles, as well as its callous indifference to the opinions of others, at least in the 2001–2004 period. What is needed, however, are clearer illustrations of how precisely lack of legitimacy and anti-Americanism have hurt U.S. diplomacy and how rectifying past mistakes in these matters would produce more good than harm.

The Uses of Hard Power

All of the chapters agree on the desirability of a general American preponderance of power, as long as that preponderance is not so great as to invite self-intoxication. The authors disagree, however, on how useful hard power is for achieving political aims and on how it should be composed and wielded. Can military power still buy influence in international relations? If so, how should it be configured and deployed, and how, specifically, can it serve U.S. interests?

In Kagan's world, conventional military conflicts among great powers are possible at any time. Little has changed since the cold war in terms of the focus on conventional military needs except that the country must also deal with terrorism. Hard power retains significant currency. Kurth is more focused on terrorism, but he also argues that the United States should maintain its traditional focus on dominant conventional war-making capabilities. He expressly warns against diverting resources to counterinsurgency strategies; at most, he insists, the United States should help train and arm local indigenous forces.

Fukuyama starkly disagrees, arguing that the Bush administration vastly overplayed "big stick" coercive diplomacy. America needs "a much greater sense of the limits of American power, and particularly conventional military force, in shaping outcomes around the world." He sees large-scale conventional military conflicts as a thing of the past. The real challenge stems from internal conflict and terrorism. In contrast to Kurth, Fukuyama recommends a "hearts and minds" counterinsurgency campaign to combat terrorism, a strategy that should be "more like a police and intelligence operation...than a war." Fukuyama would restructure the U.S. government to further enhance its soft-power capabilities by creating a department of international development and a revamped program to foster civil society abroad, mainly with the funds saved from ending the Iraq war.

Like Fukuyama, Van Evera argues that great power conflict is unlikely, but he also agrees with Kurth that counterinsurgency is not the direction the United States should take as it develops its military power. For him, counterinsurgency is undesirable because it sucks America into "brutal police work that presents an ugly face to the world." Van Evera instead calls for the country to avoid aggressive war and to refrain from violent coercion. He wants to direct national security resources toward enhancing intelligence capabilities, securing loose nukes, disseminating antiradical propaganda, modulating indigenous and regional conflicts, and dealing with failed states.

Kennedy makes this argument more forcefully than other contributors, claiming that "conventional military force may have outlived its usefulness altogether." Van Evera would seem to agree with Kennedy, with two notable exceptions: conventional military power is still needed to deter countries from giving safe havens to terrorists and to deal with "states that have violated important international norms." The rub is that these tasks would seem to require substantial conventional forces.

These debates foreshadow difficult choices in the development of military strategy and weapons and the configuration of forces in the years ahead. The United States will need to layer the challenges of Iraq onto its experiences in the cold war and in the Balkans in the 1990s in order to understand how, if it all, military power can be used. And, if such power is usable, it will need to determine how best to configure it to deal with the most dangerous threats.

The Spread of Democracy

Does the nature of foreign regimes really matter for U.S. strategy? The authors agree that the spread of political freedom is good in itself—and good for U.S. foreign policy. Wilson's legacy is alive. That general consensus quickly falls apart, however, in terms of operational strategy. What priority should democracy promotion have in U.S. strategy, and how is political freedom in the world best expanded?

Several contributors seem to agree that democracy should come into play only if there are no other significant costs. Kurth is most explicit when he says that the United States needs to emphasize security over regime type and that this may require making common cause with autocracies. If the United States needs to cut deals with Russia or China or Saudi Arabia in order to make progress on other goals, such as the stability of failing states and societies, the control of nuclear proliferation, the end to internal conflicts, and so on, then it should do so. Democracy can wait.

In part, this calculation acknowledges reality in terms of assigning priorities to the challenges facing the United States. Yet it may also reflect a calculation of what is possible politically. Kennedy places respect for sovereignty ahead of democracy promotion. One cannot force democracy where conditions prevent its success. States may have to pass through particular stages before they are ready for democracy. If Fukuyama is right, democracy is more likely to emerge after state building and the rule of law have taken root. And these, in turn, are more likely after basic social needs, infrastructure development, and economic ties to the global economy have been established. Free trade leads to political liberalization in Eichengreen and Irwin's formulation, as well as in Fukuyama's; hence "liberal authoritarianism" may make sense.

Other contributors, however, see more utility in emphasizing democracy and liberal values regardless of local conditions. In odd ways, this emphasis joins the right end of the political spectrum to the left. Kagan is the most ardent supporter of democracy promotion in the volume, yet even he recognizes that there are times when it "will have to take a backseat to other objectives." But he does not envision this as a frequent occurrence. Unlike Kurth, he advocates democracy in the Middle East and beyond, even if it initially favors radical forces ("illiberal democracies"), because, ultimately, Kagan believes it will help to resolve the clash between modernity and tradition in those countries.

The logic of Power's argument points in the same direction. The United States has to reduce the hypocrisy in its foreign policy; it must stop publicizing one set of values and acting according to another. Loyalty to liberal values may preclude the types of deals with illiberal states that scholars such as Kurth and Fukuyama deem necessary. Power, however, shies away from advocating democracy promotion; instead she focuses on how the United States can improve its own democracy at home. She, like Maier and Fukuyama, decries a focus on elections at the expense of attention to human security—that is, basic needs and political freedoms. Yet Kagan's stance on democracy would seem to match Power's advice in terms of "walking the talk" of human rights and democracy.

If this emphasis demands confrontation with regimes that are nondemocratic or that violate human rights, this orientation might have dramatically negative effects in other crucial areas. The Bush administration has pursued an alliance with nondemocratic Pakistan specifically because it felt the country was exceedingly important yet too fragile to alter its regime type. Or consider the case of China, in which assigning priority to democracy promotion over other U.S. interests may lead to the decline of one of the central economic relationships in the world economy. On this matter, Fukuyama would disagree with Kagan, arguing that excessive emphasis on democracy progress will lead to the alienation of China. Fukuyama contends that the integration of China into the global market economy could, over time, lead to the liberalization of Chinese politics and society.

In sum, both sides of the democratization debate face trade-offs in pursuing their preferred options. Values and interests are not easily reconciled, even if we accept the claim by Power that the protection of values can lead to influence that helps protect interests.

International Cooperation and Institutions

The contributors agree that the United States must seek more cooperation, but they differ on how and how much to do that. Is it possible and desirable to move beyond traditional alliances? Can the United States usefully engage international institutions in a way that serves U.S. interests, or do the latter simply bind the U.S. Goliath? What types of institutions are desirable, and can they be realized?

The chapters in this volume offer different schemes for working with other countries. Kurth suggests that the United States should collaborate with China and Russia in order to preserve stability in their respective spheres of influence and to strangle transnational terrorism. It is a Machiavellian twist to Roosevelt's "four policemen" idea. But in principle and operation, it would not be far removed from the Concert of Europe following the Napoleonic wars, when different types of regimes also collaborated to provide order.

Kagan sees limited room for collaborative deals of the sort Kurth advocates. For Kagan, the notion of an international community is a chimera; multilateral institutions cannot be designed to serve everybody's interests. He sees international-governance deals with authoritarian China and Russia as virtually unthinkable. Kagan, however, does believe that a Concert of Democracies is desirable and possible—a type of enduring subcommunity within the international system that is shaped not just by power but also by ideologies of domestic governance.

The position in starkest contrast to Kagan's is Ikenberry's argument that *the* central interest of the United States is to lead a restructuring of an international system that is falling apart. For Ikenberry, international institutions are not just a tool in the national security toolbox; they are the master means for securing U.S. interests over the long run. He proposes an ambitious agenda for "liberal order building" that would involve global social services, rebuilt alliances with Europe and Japan, reform of the UN, a new Concert of Democracies, and reconfigured institutions in Asia to embed China and other rising powers. He faults the Bush administration for squandering the opportunity to rebuild such institutions—indeed contributing to their decline—in the years after 9/11.

Other authors in the volume echo that critique. As noted earlier, many believe that the United States has to respect, and indeed expand, international law. Power, Kurth, Kennedy, and Van Evera call for the United States to comply with international norms and U.S. legal practices. Thus Power recommends closing the prison at Guantanamo Bay, restoring habeas corpus, prohibiting evidence obtained through torture, and ending extraordinary rendition. Van Evera believes that U.S. rejections of institutions aimed at the common good—such as the UN accord on small arms traffic, the Kyoto treaty, and the International Criminal Court—were mistakes. Some provisions of these treaties may have been flawed, he argues, but the United States should not have rejected the efforts altogether but should have collaborated on their improvement. Kennedy similarly sees the need to return to engagement with, and leadership of, multilateral institutions.

A central challenge, however, in pursuing new institutions is how the United States can get others to join its lead given a perceived decline in U.S. leverage and legitimacy abroad. Does America still have the political and financial capital to cut big deals in the international arena? Although there is an emerging consensus across the U.S. political spectrum (witness the views of both Kagan and Ikenberry in this volume) on a Concert of Democracies, this concept has not been embraced even by America's closest friends, suggesting how difficult it will be to configure a new institutional order. Of course, Power believes that once U.S. legitimacy is restored, it will be considerably easier to revitalize multilateralism.

Eichengreen and Irwin are not so certain. They present a fine-grained picture of the return to multilateral practices in the economic realm in Bush's second term, but they envision formidable challenges ahead. They stress that progress in the Doha Round of the world trade talks and in the reform of the IMF and the World Bank has been hamstrung not only by a clash of interests with other countries (illustrated in the contentious debates over reducing European Union agricultural subsidies) but also by domestic politics. If the United States wants to develop international institutions, it may have to accept more limits on its own actions than it has in the past, for example, with regard to its agricultural subsidies or its claim that the head of the World Bank must be a U.S. citizen. Overall, Eichengreen and Irwin believe that new administrations will have little latitude to act in constructive ways, and Ferguson warns that this could have grave repercussions.

Fukuyama maintains that the way to make progress is to focus on regional arrangements, particularly in Asia. For example, he shows that the United States has a choice between two alternative approaches to handle the rise of China. One scheme would focus on containing China; the other would seek to enmesh and socialize China into acceptable international practices and norms. Like Van Evera, Fukuyama wants the United States to follow the latter path, capitalizing on the experiences of working with China in dealing with North Korea's nuclear ambitions. He believes the United States should strengthen multilateral organizations such as the ASEAN Regional Forum and the Asia-Pacific Economic Cooperation (APEC). Yet implementing such regional-based schemes in Asia and elsewhere would not address global concerns such as climate change or nuclear proliferation or the decline of the WTO. Fukuyama's is a bottom-up approach to international standards, but the transition from the regional to the global level is unclear.

In general, the trade-offs of pursuing international institutions have to do with the feasibility and costs of their creation, the uncertain prospects that they will be effective, and the limitations they entail for U.S. freedom of action and for the achievement of domestic priorities.

The Dilemmas of Domestic Support

There is no doubt that U.S. leaders face significant international challenges and strategic choices in the years ahead. Yet if history is any guide, one of the most difficult tasks will be the generation of domestic support for a consistent foreign policy while at the same time avoiding entrapment in a particular worldview that does not fit international circumstances. A fundamental principle of effective grand strategy is having strong unity of purpose behind it.[25] Popular support for national strategy sends stronger external signals, allows countries to generate more resources and manpower, and limits attention-diverting internal disputes.

The chapters in this volume mainly focus on how to respond optimally to the world of the future. The authors pay less attention to selling their plans at home, although some of them do illuminate the domestic hurdles that will challenge effective strategy making. Eichengreen and Irwin foresee significant domestic constraints on trade policy emanating from popular opinion and from institutional devices such as the (non)renewal of fast-track executive trade authority. Power claims that strong domestic lobbies distort U.S. policy. Van Evera agrees, worrying that lobbies associated with defense contractors and with foreign governments will block his preferred concert strategy.

Both Van Evera and Power allude to an American public that is often uninformed and insulated from U.S. strategy. Americans do not appreciate how much U.S. success in the past—such as victory in both world wars—was dependent on cooperation with others. Most important, they feel little direct connection with fundamental elements of U.S. foreign policy. This is one of Kennedy's central points. He shows that although U.S. troops are frequently deployed abroad, the decisions have a direct effect on only a small part of the population. Having a professional volunteer army, therefore, has made interventions much easier. In effect, Kennedy sees the restoration of the draft as a vehicle for ensuring popular engagement with key foreign policy decisions. People need to be engaged because the separation of foreign and domestic policy is increasingly outmoded; in a world of rapid communication, porous borders, and high mobility, it is essential to involve the American electorate in issues such as global warming and disease control that will invariably affect their lives and the lives of their children.

Accordingly, Power calls for a broad-based effort to "thicken" the "domestic base for foreign policy." In the past, however, when presidents have tried to do this, they have exaggerated challenges and overpromised. The outcome of this dynamic has often had a deleterious effect on strategy. Woodrow Wilson, for example, promised that intervention in World War I would promote reform at home, end European imperialism, and spur democracy. The United States did intervene and helped to defeat Germany, a country that challenged U.S. interests. Yet people's expectations went unfulfilled; the world was not made safe for democracy. Disillusionment set in, internationalism suffered, and throughout the interwar years the United States was constrained from playing a constructive role in the international system. Likewise, after World War II, President Truman oversold the Soviet threat in order to mobilize a war-fatigued American public. The result was that many Americans did not distinguish Soviet Communism from Chinese Communism—or from revolutionary nationalism. Although the Communist movement was not a monolithic threat, the rhetorical trope that Communism was a unified challenge to the American way of life, as had been Nazism, was a simple message that engendered a domestic bipartisan consensus but often distorted policy toward such countries as China and Vietnam. After the 9/11 attacks, President Bush also sought to galvanize Americans' attention around a terrorist threat of global reach.[26] That focus mobilized a consensus behind military intervention in Afghanistan and then in Iraq, but the rhetoric also may have obfuscated critical distinctions and nurtured fuzzy thinking that has actually impaired progress not only in those two places but also in the overall effort to defeat al Qaeda.

Partisan and ideological splits in the American electorate make it difficult today to forge a domestic consensus. Growing media partisanship, religious mobilization, immigration, and generational change complicate policy making.[27] America's future leaders face the formidable task of generating domestic bipartisan support behind policies that can match the complexity of international relations. They must do so without creating popular fears that lead to pathologies of strategy; they must do so without engendering unrealizable expectations; and they must do so without blinding the American people to other threats that they will have to manage in the years ahead.

Conclusion

U.S. leaders must think about the unthinkable—be it terrorist nuclear attacks, the possibility of a global economic meltdown, or the rapid transmission of a deadly virus. They know that they cannot fully prepare to meet all contingencies. In a bewilderingly complicated world, they must assign priorities to the threats they face, plan for action, and rally the support of the American people. Passing the buck cannot help but be a great temptation.

This seems especially true as we look forward to a more complex and dynamic period in global politics. The cold war is long gone, new borderless dangers have emerged, and the world is difficult to understand simply through the lens of state-versus-state competition. The future appears more likely to resemble times in which there was little consensus on the threat—for example, the 1920s or the 1990s. Terrorism, of course, retains an important hold in American thinking. But the urgency of that challenge has faded since 9/11, perhaps because of the absence of attacks on the United States or perhaps because Americans have become more aware of other challenges that might be even more portentous, including a nuclear Iran, a Middle East engulfed by war, the rise of China, the revanchism of Russia, the warming of the planet, and the spread of disease. It is daunting to understand and to deal with any of these threats individually, let alone compare and rank them.

But decisions must be made, and the contributors have offered a series of provocative and insightful analyses. They disagree on many things: the nature of world politics, the main threats to U.S. security, and the best ways to restore American legitimacy, apply coercive power, promote democratization, and configure international institutions. Collectively, however, their disagreements are useful in clarifying the trade-offs that are inevitable in policy making. Readers may not agree with the conclusions of individual authors, but their insights and arguments should provoke deeper thinking about critically important matters. Collectively, they offer hope that American leaders can seize the initiative, overcome the reactive mode in which they have been operating since the attacks on 9/11, and tackle age-old problems that are more frightening than ever before: preventing war, feeding hungry people, improving human rights, reducing inequality, creating international community, protecting the global environment, and advancing the well-being of the Republic itself.

In order to make progress on such matters, the authors agree that the United States must retain a position of leadership in world affairs. They concur that the United States must retain its military preponderance, pursue economic openness, collaborate more closely with other nations, and nurture the rule of law, the growth of civil societies, and the spread of freedom. Moreover, these goals not only appear to have the support of much of the American citizenry but also seem to accord favorably with extant world opinion.

Such goals, of course, constitute a starting point for future action. They in no way mitigate the controversies that will arise over the implementation of a robust foreign policy. What follows the Bush doctrine, moreover, may be shaped by the unknowable and perhaps by the unthinkable. The problem of conjecture, as Ferguson aptly stresses, is forever with decision makers. But U.S. leaders and citizens will need to make sense of the world, to identify threats, to engage in agonizing trade-offs, and to plan accordingly. We hope the chapters in this volume will assist them in the ordeal and opportunity of making the United States more secure and fashioning a more peaceful, stable, just, and prosperous world.

Notes

1. See David Brooks's column after attending the conference at the Miller Center, "A New Global Blueprint," *New York Times*, June 19, 2007, and sessions from the conference "After the Bush Doctrine: National Security Strategy for a New Administration" on the Miller Center of Public Affairs Web site, http://www .millercenter.org/scripps/digitalarchive/conferenceDetail/68.

2. For one plan, see G. John Ikenberry and Anne-Marie Slaughter, *Forging a World of Liberty under Law: U.S. National Security in the 21st Century* (final report of the Princeton Project on National Security, September 26, 2007), http://www.wws .princeton.edu/ppns/report/FinalReport.pdf.

3. See Charles P. Kindleberger, *The World in Depression, 1929–39* (Berkeley: University of California Press, 1973); Robert Keohane, *After Hegemony: Cooperation and Discord in the World Political Economy* (Princeton, NJ: Princeton University Press, 1984).

4. WorldPublicOpinion.org, "U.S. Role in the World," http://www.americans-world .org/digest/overview/us_role/hegemonic_role.cfm.

5. WorldPublicOpinion.org, "World Publics Reject U.S. Role as the World Leader" (April 17, 2007), http://www.worldpublicopinion.org/pipa/articles/ home_page/345.php?nid=&id=&pnt=345&lb=hmpg1.

6. Chicago Council on Global Affairs and WorldPublicOpinion.org, "Views of the United States" (April 2007), http://www.worldpublicopinion.org/pipa/pdf/ apr07/CCGA+_ViewsUS_quaire.pdf.

7. Ibid.

8. *The National Security Strategy of the United States of America* (Washington, DC: The White House, 2002); *The National Security Strategy of the United States of America* (Washington, DC: The White House, 2006).

9. Jimmy Carter, "The State of the Union Address Delivered before a Joint Session of the Congress" (January 23, 1980), http://www.presidency.ucsb.edu/ws/index.php?pid=33079.

10. Chicago Council on Global Affairs and WorldPublicOpinion.org, "Americans Continue to Support International Engagement Despite Frustration over the War in Iraq" (October 11, 2006), http://www.worldpublicopinion.org/pipa/articles/brunitedstatescanadara/256.php?nid=&id=&pnt=256&lb=brusc.

11. See Andrew Gamble, "Hegemony and Decline: Britain and the United States," in *Two Hegemonies: Britain 1846–1914 and the United States 1941–2001*, ed. Patrick Karl O'Brien and Armand Clesse (Aldershot, UK: Ashgate, 2002), 127–140.

12. "Views of the United States."

13. Chicago Council on Global Affairs and WorldPublicOpinion.org, "The Rise of China" (May 2007), http://www.worldpublicopinion.org/pipa/pdf/may07/CCGA+_RiseChina_quaire.pdf.

14. See Michael W. Doyle, "Liberalism and World Politics," *American Political Science Review* 80, no. 4 (December 1986): 1151–1169.

15. John M. Owen IV, "Transnational Liberalism and U.S. Primacy," *International Security* 26, no. 3 (Winter 2001/2002): 117–152.

16. Ian Johnson, "The Death and Life of China's Civil Society," *Perspectives on Politics* 1, no. 3 (2003): 551–554; Alastair Iain Johnston, "Chinese Middle Class Attitudes towards International Affairs: Nascent Liberalization?" *China Quarterly*, no. 179 (September 2004): 603–628.

17. Arthur Stein, "The Hegemon's Dilemma: Great Britain, the United States and the International Economic Order," *International Organization* 38 (Spring 1984): 355–386.

18. See WorldPublicOpinion.org, "Comprehensive Analysis of Polls Reveals Americans' Attitudes on U.S. Role in the World" (August 3, 2007), http://www.americans-world.org/digest/overview/us_role/multilateralism.cfm; as well as "United Nations," ibid., http://www.americans-world.org/digest/global_issues/un/un1.cfm.

19. WorldPublicOpinion.org and the Chicago Council on Global Affairs, *World Public Opinion 2007*, http://www.worldpublicopinion.org/pipa/pdf/jun07/CCGA+_FullReport_rpt.pdf.

20. National Commission on Terrorist Attacks, *9/11 Commission Report: Final Report of the National Commission on Terrorist Attacks upon the United States* (New York: Norton, 2004), 361.

21. Andrew Kohut and Bruce Stokes, *America against the World: How We Are Different and Why We Are Disliked* (New York: Times Books, 2006); Peter Katzenstein and Robert Keohane, eds., *Anti-Americanisms in World Politics* (Ithaca, NY: Cornell University Press, 2007).

22. Ivo H. Daalder and James M. Lindsay, *America Unbound: The Bush Revolution in Foreign Policy* (Washington, DC: Brookings Institution Press, 2003), 136.

23. Keir A. Lieber and Gerard Alexander, "Waiting for Balancing: Why the World Is Not Pushing Back," *International Security* 30, no. 1 (Summer 2005): 109–139.

24. Joseph Nye, "The Decline of America's Soft Power," *Foreign Affairs* (May/June 2004): 16–20.
25. Paul Kennedy, *Grand Strategies in War and Peace* (New Haven, CT: Yale University Press, 1991), 5.
26. *National Security Strategy* (2002), 1.
27. Charles A. Kupchan and Peter L. Trubowitz, "Dead Center: The Demise of Liberal Internationalism in the United States," *International Security* 32, no. 2 (Fall 2007): 7–44.

Index

economy/economies (*continued*)

   See also currency; free trade;
     globalization; trade

Ecuador, 113, 185, 214

education, 3, 78, 147, 177, 178, 214, 256

Egypt, 59n20, 67, 116, 211–214, 216, 244

Eichengreen, Barry, 8, 181–200, 253, 255,
   256, 261, 263, 264, 268, 270, 271

Eisenhower, Dwight, 38, 62

elections, 51, 55, 76, 166, 210, 212

El Salvador, 53, 117, 129, 185

Emergency Plan for AIDS Relief in
   Africa, 194

empires. *See* imperialism

employment, 70–72

   security in, 71, 195, 196, 224

Endowment for Middle East Truth, 216

energy, 8, 23, 111

   competition for, 243

   as next U.S. administration's concern,
     197

   price rises in, 233

   threat assessment and, 89, 91, 264

   See also oil

entertainment industry, 78

entrepreneurship, 52, 71, 114, 257

environment, 12, 23, 204, 258, 259, 273.
   See also global warming

Environmental Protection Agency,
   U.S., 148

equality, 72–73, 79, 263. *See also* inequality

Ethiopia, 206, 223

ethnic groups, 115–117, 228

   rogue communities of, 109–110, 117,
     120–124

ethnic purification, 67

European Recovery Program, 79

European Union, 81, 165

   agricultural subsidies and, 195, 200, 270

   pan-European nationalism and, 43

   Russia and, 39, 42

   soft power implementation and, 216

   Westphalian system transformation
     and, 75

evangelicalism, 74

exchange rates, 189–192, 199, 232

extraordinary prisons, 263, 270

failed states, 91, 206, 267

   counterterrorism strategy and, 22–23

   Muslim world and, 112, 115

   neoconservatives and, 29

   terrorism threats and, 109, 112

Fasci di Combattimento, 178

Fascism, 69, 81, 85

fast-track executive trade authority, 271

Fatah, 136, 211, 212

Fatah al-Islam, 209

FBI, 21

federal debt, U.S., 231, 232, 233

Federal Reserve, 198, 233

Feinstein, Dianne, 142

Ferguson, Niall, 8, 77, 227–246, 253,
   255, 261, 263, 264, 270, 274

Fiume, 63

Five Power Organization, 222

flu epidemic (1918), 16

food shortages, 90, 101

foreign aid, 77, 79, 93, 147, 181, 182,
   192–194, 199

   humanitarian, 204, 212–215

foreign government lobbying, 25–26, 271

foreign policy, United States

   China and, 42, 46, 47, 52

   competence in, 133, 134–135,
     145–152, 237–238, 260–261, 265

   definition of, 60

   democratization and, 74, 267

   domestic support of, 133, 150–152,
     166–167, 229, 234–235, 271–273

   economic globalization and, 66, 69–74

   environmental concerns and, 12, 23

   explicit vs. implicit, 63

   founders' view of, 60, 158–159, 161, 165

   global public health programs and, 12, 23

   historical perspective on, 5–7

   international collaboration and, 18,
     257–259, 259

modernization and, 54
neoconservatives and, 29
nuclear nonproliferation and, 243
nuclear weapons and, 1, 15, 21, 43, 56, 77, 80, 242, 273
public opinion findings about, 235, 236
regional conflict and, 45, 56
regional predominance and, 36, 43
revolution (1978–1979), 67
sanctions and, 49, 237
Shiites and, 123, 124, 136
suicide bombers and, 119
Sunnis and, 242
Iraq, 1, 206, 220
Britain and, 116, 117, 120, 234
democratization in, 211
Islamists and, 67, 117
Kurds and, 119, 122–123, 124
oil reserves of, 243
population of, 234
public opinion on, 235
reconstruction of, 181
Shiite-Sunni split in, 8, 110, 117, 119, 120–124, 211, 242
state building and, 209
suicide bombings and, 119
United Nations and, 139, 191
U.S. future role in, 124
weapons of mass destruction and, 2, 229, 237
World Bank and, 194
Iraq Study Group, 237
Iraq war, 4, 8, 60, 62, 206, 267, 272
Abu Ghraib scandal and, 19, 142–143, 154n8, 208
alienation caused by, 19, 167, 208
al Qaeda and, 21, 110, 123, 143–144, 146
Bush doctrine and, 2, 224, 228–229, 237
counterinsurgency following, 19, 117, 118–119
Democrats' view of, 136–137
domestic support and sacrifice for, 150–151, 229, 234–235
global opposition to, 39–40, 236–237

internal Muslim violence and, 67, 117, 123–124
liberal order rejection and, 97, 98
military tactics of, 176
public opinion on, 142, 235
refugees from, 139, 140
Saddam Hussein's overthrow by, 2, 20, 29, 229, 230
U.S. competence and, 134–135, 237, 265
U.S. deficits impacting, 228–229
U.S. military deaths in, 241
U.S. spending on, 40, 149, 173, 230, 241
U.S. superpower status and, 40–41
U.S. troops in, 77, 234
U.S. withdrawal from, 45, 123–124, 136, 137, 139–140, 198, 204, 209
war on terror and, 2, 3, 208–209
as wrong war, 171, 178
Irwin, Douglas A., 8, 181–200, 253, 255, 256, 261, 263, 264, 268, 270, 271
Islam, 124, 140, 145, 242
fundamentalist, 37, 45, 54, 80
increased understanding of, 133, 145–146
in India, 67, 125
modernization concerns and, 36–37, 53–55
Ottoman Empire and, 68, 116, 117
public anti-Americanism and, 236
strong states and, 115–117
See also radical Islam; Shiites; Sunnis
Islamic law, 67
Islamofascists, 89
isolationism, 160, 162, 163, 224–225
American popular opinion on, 251, 252
Bush (George W.) and, 77–78
Israel, 25, 67, 80, 254
Beirut attacks (2006) by, 146, 155n13, 206
free-trade agreement with, 185
Hamas and, 146, 212
Islamists and, 43
lobbying by, 25
nuclear nonproliferation and, 243

NATO. *See* North Atlantic Treaty
Organization
natural disasters, 239
Hurricane Katrina as, 134–135, 148,
239, 265
natural gas, 38, 52, 124, 243
natural resources, 47, 229, 243. *See
also* oil
Nazism, 12, 87, 206, 218, 219, 272
neoconservatives, 28–30, 53, 207, 241
neoliberalism, 113
Netherlands, 68, 147
neutrality, 138
Neutrality Acts, 163
"new American militarism," 171–172
new unilateralism, 97
New Zealand, 24
NGOs, 61, 81, 82
Nicaragua, 113, 117, 185
Nietzsche, Friedrich, 66
Nigeria, 244
9/11 Commission Report, 1, 261, 264
9/11 terrorist attacks, 40, 59n20, 99,
264, 273
Bush (George W.) and, 2, 143–144,
181, 207, 208–209
costs associated with, 239
neoconservatives and, 29
speculation on origins of, 240
trade issues and, 184
World Bank initiatives and, 193
Nixon, Richard, 6–7, 118, 145, 172, 173,
197, 241
Nixon doctrine (1969), 129
nongovernmental organizations, 61, 81, 82
Nordhaus, William, 230
Nordic countries, 71–72
North American Free Trade Agreement,
56, 185
North Atlantic Treaty Organization, 7,
25, 165, 217
Afghanistan and, 122
Bush doctrine and, 3, 38, 167, 168
Concert of Democracies and, 18

contemporary crisis and, 96
creation of, 92, 93, 105, 127
Kosovo intervention by, 46, 50
liberal order building and, 94, 101–102
post–cold war expansion of, 56
Russia and, 42, 57
selective-engagement strategy and,
24, 25
North Korea, 1, 40, 71, 135, 189
autocratic government in, 56
Axis of Evil and, 235, 237
neoconservatives and, 29
nuclear nonproliferation and, 243
nuclear weapons and, 15, 21, 42, 271
public opinion on, 235
sanctions and, 49
Northwest Frontier Province, 120, 121
nuclear energy, 243
nuclear nonproliferation, 229, 242–243
Nuclear Nonproliferation Treaty, 21, 22,
77, 243, 251
nuclear proliferation, 12, 165, 267, 271
counterproliferation successes, 15
emerging threats of, 14–15, 17, 18,
20–23
threat assessment issues and, 89, 90, 264
nuclear reactors, 21
nuclear terrorism, 14, 20–21, 110, 126,
208, 261
nuclear weapons, 163, 167, 260
China and, 14, 77
deterrence and, 11, 14, 17, 75, 111–112
first-strike capability of, 14
India and, 15, 77
Iran and, 1, 15, 21, 43, 56, 77, 80,
242, 273
in multipolar world, 44
North Korea and, 15, 21, 42, 271
Pakistan and, 15
Russia and, 14, 21, 111, 124
securing of, 20–21, 22, 29, 267
threat assessment of, 91, 110, 261, 264
Nuremberg trials, 165
Nye, Joseph, 78

rogue ethnic communities and, 117,
    120–124
suicide bombing and, 53, 117,
    119–120, 138
terrorism and, 53, 89, 111–112, 119,
    124, 125, 127
Rato, Rodrigo de, 199–200
raw materials. *See* natural resources
Reagan, Ronald, 7, 53, 58n10, 62, 157,
    173, 213, 214
REAL ID Act (2005), 153n3
Reciprocal Trade Agreements Act of
    1934, 183, 184
refugees, 25, 139, 140, 153n3
regime change, 37, 38, 63, 228
religion, 8, 43
    fanaticism and, 261 (*see also* radical Islam)
    as foreign policy influence, 66–69, 76,
        79, 80
    freedom of, 228
    fundamentalism and, 15, 37, 45, 54, 80
    liberation theology and, 73–74
    millenarianism and, 15
    policy making and, 272
    See also secularism; *specific religions*
rendition, 141, 263, 270
renewable energy, 243
renminbi, 189–190, 191–192
reproductive medicine funding, 68
Republican Party, 1, 126, 136, 194, 235
    economic issues and, 73
    energy industry and, 111
    Marshall Plan and, 151
    U.S. military superiority and, 253
reserve military forces, U.S., 170–173, 176
Reserve Officer Training Corps,
    177, 178
resiliency, U.S. strengthening of, 133,
    137, 148–152
respect, 42, 43, 96, 107, 134, 142
"responsibility to protect" concept, 47
retaliation, military, 241, 245
"Revolution in Military Affairs,"
    129–130, 175–177

Rhodes, William, 190
Ricardo, David, 70, 162
Rice, Condoleezza, 63, 193
Ridge, Tom, 149
Rio Pact (1947), 127
rising expectations, revolution of, 61
Rodrik, Dani, 80
rogue ethnic communities, 109–110,
    117, 120–124
rogue regimes, 228
rogue states, 2, 21, 47, 87, 109, 261. *See
    also* Iran; North Korea
Romania, 40
Rome Statute of the International
    Criminal Court, 96, 97
Roosevelt, Franklin, 82, 127, 149,
    154n7, 163, 183, 184, 203n20, 245
Roosevelt, Theodore, 160, 168, 269
ROTC, 177, 178
rule of law, 80, 130, 274
    Bush doctrine and, 3, 228
    China and, 114
    concerts of democracies and, 103
    democratization and, 76, 210–211, 268
    promotion of, 110–111, 122, 125, 126,
        127, 130
Rumsfeld, Donald, 62–63, 129–130, 142,
    155n9, 176, 230
Russia, 8, 12, 48, 56, 64, 160, 236, 260, 273
    anti-Americanism and, 38, 40
    autocracy and, 36, 46–49, 50, 51–52, 56
    Chávez and, 223
    Chechnya and, 21, 124
    China and, 38–39, 125, 254
    democracy and, 52
    economic influence of, 111
    foreign policy of, 42, 46
    as great power, 124, 126, 127, 130
    international competition and, 36, 52
    Islamic terrorists and, 124, 125
    Kosovo intervention and, 46, 49, 50
    liberalism and, 45–46
    military power and, 38
    in multipolar world order, 44